CONVENTIONAL AND ULTIMATE TRUTH

THRESHOLDS IN PHILOSOPHY AND THEOLOGY

Jeffrey Bloechl and Kevin Hart, series editors

Philosophy is provoked and enriched by the claims of faith
in a revealed God. Theology is stimulated by its contact with
the philosophy that proposes to investigate the full range
of human experience. At the threshold where they meet,
there inevitably arises a discipline of reciprocal interrogation
and the promise of mutual enhancement. The works in this series
contribute to that discipline and that promise.

Joseph Stephen O'Leary

CONVENTIONAL AND ULTIMATE TRUTH

A Key for Fundamental Theology

University of Notre Dame Press
Notre Dame, Indiana

Manufactured in the United States of America

Library of Congress Cataloging-in-Publication Data

O'Leary, Joseph Stephen
Conventional and ultimate truth : a key for fundamental theology /
Joseph Stephen O'Leary.
pages cm — (Thresholds in philosophy and theology)
Includes bibliographical references and index.
ISBN 978-0-268-03740-6 (pbk. : alk. paper) —
ISBN 0-268-03740-X (pbk. : alk. paper)
1. Truth—Religious aspects—Christianity. 2. Philosophical theology.
3. Christianity—Philosophy. I. Title.
BT40.O43 2015
230.01—dc23

2015000693

∞ *The paper in this book meets the guidelines for permanence
and durability of the Committee on Production Guidelines
for Book Longevity of the Council on Library Resources.*

In Memory of

Padraic Conway (1962–2012) and Sean Freyne (1935–2013)

Contents

Preface

The present work is intended as a contribution to fundamental theology and sets forth as a paradigm for theology today the practice of a reflective judgment that attends to the interplay of conventionality and ultimacy within Christian tradition and in the wider interreligious horizon. The theme of reflective judgment has a Kantian background and the dyad of ultimate and conventional derives from Mahāyāna Buddhist philosophy, especially the Madhyamaka school founded by Nāgārjuna (second-third centuries), but my handling of these two topics is not confined by any scrupulous obedience to these historical figures. Open-ended critical reflection on conventions in view of ultimacy is an art of theological judgment that discovers its own principles and possibilities as it proceeds and as it relativizes or overcomes conceptions of the theological task that are less adequate to what is to be thought today.

"Conventional truth," the axial notion of this book, will strike many as an oxymoron. Surely Christian faith stands or falls by the capacity to express truth plainly in an irreducible form? To talk of a play of conventions sounds like nominalism, or nominal Christianity, in which the play of names and representations is kept up at the expense of any real encounter with or enactment of the thing itself. In the age of the Internet, Christian talk is in far greater supply than Christian faith and deeds. "For as one speaks of chattering oneself away from a subject by a long talk, so has the human race, and the individual within it wanted to chatter itself out of being a Christian and sneak out of it by the help of this shoal of name-Christians, a Christian state, a

Christian world, notions shrewdly calculated to make God so confused in His head by all these millions that He cannot discover that He
has been hoaxed, that there is not one single . . . Christian" (Kierkegaard, 127).

This danger is real, and yet I want to put in a plea for a conventionalist understanding of Christian language and views, for three reasons.
First, this approach is intellectually satisfying, and reassuring for faith,
insofar as it enables us to take in stride the flimsiness, the contradictions, the all-too-human distortions of our religious language as it has
grown and changed over three millennia and to find meaning in these
apparent absurdities. In Kierkegaard's time many theologians were
seduced by the speculative "chatter" of Hegel and Schelling about the
Trinity and the Incarnation, which promised a rescue from the broken, finite, incarnate condition of the language of faith. The conventionalism I would oppose to any such ideal of speculative transparency
is meant, not to undercut the reality of the core affirmations of faith,
but on the contrary to make them more persuasive by thorough reflection on the human historical texture of the language that has been
their vehicle.

Second, this conventionalism is liberating in that it provides a
medicine chest for healing the many forms of obscurantism, fanaticism, and violence that have attached to our religious views down
through history. Third, it is ecumenically enriching, insofar as it integrates into Christian reflection the wisdom of Buddhism, which sees
language as a source of delusive entanglement but uses it skillfully as a
provisional raft and which sees all views, especially right views, as imprisoning attachments, to be handled with skeptical caution.

There is also a fourth reason: acceptance of the conventional texture of our language leaves us free to experience the emergence of realities marked by ultimacy. We do not need to clutch at every utterance of scripture or church tradition in order to encounter the divine
word that scripture and the creeds attest. Rather, it is in letting go of
whatever is hollow or obsolete, and treating all religious language as a
convention to be skillfully deployed, that we are best prepared to discern and respond to whatever carries the full weight of prophetic truth
or contemplative vision. Christianity is based on hearing a divine word

or call, embracing it in faith, and attempting to live by it; this is as ultimate an experience as one could wish. Yet this ultimacy does not carry over to the specific cultural forms that the divine call takes in different epochs; indeed, a divine call, in its newness, will probably run athwart and subvert these previous forms. The old stories of encounter with divine reality can inspire us, but we are not obliged to take on board the archaic symbolic or conceptual frameworks within which they were located. Even the way monotheism comes to be constructed in biblical history is not a binding template. As a construct it can be tested for its adequacy to modern experience and understanding; it may be imperative to reforge the idea of God in the name of creative fidelity to the monotheistic tradition, soliciting one strand or another within the pluralistic and historically mobile texture of scriptural language. Again, the various ways in which the Resurrection has been named, imagined, conceptualized, and narrated are only pointers to a reality that is of an ultimate and incomparable order and that may summon up other languages to speak of it today.

Constructing a religious template that allows modern aspirations to be freely expressed, and that reflects the much larger cosmic context of today as compared with that of biblical times, can be seen as a "development" of the old perspectives, but this development is not achieved by logical, metaphysical reasoning whereby one tight system is reshaped into another tight system. Rather, today, we realize that no religious system is tight, that imagination or poetic vision plays a huge role in all of them, and that their truth is that of a valid convention rather than a transparent objective account of how things are. This leaves us free to look back at the history of our traditions, as a chronicle of human strivings to imagine the divine, enshrining moments of grace when the divine manifested itself in saintly figures, saving events, and holy lifestyles and communities. Doctrinal debate about who was right and who was wrong is radically relativized as we see more clearly the nature of religious constructs. The theological quest for truth takes a different turn as it deinvests from fetishized topics and brings all questions of true and false back to a basic underlying question about human understanding of ultimate reality. This frees us for a flexible hermeneutic that can pore over Christian and non-Christian traditions, tracking intimations of ultimacy among so much that is obsolete or even deluded. The construction of religious truth today cannot be directly provided by the past but demands our own creative and imaginative retrieval and overcoming of that past through fresh engagement with what was fundamentally at stake in it.

Some may feel that I have not in fact avoided the danger of nominalism and that a fundamental theology in a conventionalist key cannot provide a secure basis for a robust systematic theology. In that case, this book could be read as a statement of the difficulties encountered today in the construction of fundamental theology, the challenges to be overcome in securing the authentic standpoint of faith. It would thus retain a negative value, prompting others to provide a stronger alternative.

The first two chapters establish the general climate of the inquiry by articulating two methodological orientations for fundamental theology. First, I discuss the conditions of theological judgment today, stressing the need for open-ended reflection rather than quests for systematic closure. Historical consciousness, cultural relativism and pluralism, recognition of the autonomous values of secular reason and sensibility, and the linguistic turn in structuralist and poststructuralist thought are so many factors that impose a new context for reflective judgment. Those who reject aspects of modernity, praying for the return of a medieval universe in which theophany and sacramentality pervade the world and everyday life, have really signed off from the art of judgment, in a suicide of thought that may also issue in a suicide of faith. Reflective judgment, adjusting to the conditions of modernity, is a school of detachment from dogmatic heavy-handedness, and thus a strong antidote to fundamentalism and other pathologies of religious judgment. It does not mean that theology is content to become an inconclusive musing but rather that theology becomes truly rational through cultivating an integral critical awareness of the possibilities and limits of its categorical equipment and of the conditions under which it can legitimately proceed today.

Then I discuss the Madhyamaka topic of the two truths, the ultimate and the conventional, advocating its strategic value for theology in that it allows us to be relaxed about the conventional texture of our religious discourse, defusing controversy and anxiety and opening up a space for the ultimate dimensions of the faith to emerge. To bring this way of thought into more gripping focus I connect it with the negative dialectic of Hegel, suggesting that an open-ended Hegelianism would go halfway to meet the Madhyamaka negations and could enable their richer and more effective application to the themes of Western philosophy and theology. Talk of the ultimacy of emptiness does not plunge one headlong into a negative theology that abandons all discourse and doctrine to espouse a silent communing with an ineffable absolute. Rather, it sends us back to the fabric of conventional discourse, to be treasured and carefully tended as the indispensable vehicle for breakthroughs of ultimacy. The value of the two-truths perspective is that it can give free rein to the insights of pluralism, relativism, and historical consciousness, in constant rediscovery of the fragility and provisionality of all religious language, while at the same time remaining alert to the intimations or revelations of ultimacy that this language seeks to convey.

The remaining chapters forswear a ruthlessly linear progress and linger instead over a number of loci that enable the perspectives sketched earlier to be explored and developed in relation to different concrete topics. Fundamental theology has always been something of a ragbag, and this is even more the case with the older *loci theologici* tradition of Melanchthon (1521) and Melchior Cano (1562). My choice of topics is guided by the themes of theological judgment and the status of conventional religious utterance. Other lead-ins to theology, such as the problem of evil, or of sin and justification, or concerns of social justice, or feminist and gay questions, or frontal engagement with the church or its founder as sources of faith, have been set aside as being less illustrative in this respect.

The first locus is literary modernism, which is a privileged guide to the spiritual situation of Western humanity today, so much so that any apologetics and any fundamental theology worth its salt must take account of the vision of existence so subtly explored in the writings of Mallarmé, Proust, Rilke, Musil, Kafka, Joyce, Yeats, and Beckett. The second locus revisits the theme of "overcoming metaphysics," showing how reliance on classical metaphysical procedures, as well as on a crypto-metaphysical phenomenology, has blocked the subtler play of judgment that theology requires. The third locus is the one Barth sets at the foundation of his dogmatics, the church's experience of listening to the Word of God. I attempt to reflect anew on the interplay between the ultimacy of this experience and our keen sense of the fragility, pluralism, and brokenness of its conventional vehicles, especially scripture itself as it appears in a modern historical, literary, and ethical critique. The fourth locus is religious experience, which is so often treated as sheer ultimacy that abolishes the play of reflective critique. I focus on the way it is intimately imbricated with historical and linguistic conventionalities, though not thereby losing its character of ultimacy. Next I turn to the tradition of apophatic theology, again seeking to correct absolutistic tendencies and to reconnect this tradition with a reflective thinking taking its cue from the incarnational economy and a sense of the concrete texture of religious conventions. Comparison with Buddhist and Vedantic apophasis further serves to bring this tradition into dialogue with contemporary critical judgment.

The sixth locus, the practice of interreligious dialogue, has become a shaping context of fundamental theology, no longer something that can be deferred as a speculative luxury or treated as a problem to be mastered and dispelled in a supplementary exercise known as "theology of religions." That "the question of the 'other religions' can no longer be left until the end of a Christian systematic theology but should enter at the very beginning" (Tracy, 8) is now widely recognized, but this "question" goes deeper than differences about what is believed. It obliges us to develop a comprehensive method for assessing all religious interpretations and judgments. Finally, I ask about the status of dogma in light of the foregoing, attempting to show how doctrinal questions can be envisaged afresh in light of the fundamental-theological perspectives here explored. I sketch a method of successive "steps back": from bad metaphysics to good; from good metaphysical theology to the sobriety of dogma in its nucleus; from dogma to its alleged grounds in the world of scripture, where dogma is unsettled and new critical judgments on its achievement can be formulated; and within scripture from the Johannine vision of God and Christ to the historical Jesus and his Jewish thought-world (as an example of the many critical trajectories theology can follow within scripture in the search to demystify its dogmatic lore); and finally a Buddhist step back that assesses the entire development of monotheism, messianism, and trinitarianism as a conventional construction to be brought back to the silence of the ultimate. Some such multilayered critical mapping and sifting of our traditions allows each element to be situated perspicuously with the cluster of critical questions that specifically concern it, and thus to retell the tale of biblical and church theology in a more human and chastened key.

Each of the loci chosen takes us toward experiences marked by ultimacy: the supreme presence of a literary work of art; the reality of transcendence as discerned by metaphysical reason, or in a thinking that overcomes metaphysics in order to discern this reality more adequately; the supreme authority of the Word of God; the immediacy and ultimacy of religious experience; the silence at the heart of negative theology; the horizons of ultimate mystery that open up when religions share their insights; the certitude and rootedness of faith, creed, and dogma, understood as a rootedness not in formulas but in the "divine milieu" they point to. In each case the ultimacy refers back to earthly conventional vehicles, in an incarnational twist. All seven loci are concerned with the texture of ultimate reality, and the different roles of artist, philosopher, preacher, contemplative, and ecumenist are anchored in the quest of ultimacy. Yet all seven loci are fields of conventional discrimination and are searingly skeptical about their own status. The artist trades in fiction; the metaphysician undercuts the traditional claims and methods of the discipline; the preacher attentive to the Word of God will constantly relativize the letter of scripture; the mystic's immediacy cannot shake off its conventional mediations; the apophatic theologian is thrown back on cataphatic conventionalities; the religionist seeking a shared contemplative core of different traditions is embarked on an unending dialogue between finite histories, in which breakthroughs of ultimacy become as elusive as ghosts; the dogmatist proclaims his or her creed with adamantine conviction, but close examination of any given proposition leads to a blurring of clarities and a crumbling of definitiveness. The to-and-fro between ultimacy and conventionality in all seven fields generates a dynamic critical dialectic that is the hallmark of the activity of the spirit (or the Spirit) in the world of history, the flesh, the letter.

In keeping with this incarnational dynamic I have sought to give each of the loci a determinate historical profile. I discuss not literature in the abstract but twentieth-century literary modernism; not metaphysics in the abstract, but metaphysics in its historical trajectory and present status as discerned by Heidegger; not the Word of God in its constant abiding, but the historical shifts generated in our relation to it by the crises of Modernism, dialectical theology, and their continuation in current questioning. The historical fulcrum in these three loci is the early twentieth century. In dealing with religious experience, negative theology, and dogma I go back to the patristic epoch, which played a foundational defining role for each of them. For Oriental apophasis and interreligious dialogue, too, I keep in mind a particular epoch, that of early Indian Mahāyāna (the first centuries of our era), when the Buddhist ideas that most attract Western philosophers and theologians today found their classical formulation.

"Here then I conclude my entire critical enterprise" (Kant, 20), under the happy auspices of the University of Notre Dame, where I began writing *Questioning Back* in 1982. Rather than "stride forward without delay to the doctrinal" (20), I hope to sustain a leisurely study of Buddhist sources, in ongoing debate with the friends to whom the following pages are so clearly indebted. Since the hour of doctrine has not yet struck, it is best to continue theology in the form of conversation. May it be an increasingly civilized, tolerant, imaginative, and reflective conversation, so that religious ideas become again a blessing rather than a bane to humankind.

Abbreviations

GA   Heidegger, Martin. 1975–. *Gesamtausgabe.* Frankfurt: Klostermann.

KD   Barth, Karl. 1939–1970. *Die kirchliche Dogmatik.* Zollikon: Evangelischer Verlag.

LW   Eckhart, Meister. 1936–2007. *Die lateinischen Werke.* Ed. E. Benz et al. Vols. 1–6 of *Meister Eckhart: Die deutschen und lateinischen Werke. Herausgegeben im Auftrage der Deutschen Forschungsgemeinschaft.* Stuttgart: W. Kohlhammer.

MK   Siderits, Mark, and Shōryū Katsura, trans. 2013. *Nāgārjuna's Middle Way: The Mūlamadhyamakakārikā.* Boston: Wisdom Publications.

WA   Luther, Martin. 1883–2009. *D. Martin Luthers Werke: Kritische Gesamtausgabe* [*Weimarer Ausgabe*]. Weimar: Hermann Böhlau.

WA TR   Luther, Martin. 1883–2009. *D. Martin Luthers Werke: Kritische Gesamtausgabe* [*Weimarer Ausgabe*]. Weimar: Hermann Böhlau. Subser. 1. *Tischreden.*

Chapter One

THEOLOGICAL JUDGMENT
AS OPEN-ENDED REFLECTION

In two earlier contributions to fundamental theology I tried to show how the situation of religious belief today is shaped by a new "regime of truth" that obliges us to undertake a critical retrieval of Christian tradition in dialogue with the other religious traditions, appraised as partners rather than rivals. *Questioning Back* (1985) tackled the heritage of metaphysical theology and asked how the old question of "Athens and Jerusalem" might be rethought in light of a critical reception of Heidegger's "overcoming of metaphysics" and Derrida's deconstructive radicalization of it. The syntheses between biblical event and metaphysical concept produced in so many forms throughout Christian history are always marked by tensions and flaws which a deconstructive reading builds on. "Every synthesis," psychoanalysts tell us, "is defensive" (Laplanche, 84). What holds for the story of an individual subject holds also for the history of a religion. The synthesis of Athens and Jerusalem, going back to the Septuagint, or more radically the monotheistic synthesis itself, or the Islamic one, or Christianity itself insofar as it presents itself as a synthesis—each of these is a defensive construction which needs to be interrogated to let its buried truth emerge. What particularly emerges is a phenomenological

I

regrounding of monotheism in the experience of the individuals addressed and claimed by the divine command of Deuteronomy 6:4 (Casper, forthcoming), and a corresponding "reduction" of trinitarian theology and Christology through a retrieval of their biblical basis. Reduction involves overcoming and demystification, but it is not a matter of whittling down ecclesial faith in the divinity of Christ, the Resurrection, redemption, the Eucharist; rather, it retrieves the horizon or event (the biblical horizon as currently accessible) in which such faith emerges and whence it draws its meaning and persuasive force.

Religious Pluralism and Christian Truth (1996) reflected on religious pluralism as the governing horizon of thought to which theology today must accommodate itself. In this area of questioning, too, I noted how much the texture of Christian history and language and of their relation to other traditions imposes sharp limits on speculative reason in theology. With this suspension of trust in speculative reason grows an obligation to exercise constantly another form of reason, namely, reflective judgment. Speculative reason can get going only by using a sort of shorthand, speaking summarily of "the divine attributes" or "the Trinity" or "scriptural revelation" as if they were fixed and clear matters. Reflective judgment, facing historical contingency and pluralism, instead multiplies nuances so as to keep open the questions that speculative reason simplifies and too hastily solves.

Reflecting on reflection may seem a rather abstract exercise, but a review of how reflection was afoot in these previous investigations may help give a sharper profile to the task before us in the present book. Setting out on Heidegger's quest, which was Luther's before him, for *die Sache selbst*, the matter itself, the phenomena, and practicing the step back, *der Schritt zurück*, that takes us back from the enclosure of metaphysics to the "truth of being," or, in its theological application, to the truth of the biblical vision, was a problematic process from the start, and Derrida both invited and enabled a probing articulation of the doubts that undermined it. For "metaphysics" and "phenomena" and "truth" turn out to be very mobile expressions. A return to bedrock sources, such as Luther and Heidegger in their different fields envisaged, cannot be achieved by a single sweeping gesture but demands a series of reading strategies that track the tensions between rival orientations in the classical texts of philosophy or of theology. The idea that there is an originary Word of revelation or an originary poetic speech needs to be countered by the reflection that both scriptural and poetic language are the highly structured results of centuries of tradition. As in classical music, the labor of form is the condition of the spontaneity of what seems an originary utterance. It is a second originarity, the fruit of art, not a primitive cry. (Luther often attains such well-grounded originary utterance but, alas, also multiplies ill-conceived sweeping gestures that muddy his thought instead of bringing the desired clarity, immediacy, and definiteness.)

Inflecting the semi-Heideggerian project toward the "errance" of "writing," in the wake of Derrida, meant blocking the path to any premature understanding of being or of revelation, any fetishization of the phenomenon. The phenomenon withdrew behind the swarm of interpretations, all of them caught up in the destabilizing effects of what Derrida named "dissemination." Such deconstructive critical sensibility threatens to undercut and dissolve what was radical and decisive in the thought of Heidegger and Luther (or Eckhart before him). It also further devalues the lucidity attained by the thorough cultivation of logical and literary form in classical philosophers and authors, such as Augustine and Aquinas in the field of theology. Neither Heidegger nor Derrida provides a fully adequate hermeneutical key to a critical retrieval of the philosophical or the theological heritage.

The orientation to the phenomenon is fecund and sharpens one's critical perceptions, but it leads to an impasse. The promise of Husserl's "philosophy as a rigorous science," of Heidegger's originary phenomenality of being, of Jean-Luc Marion's "givenness," if pushed too hard, shows up as just another quest for a *fundamentum inconcussum* that could abolish the disturbing pluralism of all perception and language. Marion's sighting of givenness as the irreducible bedrock of phenomenology, somewhat like the *ens communissime* (*Quodlibetum* 3, a.1) identified by Duns Scotus as the first and most universal object of thought, promises a regrounding of phenomenology analogous to the "second beginning of metaphysics" achieved by Scotus (see Honnefelder). Marion develops an analogy of givenness, somewhat reminiscent of the Thomistic analogy of being, that culminates in the supreme givenness of "revelation," a bridge concept between philosophy and theology. (See the exchange with Derrida in the last chapter of

Marion 2010.) So fundamental is the universal phenomenon of givenness that it is immune, Marion claims, to the relativizing impact of hermeneutics and deconstruction, which would undercut any "metaphysics of presence" or of "givenness" by showing all immediate givens to be caught in the dissemination of language, the deferral of any final signified. But the wound that structuralism and deconstruction inflicted on the immediacy and transparency of philosophical and theological speech is not easily healed. These movements correspond to "the demand for a radically changed mode of philosophizing," capable of "giving its appropriate means of thought to the process of modernity" (Sloterdijk, 177).

Phenomenology in its first overcoming of metaphysics—in the three successive "reductions" to a purified consciousness, the event of being, and the arrival of the gift—still remains metaphysical in its basic shape. It inhibits the play of critical reflective judgment. The study of literature, such as the poems and novels of early twentieth-century modernism, reveals the gap between the unitary schemes of Husserl, Heidegger, and Marion and the unmasterable diversity of the empirical phenomena of life and art. This sets off a play of reflective judgment that can never be overtaken by the philosopher's insistence on supreme principles, be they metaphysical or phenomenological, or by the theologian's urge to map human experience in reference to dogmas such as original sin, the Incarnation, or justification. Phenomenology claims to return to basic essential structures of experience, but when it is drawn into conversation with the literary treatment of experience in such philosophical-minded writers as Mallarmé and Rilke, Henry James and Proust, Joyce and Musil, its presumption that essential structures can be apprehended and mastered comes to grief against the dense singularity of each writer's vision, so that it is menaced with the fate of becoming a mere adjunct to commentary. To be sure, phenomenology lights up objective structures in the experience of sound, color, time, but "the more the description progresses, the more complex it becomes, and the less plausible it seems to maintain that it proceeds to a simple discovery of legalities of essence" (Romano, 67). The myriad facets of consciousness, the world, and being, multiplied in imagination and interpretation, are as resistant to phenomenological reduction as to metaphysical concept. Yet the Hegelian quest of the concept (reality as grasped) and the Heideggerian quest of the phenomenon (reality as given) express a longing of the human mind that will not go away. They are deep-seated "regulative ideals," as Kant would say, powerfully orienting our thought even if always disappointing when they come up with concrete "results."

If the establishment of Husserlian essences is a strenuous exercise, impeded at every turn by its linguistic embeddedness, and so difficult to keep at the rigorously philosophical level, so prone to be eaten into by a hermeneutical sense of contingency, religious phenomena, including those attested in scripture, are still more resistant to definition of their essence, and it is strange to see philosophers turning to them as if they offered a simplicity, immediacy, and transparency lacking in ordinary data. The pluralism and ambiguity that troubles philosophers is not resolved but rather augmented when one passes to the realm of religious discourse. Though religious thinkers may be tempted to appeal to the purity of mystical experience, or "the essence of Christianity," or some other such theophanic datum, or to some general unquestionable principle such as justice, liberation, or love, such gestures cannot override the everywhere recurrent experience of pluralistic, relative languages and contexts. To be sure, a general appeal may be made to the quality of depth, or of ultimacy, attaching to religious phenomena, which brings together religious figures from the most diverse backgrounds. Pluralism and cultural relativism need not discourage us from welcoming phenomena as they manifest themselves, using the arts of phenomenology to uncover them, or from interrogating classical texts in view of their phenomenological yield. But these procedures become more diffuse and variable than in the Heideggerian ideology of metaphysics and its overcoming or than in theories of religion that seek to anchor the multitudinous phenomena in some single central theme. Theologies that survey human experience from on high are themselves imaginative products that creatively shape the experiences they analyze. Even the biblical presentation of human experience, though fashioned for theological purposes, is so rich and complex that it perpetually eludes theological closure.

Reason, faith, phenomena of perception or religious awareness, are never given except as embedded in culturally and historically shaped situations, narratives, and texts, all with their particular constrictions and blind spots. This makes them difficult to handle in straightforward conceptual argument, as is attempted when the ahistorical procedures of analytical philosophy are let loose on historical texts. An inescapable precondition for tackling religious traditions is a full-blooded hermeneutics, in the manner of Dilthey's critique of historical reason, reinforced by whatever literary criticism can teach us about the interpretation of texts. There are still theologians, and of course there are many philosophers, who treat historical and cultural pluralism as a mere grace note, a preliminary complication to be quickly resolved, or something best left to the care of sociologists, cultural theorists, and the like. Such an attitude ensures that encounter with cultural variety can never produce a paradigm shift, dislodging one from Eurocentrism, for example. To lay a reliable foundation for theology it is necessary to set up a style of thinking that ensures an ever-increasing openness to the pluralistic texture of language and experience. Any defensive foreclosures at this basic level will be paid for by a loss of credibility in the long run.

REFLECTIVE RATIONALITY

Like the Heideggerian step back in the first phase of our inquiry, the opening up to pluralism in the second phase was in its turn seen to be riddled with problems from the start. The very notion of pluralism tends to level differences, setting up the same frames of understanding everywhere so that all "others" may be fairly processed. A leveling theology of religions, in the style of John Hick, has become a dogma in some places, a virtuous democratic prescription that all religions are created equal and that claims of one religion that might clash with others must be toned down. Unless carefully interrogated, "pluralism," like "democracy," can become a formula for violent simplifications, a hegemonic Logos dictating that the mode of subsistence of truths and beliefs is everywhere the same, belonging to the single universal play of historical and cultural perspectives. The art of mature theological judgment demands the renunciation of such convenient all-purpose ideologies, which have at best only a relative, conventional, and pragmatic validity.

The question to be clarified here, in the third phase of our inquiry, concerns the kind of rationality that theology must seek out and practice. Against the still widespread trust in metaphysical speculation as the basic mode of theological thought, we have argued that theology now finds itself in a postmetaphysical situation—in the sense that metaphysics, be it Thomist, Hegelian, analytical, or phenomenological, seems unable to impose itself as the dominant horizon of thought. Science, technology, and economics could be seen as the present most powerful embodiments of metaphysical reason, prompting Heidegger to say that the world is more in the grip of metaphysical reason than ever. It might also be argued that metaphysics in the formal sense has always been a ghostly presence anyway, a Sleeping Beauty; Aristotle himself may have let his metaphysical writings slip into oblivion, from which only a lucky find rescued them centuries later (Aubenque 1997:27). But even if it were conceded that the metaphysical instinct is unstillable, the shape it effectively takes in our world is that of a pluralistic dialogue among different metaphysics, a space of free commentary on the margins of the world's business. No one metaphysics can any longer set itself up as the "truth" of all the others. Hegel was the last great defender of such a claim, and the most successful, though he understood metaphysics as a flexible opening of mind, a method, and was always breaking the mold of the system set forth in his *Encyclopedia* as he nourished his lectures on political theory, history, religion, and aesthetics with infusions of empirical research and as he kept on rethinking the logical structures he discerned. The publication of the successive versions of his lecture courses in recent decades has made this open-endedness apparent, giving us a more living and human image of the thinker, albeit a less imposing one than in the monumental syntheses put together by their first editors. We see, for example, that his systematic logic functions in his lectures on aesthetics as a regulative idea in Kant's sense, "a methodological sketch for reflective consideration of the arts and determination of their cultural significance in the past as well as the present" (Hegel 2004:29). The scholarly rediscovery of the philosophers of reflection, who resisted the system building of Fichte and Hegel, has also contributed to bringing the classic period of German philosophy (1781–1831) into new perspective less as a resource for building metaphysical or theological systems than as a reservoir of strategies of reflective judgment (see Frank 1997). Despite its elements of reflective open-endedness and flexibility, the Hegelian style of metaphysical reason is still vulnerable to the critics such as Kierkegaard, Marx, Husserl, and Heidegger who have hemmed it in, pluralized it, relativized it, or brought it down to earth, and from whom we may draw encouragement for a more thorough retreat from the rigors of the system to a more Kantian culture of reflection.

The rationality of religious belief is no longer defended within the framework offered by the regnant metaphysics but has to take its stand on judgment, that is, a more comprehensive and concrete thinking, able to live with ambiguities and unresolved questions. To accept this is not to fall back into a fuzzy existentialism or the Hamletian paralysis of a *pensiero debole* but on the contrary to advance to a reflection more in accord with the full complexity of rationality today. Such reflection is not the application of preestablished principles, nor does it aim to erect a system, nor is it an inspired divination free from all regulation. Guided by the perception of certain concrete realities— the questions and hopes of the contemporary world, the Christian faith in its deep movement, in which it is connected with the Spirit moving in all hearts and in all cultures—theological judgment weighs these realities and responds to their pressure appropriately, adjusting the traditional methods of theology to present needs. This means broadening the categories of theology, which so often fall short of the human and divine realities they claim to deal with. The witness that flexible and open theological judgment gives to the rationality and credibility of the faith cannot be reduced to logical or systematic form, yet the integrity of this perpetual movement of the reflecting mind, and of communal debate, learning, and mutual challenge, is perhaps the best apologetic for faith today.

Theologians have been too fascinated by Kant's *Critique of Pure Reason.* To reground and reconstruct religious consciousness according to the precepts of transcendental rationality is a project that misses not only the pluralism of the religious but also that of the rational. Neither can be entirely purged of the contingency of its particular incarnations. Seeking the rationality of religious constructions in their historical variety, one must leave aside such metaphysical schemas and adopt the more groping, empirical approach of a *critique of judgment*, which will bring out the labor of rational thought going on within each set of religious representations and articulate a contemporary appreciation of that labor. Even in pointing out errors and weaknesses in religious traditions, this critique will resemble the procedures of artistic and literary criticism more than the constructions of philosophy. That is, we do not summon religious traditions before a superior and neutral bar of reason but listen to and interpret them, seeking to liberate their superior wisdom and rationality from the fixations and distortions that beset them, whether these are due to limitations of the original historical context, or to obsolescence brought by the emergence of new horizons, or to a reception history that has subjected these traditions to rigid dogmatic, metaphysical, or sectarian formats or that has failed to find an adequate imaginative and spiritual response to them.

Hegel, perhaps less canny than Kant in this, did not linger on the question "What does it mean to orient oneself in thinking?," being convinced that the art of judging could be embodied in and entirely sublated into a logical dialectic, albeit one in perpetual reconstruction. Like Fichte and Schelling, Hegel found in Kant's mysterious reference to the "common root" of theoretical and practical reason the charter for an integral rationality that eluded Kant himself. Kant gave to his reflections on a teleology in history a purely subjective and moral status, whereas Hegel sought a constitutive rationality in the historical process, as the agon of the spirit finding its way to freedom; he banished mere reflective understanding from the realm of truth (see Horstmann, 165–244). Likewise, in his treatment of aesthetic judgment he introduces subtle distortions of Kant's account. The contingency of beauty, essential to Kant, is mere *Schein* for Hegel and masks the intimate and necessary connection between the beautiful object and the concept. The object is seen as containing a concept or an end in itself; the perception of beauty is no longer disinterested play but is subordinated to grasping conceptual necessity. Whereas Kant delighted in contingent harmonies between reason and nature, which nourished a delightful play of reflection (see Guyer), Hegel's antireflective reading of Kant milks his texts for evidence of constitutive reason at work, a reason for which the subjective activity of judgment can only seem superficial and deficient in rational necessity. From the moment when Hegel decided that his philosophy demanded the form of a system, he began to play down reflection as belonging to the lower realm of "understanding" rather than "reason," notably in his 1802 work *Glauben und Wissen*, the full title of which reads: *Believing and Knowing: The Reflection-Philosophy of Subjectivity in the Completeness of Its Forms as the Philosophy of Kant, Jacobi, and Fichte.*

Hegel never liked to say, "I believe," in reflective, exploratory tones; a philosopher, he thought, should always say, "I know." But today even "hard science" seems to take on the form of a reflective play with hypotheses and to be constantly putting its own status in question. Hegel's own practice reveals that even the most imperialist dialectic finds itself forced to undergo perpetual modifications, which it seeks to justify as developments inscribed in its own inherent dynamic. That is why it is a caricature to present Hegel's "absolute knowing" as narcissistically self-enclosed and self-sufficient (see Kimmerle); rather, it is a knowing that is free for demystified engagement with historical reality, so that Marx may be seen as in fundamental continuity with Hegel in this respect. Dialectic could be seen as an art of judgment that misunderstands its own nature. Up to a point the master of dialectic will triumph on every front, staking a persuasive claim to a more capacious, enlightened, and objective judgment than can be attained by amateurs who entrust themselves to the currents of free reflection. But it may happen that the dialectic is suddenly seen as a cumbersome old machine that prevents intelligence from going forward. When Hegel expounds law, morality, and politics according to the schemes of his *Logic* in the *Philosophy of Right*, he seems to aim at a pharaonic completeness of Reason that could easily become "the most stiff-necked enemy of thinking," as Heidegger observed in a different context. Reflective thinking on the ever shifting forces of law and politics is helped only up to a point by elaborate logical differentiations. With the critical edition of Hegel's different lecture series on the topic, we can see that the glacial appearance of the *Philosophy of Right* (1820) is untrue to the perpetual critical movement of his actual reflections. Even the ideal of systematic logical completeness, as opposed to its actual realization, is a misguided one. Logic serves for critical clarification of the concrete movement of the whole mind, which is always involved in complex unmasterable contexts. A methodology that accompanies thinking on its way (*met-hodos*) sights other patterns of rationality that do not reach closure in logical determinations.

In German idealism, dialectic takes shape as the most comprehensive and systematic way of thinking. Heidegger, who in *Sein und Zeit* dismissed dialectic as the mark of a philosophical embarrassment, thirty years later, in his lectures entitled "Grundsätze des Denkens" (1957), celebrates the way that "thought becomes knowingly dialectical" (*GA* 11:128), not only in Fichte, Schelling, and Hegel, but also in Hölderlin and Novalis. "Thinking has entered the dimension of dialectic" (130), which "we must recognize as the highest dimension of thought in the historical course of metaphysics" (131). Now the supreme principles of thought such as the laws of identity, noncontradiction, and the excluded middle become dynamic and mobile; living thought, as Hegel showed, does not follow the laws of thought, since "everything that is has contradiction for its foundation" (132). But Heidegger remains ambivalent and questionably links dialectic with the triumph of science over nature in the atomic age (134), failing to stress how dialectic seeks to break the grip of standard, atomistic logic (Hartkopf, 12). Heidegger insists that scientific thinking cannot reach the place of origin of the laws of thought; it is a place that is dark to us (137–38). The scholastic shining self-evidence of the laws of thought is deceptive (138); we must think back to their obscure ground. Hegel, too, overcame previous metaphysics and brought thinking back to its original ground, through the ever richer and more integrated development of the Concept; Heidegger takes one step further, seeking "to return to the ground of metaphysics" (*GA* 9:368) by a step back "out of metaphysics into the essence of metaphysics" (*GA* 11:60), or the unthought of metaphysics, acceded to by a preconceptual phenomenological thinking that is reinforced by critical soundings of the blind spots of metaphysics and technology. Hegel's dialectic is led by the ideal of thinking the whole, and it is a heuristic method, a "logoid" rather than seamlessly logical way of thinking (Hartkopf, 15–17), serving to organize in the most illuminating way what has already been thought and thence to break through to new horizons. While dialectic aims to be as logical as possible, it is misguided to attempt to reduce it to a strictly logical form, as some analytic philosophers have attempted; their logical restructurings of Hegel begin by sacrificing large swaths of his work as too untidy, and they lose what is essential, the dynamic forward propulsion of his thinking. While Hegel's dialectic is poles apart from the reflective, open-ended dialectic of Plato, it is not a method of thinking that is generated by the foolproof application of rules; creative imagination is required for its development, and it changes shape in accord with each new field of inquiry in which it is deployed. The art of reflective judgment, despite the subordinate status it is given, continues to accompany the dialectic at every step. Reversing Hegel's priorities, one might present the logical and "logoid" achievements of the dialectic as instruments ultimately at the service of exploratory questioning and divinatory judgment. Thus perhaps even in its final form Hegel's dialectic remains true to the creed expressed by Schelling in 1795, that freedom is "the alpha and omega of all philosophy" (Beiser, 479). Even the sciences, when they are thriving, are led by the *Sache* along paths of inquiry that cannot be mapped logically, even in retrospect.

Theology has followed Kierkegaard in using dialectic to open the human mind to the otherness of the Word of God. Just as Heidegger draws on dialectic only to step beyond it to a phenomenological thinking, so Kierkegaard and Barth use dialectic to step beyond it in the leap of faith or obedience to the Word. Yet shadows of dialectic are allowed to play within their thinking (or in Kierkegaard's case to shape it in depth) even when it is at its farthest from the Hegelian Concept. They give dialectic a more thoroughly negative cast, confirming that the power of Hegel's thought resides in its negative thrust rather than in the turnabout whereby the dialectic is enabled to build a speculative castle. Or does dialectic here become an opportunistic shadow play, abolishing the processes of critical mediation, *Vermittlung*, to fall back on an emphatic immediacy, fixated on the "unhappy consciousness" of solitary inwardness, or on the theological front subscribing to a "positivism of revelation" that freezes the divine Word into an abstract or absolutized Event?

Theology has drawn rather less on Marx's application of dialectic to the material conditions of social existence, though the concrete texture, and the contradictions, of the church's life in the world would give ample scope for such an application. The Gospel does not stop with Kierkegaard's depoliticized, dehistoricized, atomized individuality, "the historical situation of objectless inwardness that he embodies" (Adorno 1966:302). The Christian community, in pursuing the project of the Kingdom, needs to take on board Marx's awareness that the true relations among human beings are presented in a distorting mirror of reification and commodification and thus to acquire critical insight into the many forms of fetishization that block access to the social relationships of freedom that the Gospel is intended to actualize. Currently an anxious laity is crying for a return to "transparency" in church affairs, but this cannot be achieved by moralistic reforms driven by media campaigns. It means exchanging a mindless "communion" or a pastoral populism for a truly communicative adult community. Marx denounced the reification of social activity, "this consolidation of our own product into a factual power over us, which escapes our control, thwarts our expectations, reduces our calculations to naught" (quoted in Ternes, 34). Christians struggle with mystificatory petrified reifications of their communal project, routinized sacraments, frozen authorities, bugbears of privatized conscience, shibboleths used as litmus tests of identity, inbuilt tribal and atavistic reflexes, past vestiges that carry illegitimate weight in the present and serve only to quench the Spirit. An unfree church, everywhere in chains, can hardly be a vanguard of the Kingdom, liberating for the world. But a church that works through its own mystification and bondage dialectically, in debate and concerted reform, could become such a vanguard.

Schleiermacher, steeped in the Greek understanding of dialectic as a practice of dialogue and debate, presents it as the highest theological art. "Faced with the existence of numerous, competing systems, it does not make sense to add to their number or to outbid them by constructing yet another system. It is more meaningful to develop a 'methodology of dispute' [*Kunstlehre des Streitens*]. It would be the goal of dialogue to lead out from the situation of difference and to attain a knowledge binding for all" (Pleger, 5). "With the recognition of relativity, disputes do not vanish from the world, but we have found the condition of possibility of a dispute with chances of success" (159). Success in ecumenical and interreligious debate is not measured, in any case, by the resolution of controversial issues but by the human, intellectual, and theological yield of the ongoing dialogue. Like Talmud study, this has great value and dignity in itself, and it produces "a knowledge binding for all" that is no longer a matter of doctrines or propositions but of lived wisdom.

It is clear that my present attempt to tackle directly the question of the rationality of theology, like the previous orientations to phenomenality and pluralism, will in its turn run into limits and perplexities. The gap between conceptual reason and the phenomena to be thought, and the irreducible pluralism of the historical forms of reason, make it impossible to settle down peacefully in any system of rational principles, so as to manage the phenomenological and pluralistic complexities while admitting their irreducibility to the rational. Not only is it hard to find a secure rational home base from which to launch reflective sorties, but the status of reason itself is put in question. The old Kantian suspicion that reason, in its bid to establish ultimate principles, is doomed to fall into antinomies and contradiction might be dispelled by a dialectical leap forward. More likely, philosophy is fated to remain a reflective discipline, unable to establish its foundations in a definitive, foolproof way. Theology would benefit from embracing such a regime of reflection, no longer hankering after the definitive foundations that would allow it to become a more solid and systematic discipline. To speak in Kantian terms, the faculty of judgment in contemporary theology depends less on determinative judgment, which grasps the data by subordinating them to a concept acquired in advance, than on reflective judgment, which traverses the phenomena in their always changing diversity while inventing concepts that allow them to be better understood. When theology proceeds by determinative judgments it becomes an inquisition applying to suspect discourses ready-made categories to assess how far they accord with the system of orthodox ideas. Reflective judgment, in contrast, begins by stepping outside the enclosure of what is already understood, seeking new categories more adequate to what is met with out there. A free critical play of the mind, reflective judgment is not the prisoner of any dogma, even if it recognizes provisionally or definitively the truth of dogmas, treating them as instruments at the service of the labor of reflective understanding. Recognizing how dogmas are born of previous reflection, it seeks to modify the status of automatically applicable principles that has been given them and to reimmerse them in the movement of reflection that engendered them, rethinking them from their origin to allow their development and eventual "overcoming" in a later, more supple reflection.

But is the appeal to judgment and reflection an ultimate panacea, offering the master key to the entire theological enterprise? No doubt it needs to be relativized in its turn. But given the current theological situation, we may claim for it at least a strategic significance in the task of advancing the discipline in a constructive fashion.

PATHOLOGIES OF THEOLOGICAL JUDGMENT

It may seem harmless to encourage freedom of theological judgment; but a look at the mind-sets opposed to that freedom shows that the struggle for it involves a strong dialectic. That the cultivation of theological judgment is not a matter simply of taste or fashion, just another name for indulging the kind of theological judgments one happens to approve of, can be demonstrated by considering these opposed mind-sets and demonstrating why they fail. This enables a more concrete profiling of the character of legitimate theological judgment. Of course there is an element of choice in the style of judgment we advocate. The choice is rooted in a concrete context, namely, the theological method of Vatican II, with its recourse to scripture, experience, history, and dialogue, over against previous approaches which denied primacy to these factors. "The council has left as a legacy the best theology since the Tridentine period, not only as regards conclusions on specific questions but particularly as concerns theological method. The theological method of the council—attention to history, valuation of experience—cannot be renounced" (Massimo Faggioli, *La Stampa*, 4 October 2012). A fuller grounding of this shift in theological style, and an attempt to draw out its further implications, are what the present inquiry proposes. Moreover, the inaugural insights of the Protestant Reformation, as well as those of Buddhism, can instruct and guide our theory and practice of theological judgment; Vatican II has opened the way to a new appreciation and use of these traditions.

The world of religious thought bears many pathologies demanding diagnosis. Fundamental theology has to negotiate a path of sane judgment between fundamentalism, sectarianism, fanaticism, dogmatism, alienated bureaucratism, and scholasticism, on one side, and relativism, indifferentism, New Age woolliness, ideological hijacking of faith, and deafness to the authority of tradition, on the other. A critique of theological judgment must search out the roots of these many distortions and establish over against them the principles of a viable and progressive procedure. The proliferation of folly must be analyzed so as to become a source of instruction in wisdom, just as in the early church orthodoxy was attained by the analysis and overcoming of proliferant heresy. Fundamental theology thus becomes a medicine chest for all the intellectual ailments to which religion is so prone.

While Hegel, in the *Phenomenology of Spirit*, tackled many deficient forms of rationality and exposed their inner contradictions in an odyssey of mind that opened up the riches of the highest and most integrated forms of thought, the pathologies I shall now discuss do not offer such nourishing fare for dialectic or deconstruction. Their ideological tawdriness and intellectual penury seem to put them outside the pale of theological or philosophical critique. Indeed, the academy and its respected publications generally exclude them as vigilantly as biblical fundamentalists are excluded from self-respecting societies of biblical studies. Yet influential theological movements often allow these pathologies to infiltrate them in subtle ways, and without a thorough understanding of their roots and motivations theology is ill defended against them. A critique of judgment at this level is thus an ungrateful yet necessary task.

Fundamentalism clings to certitudes drawn from a narrow reading of biblical or ecclesiastical sources, which has signed off from attention to contexts and historicity and from participation in a dynamic process of developing understanding. Most Christians probably start

from a fundamentalist attitude to the sources and are only slowly persuaded to adopt a historical and developmental attitude that at first
seems profane. Study of this pathology in the present and in history is
a precondition for clarifying how strong faith can be conjoined with
critical thinking. A culture of judgment would develop systematically
the antidotes to fundamentalism. Fundamentalist narrowness tends to
prompt a tit-for-tat response, a mirror image of the pathology, and
the therapist of fundamentalism should analyze this "transference" to
discern what insecurities underlie both the fundamentalist attitude
and this tit-for-tat reaction.

A first antidote to fundamentalism is hermeneutical awareness,
which realizes the imperfect and provisional nature of every historical
structuration of religious vision, and which undertakes critical rereadings that allow the present value of ancient traditions to be discerned.
Studying his or her own resistances to such awareness, the theologian
will better understand the roots of fundamentalist rejection of it. On
a deeper level, one can engage the lack or anxiety that confines minds
and communities to the fundamentalist attitude; here fundamental
theology comes close to pastoral therapy. As the style of Pope Francis
shows, pastoral theology is not a supplement to dogmatic theology,
mere icing on the cake, but a presentation of evangelical truth in its
integral concrete shape. It would be pastorally as well as hermeneutically unwise to dismiss or ridicule the fundamentalist in the name of a
blithe relativism; rather, one must hold out the invitation to the integral vision from which fundamentalism falls short, weaning the believing mind away from an obsessive focus on particular texts or doctrines
that misses the broad sweep of the vision these subserve, whether
today or in their past contexts. The patient dismantling, one by one,
of the fixations that are the cement of fundamentalism is instructive in
itself and the only efficacious barrier to their reconstitution. One
must assess the objective or subjective conditions that give rise to fundamentalism if one is to achieve its reflective overcoming and its replacement by a sober and rational respect for the sacred authorities.
To be tackled especially are the principles at the basis of fundamentalist outlooks, for the defense system of fundamentalism cannot be
penetrated by surface skirmishes about particular issues. It has deep

foundations, for instance, in the premise that any normal, undefensive historical approach to scripture is inherently sacrilegious, or that critical questioning must be suspended in face of divine authority, or at least kept subservient to obedience to that authority. Protestant Christianity draws its strength from the wholehearted embrace of scripture by Luther and Calvin, and this continues to animate and galvanize evangelical communities throughout the world. To combine this love of scripture with critical consciousness is a difficult art, on which the health of biblical religions depends.

Of course, as Johannes Zachhuber warns, "The increasingly aggressive tone dominating the internal discourse of many major Christian denominations" cannot be simply blamed on "fundamentalism": "In fact the career of this term is in itself a powerful example of contemporary rhetoric of exclusion practised by those who, in their own view, intend to be perfectly inclusive" (210). We must avoid a dualistic attitude to those groups we see as misguided, not making them scapegoats to shore up our own identity; rather, let us see the pathologies of theological judgment as temptations inherent in the enterprise of religious thinking as such, lying in wait for the would-be enlightened and progressive theologian as well.

Sectarianism invests in denominational positions at the expense of a vision that would stress what all churches or all religions have in common (be it only a space of questioning) and that would open up to an eschatological future that surpasses them all and toward which they are under way. Most religious people start with a conception of their identity that is narrowed in a sectarian way. To develop flexibility of judgment one must cultivate transdenominational thinking, aware that one can do justice to no religious theme if one confines oneself to the optic of a single tradition. The more one advances in dialogue with the religious or nonreligious other, the more one senses the painful penury of one's initial sectarian position. This dialogue is the very element of theological thinking. It is based on recognition of a revelation of the divine on the scale of human history in its totality, whatever prerogatives theologians may still claim for Judaism and Christianity, or for their own denomination within the latter.

Sectarian notes easily infiltrate theologies that are self-consciously denominational. Scholars advocating the alleged ongoing value of allegorical exegesis sometimes suggest that failure to recognize it is the result of a Protestant blindness, although Vatican II makes no mention of allegorical exegesis in *Dei Verbum*, and although it is rarely practiced by post–Vatican II exegetes. As Sean Freyne noted in 2012 at a Dublin conference commemorating the fiftieth anniversary of Vatican II, the document of the Pontifical Biblical Commission entitled "The Interpretation of Scripture in the Church" (1992) gives a minor place to patristic exegesis, but the *Catechism of the Catholic Church* (1994) persists in regarding it as a live option. Indeed, on many points the Catechism, largely by virtue of its very format, is unconducive to theological judgment, sometimes recounting scriptural matters such as the story of paradise or the Resurrection narratives in what seems a woodenly fundamentalist way, perhaps practicing a prudent suspension of judgment that ends up in a total lack of it. It is not only Catholics who clutch at past convictions and notions long after they are emptied of vital meaning. Lutheran reverence for the doctrine of justification by faith can also degenerate into its invocation as a sectarian shibboleth. Denominational identity in Christian theology today is more responsibly enacted through a conscious effort to overcome inherited blind spots and fixations than in anything resembling a proud assertion of identity. What should be passionately affirmed is the Christ we have in common, for he is the most valid component of the identity of any Christian group. To make reflection on the sectarian temptation fruitful for theological judgment, the theologian should assume that no one is immune from provincial restrictions of his or her horizon, that overcoming narrow identity fixations is a constant task for all, and that even transdenominational or ecumenical postures can be taken up as a party line that reflects a sectarian dynamic in its very antisectarianism. Any pathology of judgment that we succeed in clearly identifying must be treasured not as an enemy to be targeted but as a revelator of the dangers besetting religious thought, of which the theologian must cultivate a heightened awareness, thinking against them more and more self-consciously.

Bureaucratism administers matters of faith with an excess of attention to order and control, becoming cut off from living faith and the possibility of addressing any positive glad tidings to humanity. The antidote is dialectical engagement that connects every datum of faith

to the questions of the contemporary world, which will always prescribe some rethinking of the datum. Such engagement teaches that to
recite orthodox propositions cannot guarantee possession of truth
and that true speech is a richer event than the formulation of a true
proposition; the latter is not fully true, fully connected with the real,
if it cannot be enfleshed as true speech. A propositional disciplining
of living speech may be necessary, but it is the living speech that is the
ultimate judge of the relevance of propositions. The stereotypical un-
imaginative bureaucrat is a "control freak," suspicious of any stirring
of life that escapes his or her control, and thus perpetually quenching
the Spirit. Useless to tell the Spirit "blow here" or "blow there," for it
blows where it wills. Yet theologians should not delude themselves
that they have attained an imaginative vision far beyond bureaucratic
dullness. To the contrary, their comfortable processing of theological
topics and their history can stifle imagination. This variety of clerical-
ism is the most persistent occupational hazard of theologians. Often
what the theologian imagines to be a daring leap of insight comes
across to the outsider as just a bureaucrat's purr of satisfaction when
shuffling old files.

Obsession with orthodoxy is a kind of bureaucratism. Orthodoxy,
or sound judgment, is a beautiful ideal, but from which we decline
when we overstress the defense of creedal landmarks. These may be
of immense strategic significance in a battle of ideas, yet they should
not be taken as the living presence of ultimate truth. They are claims
built up in history, tried and trusted conventions, to be handled with
a certain wise detachment. They should be held in a modest and reflective way, as one holds real convictions, calmly, without shrill emphasis. In the Vatican's penitential utterances of 2000 the excesses of
some Christians in their zeal for truth were deplored, but the great
bureaucratic institution of the Inquisition, so central to the polity, theology, spirituality, law, and constitution of the church for centuries,
was not explicitly rejected. There are several apologetic writers who
celebrate this institution for its civilized and equitable handling of the
problem of heretical deviation. But when orthodoxy crumples into
worry about deviation it becomes itself a heresy factory. Indeed, the
Inquisition needs to be unmasked as the supreme heresy of Christian

history, built on the reduction of truth to correct views, the objects of violent attachment, and turned into weapons against those who appeared to question or doubt them. The real heretic, however, is not "out there" but lodges in the orthodox breast, materializing when love of truth changes into zealotry about claims and views. The current failure to address in depth what went wrong in the Inquisition allows an eerie atavism to take over: inquisitorial attitudes resurface even in this new millennium; faith is still confused with fanaticism, while openness of mind and open discussion are identified as the spirit of heresy. Such reactions generate a circular discourse feeding on itself, in unprofitable strife with imagined foes, thwarting any liberative actualization of the élan of faith.

The antidote to this obsession is the confidence of evangelical faith. Theologians may be so conscious of their duty to be critical over against traditions suspected of being oppressive that they have trouble assuming a full-blooded ecclesial faith. But equally a professional, clerical concern with points of doctrine also alienates theology from the large biblical horizons that call forth generous imagination before crystallizing in theologoumena. Orthodoxy is not in the first place a matter of the past; it even becomes a poison if it does not express the vision of a church open to the future and to dialogue with the diverse voices that are calling to it in the present. In any case orthodoxy is a secondary virtue, remaining at the service of the vitality of a vision of faith. To give it primacy is like killing a living language by worrying at every moment about the correctness of its grammatical rules. If "error exists nowhere in and for itself but always only in relation to truth, and is not fully understood until one has found its connection with the truth, and the true, to which it adheres" (Schleiermacher, 1:50–51), to suppress error without discussion is to close off access to truth. When something that seems obviously an error keeps on surfacing, insistently, as in the various flash points concerning ministry and the Eucharist that currently create tension between theologians and the Vatican, this is an indicator that something needs to be thought out more thoroughly, that vigilant stressing of the points of orthodoxy is not enough to provide the integral and persuasive vision required, which can ripen only in open discussion. Nor is there any orthodoxy that is sheltered from error and in full possession of truth. The health of our religious ideas is only relative and is preserved only in the mobility of dialogue. Sometimes, in their eagerness to combat an unacceptable statement of a theologian, the guardians of orthodoxy carry their critique too far, trying to build up a case against everything the theologian says and thus missing the valuable contribution he or she may be able to make in spite of unorthodoxy on some points. Or an entire theological method may be marked as dangerous or deviant because some of its adherents end up opposing church doctrine. But orthodox faith is ill defended by simply cutting off paths of thought perceived as threatening. It should not fear to be immersed in the dangerous element, bearing its stresses and reacting to them in vigorous but undefensive debate, in the confidence that the truth will reemerge, no doubt transformed, within the practice of this open dialogue. Historically, the Reformation offered the church a great opportunity to practice such openness—to formulate differences sharply but discuss them calmly. Can the serenity of faith and reason that was lacking then prevail in our more jaded times, so that we can revisit the sixteenth-century theological battlefields together, ecumenically, in order to learn the wisdom of hindsight?

To be sure, none of this will cut much ice with those who nag and fret about orthodoxy, and indeed it is not a fully adequate response to them. A dialogue that goes beyond tit-for-tat should espouse the concern for truth that is the noble core of heresy hunting. Not just diplomatically, or as a token gesture aiming to secure ecclesiastical respectability, but speaking from that depth where an ultimate, truth, is at issue, the theologian should say: "I truly appreciate your concern for the truth and integrity of the Christian faith, and I seek only to translate it into categories that show it better, in all its splendor, for today." To coax the interlocutor away from a concern with truth as grasped in terms of a narrow framework to a broader embrace of truth that integrates all that was valid in the narrow concern, the theologian must again look inward and assess how broad and narrow notions of truth jostle within his or her own religious thinking.

Scholasticism, in the bad sense, is preoccupied with theoretical questions that are tangential to the thought and experience of the contemporary world and offer no point of articulation of theory with praxis. Should we subscribe to the judgment of John Colet on Aquinas, as recalled by Erasmus: "He must have been very arrogant, to define everything with such temerity and superciliousness, and he must have had a rather worldly spirit or he would not have contaminated the entire doctrine of Christ with his profane philosophy" (quoted in Renaudet, 34)? Colet, Erasmus's spiritual guide for twenty years, was himself one of the most eloquent advocates of a return to scripture, a plea long associated with schism and heresy but favorably received at last at Vatican II. The role of scripture, history, and experience in theology now, a role which Erasmus pioneered, must certainly be invoked in judging the strengths and limits of scholasticism, and this opens a critical perspective even on Aquinas which can never again be closed.

The antidote to scholasticism is a quest for the real that steps back from speculative constructions to the heart of the Gospel, as attested in the sources and in contemporary Christian life. To discuss classical theological issues as if we were still living in the days of Augustine or Aquinas (or in those of Hegel and Schelling) is not a prophetic resistance to modernity or postmodernism but an avowal of incapacity for integral reflection. A theology based on archaic categories, be they those of the Greek fathers, of Thomism, or of German idealism, is not a real theology but a pastiche, like a work of literature written in a vanished style. Even a theology holding fast to biblical concepts may soon lose its freshness and become another escape from the present task of thought. To some extent theology has always built itself a Noah's Ark of Christian representations, refusing to take quite seriously the questions and values of those outside. This is a good strategy for identity building but implies a violent repression of unsettling questions and their bearers. This dark side of Christian identity, apparent even in the patristic centuries, calls for vigilant scrutiny. A common feature of thinkers ensconced in scholasticism is what Heidegger calls "blindness to being," an inability to open up to phenomena not accounted for within their speculative set of categories, and the theological equivalent of this is "blindness to God," an inability to think of God—"*Dieu sensible au coeur*" (Pascal)—from contemplative experience rather than through manipulation of categories. Theological judgment never ceases to assess the adequacy of its categories at this basic level, with an almost literary anxiety to find *le mot juste*, to give persuasive voice to its themes. The many linguistic debacles in contemporary presentations of the Gospel, including in translations of the Bible and the Missal, can be studied as instructive counterexamples, which show that failure of theological judgment begins at the level of our everyday language.

The new discipline of comparative scholasticism reduces the distance between the intellectual profiles of Buddhism and Christianity (see Cabezón, Griffiths), in that both religions developed a scholastic culture allowing a great space for the free play of the mind. Yet scholasticism disappoints today's questioners in all religions by its neglect of such factors as feeling, mood (*Stimmung*), contemplative attention, and existential authenticity, as well as by its estrangement from historical vision. Scholastic reasoning would like to reabsorb and reintegrate the soil that nourishes it. Aristotle warned that abstraction (*aphairesis*) should not become separation (*chōrismos*), but insofar as he failed to follow his own advice he became the father of scholasticism (Vaihinger, 389). When Hegel identified the movement of the categories with that of reality itself, he robbed thought of its human, contingent, makeshift character to make it the necessary unfolding of essential structures (10–11). A theology that made itself a fortress of well-defined categories, mastering and unifying the biblical data, would be a prisoner of that Hegelian myth, even if based on the hearing of faith, for the hearing would be structured in advance as a project of control. The ideal of Vatican II, to interpret the Gospel in light of the signs of the times, gives a very different charter to theology, summoning it to the service of a renewed church rooted in scripture, building collegiality, engaged in work for justice and peace and in warm ecumenical and interreligious sharing, cherishing freedom of conscience, and able to worship in a joyful and creative liturgy in which all the arts of today have a place. Some have attempted to reduce the shift to an open-ended practice of theological judgment, which the Council enacted and encouraged, to mere "pastoral" accommodation without serious "doctrinal" relevance. In dealing with this and other skirmishes, the theologian should seek to bring out the underlying epistemological framework of both sides, uncovering under the foreground controversy a more fundamental, albeit unarticulated, one bearing on the very nature of religious truth and its transmission and development.

The paradigms that prevailed in the long scholastic era of theology are often invoked out of season in a way that mystifies theological thinking today. These too must be assessed and overcome when they are obsolete. The honored role given to a quest for speculative insight in the early church oriented theology toward a systematic enclosure that it keeps falling back into today even as richer and more promising horizons are opening out on every side. For many of the fathers, speculation was an evil made necessary by the needs of apologetics or the correction of heresy. However, Gregory of Nyssa and Augustine associated the speculative *intellectus fidei* with the sixth beatitude, "Blessed are the pure in heart, for they shall see God" (Mt 5:8), and set it up as the highest goal of Christian thought. It was still a spiritual ideal but in time became an intellectualist one, animated by a kind of rationalism. Augustine followed Origen in declaring that the role of the *minores* in the church is to believe while that of the *maiores* is to understand (*intelligere*). Commenting on the sixth beatitude, he says that love of truth is what purifies the mind and that the act of *intellectus* carries this pure intention to its fulfillment in the joy of understanding (*De Sermone Domini in Monte* 2.14). Influenced by the model of the Plotinian *Nous*, which completed the identification of Plato's intelligible world with Aristotle's self-thinking mind, Augustine grafted a speculative pathos onto biblical faith, giving theological judgment the metaphysical cast that would flourish in scholasticism. He launched the quest for *intellectus*, seen as a necessarily edifying spiritual activity, with a candor that would not survive the centuries of scholasticism that made this quest a vast academic industry. But he also underscores, especially in the *De Trinitate*, the eschatological tension inherent in the quest for *intellectus* and even in the attainment of it; the effort to penetrate intellectually the mysteries of faith shares the dynamic existential condition of faith itself, "forgetting what lies behind and striving toward what lies ahead" (Phil 3:13). Each advance in insight opens a still greater range of what remains to be understood.

Augustine's speculative tour de force, the psychological analogy of the Trinity, is an inconsistent and broken-backed construction (Horn, 210–17), and he himself seems intent on demonstrating its inadequacies, in book 15 of *De Trinitate*, so that they serve to point to divine inscrutability and are reinserted into the existential, eschatological striving forward to the heavenly knowledge of God "face to face." Thus theological dignity is conferred on the failure of the speculative quest. The scholastic theologians sought to iron out the flaws in Augustine's constructions and in doing so lost the reflective open-endedness of his inquiry. Developing the most metaphysical dimension of Augustinian rationality, which Augustine himself held in check, they neglected the wider exercise of theological judgment, which focuses on scriptural and experiential *sapientia* rather than on speculative *intellectus*. The blame lies partly with Augustine, in that he failed to make his biblical material as interesting as his speculative ventures. In Aquinas the pyrotechnics of his constructions of the immanent Trinity are again far more gripping than his handling of the scriptural data. Thus in the two great Latin theologians scripture risks being pushed back to a secondary place, to the domain of the merely homiletic. Within scientific theology, it fails to breathe freely and to establish its primacy. This is much more the case with resolutely intellectualist theologians such as Duns Scotus. It took the Reformation to correct this metaphysical captivity of scripture, establishing new canons of theological judgment that show up inadequacies in the scholastic regime of truth.

To save speculative medieval theologians for theology today, it seems a worthwhile strategy to reread them against the grain, highlighting the underdeveloped biblical aspects, as in Barth's revisionist reading of Anselm. Anselm was steeped in the pathos of the speculative quest, seeking to put the truths of faith on a rational footing, yet Barth boldly claims that the only *intelligere* he was concerned with was that "desired" by faith (Barth 1958:15). But faith is not an ahistorical reality seeking only one form of understanding. Barth would make Anselm's *intellectus* the self-understanding that biblical faith seeks in Protestant culture. A more radical overcoming of the ideal of *intellectus* is required. It would not suffice to say that the *intellectus fidei* should remain integrated into the inner dynamic of faith, so as not to become a metaphysical speculation cut off from the being-in-the-world proper to faith. One must put in question the idea that faith is called to perfect itself in speculative understanding or that deeper familiarity with the divine necessarily comes about through conceptual lucidity. It could be the case that the understanding of faith has very little to do with conceptual mastery. It has to do more with interpretation than with explanation, more with thinking than with reason, more with reflective assessment than with diremptive definition.

"It is more difficult to put solid thoughts in flux than to make sensible existence fluid," said Hegel (1988:27). The path to the understanding of faith will involve grasping classical dogmas and theologoumena as traces of the movement of the believing mind in the past—"What was the matter itself is no longer anything but a trace" (22)—or scars of ancient mental battles, so that they are caught up into the more flexible thinking now required of us. If dogmatism is "the opinion that the true consists in a proposition that is a solid result or that is immediately known" (30), it can be surmounted only if one recalls dogmas to the context of their initial formation, which provides their meaning and at the same time limits their bearing, as moments in a historical process. Those who embrace Aquinas's trinitarian theology and his Christology as the secure foundations of all further theological thought are obliged to see his categories ahistorically, as transparently connecting with the contemporary mind. If the same attitude were adopted toward Thomist cosmology and psychology the anachronism would be apparent.

The danger of a paralyzing closure threatens all theology. Even a sophisticated hermeneutics can be a lure, trafficking expertly in traditions and interpretations but failing to secure a link with the real. Just as accomplished bureaucrats can fail from incapacity to see beyond the culture of their class, so theologians have trouble finding the exit from the labyrinth formed by the habits of their discipline, instilled over centuries. Bonhoeffer, in prison, glimpsed the exit, whereas Barth, in the same grim years, wrote a treatise on predestination, replying too late to a question no longer asked (in a masterly deconstructive retrieval of centuries of theological thought), later adding four tomes on Creation that manage to avoid any reference to contemporary cosmology or biology. Likewise, Hans Urs von Balthasar, after Vatican II, built a baroque edifice that for all its spaciousness shows little cognizance of the horizons the Council wanted to open. Balthasar slights and by-passes the theological method of the Council, in a theology "from above" that "does not seem to hold itself accountable to Scripture, tradition, or its readers, but somehow soars above them all" (Kilby, 40), scorning liberation theology, interreligious theology, and critical scriptural scholarship that seeks to approach the biblical God and his Christ "from below." The decades-long overdependence of many students of theology on the massive corpus of the Swiss master has alienated them from authentic hermeneutics and left them unpracticed in its methods. Grasping revelation in a mystical aesthetics as a unitary phenomenon, this theology underestimates the degree to which biblical knowledge of God is knit together with the obliqueness and elusiveness of language and history, and the play of judgment these elicit. Perhaps the riches of Balthasar can be retrieved in this key, but the key needs first to be securely established.

OPEN FAITH

A culture of theological judgment that can overcome the pathologies listed above must nourish itself from the broad reaches of scriptural and ecclesial tradition, learning to think as scripture thinks and as the church thinks (*sentire cum Ecclesia*)—the church not of catechisms only but in the totality of its prophetic and pastoral instinct as it meets the challenges of the times. Theology receives the heritage of faith with generous trust, but at the same time it opens up to questions that make necessary a reinterpretation of this heritage. If Christian tradition is currently undergoing a paradigm shift or a change in its "regime of truth" that demands a radical change of mental habits, then the strategies of restoration are misplaced and we need to advance further along the critical paths that came into view after the Council. For this purpose we need a culture of *open discussion*, which provides the oxygen necessary for the thinking and imagining that is required. To a certain extent, all religions in their institutional embodiment want to control open discussion, keeping it on a leash of orthodoxy. While it is true that the spirit of collegiality promoted by Vatican II belongs to the essence of the church from New Testament times and is not to be confused with modern democratic culture, nonetheless the human rights of freedom of opinion and freedom of expression, as defined in the Universal Declaration of Human Rights, are slowly winning recognition within the ecclesial enclosure, as reflected in Canon 212 in the 1983 Code of Canon Law, which recognizes that the faithful, according to their competence, have the right and sometimes the duty to make known to their pastors and the other faithful their opinion on matters concerning the good of the church. The right to public opinion, even through the media, is recognized for the first time in church law. However, when a review of canon law offered critical reflections on the motu proprio *Ad tuendam fidem* in 1998 the competent Roman congregations told them that the document was not subject to debate. "The legislative text forbidding that certain burning topics be spoken of is itself excluded from any discussion" (Werckmeister, 141). A true ecclesiology of communion has to treasure the behaviors that most strengthen bonds of community in the modern world: free exchange of opinions, mutually enriching communication of ideas, even of ideas that can disturb or shock. While canon law affords rights and freedoms of which people, including the lower clergy, are often ill apprised, one might ask whether such fundamental rights as freedom of speech can be parceled and measured in a limitative legal code. The voice of the faithful, and the voice of bishops expressing their collegial authority, are theological realities before they are given legal embodiment. A more collegial church would cultivate patient reflection rather than peremptory judgment, and the judgments that would ripen through its deliberative processes would be better founded and received.

It is not wrong to insist that theology should be at the service of the church's kerygma, but this should not be used to repress the critical aspect of that service or to enfeeble the dialectical relationship between magisterial teaching and theological questioning. There is no foolproof method for harmonizing the duty of respect and the duty of criticism; criticism seems to annul respect, respect seems to blunt criticism. Theologians deploy a wide range of approaches, with many tensions and unclear points. Here again the play of judgment is indispensable. Theology is responsible not only to the magisterium, or even to the prophetic insights of the people of God, but also to the questions of the world. If the church judges the world, guiding it to its good, the world in turn judges the church, not only morally, but in reminding it of realities to which its teaching must do justice.

Sculptors uncover form by cutting away; scientists work toward truth by falsifying previously accepted hypotheses. The judgment that seeks the vital dynamic of faith today must negate what hides or encumbers this, as in previous periods when Christianity defined or redefined its basic thrust—the fourth-century formation of dogma, the sixteenth-century reforms, the restructuring of theology from a hearing of the biblical Word in twentieth-century dialectical theology. Perhaps the present kairos is an even more radical turning point: "From the point of view of systems theory, all the religions are now living a phase of 'fluctuation.' Rules and bounds seen until recently as sacrosanct are losing their status at great speed. Even the important 'doctrinal contents' of the tradition are no longer known or are only scantily attended to, while instead one finds a growing curiosity about and absorption in new spiritual arrangements. This phase of the present development, clearly marked by breakdown and transition, is an inevitable process, full of opportunities, but not without dangers either" (Drewermann, 214). One of these "dangers" is the reduction of faith to New Age spirituality or psychotherapy. Theology needs to link current spiritual breakthroughs, if such they are, to the tradition, by rereading it with an eye to its depth-insights, hidden by a language that has grown overfamiliar. No revolution in structures or spiritual vision can eliminate, though it may recontextualize, what is true and living in the ancient sources.

The health of theological judgment depends on the health of a faith that is both lively and critical. Faith is the first theological judgment and orients the whole discipline. But faith has become a monolithic notion that needs to be reimmersed in history, so as to uncover the pluralism of usages hidden by that deceptive homonym. *Faith* can signify basic existential trust or a mistrustful clinging to a slogan or a fetish. If it is contrasted with *reason*, one must note that this word, too, masks a pluralism of historical usages. The judgment of faith can be a mobile and differentiated investment of trust, rather as aesthetic judgment is a flexible and critical response to the artworks that fix its

attention. A faith not frozen in a posture of absolute certitude but reacting to the objects to which it relates, registering their real rather
than merely claimed credibility, would be a generous opening of the
mind, and its judgments would be no less responsible and intellectually respectable than those of ordinary rationality.

It is an apologetical commonplace that all human action and
knowledge is rooted in the soil of belief, an idea that brings the notion of faith as principle of perception and knowledge of things divine
back down to earth. Contrary to the perception of good and evil or of
beauty, faith is said to be a supernatural gift; but this idea can be
spelled out in fairly realistic terms if we think not of an invisible magical process but of the concrete effect that the object of faith has on the
believer. Like moral and aesthetic perception, religious perception
brings about a change in the existence of the subject, opens up a new
possibility of life. Faith exists only as response to its object and is "lost"
when that object is forgotten. Far from being a monolithic virtue, it
takes as many forms as there are objects to which it adheres, from
"philosophical faith" (Karl Jaspers) that affirms general convictions on
the meaning of life (and that no doubt underpins rational arguments
for the existence of a God or the immortality of the soul) to the different cultures of faith in revealed religions, in which the element of belief
is but one component in an ensemble of praxes and feelings.

Faith is not a fixed starting point to be followed in a second phase
by the quest for "the understanding of faith" (*intellectus fidei*). Rather,
it is a mobile and dynamic outlook that grows and deepens, nourished
by scripture, liturgy, and the experiences of Christian life. This mobility
complicates the role of faith as first principle of theological judgment.
It no longer orients theology in the form of a set of propositions *de
fide* which are defined by the magisterium and which theology is supposed to defend and elucidate. A dynamic and changing faith gives
theology another task, that of negotiating between the past heritage
and the new possibilities now dawning, situating that heritage in relation to the life of faith that produced it and that surpasses it. Theology
has thus to reevaluate the function of dogma and weigh the contribution and the capacity for development of every path of faith that opens
up. Theology becomes a critique lodged within the life of faith in the

diversity of its forms, rather as literary criticism lodges in the texts it studies. One might say that faith comes first and that critical judgment is merely auxiliary, just as literary criticism is merely auxiliary to literature. But that division is too neat. Faith itself is often a critique— consider the prophets, Jesus, Paul—just as literary works critique one another. Theology shapes and develops this latent critical or iconoclastic dimension of faith, blurring the distinction between believing affirmation and theological critique. Theology lodges in the discourse of faith not only to study and appreciate it but to become an essential aspect of it, just as literary criticism has from classical times been an essential component of literary creation. Theology frees faith from its shackles and is in turn freed by faith. The critical judgment of faith is prolonged in theological judgment, which may become an expression of faith in action, a prophetic activity.

Thus conceived, faith is no longer the rival of free reflection but invites that reflection to a larger horizon. The enemies of theological liberalism in the nineteenth century such as Newman and Scheeben stressed that faith is an act of obedience crushing our pride, a *sacrificium intellectus*, welcoming the gift of a new, supernatural principle of knowledge (see Murray, 21–23). This is an Abrahamic exodus out of narrow worldly categories, through encounter with an external reality and the hearing of a word that opens a perspective wider than what skeptical reason could envisage. The very breadth of this vision is what prompts faith to undertake critical reflection on its own tradition. Faith is attuned to what is worthy of faith, taking this, dropping that. To some extent it entrusts this discernment to the church magisterium, but it reserves a margin of critical freedom over against magisterial formulations, not only as regards their adequacy, but sometimes as regards their substance. A critique in the name of faith, like Luther's, surpasses the negativity of a purely rational critique by its exercise of prophetic judgment, its claim to perceive a concrete aspect of the revealed that official teaching has occluded or neglected. Theological judgment seeks to do justice to the two poles of magisterial and prophetic teaching, espousing the tensions between them. Full acceptance of this dialectic could release the church from anomie and make its conflicts more fruitful.

RELATIVISM

The church, Benedict XVI once remarked, is not a club for free-thinkers; the liturgical community is not a discussion group. Yet in a democratic culture, which is a culture of discussion and reflection, it is normal that church life, too, should be impregnated with those virtues. The alleged "tyranny of relativism" is sometimes perhaps a misnomer for the reflective reason that has been for centuries in Europe the vital milieu for all alert and responsible thought—here is an Enlightenment heritage that must be cultivated and developed, let the chips fall where they may. The free exchange of ideas need not thwart decision and action, or, in the church, unity in the act of worship; rather, it protects their authenticity, grounding it in mutual recognition. Fundamental theology has a role in guiding such debate, mapping its parameters, taking stock of its major questions, and so promoting the formation of a dialogal culture in the church. Casting out fear, it can show that open discussion is not a threat to faith but the condition of its proper exercise.

The debates of Vatican II were the happiest demonstration of teaching authority in recent times, and the continuation of that debate at the local level brings an experience of the learning church, *ecclesia discens*, in which the teachers learn and the learners teach. If bureaucratic fears block this process, fundamental theology has to plead for a new model of church life, for in exploring the paths of judgment it discovers as well the conditions required for its free and healthy exercise. A church that had suppressed freedom of reflection would, and did, produce the corresponding fundamental theology, a fortress-style apologetics. Choosing free discussion as the necessary milieu of its reflections, fundamental theology sets the tone for all other theological domains, which in turn acquire the questioning and reflective hue of fundamental theology. The questions of the latter can no longer be treated as preliminaries, to be solved and laid aside as one enters the labyrinth of particular dogmatic treatises.

People are troubled by moral relativism, the replacement of clear moral rules by a hortatory appeal to conscience, now seemingly obliged to practice a subtle calculus of results, feelings, or intangible values such as authenticity, sincerity, and fulfillment. This seems a formula for Hamletian paralysis. People also worry about religious relativism, the pervasive sense that all religions are more or less equally valid spiritual paths. Doctrinal relativism is closely linked to this and holds that dogmatic language has no objective content—certainly not one that remains invariant over time—but merely gives expression to religious intuitions. Religions become imaginative webs of interpretation rather than secure sets of certitudes. Cultural and historical relativism recognizes that all truths and meanings are constructed within a particular cultural and historical horizon and must undergo huge change when transferred from one horizon to another. The more radical, but self-refuting, movement of philosophical relativism holds that no truth can be stated at all, even the truth that no truth can be stated. All of these movements are laced with a "hermeneutics of suspicion" that in the wake of Feuerbach, Nietzsche, Marx, and Freud queries the genealogy of religious traditions as human inventions whose real motive and function must be brought to light. Relativism goes hand in hand with secularism and with a naturalist view of religions as ideologies jostling for a place in the market of cultural products.

I would argue that a reflective and differentiated response to these movements of contemporary thought can recognize their promise as well as their danger, even to the point of adopting an alternative mantra: "the blessings of relativism." In fact, the impact of all these movements is not to license a free-for-all of gratuitous interpretations but rather to impose a severe restraint on what theologians can legitimately say. Yes, a skeptical relativism can sap moral and religious conviction and even devalue scientific and philosophical thought. But full recognition of the relativizing factors at work in modern religious, moral, philosophical, and scientific consciousness has a bracing effect, too, inviting a more intelligent handling of our traditions of insight and founding a riper judgment in our humble acknowledgment of the shape of contemporary regimes of truth.

What is called relativism, in the moral sphere, is often merely an acceptance that a shift is taking place in the anthropological paradigm, with the emergence of a subtler understanding of the values involved in sexuality and marriage, birth and death, natural environment and

social coexistence. But an aprioristic construction of a new paradigm—
in the fields of psychology, philosophy, law—needs to be supplemented by cross-cultural study. William LaFleur studied traditional
Japanese attitudes to miscarriage, abortion, and infanticide (sending the
baby, regretfully, back to the gods), showing how these human realities
can be situated within a moral and spiritual horizon far from that of
the Christian West. Maurice Pinguet similarly reviewed attitudes to
suicide in Japanese tradition. Here the relativization of a paradigm
proceeds not by abstract argument but in dialogue with those who
live or lived by other paradigms. "Thou shalt not murder" (Ex 20:13)
is an ethical universal, but its formulation and application in diverse
cultural and religious contexts require an art of judgment responsive
to the ethical claims and pressures of these contexts, which cannot
simply be written off as benighted.

Will such exposure to other cultural frameworks result in a relativization of the Enlightenment itself and all the subsequent movements in which modern rationality has unfolded? Will it replace the
Western ideology of progress with a pluralistic attitude to the interpretation of history? Will it undermine our absolutization of freedom, democracy, tolerance, and human rights? That would indeed be
a bitter reward for reveling in the relative. François Jullien (155–56)
suggests that since "we can no longer see ourselves henceforth other
than as *cultural subjects* (thus marking at least a partial breakdown of
the 'transcendental subject')" the universality of our ethical judgments must be rethought along the lines of the universality of aesthetic judgments in Kant: "When I judge that something 'is beautiful,'
though I am indeed making a singular judgment, at the same time I
claim that all people necessarily agree thereon; in other words I do
not allow anyone to be of a contrary opinion." When Europeans assert human rights for all peoples as an unconditional principle, they
do so without being able to formulate a transcultural definition of this
value. Our formulation of human rights and other Enlightenment values is conditioned by the history of their emergence, particularly by
the presence of Christian theology both as matrix and as that against
which these values had to struggle for autonomy. Nor is this tradition
without its inner tensions, contradictions, and themes for ongoing

open-ended revision. Awareness of this cultural and historical embeddedness checks a naive universalism but does not undercut the legitimate element of universality in the judgments formed with such immense intellectual and political effort in European and American history. These judgments, Kant would say, appeal across cultural differences to a common human sense (*Gemeinsinn*) and a "general communicability" that is experienced in all dialogue, though it eludes formulation as a concept.

In the sphere of religion, the factors making for relativization are more sharply marked. Modern historical consciousness has some impact on moral discourse but a great impact on religious discourse, for the changes undergone by religious ideas even within a single tradition and within the constraints of orthodoxy are even more dramatic than the variations of moral judgment. The modern awareness of cultural pluralism finds more food for thought in the garish variety of religious universes than in the quieter differences in ethical understanding. Insight into the inherent conventionality of religious language and gestures also goes much further than attempts to show the element of conventionality in moral reflection.

"The historical sense is altogether new in the world," wrote George Sand. "People are going to set about studying ideas like facts, and beliefs like organisms" (quoted in Chrétien, 302). The historical consciousness that has been growing in the Western world since the early nineteenth century is no longer a preserve of scholars but has begun to infiltrate ordinary religious awareness and practice. Increasingly, when believers use the words and gestures of their religion it is with the historicizing awareness that they are inscribing themselves in a tradition—or that they wish to do so, despite a sense that the gestures it prescribes are archaic, unreal. Today this historical self-consciousness embraces not only one's own tradition but also the wider community of faiths, bringing a critical sense of the nonabsoluteness of any one mode of engaging with ultimate reality. The community that recites the Lord's Prayer is increasingly aware that it is enacting a specifically Christian convention, while neighboring communities enact conventions no less efficacious for them. Such "etic" awareness might undercut or dilute "emic" participation at first, but subsequently it can renew one's relations to the forms one uses, as they are reappropriated in their fragile status as historically tried and tested means of opening to the divine. Such a reflective, self-conscious, and modest reappropriation of one's religious culture is becoming a hallmark of adult faith.

In the past, the moral, dogmatic, and sacramental structures of Christianity were absolutized, as embodying a permanent and universal cosmic order. But a critical sense of historicity that "goes all the way down," breaking with convenient providentialist patterns, will take seriously the fact that all of these sacrosanct institutions were set in place and perfected by human reflection, born in specific times and places, and developed over centuries. Believers trust that the Spirit is at work in this process, but that conviction cannot alter the fabric of history, always made up of human interpretations and decisions. Divine action is primary, in Creation, in redemption, in the new creation founded in the Resurrection, but our human ways of discerning, interpreting, and narrating this divine action are always exposed to reassessment. A wider historical perspective will inevitably affect our interpretation and assessment of the entire history of Christianity so far. As believers reappropriate their history in a demystified style, they will come to a more lucid appreciation of how their religious culture has forged its creative trajectory through the ages. As ritualizations of human activity, orienting it to God as the source of its ultimate significance, the Jewish Torah, the Christian sacraments, and all other such religious patterns of behavior emerge from within that everyday human activity, shaping it in forms and conventions that become symbolically expressive of human finitude and hope. The claim that they are revealed from above points to their "ultimate" dimension but their concrete historical formation throws us back on the conventional, and the mutual imbrication of the two aspects never permits them to be definitively disentangled.

The metaphysical account of God is contextualized as a specifically Western or Greek speculative project, richly developed by the biblical input in Jewish, Muslim, and Christian scholasticism. At the same time the concrete faith in the God of Abraham, the God who made heaven and earth, shared by these three religions is contextualized as the product of a particular history. When we say, "We believe in God," we inscribe ourselves in that history, accept its conventions for expressing a basic trust, and appropriate its memories of deliverance that ground the conviction that this God is present and active in history. To say that God or the Spirit of God is at work in history is to adopt Jewish prophetic rhetoric, used by the early Christians to express their conviction about the significance of the life, death, and ongoing life of Jesus. The rhetoric will create an idealized account of the historical events that seem most to substantiate it, as in the many wondrous tales enhancing the four evangelists' vision of the life of Jesus and the early church. That *something* of ultimate significance was afoot in these commemorated events is warranted by their enlightening, strengthening, overjoying impact on the witnesses and on the later hearers of their message. To some extent a dramatic story of God acting in history may be rewritten as an account of humanity crossing thresholds in consciousness of the divine. In that case, the biblical and Islamic tales of revelation would be exemplary instances of a universal process of realization of divine presence. Even the salvific uniqueness or primacy and the divine status claimed for Jesus could to some extent be reinterpreted as a special completeness, universality, and providential timing of the breakthrough to the divine, or of the divine, that took place in and through him.

Theologians have come to terms with the gulfs between archaic and modern contexts thanks to the inventive discipline of hermeneutics, which permits a flexible and revisionist approach to the ancient sources. Feuerbach scoffed at this as an opportunistic method for glossing over contradictions. Today, not only theologians but believers in general are willing to recognize that any history is likely to be a tissue of contradictions and that there is no need to iron out the oddities of the past in order to assure ironclad consistency. Such a change in attitude establishes a more comfortable relationship to scripture as a collection of tales to be appreciated for its imaginative power rather than assessed for its claims to literal truth. It also permits the same tolerant appreciation of the myths and legends of other religions, all viewed as productions of the human spirit in its reaching after ultimate depths.

It can be unnerving to sense the pastness of one's religious culture, to feel that one is enacting a historical drama, that one's religious

speech is placed within quotation marks and threatens to become unreal, nothing more than a pious homage to a vanishing tradition. Then
one asks: "Why do I utter these words, make these gestures? What is
their relation to the actual conditions of life?" Liturgical discomfort
has made many aware of the conventional texture of the languages of
faith and forced them to practice discernment in regard to the conventions, in the ordeal of a double constraint: on one hand, ritual calls
for a direct investment of faith; on the other, a scruple about authenticity obliges one to register its inadaptation to the contemporary
world. Instead of deploring this tension and seeking to manage the
"crisis" by busy-busy adjustments, one should recognize that a muta-
tion is afoot, that awareness of historical relativity and the free play of
judgment that this awareness permits are becoming intrinsic to Christian existence. This recognition allays the unease caused by the elements of archaism, conventionality, and inadequacy in Christian language and gestures, letting us perform these gestures in the double
awareness of their provisional nature and their spiritual aim. And of
course it clears the ground for creative innovation, which could make
our modern doubts and questions themselves a locus of imaginative
prayer, in the style of Job and the psalmist pouring out their trouble
before God.

JUDGMENT AND METHOD

A theology in the key of dialogue and reflective judgment will use
systematic methods and procedures, seeking to give them a valid role
within reflection and debate but not to leave behind the mobility and
openness of dialogue by imposing systematic closure. A thinking theology will not be content to apply methods, such as Lonergan's "functional specialties," in an automatic way. Lonergan's *Method in Theology* overcomes the scholastic horizons within which his own courses
at the Gregorian University were composed by regrounding theology
in a transcendental study of human consciousness both noetic and affective and by taking on board in this perspective the modern experience of historical and cultural pluralism. But his analyses do not quite

rejoin the living practice of theology, as an art of concrete judgment, either as it was developed within Protestantism or as it was being renewed in Vatican II Catholicism. Written at a time of transition and flux in Catholic theology, the work had the merit of instilling a subtler methodological self-consciousness among theologians, reminding them of the plurality of instances to be respected in their autonomy and held together in a dialogal and dialectical interaction: scriptural exegesis, hermeneutics of dogma, reference to the existential and spiritual context, pastoral communication. Much theology has fallen short of this sharp awareness of the plurality and distinction of the different disciplinary horizons, allowing the theological enterprise to collapse back into the narrowness of a single horizon, whether supplied by dogma, scripture, ideology, spirituality, or philosophy. However, theological rationality must go beyond Lonergan's vision in a fuller exposure to pluralism that would call in question the authority of a single founding transcendental philosophy. In face of Christian divisions Lonergan prescribes that "the needed solution to such ongoing differences is a theological method radical enough to meet head on the basic issues in philosophy. What is one doing when one is knowing? Why is doing that knowing? What does one know when one does it?" (297). But the historical movement of Christian thought, with its inherent pluralism, is recalcitrant to clarification on this basis. Even opposing theses within mathematics are not easily resolved by appeal to pure reason, and the texture of religious vision and articulation is even less amenable to such appeal. Accepting the contextuality and conventionality of religious language, one can deal with differences dialogally, in ongoing shared reflective judgment, with no need to ground the process in a transcendental philosophical theory.

Theology will always retain firm methodological bearings, given the necessity of a critical handling of scripture and doctrinal tradition as well as its accountability to current questions and the church's apologetic and missionary task. Theological judgment uses systematic methods and procedures but can never be reduced to them. To judge is a free and creative activity, never simply the application of methods. In theology as in all humanistic disciplines the "results," established by reflective judgment, have less to do with discovering particular truths than with enlarging the horizons of awareness. Beyond the data and their treatment by various methods, judgment supervenes as the sovereign authority. If judgment is preempted by conclusions fixed in advance, this is as inauthentic as it would be in other sciences. Theological judgment cannot, then, foreclose the possibility of reaching results that exile it from orthodox faith; but given its initial foundation in faith this should be a rare event.

Each method used in theology retains its particular autonomy, which prevents theological judgment from taking shortcuts. Methods inflict a certain alienation on theology, forcing it into infinite detours. In fact, however, the only discipline by which theological reflection as currently conducted is likely to feel intimidated by the weight of scientific method is exegesis. Theologians fear embarrassing blunders when they speak of scripture, whereas they are prone to discourse freely on psychology, society, other religions, and even science, as in the days when theology was still queen. Theology handles a language—the entire set of religious notions, scriptural texts, historically constituted dogmas and theologies. Can it measure this language against the "thing itself"? No, but it can discern, by immanent critique, that some elements in the languages it examines are more adequate than others. This discernment obliges it to work from below, without jumping to a "God's eye" point of view. For Stanislas Breton: "Theology can no longer be 'dogmatic,' for it can no longer be a set or body of 'determinative judgments' (or rather propositions) on the being of God. It can finally be only a set of regulative principles bearing not on the existence (or essence) of God but on our existence in God" (Castelli, 372). Even the latter theme can be approached only through textual, historical, disciplinary mediations in which one always risks losing the thread.

At the threshold of theology there must be a place for a free reflection moving among different disciplines, open to culture, the human sciences, and interreligious encounter, and abiding in an essayistic mode that cannot aspire to build a system. Such groping provides the vital milieu of fundamental theology as it seeks the path from the old structurations of the situation of faith toward the emergent new paradigms. The freedom of the essay is suited to divinatory anticipation of the new, as well as to the concern with putting theology in contact with its contemporary interlocutors, building bridges by following its hunches rather than seeking methodological safeguards. This may expose it to censures like that of *Dominus Iesus* (Congregation for the Doctrine of the Faith, 2000), which refers to "the eclecticism of those who, in theological research, uncritically absorb ideas from a variety of philosophical and theological contexts without regard for consistency, systematic connection, or compatibility with Christian truth" (#4). The question is whether the systematic coherence here desiderated fits the actual landscape of religious awareness and thought today. To be sure, the current epistemological context, that of "the hermeneutical age of reason" (Greisch 1985) and of a new "regime of truth" of which Wittgenstein, Foucault, and Derrida help us grasp the constraints, must be reflected as thoroughly as possible, so as to show how the Christian message must be rearticulated in this new context. Some recent theology has been intoxicated by the wines of postmodernism, as Clement of Alexandria was by those of hellenism. But even more drunkenness might be desired, since theology has still a lot to absorb from modern culture; a tighter and more systematic vigilance, like that which Origen imposed on the revels of Clement, could be premature. Happily, theology is hardly likely to find itself in a position of mastery over the currents of contemporary thought, which would then lose their power to solicit the stability of its positions and claims.

Judgment is sovereign in every field of reflective thought. In ethics, it takes the form of conscience, which can be informed by laws and their methodical analysis but which shows its finesse in free reflection, the matrix of ethical decisions. A moral thinking that would accord conscience only the task of applying laws placed above criticism would have rather immorally signed off from mature, adult reflection that weighs all the factors in play. In aesthetics, judgment is taste and the reflection based on it. It is informed by the principles of the arts and the frequentation of many works, but it proceeds freely, beholden to no authority but its own.

One cannot get rid of the freedom and duty of judgment by consigning them to some method or authority. Those who swear by the phenomenological ideal of a return to the phenomena themselves tend to forget that this too is a method or strategy, which cannot usurp the role of judgment. In practice phenomenology has hardly remained a pure science such as Husserl envisaged, for it begins with and lets itself by guided by choices and priorities decided on by judgment. It creates techniques at the service of paths of thought that construct, in a great variety of styles, what is going to count as an essential phenomenon. Theology turns to the phenomena in order to keep its discourse in touch with its theme, but the role and weight given to that phenomenological investment are determined by theological judgment, sovereign over whatever method or strategy it adopts.

Inspired by Heideggerian phenomenology, some theologians insist too much on the primacy of intuitive givens and underestimate the role of judgment and dialectic. Francesco Gonzalez shows how from his first courses Heidegger, mistrustful of the occulting power of language, opposed linguistic expression and dialectic to the idea of a pure *noein*, though doubting the possibility of the latter and admitting that dialectic at least attempted to free itself from linguistic captivity to point to the phenomena. According to Jacques Taminiaux, Heidegger, following Husserl's faith in the primacy of the intuitive given, claimed "the status of an ultimate visionary *aneu logou*" (quoted in Gonzalez, 370). Heidegger inherited the choice or destiny of the later Husserl, who invested totally in the intuitive, leaving behind the exercise of judgment that is still found in the *Logical Investigations* (see Devynck). Admittedly, the word *intuitive* can facilitate a caricature of Husserl and Heidegger, whose interest was in the texture of reality itself.

Theology does not live from the given alone but must determine its principles and deal with its many open questions by an exercise of reflection. The cult of the originary phenomena of revelation easily falls into mythic accounts of how God's presence is discerned in history. Contemplative attention is needed to allow the language of scripture to breathe, but it should not mask or paper over the historical diversity, incompleteness, or brokenness of that language. Scripture opens up a field of intellectual inquiry and ethical discernment, awakening fundamental questions rather than suspending them with blanket answers. The phenomenological step back to originary biblical realities must thus be conjoined with an effort of reflection that connects these realities with today's horizons of understanding. The focus on dogma and metaphysical speculation in much contemporary theology is an obstacle to the kind of reflection that is needed. Critical interpretation of the history of faith, in its varied imperfect structurations, as an aid to finding viable expressions of faith and hope today is a task requiring flexible and open judgment at each step. It surveys and assesses the different investments of theological thinking past and present, giving none of them an undue hegemony.

This theological judgment should not be identified with hermeneutics, for hermeneutics is itself a method, even if with Gadamer it puts in question the primacy of method. It is the most comprehensive of methods and the one that furnishes the most propitious context for theological judgment, but it remains an auxiliary of judgment and does not predetermine its outcome. If one were to say, "Theology is hermeneutics," subsuming the whole art of judgment under the rubric of interpretation, one would either dissolve the specificity of hermeneutics or reduce theological judgment to the application of a method. True, hermeneutics, as the understanding and assessment of historical and contemporary discourses, demands a continual exercise of interpretative judgment, and it is hard to sustain a sharp distinction between this latter and theological judgment in a strict sense. Nonetheless, hermeneutics has a specific role as a counterbalance to the free movement of theological judgment. One can actualize past traditions for contemporary understanding in two different ways: by critical and methodical work on the past with a view to understanding it, or by direct response to contemporary questions. In formulating that response, theology consults hermeneutics to verify or nuance its judgments. The role and weight that a theologian accords to hermeneutics depend on his or her judgment as a theologian, not as a hermeneut. Conversely, the exercise of interpretative judgment in hermeneutics is enriched by the suspension of final, properly theological judgment. Methods in theology are well deployed only when given their orientation by a theological judgment. One should accord maximum autonomy to hermeneutics, exegesis, and all the other functional specialties, since the methods, when sophisticated and professional, give weight and force to theological judgment, keeping it from being squandered in indecisive essays.

A mature theology must adopt the stance of judgment, independently of every method and every set of established propositions. In doing so it reflects the collective enterprise of the Christian community seeking its way under the guidance of the Spirit at a time of profound readjustments of human and religious understanding. Whatever the exactness and weight of dogmatic determinations concerning God, the Trinity, Christ, redemption, or grace, theological reflection seeking to orient itself to the fundamental issues of faith knows that these determinations are not the last word ending all reflection. Whatever the rigor of reflection in moral theology and the hierarchy of authoritative sources it takes account of, from natural law to the teachings of the magisterium, there is an authority beyond them, that of personal conscience (always of course obliged to take into account the common good). Whatever the acuity of scientific exegesis and the authority claimed for scripture, there is an instance that judges them, namely, the Spirit that enables one to discern the meaning and use of scripture.

This judgment that transcends method is exerted on a communal level, at the heart of ecclesial life, and is not reducible to the private judgment abhorred by the old anti-Protestant apologetic. In a first phase, Protestants maintained that the evidence of scripture requires no examination and no "judgment of authority" but is grasped "by a judgment of discretion, as one judges the taste of foods" (Du Moulin, quoted in Voeltzel, 139). Then it was argued that the examination required by scripture is less complicated than that imposed by the mass of ecclesiastical documents and that even if one conceded infallible authority to the church, to determine where it is exercised and how it is applied would demand an infinite examination. A reasonable compromise: the recognition that the church has a long tradition worthy of trust. No need to claim "that each individual can examine the meaning of scripture in a rigorous way . . . nor that an individual can judge better than the church as a whole taken in all its communions by that judgment that is born of unanimous consent" (Jurieu, quoted in Voeltzel, 146). The judgment required for faith is the fruit not of a long theological discussion but of "attentive examination": "The catechumen receives this light from the mysteries and the motive that one proposes to his faith. But neither the mysteries nor the motives are proposed to him in the degree of evidence needed to give a certitude that excludes doubt. What the mysteries and motives do not do, the spirit and operation of God effect" (Jurieu, quoted in Voeltzel, 147). Thus church teaching can be received as that of Christ himself in what concerns the foundation of faith. But if one seeks to give the note of infallibility to secondary and contested theologoumena and particular ethical positions, one makes infallibility the hostage of quarrels it cannot terminate. The failure of that strategy, born like the whole debate on private judgment from the epistemological anxiety characteristic of modern times, leaves the field open for a rethinking of church authority starting from its bases in the Gospel kerygma.

Theological judgment is not arbitrary, for it is informed by frequentation of the sources and respect for the authorities. But no method, strategy, or church discipline or doctrine can guarantee the correctness of theological judgments and render superfluous the supreme art of thinking that resides in the faculty of judgment. Hermeneutics opens up the field of questioning and traces paths toward clarity, but to find one's way there, decisions that depend on judgment are necessary. Judgment is influenced by character, habits, circumstances, and ideological pressures, and the self-critique necessary to correct such prejudgment is again a task of free reflection, which no methodology can accomplish.

Before discussing any thesis, fundamental theology elucidates the basic orientation of Christian thought. In principle it has surpassed the neutral skepticism that treats religious ideas as problematic themes. But in seeking to illuminate the horizon of faith, it cannot take its bearings solely from a particular confessional conviction but must occupy a transdenominational position. It explores the space that is the condition of the correct formulation and use of confessional ideas. These first orientations of reflection determine the aims of research in fundamental theology, the basic rules of the discourse, the paths of dialogue to be explored, the perils to avoid, and the respective status of the various instances, such as scripture, religious experience, dogma, reason, and judgment. Dogmatic judgment is not the last judgment of theology, even if it usually claims that status. The final instance of judgment can only be the faculty of discernment inherent in faith. This discernment decides how to use scripture, so as to find there a God of liberation and salvation, in a judgment at once pragmatic and pneumatic, and is ready to bend the rigidity of dogmas and the letter of scripture so that they too can serve this liberative movement. The human judgments of theology are an effort to make straight the paths of divine judgment. The combination of generous faith and probing critique that this requires is supremely exemplified in theological thinkers who have broken through to the prophetic level, such as Luther, and in the movement of the whole people of God when they make new discernments, as at Vatican II. The ordinary exercise of theological judgment, navigating between conventions and ultimacy, is more sedulous and critical and will be loath to arrogate to itself the authority of original prophetic utterance.

Chapter Two

THE TWOFOLD TRUTH

Fundamental theology is concerned more with the method of theological judgment than with its content, though of course it is impossible to make a clean separation between the two. Some methods conduce inevitably to the abyss of skepticism, others to the fortress of dogmatism. The Buddhist-inspired quest of a middle path avoiding these extremes is perhaps itself not ultimately justifiable other than as a sage choice based on an act of faith. The skeptic will reject it because of its generous respect for religious traditions, while the dogmatist will reject it because it tends to defer and relativize fixed certitudes. But as we cultivate this path, focusing on the epistemological lay of the land rather than taking sides on disputed issues, and envisioning doctrines from the aspect of their mode of presentation and articulation, we can build up a reservoir of therapies to tame and heal both skepticism and dogmatism. Skepticism is undercut by the necessity of investing in some affirmations in order to say anything at all. Dogmatism is undercut by the necessity of making those affirmations understandable and credible. The tensions thus manifested at the two extremes are taken on board and handled patiently in an art of judgment that attends to the fundamental conditions of religious affirmation and negation, vindicating the former as radical trust, the latter as puri-

fying critique, and assessing the limits of both in view of the constantly changing contexts in which they operate.

If rationality in theology must go beyond Hegel to a new appreciation of open-ended, dialogal reflection, it must also link up with
sources of rationality in traditions beyond the European or Christian
fold. As Christian thinking negotiates its way from a systematic rationality dominated by concern about dogma to a reflective rationality
that puts dogma in its subordinate and functional place in order to set
up instead an interplay between the basic Christian message and the
complex world to which it is supposed to be directed as good news, it
can learn much from Buddhism in particular. In a style very different
from that of the early church, Buddhism has carried on a radical reflection on the status and function of language, concepts, and doctrinal
views, in the process acquiring a type of credibility that Christian
reflection can also attain as it deals with the poisons of skepticism and
nihilism, not in a clumsy dogmatic reaction, but in a subtler, lighter,
and more flexible way.

Madhyamaka Buddhism connects the lighting up of ultimate reality (*paramārtha-satya*) to the skillful deployment of a given conventional setup (*saṃvṛti-satya*): "The ultimate truth is not taught independently of customary ways of talking and thinking (*vyavahāram*).
Not having acquired the ultimate truth, *nirvāṇa* is not attained"
(*MK* 24.10, trans. Siderits/Katsura). The word *saṃvṛti* has the connotations of something that covers, a surface reality that occludes the
true nature of things. The word *vyavahāra* refers to the conventional,
pragmatic realities of everyday life. Conventional truth is a truth
agreed on for practical purposes. All the realities of our world have a
merely conventional existence; the ultimate truth about them is their
emptiness; yet the truth of emptiness is realized only in constantly
dismantling the delusions of substantiality to which the conventional
world gives rise. The two-truths doctrine "establishes the ontological basis of Mādhyamika and at the same time its soteriological basis:
to understand the two realities correctly means to know the world
and its true essence, and this is the knowledge that brings redemption. . . . Every other theme is related to this, directly or indirectly"
(Tauscher, 3).

While there are antecedents for the notions of conventional truth and skillful means in earlier Buddhism, it is only in the Mahāyāna that these themes determine the very nature of Buddhism in an explicit, reflective way. Both notions are "metacategories of the tradition-immanent hermeneutical process of reflection on the essential character of the Buddhist teaching" (Schmidt-Leukel 1992:549). Buddhist teaching is valid and efficacious only when it grasps itself as conventional truth, a skillful means for guiding the unenlightened to liberation. To what degree can Christian theology learn from this radical relativization and functionalization of religious doctrines?

It is essential to fully rounded theological judgment to be clear about the status and function of its own discourse. The Buddhist account of religious discourse as a provisional, conventional means, whose value is measured by its practical, liberative bearing, can surely aid Christian theology to attain a more integrated critical self-consciousness. Classical negative theologies, as well as efforts to re-ground theological reflection in the kerygma or in pastoral vision, point in this direction too, but the Buddhist tradition invites us to carry such reflection much further, overcoming models that are no longer adequate to current epistemological conditions. If it is objected that the Buddhist view of religious language is too closely tied to a specific doctrine to be of use to Christian thought, one might answer that the same could have been said of the Greek philosophical equipment that the early church adopted so discerningly and used so skillfully.

The two-truths theory, it must be admitted, is a logical and historical quagmire. But, again, the same might be said of the Greek metaphysical doctrines on knowledge and being, which nonetheless, in their very diversity, proved so powerful a stimulus to classical Christian theology. Within Madhyamaka, the twofold truth becomes a systematic and authoritative doctrinal construction for the Tibetan Gelugpa, in the formulation of their founder Tsong Khapa (1357–1419); yet even within the Gelugpa there is a great variety of interpretations of its meaning. Some Buddhists have a "sliding-scale" conception of the two truths: what is the ultimate truth at one stage of analysis turns out to be a conventional truth at a higher stage (see Dunne). As Madhyamaka reflection advances, the ultimate truth becomes increasingly elusive, so that in the end we seem left with little more than a skillful play with conventions. Even if it were a purely skeptical philosophy, as some postmodern interpreters seem to wish, the two-truths theory could still free up our thinking on the historical and textual embeddedness of faith, doctrine, and mystical experience. But in fact it has a further value for the challenges faced by theology, in that it shows how the most radical criticism can be placed in the service of a positive religious vision and enactment, restoring the validity of religious views and practices in a new key. Views and practices are chastened by the realization of their mere conventionality, but they are also liberated for more intelligent and flexible application, guided by a tacit discernment of what ultimately counts.

It is not necessary to sort out the details of historical Buddhist debates about how to interpret Nāgārjuna, a daunting task in any case, given that even central texts such as Candrakīrti's commentary on Āryadeva have not yet been edited. Without being intimidated, one may draw freely on the ancient and contemporary debates in order to allow a general sense of the interplay of the two truths to nourish theological discernment and reflection. The best contemporary experts on the topic, united under an ironic sobriquet denoting ignorance, forgo historical controversy in order to ask bedrock questions (The Cowherds, vi). Standard Gelugpa summaries may be queried by scholars as to their accord with Nāgārjuna or Candrakīrti, but that need not prevent the theologian from benefiting from them. When we read that "the two truths, although mutually exclusive, are a single entity because emptiness (ultimate truth) is the mode of subsistence of conventional phenomena (concealer-truths)," or that "concealer-truths are objects found by conventional valid cognition, while ultimate truths are objects found by ultimate valid cognition. Conventional valid cognition is not superseded or invalidated by ultimate valid cognition" (Newland 1992:3), theological resonances press upon us.

Madhyamaka thinking is a mobile dialectic that never comes to rest. It cannot rest in an intuitive contemplation of emptiness, since emptiness undercuts such stability and reification: "When Jñānagarbha turns the ultimate on the ultimate and finds it no different from the relative, he is giving the classic Madhyamaka argument for the return to the relative. The emptiness of emptiness itself compels a person to reappropriate and affirm, in a transformed way, the distinctions of the relative world" (Eckel, 41). Neither can it rest in any propositional statement of the doctrine of emptiness, since this is an entirely functional doctrine, serving only as a skillful means for reconnecting us with the texture of reality by undercutting our illusions and reifications. As a school of critical awareness, Madhyamaka does not replace the philosophical frameworks for theology proposed in the West, such as Hegelianism or Lonergan's transcendental analyses. Rather, somewhat like deconstruction, it alerts theology to the limits, even the ultimate impossibility, of its own discourse, in order to free it from heavy-handed attempts at securing substantial foundations, so as to let the conventional play of its concepts proceed in a more lucid and effective way. This is not so much the replacement of a philosophical framework as a change in the style or texture of thinking. Philosophical frameworks, and even dogmatic frameworks, undergo a change in status in this new style of thinking, as they too, however valid and well founded they may be, are treated as conventional constructs and skillful means and are queried as to their practical, soteriological bearing.

The frequent objection that if all is conventional the beliefs and precepts of religions become baseless is countered by Śaṃkara, under Madhyamaka influence, as follows: "The entire complex of phenomenal existence is considered as true as long as the knowledge of Brahman being the Self of all has not arisen. . . . As long as true knowledge does not present itself, there is no reason why the ordinary course of secular and religious activity should not hold on undisturbed" (Thibaut, 1:324). Conventional truth, even religious doctrine, is based on ontological ignorance and is as flimsy as a dream. St. Augustine frequently reminds his readers that we know only "through a glass, darkly"; in this sense all our doctrinal and theological understanding is a matter of flimsy, provisional convention, to vanish when we see "face to face"—an experience partly anticipated in the breakthroughs to intuitive *intellectus*, which are the rare reward of theological labor, and which are closely related to the contemplative breakthroughs recorded in *Confessions* books 7 through 10. Many theologians, such as Meister Eckhart, have been haunted by a sense that the finitude and brokenness of our doctrinal categories must ultimately yield to a supreme simplicity to which silence is the best pointer, and that the processes of concrete spiritual life are ultimately uncontrollable by cut-and-dried categories.

Whatever we say of God depends on the limitations of our mental and linguistic makeup. For Śaṃkara, "The Lord's being a Lord, his omniscience, his omnipotence, etc., all depend on the limitation due to the adjuncts whose Self is Nescience; while in reality none of these qualities belong to the Self whose true nature is cleared, by right knowledge, from all adjuncts whatever" (Thibaut 1:329). In Christian discourse the distinction between Creator and creature no doubt withstands reduction by this kind of ontological explication (except possibly in Eckhart). Nonetheless, the fabric of our talk about the Creator proclaims its makeshift quality at every turn, both in its basic anthropomorphism and in the antinomies courted by every effort to give it a coherent explication in terms of ontology. This flimsiness casts us back on a silent committal, in trust and praise, to the ultimate silent source of all, in an emptying out of all the concepts and determinations that our conventional theologizing shapes about it. The emptiness of the ultimate makes itself felt in Christian as much as in Indian tradition, not only in mystical states, but in the very fabric of our imaging and conceptualizing. Images and concepts can be skillfully deployed only on the basis of this sense of their radical inadequacy and conventionality. Medieval scholastics showed that the trinitarian relations and the doctrine of Creation do not conflict with the divine unity and simplicity. But that entire argument proceeds in a negative key, as a demonstration of noncontradiction between tenets that are themselves negatively constructed. While classical theology appears to marshal a rich, positive, analogical language on ultimate reality, it is possible to analyze the texture of that language in such a way as to bring it into close proximity to what Indian wisdom would identify as conventional truth.

In using the twofold truth as a theory of how conventional historical religious languages can serve as vehicles for insight, or revelation, having the quality of ultimacy, I use *ultimacy* freely as a phenomenological term, meaning that which is recognized as supremely, undeniably, unsurpassably, incomparably real. It need not carry the metaphysical implication of terms such as *absolute* or *transcendent*, nor need it have the status of a unitary principle. More adjectival than substantive, it can attach to a great variety of experiences. Yet it is not merely subjective: it is recognized by the subject as irreducible bedrock reality. I shall suggest that we should conceive not only the conventional languages of religion but even the experience of which they are a vehicle as a pluralistic, culturally contextual phenomenon. I mean that ultimacy comes into view in function of the conventional setup that stages its emergence, so that if it transcends the conventions, it does so in a way that is intimately related to them. God, emptiness, Brahman, the Resurrection, are all marked by ultimacy, yet each of them emerges within a complex historical language, in perfect harmony with that language, and we are unable to envisage a space of ultimacy beyond those languages.

NEGATIVE DIALECTIC

In Hegel's logic of reflection (the most interesting part of his *Science of Logic*), being, which earlier appeared to be given immediately, is revealed as posited by the negative movement of reflection, and to subsist only as show (*Schein*). Show is "being only as *moment*, or being affected by nothingness. . . . Show is a nothingness—not a reality on its own, but only the *illusion* of being" (DiGiovanni, 146). Reflection nihilates the initial positing of being, reduces being to a moment within a movement from nothing to nothing. This stage in Hegel's logic can be read as a critical exposition of the status of phenomena in Greek skepticism and in the idealism of Leibniz, Kant, and Fichte. It is surpassed in the final stage of the *Science of Logic*. But even there, in the dynamic structure of the Concept, being continues to be penetrated by the negative movement of thought: "The essence is the *first negation* of being, which thereby has become *show*; the Concept is the *second*, or the negation of this negation, thus reestablished being, but as its infinite mediation and negativity in itself" (1934:235). This all-pervading movement of negation is the oxygen of Hegel's thought, ensuring that it remains an enactment of intellectual freedom. Whenever he stops short at some positive, unreflected assertion, his thought dies; it lives only by pulverizing purportedly solid points of departure and by rendering purportedly clear goals elusive and fluid, thus remaining a movement from no-thing to no-thing.

The purely negative dialectic of Madhyamaka Buddhism, which issues in emptiness, can solicit Hegelian thought to new horizons, to a "letting go" in which it fully accepts its own fragile and provisional status. Nāgārjuna's *Mūlamadhyamakakārikā* or *Stances of the Middle Way*, by dint of dialectical quizzing and *reductiones ad absurdum*, bring all claimants to substantial identity (*svabhāva*, "own-being") to confess their self-contradictory and ultimately empty nature. Thus every clinging to them is cut off at the root and the mind is released from bondage to rigid, uncriticized concepts. Could a Hegelian dialectic, hospitable to the power of the negative, take this in its stride as well? Or is reason shown up as merely a strategy for regulating truths of a conventional, world-ensconced, provisional order, its highest role being to allow ultimate emptiness to show through the web of conventionalities—an emptiness on which reason has no grip? If reason succumbs to such a radical crisis, this could paradoxically constitute a triumph of reflection; speculation is thwarted but judgment thrives. Integral rationality, Hegel would agree, is that which recognizes its weakness and does not lean with illicit certainty on any of the theses or presuppositions with which it finds itself provisionally furnished. But more than that, it renounces all illicit groping after system, completion, absoluteness, where its weaknesses would be eliminated. Speculative ambition cedes to espousal of the wisdom of emptiness. The deconstructive movement of reflection realizes that it can never go back, never heal the wound it has opened. Analysis shows every proposition to have but a fragile and provisional validity. Hegel might object that it cannot do this except in light of some ultimate yardstick. Nāgārjuna would say that no such yardstick is given. In Hegel the power of the negative generates from the collapse of one set of assertions a new and richer set to replace them, but for Nāgārjuna a nonimplicative negation (*prasajya-pratiṣedha*) prevails, which dismantles various illusory objects of mental attachment but asserts nothing.

If we wager that Nāgārjuna's dialectic of emptiness can prise the Hegelian system open, instead of being reabsorbed into it, this need not entail that Hegel's thought is vain and delusive. Emptiness, which a Chinese adage calls "a fasting of the mind," does not end thought but rather redirects it. Nāgārjuna and his followers constantly generate subtle arguments in the service of emptiness, and many of these have affinities with the negative aspects of Hegel's thought. Unlike Kant, who proves contradictories to show the futility of speculative reason, and who fails to put in question the categories of substance, space, or time that the proofs presuppose, albeit giving them a transcendental interpretation, Hegel is more radical and admits no givens that cannot be explicated and surpassed in logical terms. Nāgārjuna, too, would say that neither of Kant's contradictory theses can be established, for the categories of time, space, and self are inconsistent, and this inconsistency can be resolved only by recognizing their emptiness of substantial identity. The same is true of all other phenomena. Even the Tathāgata is empty of identity, neither eternal, nor noneternal, nor both, nor neither; neither having an end, nor not having an end, nor both, nor neither (see *MK* 22.12). This negative procedure may seem to repeat over and over again the thesis that all dharmas are empty, discouraging differentiated thought about the various levels of reality and of conceptuality. But each class of dharmas offers a different handle for the negating analysis, and the ultimate sameness of all dharmas insofar as they are empty does not exclude a great variety of strategies to be employed as the mind gently leads each kind of dharma back to the quiet of ultimate reality (or to demystified mindful engagement with the dependently arising here and now).

The sameness (*samatā*) of dharmas is not a dull leveling but corresponds to a vivid savoring of their thusness, *tathatā*, which might be compared with Hegel's reestablishment of the immediacy of being. Murti (301–6) holds that conventional truth in Nāgārjuna is absolutely false from the vantage of the ultimate, whereas Hegel preserves the truth of "show" in its entirety in the realization of the Concept. Madhyamaka dialectic proceeds by the negation of views, not by their addition. But if the *Science of Logic* is read as dissolving traditional metaphysics by expounding its categories in critical dialectic, then the role of negation in his thought brings Hegel into proximity with Buddhism. In Hegel, every thing, every state of consciousness, is the negation of itself. It is thanks to the negative work on the logical determinations of thought that a finally free thinking emerges in the Concept or the Idea. In Madhyamaka, all thinking belongs to the conventional level and the ultimate is presented as the dissolution of conceptual distinctions. If Hegelian dialectic is read as concerned not with establishing correct positions but with freeing the mind from bondage to fixed mind-sets, it comes close to a Buddhist sense of conceptuality as functional and conventional. If one carries further Hegel's critical activity of putting a halt to reifying fabrications, it opens onto emptiness and can expand and enrich Madhyamaka insight into the fragile conventionality of all categories and propositions. Such a prising open of Hegel will also connect with the reassertion of real existence over against the closure of the Concept that is variously expressed by Schelling, Kierkegaard, Marx, and Heidegger.

Buddhist emptiness accepts the nothingness at work in the heart of being and thereby discovers that in their very fragility and mutual dependency phenomena become the vehicles of a new freedom. If we think of conventional or "screening" reality, *saṃvṛti*, as inessential appearances over against the essential reality of emptiness, we miss a more intimate mutual co-implication of conventional and ultimate, in which to see the conventional as conventional is already to see its emptiness. The wisdom of emptiness arises from reflection on the conventional; it is that reflection itself; or it is the conventional's self-reflection. The empty "thusness" that survives the ordeal of the negative cannot be the self-satisfied reassertion of delusive *svabhāva*. Rather, it is being that is totally identified with emptiness or that has become a moment of emptiness. "Form itself is emptiness, emptiness itself is form" (*Heart Sūtra*). We know emptiness only as embodied in dependently originating phenomena, and we know these in their thusness only when we grasp them as self-negating or self-deconstructing, thus confessing their own emptiness. Deepening this insight, one discovers that the frail world of *saṃsāra*, the realm of pain and impermanence, is not different from *nirvāṇa*, the realm of blissful emptiness. That was Nāgārjuna's culminating insight: "There is no distinction whatsoever between *saṃsāra* and *nirvāṇa*. There is no distinction whatsoever between *nirvāṇa* and *saṃsāra*. What is the limit of *nirvāṇa*, that is the limit of *saṃsāra*. There is not even the finest gap to be found between the two" (*MK* 25.19–20). The discovery of emptiness is itself blissful *nirvāṇa*, the quiescence of all grasping and all conceptual fabrications (25.24). Even ordinary everyday life can be the locus for *nirvāṇa*, and even a nirvanized person can continue to live everyday life, using it as a convention to lead others compassionately to ultimate reality. A retrieval of all Hegel's arguments in this key would give a new lease of life to his thought.

The many superimposed layers of Hegel's argumentation and the way in which the solution reached at a given level is relativized and overcome at the next, higher level recall similar structures in Madhyamaka, such as the rather schematic arrangement in Tibetan debates where what appears as ultimate truth in one of the lower schools (Vaibhāṣika, Sautrāntika, or Yogācāra) is seen as merely conventional in a higher school, with Madhyamaka as the highest. Original ignorance (*avidyā*) generates a cascade of false conceptions, amid which we live, and without which ordinary life would become impossible. Madhyamaka distinguishes ever subtler forms of delusion, both in metaphysical ratiocination and in an underlying subconscious investment in mental habits and presuppositions, cemented by tenacious clinging. Hegel arranges the categories that seek to name the true nature of reality from the simplest to the fullest. Each of them (being, *Dasein*, essence, identity, ground, existence, power, actuality, absolute, substance, necessity, cause, concept, judgment, conclusion, objectivity, life, teleology, knowing) reveals its limit through its inner contradictions, until in the end the absolute idea emerges as the complete, integral actualization of logical truth. This process should not be seen as a purely positive accumulation. Rather, the labor of dialectic is negative, working not in the direction of ever richer substantiality but in that of subjectivity and freedom. The categories become lighter and more alive and take the form of an open movement of relating rather than a closed self-sufficient solidity. To each category corresponds an idea of God, from the primitive level of "God is being" or "God is the essence" up to the richly reflected content of "God is idea" or "God is life."

Hegel's logic enacts "the activity of the determinations of thought" and shows how in their dialectical movement they "investigate themselves" and "exhibit their lack" (quoted in Theunissen, 15). Previous metaphysics, composed from these determinations of thought, is put in movement and overcome. Nāgārjuna does the same for Buddhist conceptions. His critique has two phases that might roughly correspond to Hegel's logic of being and logic of essence. In the first phase he tackles hypostasized notions of simple independent realities such as "time" as a unitary substance or power, or "past," "present," and "future" as independent realities. This can be compared with Hegel's "critique of an ontology that asserts only beings and indeed beings in themselves" (Theunissen, 25). In a second phase the mutual relationship of the three dimensions of time brings a reflected apprehension of time. Temporal concepts have meaning only in relation to another, be it the alleged temporally existing thing or other temporal dimensions. In reflection each temporal dimension is successively the dominant one. Present and future exist only in dependence on past and thus have no real existence. The same holds for the other two permutations. The three relations of dominance between the temporal dimensions subvert one another. The same logic applies to triads such as "above, middle, below" and to dyads such as "one, many" (*MK* 19.4). Similar arguments are used for the relations of seer, seen, and sight (*MK* 3), an element and its defining characteristic (*MK* 5), desirer and desire (*MK* 6), fire and fuel (*MK* 10). Reciprocal relationships betoken the nonexistence of the *relata*.

In the logic of reflection all these categories are conceived in purely relative terms. But in a further movement of critical analysis these relative determinations are themselves unmasked as *svabhāva* and their reciprocal dependence is problematized. If two of these moments already exist in the third (or, in the case of a dyad, if one already exists in the other), they lose their own identity (versus the Sāṃkhya philosophers' *sat-kārya-vāda*, the claim that the effect is preformed in the cause). If they do not already exist there, how can they depend on it (versus the Vaiśeṣika school's *asat-kārya-vāda*, the claim that the effect is not preformed in the cause)? Relativity must be thought through to the end, so that every claimed identity of the *relata* vanishes and what remains is only a play between conventional designations. Similarly, in Hegel, "The logic of essence unmasks the metaphysical categories as products of the reflecting understanding, which, as we have heard, 'posits' the 'relativity' of the distinctions. It is to that extent untouched by the critique of indifference in the logic of being, for to the contrary the positing of relativity removes the foreignness in which the relata stand over against each other as long as, on the basis of the assumption of their subsisting for themselves, their reciprocal relation appears as external to themselves" (Theunissen, 26).

Why does the concept of time succumb to the critique of *svabhāva*? The critique of metaphysics in the logic of essence is directed against the way that "understanding, despite its insight into relativity, holds fast to the independence of its determinations." Nāgārjuna directs a similar critique against the conceptual web of Abhidharma scholasticism. The relative understanding of temporal categories is still tied to *svabhāva* thinking in that "reflective understanding assumes the independence of its determinations and at the same time posits their relativity" (Theunissen, 28). The logic of reflection is thus a structure of dominance insofar as "the one that stands over against 'its other' is at the same time the totality that contains the other in itself as its own moment" (28). The relational account of past, present, and future still attempts to control the reality of time and repress its inner contradictoriness. It unmasks the physical instability of time only to set up an irreproachable metaphysical concept of time. For Hegel the only true reality is one "in which relationship is everything and the *relata* keep nothing back for themselves" (30). This ideal is not attained by the co-implication of the three temporal dimensions. Only in emptiness can the sameness (*samatā*) of all dharmas (or their mutual interpenetration, as in the *Avataṃsaka Sūtra*) become manifest.

As the logic of essence falls back into the logic of being (Theunissen, 35), so, too, are the determinations of reflection in Nāgārjuna unmasked as having the same significance as the more naive determinations of being. The mutual dependence of the three dimensions of time is not the dependent co-arising that is identical with emptiness. It is still a hypostatizing fixation of a claimed identity of time. To seek the *essence* of time was already a mistake. The relations of the time dimensions must be recognized as riddled with contradictions in order to prove the nothingness of time.

All of this may sound drily logical, but it carries a phenomenological impact as well. To see starkly dialectical reason as fundamen-

tally opposed to a phenomenological step back to the things themselves would be to miss the strong affinities between Heideggerian
phenomenology and Hegelian dialectic, and between meditation and
dialectic in Buddhism. Hegel's logic of being and nothingness often
carries phenomenological undertones, more marked in the *Phenomenology of Mind*: "For we call show the *being* that is in itself immediately a *nonbeing*" (1988:100–101). Conversely, traces of dialectic haunt
Heidegger's discourse on the intimate conjunction of being and nothingness, represented as the unfolding of a phenomenological insight:
"Nothingness is what makes possible the opening of beings as such for
human *Dasein*. . . . In the being of beings the nihilation of nothingness
is taking place" (*GA* 9:115). Both Hegel and Heidegger offer their
readers a breakthrough to a free relationship to being. The freedom of
meditative thinking, which has relinquished the attempt to subject the
phenomena to metaphysical grounds and reasons, is perhaps not so
far as it seems from the freedom of the Concept. The Concept, too,
has abandoned the painfully constricted forms of metaphysics whose
inner logic is exposed and critiqued throughout most of the *Science of
Logic*. In stepping back from the Concept to the primary thinking of
being, Heidegger may be opening the ground for a more vital and
rooted deployment of the power of the Concept. Analogously, Madhyamaka opens the ground for a more vital deployment of conventional Buddhist concepts. It might be objected that Hegel could never
agree that concepts have a merely conventional and functional status.
Yet the vast majority of the concepts he expounds are shown caught
in a process of deconstruction, and the conceptual framework that
emerges intact from this battle can be seen as a methodology for thinking, constantly reconstructed, rather than a definitive system. In any
case, what is to prevent a critical Buddhist revisioning of Hegelian
conceptuality?

Buddhism thrusts human existence into the experience of nothingness, constantly stressing the impermanent, painful, and insubstantial character of all phenomena. The whole world is imaged as a
burning house, a situation bound to inspire panic. But nihilating nothingness that marks all beings as impermanent, painful, and lacking
in self-identity transforms itself into a gracious emptiness, just as in
Heidegger nothing reveals itself as "the veil of being." Tossed about

between being and nothingness, clinging desperately to the former and dreading the latter, enslaved to instinctive desires and fears, we can transcend that situation and establish ourselves in the freedom of emptiness, the middle path between the extremes of being and nothingness. Beings survive with a merely conventional and functional existence (*saṃvṛti*). One's own perpetually changing being is a merely conventional existence, yet it becomes the locus of awakened insight. Far from suppressing logic and dialectic, this situation prompts a sharper and more critical exercise of reason, a reason all the keener because knowing the limits of its reach. Very often Buddhist texts play down the rhetoric that their vision of radical impermanence might seem designed to inspire and content themselves with cool, logical analysis instead.

Christian theology, especially in Germany, has been more willing to embrace "constructive" aspects of Hegel's thought than what is most alive in it, the power of its negative dialectic. Even the kenotic theologies inspired by Hegel are lofty speculative constructions that do not explore the "empty" texture of Christian language. Even Buddhism has been dragooned into a speculative kenoticism, instead of being allowed to bring about a general conversion of theological thought and language through relinquishing substantialism and attachment to views. A fuller kenotic expropriation of Christian language depends not on any esoteric speculative leap but primarily on a nondefensive insight into the flimsy, makeshift, functional, provisional, conventional status of religious and theological words, images, and concepts. Both Hegel and Buddhism assure us that this opening up to the power of the negative need not issue in nihilistic disillusionment but can attune us to a reality that is mobile, dynamic, vital, and spiritual.

CONVENTIONALISM

Our reflection on the art of judgment must not stop at a standoff between pure principles and systematic mastery on the one hand and an experiential pluralism to be handled by the endless play of reflective judgment on the other. The twofold truth offers a comprehensive horizon that reconciles openness to pluralism with the quest for ultimate grounds. In everything there is a core, an ultimacy, which demands the fullest philosophical, phenomenological attention. Art and religion bring this out in their different ways, especially at the moments where they touch the sublime. But everything is also relative and conventional. Ultimate realities themselves are incomparable, but any language in which they are expressed instantly enters the web of conventionality. The supreme task of theological judgment is to do justice to both dimensions. When it finds itself celebrating pluralism and conventionality too enthusiastically, it needs to draw back by reflecting on the unchanging core of truth at the heart of religious traditions. When it savors the archaic quality of the Nicene Creed, consigning it to its historical context, let it correct that thought by attending to the powerful way the Creed still speaks. Theology is thus caught in a to-and-fro between the two poles, a situation not very satisfactory to the determined systematician, but one that accords with the dynamics of faith, committed to the ultimate but having access to it only in fragmentary glimpses. The art of reflective judgment in theology consists, then, in skillful navigation between the ultimate and the conventional, shunning both the Scylla of dogmatic fixity and the Charybdis of skepticism. It sustains a double consciousness, cherishing the transcendent impact of its source events, experiences, and texts and at the same time recognizing their fragile, fleshly, provisional texture. It unmasks the human, historical, relative, deconstructible character of every witness to an encounter with ultimacy, and at the same time, in a "negation of the negation," it sees this very brokenness and open-endedness as a mark of authenticity, intrinsic to the logic of religious insight and religious communication. (No doubt a similar to-and-fro can be observed in study of art and literature.)

For Henri Poincaré geometry is not an immediate datum of experience; neither is it a Kantian a priori structure, an inbuilt necessity of the mind. A geometry is freely chosen, as a conventional construct, constrained only by the necessity of avoiding contradictions. "Our Euclidian geometry is itself only a convention of language; we could enunciate mechanical facts in relation to a non-Euclidian geometry that would be a less handy frame of reference, yet just as legitimate as our ordinary space" (Poincaré, 112). When the purely theoretical conventions of mathematical geometry are put to practical use, we are forced to recognize a specific, complex geometry as that of our cosmos. Einstein showed that this geometry is constrained in addition by the empirical reality of solid bodies. The space-time continuum is "a manifold of variable curvature—and, in fact, a curvature that depends essentially on the distribution of matter" (Friedman, 79). Since the universe is non-Euclidian, Euclid is a viable convention only for a fictional space, and in the real world Euclid is false. All the confirmations of Euclid and of Newton that centuries of experience provided now need to be recontextualized.

Whatever the fortunes of Poincaré's specific claims, conventionalism continues to play a major role in assessments of the status of scientific discourse. If scientific frameworks can be seen as conventional, this is likely to be much more the case for philosophical systems. "In the endeavour to live up to traditional ideals of completeness and ultimate justification, a philosophical tradition or school tends to define and explain its basic notions in terms of the notions belonging to its own terminological core. Its arrangement of basic notions is in that sense circular, and it is by training and by allowing oneself to become convinced of its trustworthiness that one gets into that circle" (Stenlund, 196–97). The world yields to the analytic methodology of a strong philosophical system, but the bulk of the system's progress lies in its internal self-confirmation and self-perfecting, sometimes to the point where it seems to exclude worldly reality from the crystal palace of its own purified reconstruction of the world.

Analogously, Jonathan Z. Smith once compared religions to packs of cards. They are systems of conventional symbols and rules for playing with them. This conventionalist reading of religion has become very tempting as we take religious pluralism seriously, realizing that no one religion can set itself up as the ultimate norm whereby all the others are judged. Humans have forged religious systems from the materials available in their different cultures in complex historical trajectories. Faced with the contradictory variety of the results, we are forced to wonder if religious discourse has any substantial referent. Even the card "God" retains its value only within a certain game, one that is becoming ever more remote from the grammar of our experience of a secularized world, in which the word *God* designates rather an eccentric element, something like the Joker.

For Poincaré the question "Is Euclidean geometry true?" had no meaning (though as we have seen, contemporary physicists would answer the question, in the negative). Similarly the questions "Is Buddhism true?" "Is Christianity true?" could be construed as having no meaning. Both religions are "skillful means" (*upāya*) for lighting up a spiritual space and traveling in it. Any other religion that works as effectively and as consistently would do just as well. We do not ask, "Is Mozart true?" "Is Beethoven true?" as we travel in the space they open up. A conventionalist would say that within a certain geometrical setup there are true and false propositions, while the question of the truth of the geometry as a whole cannot be asked, for there is no external, objective "space" with which one could compare it. A religion preoccupied with proving its truth has failed to establish its authority by transmitting a contact with the ultimate.

For Poincaré any noncontradictory geometry can be made to fit our spatial experience, and the question "Which fits best?" reduces to the question of which is of most pragmatic value in a given context, or which best serves the evolution of the species. A religious conventionalist, analogically, could say that within a certain religious language game there are true and false propositions, but the question of the truth of the religion as a whole cannot be asked, for there is no external, objective religious space against which one could assess it. A religion is a human method of tuning in to ultimate mystery. Its language generates propositions that have their own inbuilt, autonomous logic, just as those of geometry have. In Euclidean space it is true that the angles of an equilateral triangle are equal, and false that they are not. The truth-effect is embedded in a context, inscribed within a web of writing that exceeds and encompasses it; and this writing itself eludes the question "True or false?," as Derrida argues.

Religious experience confirms religious systems as the physical world confirms geometric ones, that is, by confirming their practical usefulness. That the religious system can enable a privileged experience, an enlightenment, even the shock of an encounter, shows that it is a game that sets in motion forces in the depth of the soul and of being and is not an insignificant formalism. Compare the relation between experience and theory in science: "One does not limit oneself to generalizing experience; one corrects it; and the physicist who would want to abstain from these corrections and really be content with raw, naked experience would be forced to formulate really extraordinary laws" (Poincaré, 159). Buddhist and Christian theories correct the sparse experiences on which they are based to construct a comprehensive and coherent vision of the spiritual universe. The extravagance of religious imagination overflows what could reasonably be induced from experiential data, and a good part of the labor of theology consists in recalling religious thought to its real bases. Its critique goes deeper when it questions the best-founded religious constructions. The experiential bases resist skepticism, but the construction drawn from them is not thereby rendered incontestable or unsurpassable. Even a generalizing phenomenology of "sin" or "ignorance" is a construction shaped in depth by the particular values of biblical and Indian traditions respectively, and when that phenomenology is invoked as the basis for complex ontological theories on the origin of evil one is still further from the basic data.

The theories of physics "teach us, before and after, that there is such and such a relation between one thing and another; only that something that we once called 'movement' we now call 'electric current.' But these appellations were only substituted for the real objects that nature will forever hide from us" (Poincaré, 174). The system of relations thought in terms of substances and natures in classical dogmatics is thought in terms of event and process in modern theology. When Carnot's principle gave place to the second law of thermodynamics, "the same relations still held, even though the relations did not take place, at least in appearance, between the same objects. . . . Carnot's reasonings . . . were applied to a material vitiated by error, but their form—which was the essential—remained correct" (177). The relations are not quite the same, but we have a dynamic equivalent of them. The questions the discovery of the system resolves are not the same either. Contradictions between two religious systems become intellectually tolerable in light of scientific practice: "When a physicist registers a contradiction between two theories equally dear to him he will sometimes say: Let's not worry about that but let's hold firmly the two ends of the chain even if the intermediary links are hidden from us" (175). The two religious systems express true relations but dressed in images or mental frameworks that introduce contradiction into the expression. A larger ecumenism that embraces the major contradictions between religions—between Christian trinitarianism and Islamic monotheism, for example—is not as irresponsible as it seems to those who cling to a transparent objectivity of doctrinal systems. One labors to reduce these contradictions by interpreting the rich historical context that determines their meaning and by critiquing the inadequation of the frames of thought on both sides. Jewish monotheism, Christian Trinity, Buddhist nontheism, Greek or Japanese polytheism, all express true relations that contradict each other only as dogmas made autonomous in regard to their phenomenological basis.

A conventionalist would say that within a given geometry one can judge propositions true and false but that the question of the truth of the geometry itself does not arise, since there is no external and objective "space" with which it might be compared. Any noncontradictory geometry will fit our spatial experience, and the question as to which of them best fits it concerns the pragmatic efficacy of the system in a given context, or its value for the evolution of the species. If a Euclidean insisted to a Riemannian, "No, two parallel lines can never meet!," it would be absurd, given the conventional status of the axiom in question. Similar absurdities dog religious debates. Axioms such as "God is love" make sense within a system of living representations. Exported out of this context they change their meaning or lose it and can become unintelligible even to longtime believers. A conventionalist would say the truth of such propositions can be asserted only with the language game of faith; this is a system which functions, but there is no "outside the text." Thus the religious approach to truth is subject to constraints, laws of style. A mythical language cannot be sustained without constant attention to its poetic and contemplative resonances. A positivistic recension of the contents of the myth kills it stone dead. Dogmas, too, cannot afford to be unmoored from their imaginative and contemplative matrix. When Philo and his Christian heirs began to ask speculative questions about the conditions and foundations of biblical language about God, Word and Spirit, they had perhaps already lost touch with the stylistic features essential to the use of these biblical names, and with the original imaginative and contemplative sense of this biblical language.

The construction of doctrinal orthodoxy is a performance brought off within an intellectual framework that is ill accorded with the world of the biblical texts and does not provide the ideal space for exposing the elements of faith. Melanchthon and Calvin sought to supplement or replace it with a biblical mode of exposition in which the world constructed according to dogmas would gradually be replaced by that of the biblical kerygma. As the contours of the latter emerge, the dogmatic epoch comes to appear as only an episode in the reception of the biblical vision. The pluralism of scripture is recovered, and this enables a corresponding pluralism in the present reception of the biblical heritage. A plurality of Christian visions is constructed, with an unprecedented awareness of their constructed character. Arbitrariness is held at bay not by dogma but by a general fidelity to the values of the tradition, especially those of the Gospel. Such a pluralized Christianity loses the unitary force of the past but gains in persuasive presence within the contemporary world.

We tend to suppose that adherents of beliefs that seem primitive to us did not really believe them at all. But recollection of one's own younger years suffices to show that the human mind can be convinced of any miracle. For many contemporary Japanese, as for the ancient Romans, outworn beliefs survive as social and civil customs; yet what looks like a mere convention from afar can be for those who live within it a reality one does not think of questioning. Conversely, the armor of dogmatic faith may be less robust than it seems, and a gap can grow between the clarity of doctrinal formulas and catechisms on one hand and the fuzzy ideas actually held by people on the other. Even those who master a coherent set of convictions may rely on elements of conventionality that are not questioned as to their ultimate truth. Any system of human thought is a cultural construction, a provisional arrangement, enabling one to live and to think, even if this conventional texture comes to light only in a time of crisis that shakes one from dogmatic slumbers. In a time of religious pluralism all the worlds of religious thought are invited to suspect that their status is nonultimate. To expose everything to the light of criticism, recognizing the constructed and provisional nature of each element of the discourse of faith, is the posture of radical vulnerability needed for honest dialogue between faith and the world or between faith and faith.

I shall return to the topic of dogma in the last chapter of this book, seeking to show that both creedal affirmations and the largely negative constraints with which dogma and the theological defense of dogma surround them can retain their validity and force even within the regime of the twofold truth.

FREEDOM FROM VIEWS

One of the most salutary lessons of Buddhism for Christians is its warning against attachment to views. "Right view," the first member of the Eightfold Path, is opposed to sixty-two kinds of wrong view, which tend to the extremes of eternalism or nihilism. But even right views can imprison; views (*dṛṣṭi*) as such are seen as a form of attachment (*grāha*). Constructivist epistemologists show that "the real reason people maintain beliefs and views usually has very little relationship with any objective facts, but rather, on whether or not they seem to 'work well'—if they are effective, skillful (*kuśala*!) and so forth. Therefore, if someone believes that his own views are working well, it will usually matter little if you present him a solid array of facts that run contrary to his beliefs" (Muller, 31–32). Views occasion attachment even when they are carefully articulated doctrines, proving unexpectedly resistant to rational argument; this is even more the case with the subconscious investments that govern our daily lives, and without which we cannot live. These rest on *satkāya-dṛṣṭi*, which Charles Muller translates as "identity-making" or "reification," resulting in belief in a self (*ātma-dṛṣṭi*), bifurcation of self and other, and attachment to dharmas (*dharma-grāha*). At a level below the threshold of consciousness we gather experiential data into unitary formations, named as "I" or "mine," for example. To deconstruct these fixated identities more than intellectual acumen is required. The bodhisattva has overcome the distorting effect of these views and rejoined the phenomena they occlude. The bodhisattva can handle views lightly with salvific intent, but he knows their flimsy status and is not taken in by them.

It seems that many religious people today devote a lot of energy to filtering out wrong views in their own minds and especially in the minds of others. This inquisitorial mentality is a blockage of authentic theological judgment. It is one of the merits of Buddhism that it discourages people from getting excited about views. To be sure, a number of views are denounced as wrong or heretical, and thus as obstacles to liberation. But right views can be just as much an obstacle, or a more subtle and insidious obstacle. In the Gospels, the scribes and Pharisees have all the right answers, yet their orthodoxy seems only to harden their hearts. Countering this, the *Vimalakīrti Sūtra* encourages bodhisattvas to indulge false views, not only in the sense of compassionately understanding them in order to save those entangled in them, but perhaps also in the sense that Lacanian psychoanalysts might tell their patients, "Enjoy your symptom." "You're looking for emptiness?" Vimalakīrti might say. "Just revel in your false views and delusive imaginings, pursuing them to their last consequences, and you'll find emptiness at the heart of them."

Because all of the false views are empty imaginings, their failure to grasp a coherent object is a demonstration of emptiness. But emptiness itself is not to be imagined or treated as a substantive view that could be further built on. This suggests a question to Christian thought, which has often taken the most intangible and ineffable realities, such as "God" and "grace," and proceeded to treat them as solid premises for long strings of argument. But perhaps the notions of God and grace, like the notion of emptiness, are incapable of being categorized and conceptualized and are best perceived in silent contemplation that stills the busy beat of the mind.

Buddhism is chary of advancing even "right" views, since all views become the focus of enslaving attachment. Rather than glorify firm dogmatic views as a guarantee of spiritual health, Buddhist analysis probes the nature of our commitment to these views and queries its underlying motivation. Views are to be held lightly, used functionally and therapeutically, and put aside when they have served their purpose, and ultimately, it seems, the highest religious insight in Buddhism is one in which all views have disappeared. To be sure, the ontology of dependent co-arising, central to Buddhist doctrine, might be characterized as a correct view. But the Madhyamaka dialectic, building on the outlook of the Perfection of Wisdom sutras and the *Vimalakīrti Sūtra*, denies it such a stable status. What appears conventionally as dependent co-arising is ultimately nondependent nonarising. Is nondependent nonarising then the correct view? No, for its negative character makes it again a denial of views rather than a positive assertion. Dependent arising is a provisional designation of the way things are, but ultimately they are neither dependent nor arising. Dependent arising opens up awareness of emptiness, but emptiness does not refer back to dependent arising, except as a conventional vehicle. In its ultimate reality emptiness eludes all categories.

In this philosophy, right view is established, or at least provisionally accepted, at the level of conventional truth, whereas on the level of ultimate truth there are no views. Nāgārjuna denies that he is putting forward any view or proposition at all, confining himself to demonstrating the emptiness of all views. "If I had any thesis, then I would have some fault. Because I have no thesis I am entirely faultless" (*Vigrahavyāvartani* 29, quoted in Huntington 2003:73). Yet at the conventional level he does seem to advance the "view" that "everything is empty of substantial existence." At the ultimate level, he washed his thought clean of theses or terms that would have more than a totally provisional function. "Emptiness" itself is a conventional expression, and ultimate reality is neither empty, nonempty, both, or neither. "Nothing is to be called empty or not empty. . . . The word is used in conversation as a conventional designation" (*MK* 22.11).

Christian orthodox views should be maintained in the same spirit. Realizing the amount of projection, craving, and clinging that goes into the composition of our religious views, and the inevitability with which they give rise to bitter dispute, we should let them go, treating them as formations that can be deployed strategically in given contexts but that do not have the substantial solidity that we are so prone to lend them. Creedal articles must not become idols or fetishes; they are at best crutches, prompters to religious consciousness on its path to enlightenment. A mind secure in faith-consciousness will meditate on the articles of the Creed only to deepen that consciousness, without busily seeking to adjudicate what degree of credibility the archaic language of the Creed possesses. Enlightened consciousness of itself performs the demythologization and the overcoming of metaphysics that theological hermeneutics requires, for it brings everything back to the deepest intention of the Creed, an opening up to the mystery of "God with us."

A relaxed recognition of the conventional character of religious ideas may now be a key component in the stewardship of our religious heritage. Change in the texture of religious consciousness at the basic level of worship and catechesis is not being brought about by the conscious application of sophisticated theological hermeneutics. Rather, what is happening is that while the old forms are retained, they are functioning in a subtly altered way. They are treasured, but no longer as simple, direct expressions of faith; rather they begin to be understood as skillful means for indicating, obliquely, allusively, that divine realm to which religious ideas and practices attune us. A certain looseness of connection has insinuated itself into the believer's relationship to the acts and words in which his or her faith seeks expression. Theology should pursue the reflective integration of the elements of vagueness and questioning inherent in belief, which take an especially pointed form today, when inherited religious forms can seem like ghostly relics in a secularized environment. Such reflection would dedramatize the angst of those harassed by agnosticism or moral incertitude. It would accept that those elements of doubt and hesitation are not opposed to faith as what annuls it but are part of the very landscape of faith.

The pressures of modern awareness and the experience of interreligious thinking are deepening our sense of the conventionality of religions, for good or ill, and it has become impossible to foreclose reflection on the topic. "But if religions are just sets of conventions," it may be objected, "what happens to the absolute authority of divine revelation?" However, the rhetoric of revelation is particularly difficult to handle. "Revelation" is a subtle, transcendental notion, not to be used as a knockdown argument in debates on the status and texture of religious language as it has developed in history. Words such as *God*, *revelation*, and *resurrection* point to ultimacy, to an incomparable reality that cannot be encompassed in the web of the conventional; but the words themselves function at best as mere pointers to this ultimacy.

We may understand *revelation* to mean the emergence of ultimacy within a given tradition of conventional representations. It would not then consist in new information or the happening of a supernatural event that cuts across the normal unfolding of the human quest of ultimacy. There are revelatory breakthroughs or thresholds within the laborious development of a tradition of religious words, concepts, stories, and practices, privileged moments when things click into place, when there emerges a luminous perspective that both perfects the previous religious framework (through clarifying the ultimate sense of its conventional designations, or though making a breakthrough in the direction of ultimacy) or that exceeds the previous framework (through an immediate tasting or touching of ultimacy that shows up all the conventions of discourse as "mere straw"). Most religious activity consists in a scrupulous tending of the language and practices that have served as vehicles of such revelatory breakthroughs. But even the most hallowed traditions may need to be overturned when they grow stale or archaic. Religious authority may absolutely forbid any tampering with the sacred vehicles: not a jot, not a tittle may be altered. Yet conventions remain intrinsically subordinate to the ultimacy to which they are supposed to keep us attuned. True revelation is thus likely to be subversive rather than conservative. It is in the name of the ultimate significance of the Torah that Paul can radically redefine its status; the same is true of Luther's rethinking of the sacraments. Breakthroughs to ultimacy can lead to a prophetic overhaul of the pregiven conventions, in that their merely functional status becomes apparent.

The specific function of religious language is to awaken a sense of the limits of the conventional and a thirst for the ultimate. It is a language built at the frontiers of language. Even if it becomes very down to earth, it still refers each topic it deals with to the ultimate, thus signaling the conventionality of that topic. A religious act resumes and symbolizes the totality of one's being-in-the-world. It redoubles the conventions of life: sacrifice redoubles gift, sacred meals redouble everyday ones. Nietzsche noted this parasitism of religion but missed its revelatory effect. The doubling reveals conventions as conventions, marking them as such before the ultimate. Ultimacy is nothing other than the reality of the conventional, which passes through the looking glass of religious representation to discover itself as empty of own-nature and thus to come close to the ultimate. For this transformation to take effect, the conventional basis should be as real as possible. An archaic or sentimental basis should not be accepted on the pretext that religion surpasses the conventional in any case, for if the basis is hollow every effort to indicate the ultimate beginning from it will be enfeebled. There is a place for tolerance even of tawdry and undernourished religious culture, since some people can use these conventions in inspired ways. Some have recovered Christian faith because of pseudo-Christian productions such as Wagner's *Parsifal* or Mel Gibson's *The Passion of the Christ*. But a church that wallows in vulgarity does not go unpunished. Respect for conventions carries the duty of working on them to make them more coherent, expressive, and well founded. Theology can be seen as such a therapy of religious conventions, seeking to reawaken their hidden force.

Perhaps one should reformulate religious affirmations in an optative tonality. To affirm that "God is good" would then mean to orient oneself toward an ultimate reality by taking the notion of goodness as a guiding thread. The cognitive yield of the proposition is oblique and context dependent, yet it has a positive truth-value and excludes the opposing proposition, "God is not good," as objectively false (in normal usages). The flat declaration that "God is good, he is goodness itself" is rather ineffective, even when girded with the metaphysics of the Good and the convertibility of goodness and being. It requires to be contextualized as doxology, as in "How good God is to Israel!" (Ps 73:1). The referents of such first-level religious utterance should not be defined prematurely. The spectrum of its connotations should be allowed to unfold. Clearing the language of metaphysical investments in order to let it function in a lucid and demystified way, one preserves its openness to the ultimate reality toward which it points. Metaphysics offers to protect and prop up the language of the Psalms, injecting cognitive reinforcement. Yet it may be that the unprotected psalmist best expresses the human situation before the divine and that theology best finds its bearings by rejoining that situation.

A paradigm shift condemns an old world to disappear, like that of Newton when Einstein came along. Yet the truth of the old world can be preserved in a way, as the Newtonian cosmology survives within the new one: "According to Feyerabend, to say that Einstein's and Newton's theories (or paradigms) are incommensurable is to say that the principles for constructing concepts in one *suspend* the principles of the other. That is, the relativistic ideas used to understand mass, length, and time do not permit the use of the alternative Newtonian ideas" (Munévar, 73). Likewise, we can no longer construct the concept of God along the lines of mythical narrative or ontotheological metaphysics. Rather, in the relativistic perspective of reflection on religious pluralism, monotheism emerges as one historical convention among others. If we continue to use the word *God* in our actual religious discourse, its meaning has changed somewhat as the meaning of the word *mass* has changed in Einstein's discourse. Newton's mass is conserved; Einstein's is convertible with energy. Classically *God* refers to a single immutable entity; today *God* is a flexible pointer, used as a skillful means for indicating the empty realm of Spirit. One might say that *God*, along with other highly charged religious expressions, is destined to be converted into a rhetorical stratagem for unleashing the energy of religious awareness, or for tuning in to the creative, transforming energy of Spirit that all religious traditions have felt in one way or another. The biblical identification of God as the God of Abraham, Isaac, and Jacob, or as the God and Father of our Lord Jesus Christ, points to places where God is encountered and thus identifies God at a second remove, through a detour through these places. One might say: "Supreme gracious reality was known as 'God' in Israel, and any quest for this reality can find secure bearings by linking to the Israelite tradition and its Christian development, tried and tested vehicles of ultimacy." Direct identifications of God without reference to a concrete locus—as when God is called holy or righteous—mark how God transcends the places of his manifestation; but even here, more often than not, the holiness and righteousness are seen as dwelling in or attested to by a concrete locus: the angels, the Temple, or the holy, righteous community. Both kinds of identification spur the mind to seek the figure of the divine in today's world, both the concrete places where the Spirit is at work and the modalities of divine distance or transcendence that can claim a contemporary mind. The objective truth about God contained in the long history of such oblique and contextual identifications cannot be extracted in a pure form. The word *God* thus functions both to inscribe one in a particular tradition and to open one to the wide empty reaches of the divine that have always been an ultimate bourne for human thought.

The biblical God need not disappear in this pluralistic horizon any more than gravity has ceased to function with the transition from the Newtonian to the Einsteinian framework for understanding it. Like Newton's mass, length, and time, God—or the function of the name *God*—faces redescription rather than demise, in accord with the new, different principles now governing the construction of religious language. Within this economy, this new regime of truth and revelation, the biblical language about God is allowed to breathe freely, so that despite the altered coordinates it is still of the God of Abraham and of Jesus Christ that we are speaking.

A new culture of faith, which has learned to play with conventions, the products of a complex history, without taking them for more than they are, can handle even such expressions as *God* or *Our Father* as useful props, deployed to open the space of prayer. They become cumbersome if one insists too much on their literal reference. What counts is the openness of spirit they express, loving trust ("Our Father"), reverence ("Hallowed be thy name"), hope ("Thy kingdom come"), docility ("Thy will be done"). To use with the same lightness the other institutions and disciplines of the church, in what is too quickly denounced as "cafeteria Catholicism," is not decadence but the flexibility required to accord the claims of tradition with those of present reality. When one recites the Lord's Prayer, one is conscious of performing a specifically Christian act, quoting an ancient text, just as Jews, Muslims, Buddhists do. The disenchantment this leveling and relativization creates can be overcome by reappropriating the gestures and quotations in their fragile status as means of opening to the divine, which have proven their value in the course of a long history.

The most comprehensive and reflected reappropriation of a tradition is that which sees the most clearly the conventionality of religious discourse and the tangentiality of its relation to the ultimate. Karl Barth, faced with the contextuality of all religious thought and the relativization this entails, sought to master it dialectically, so that true faith emerges beyond the contradictions of religion. Thus he gains an "absolute" position, grasping the totality of traditions in a contemporary key—though in a negative characterization, not with Hegelian inclusivism. He knows that the human texture of religions does not yield a luminous unfolding, a providential order, which are mythic constructs not to be found in human history, yet he marks one corner of history as the sacral time of Christian revelation, a privileged breakthrough of ultimacy, and this is immunized against the laws of normal historicity.

What is called salvation history can be real only as a crystallization emerging within history as such. Reinserted in the pluralist horizon in which all religions deploy their interaction of conventional and ultimate, this biblical history is seen not as cutting across the common human question of the ultimate, communicating new knowledge from outside that process. At privileged points, the long labor of traditions yields a perspective in which everything seems to fall into place. Living religions draw their inspiration from the memory of such moments. Christianity is not related to other religions as revelation to its absence but as one historical vehicle of revelation to others. Whatever primacy it may enjoy is discerned neither through dogmatic logic nor through comparative evaluations of biblical language and the language of other faiths. Such debate on the conventional plane cannot dictate what will happen in the concrete encounter between revelation events, which is not a dialectic between rival claims but a convergence of practices of contemplative listening. Each tradition listens for the word or the silence that founds it, beyond the noise of its conventional embodiments, and in the mutual listening of the traditions this discernment of ultimacy is reinforced. Just as naturalist theologies accept the fabric of the universe and its exclusion of interruptions by a divine cause, so a historical grasp of religions excludes the possibility of revelatory interventions coming from outside. The divine makes its presence and power felt, as source of all, without the need to cut across the fabric of creation, on both the cosmic and the historical levels. But just as there are thresholds of evolution, there are breakthroughs of ultimacy in history, moments of revelation.

The historical view of religions as formations specific to different cultures and irreducible to a common core is in tension with the witness of religious apostles convinced of having seen things as they truly are. Ultimacy is always the ultimacy of a given conventional basis, that is, it is revealed as surpassing or "saturating" a given concrete horizon, emerging in a different perspective in each case. This pluralism of languages and perspectives need not contradict the conviction of believers in each case that they have come in contact with something ultimately real. Each naming of the ultimate projects an entire world, and the affinity that is found among the different namings does not prevent these worlds from remaining irreducibly different.

Religious claims prompt controversy and commentary, which become very complex when views formulated in remote traditions and epochs are confronted. The presence of ultimacy cannot become the toy of this vast hermeneutical activity, for it is that presence that gives to religions their vitality and value and that constitutes the final criterion for the critique and reform of traditions. Contradictions and comparisons between different breakthroughs of ultimacy depend on a reification and on the imposition of a common horizon that flattens the contours of traditions. A religion is its world grasped in its ultimate aspect or opened to the ultimate in the style proper to it. Worlds cannot be placed in mutual contradiction. Within these worlds and between them, clashes between contradictory theses take place on the conventional plane only, for the theses do not reach the level of the ultimate; yet to correct the false theses of religions is a service rendered to conventional reality in order to keep it open to ultimate reality.

Chapter Three

THE RELIGIOUS DYNAMIC
OF MODERNIST LITERATURE

The ultimacy that makes itself felt in art is consubstantial with the forms that are its vehicle; in religion, the relation between the two is more tangential, and the vehicles are at the limit merely provisional means to be cast aside when they have served their purpose. It is not easy to trace a clear border between art and religion. The dialogue between religious ultimacy and aesthetic ultimacy would be an important element in a mature culture of religious pluralism, especially at a time when for many art is the principal access to ultimacy. It is useless to inquire how religion in general relates to art in general, for the historical interferences between artistic labor and religious inspiration are multiform and unpredictable. At most one can observe that in a given period—that of twentieth-century modernism for example—some promising conjunctions or alliances of art and religion can be identified.

Since fundamental theology attempts to present the basic intelligibility and credibility of the Christian message under contemporary conditions, it is obliged to engage with the shaping horizons of the contemporary world, not only as these horizons are mapped and processed by philosophers, but also as they emerge more concretely and directly in the social, political, economic, ecological, cultural, psycho-logical, and anthropological realities that press upon human beings and their quest for meaning today. Modernist literature remains a foremost definer of the horizon that fundamental theology must ad-dress. It is rooted in the deepest questions that citizens of the modern world, seeking the meaning of their existence, have asked themselves. In turn it provides roots for its readers, giving them a language and an imaginative space with which to pursue their questioning. Originally the product of advanced, highly reflective literary enclaves in Lon-don, Paris, Vienna, Prague, Berlin, New York, St. Petersburg, this litera-ture has long become a lingua franca, a spiritual grammar, for educated and reflective people far beyond the borders of its countries of origin. If it is objected that the elite preoccupations of aesthetes have nothing to do with the down-to-earth, no-frills language of the Gospels, one may point to this wide interaction between high literary modernism and modern human experience on the one hand and the esoteric sub-limities of some parts of the Gospel on the other. The Christian mes-sage reaches out to the poor in a way that modernist literature does not, but this does not mean that it would consign its hearers to a flat, prosaic outlook that would be a dire form of mental impoverishment.

It might be feared that theological reflection on modernist litera-ture can only be lame and flat in comparison with the intensive labor of the literary critics. Psychoanalysts can bring an unexpected per-spective to it, as they read between the lines and listen for what is being voiced in the language of the unconscious. "The analyst's inter-ventions aim to reconstitute the coherence of the signifying chain at the level of the unconscious" (Lacan, 351), making sense of obscure texts and also revealing unsuspected layers of meaning in seemingly clear texts. Does theology have any similar techniques for bringing a lateral interpretation to bear on literature?

Philosophers have been stimulated by modernist literature (De-leuze on Kafka, Derrida on Mallarmé and Joyce) and have shed light on it in return. Few have risen to the construction of a philosophical aesthetic, grasping the meaning of literature and the other arts in broad philosophical terms; to do so they would first have to establish a gen-eral philosophical horizon, such as lies behind Heidegger's essay "The

Origin of the Work of Art" or Sartre's existential interpretation of modern literary projects. Richard Kearney (2011) assesses as a philosopher the religious bearing of modernist literature as he explores the "anatheistic" horizon opened by Proust, Woolf, and Joyce. He finds in these writers not a blank atheism but a new kind of faith or spiritual openness, an anonymous searching for a divine depth in things, after "the death of God." Their art labors to transform the everyday, to give it an epiphanic status. This rediscovery of wonder and grace in everyday experience is a powerful positive contribution of modernist literature to a renewed spirituality, Christian or other. What fundamental theology can add to the philosopher's reflections is a more explicit assessment of literary modernism in light of biblical revelation, as well as a reshaping of theological categories themselves in light of the questions this literature poses.

At first sight the modernist writers seem simply to turn their back on any theological approach. Even the great Christian modernists Eliot and Claudel come to meet Christian discourse only when their modernist vision is already on the wane, and what is living in their great Christian works may be something murky, chthonic, perverse that is not easily brought into accord with the Gospel. The atheism of many modernist writers is a bleak affair, and in its apologetic role fundamental theology must argue against it. Modernist writers are less interested in cosmic religious vision than the romantics were; their concern is with the texture of human experience and human existence. Theologians are tempted to measure their literary vision by pregiven biblical and church criteria, rather than seeing them as creators of new horizons that prescribe a rethinking of those criteria, for instance through a renunciation of their millennial patriarchal cast.

Against Alain Badiou's claim that the task of contemporary poetry is to "win its proper atheism," Jean Greisch points out that lyric poetry like that of Paul Celan or Ossip Mandelstam "opens a space of questioning address," and that this is intrinsic to its nature as poetry (1999:61–125). Analogously, the seemingly thorough secularization effected by novelists since Flaubert can show breaches that are not a betrayal of the novel's exploration of real experience but an opening of that experience itself onto unsettling depths. Of Henry James's novels, *The Wings of the Dove* is the one that most manifests such a thrust to transcendence. The work is not as formally self-enclosed as its rounded companions *The Ambassadors* and *The Golden Bowl*. Its rather jagged construction opens up a space of questioning beyond the well-defined issues of the other two novels and allows it to reach further, at least by suggestion, into moral and spiritual possibilities. The characters have the conatus of the urge to life (which may stumble on ultimate futility), and the conatus of style and form redoubles this and extends its energies. The story of Kate and Densher's plot to exploit the dying Milly could have been treated as a self-contained psychological ballet; but the brunt of ethical guilt and the emergence of forgiveness as a major theme break it open in a way that owes nothing to a religious incursion from outside but emerges from the dynamic inherent to the novelistic project. "The imaginative force is outward, straining toward a meaning not to be found within the work, but beyond it, escaping the constrictions of Kate's mean world and of Milly's death-bound 'box': a meaning Densher will come to recognize only in its absence, as an opportunity passed: the state to which those who can never be again 'as we were' might have aspired" (Bradbury, 72, quoting the last words of the novel). Looking back from this novel to what seem the purely this-worldly concerns of his other works, one might interrogate themes such as deception, inauthenticity, failure to love, and startling gaps between appearance and reality as exposing the texture of human finitude and guilt, and one might take the moments of gracious resolution in both the human plots and the literary structures as ciphers of grace.

A theological critique of the great modernist writers may reach back to the romantics for a more robust religious vision, as Romano Guardini reaches back behind Rilke to Hölderlin, whose verse is pervaded by a sense of *der Fehl Gottes*, the lack of God. For Hölderlin this lack is an ordeal to be endured in the spirit of hope—hope for a universe that will once again be flooded by divine presences, with Christ as one of them, a Dionysian wine-god, hope also that the "divine God" will be manifest. Heidegger took up this vision and tried to think it through in phenomenological terms. Biblical monotheism did not satisfy Hölderlin's thirst for divinity. He sketched an ideal of transcendence that perhaps calls for a transformation of monotheism in light of modern experience (though his de-Judaized religious vision also needs to be queried and resisted). His contemporary Wordsworth, too, had a vision of divinity dwelling in nature that he failed to square with biblical orthodoxy and that challenges that orthodoxy. The "atheist" Shelley rhapsodized about the Neoplatonic One, rejecting the conventional forms of religion, yet curiously rejoining them at high points in his inspired verse. The "Oriental Renaissance" was in full swing at the time, and traces of the influence of Charles Wilkins's 1785 translation of the *Bhagavad-gītā* and the researches of Sir William Jones can be detected in the English romantics. Theologically, one might discern the Spirit at work here, birthing an ecumenical religion that embraces love and freedom in an untrammeled way and that is steeped in wonder at the enigma of human existence and the quiet majesty of nature. A stern biblical monotheism might anathematize all this, but a ripe religious judgment here demands close dialogue with these poets and the modern sense of existence and of nature that they express.

Our access to the romantic chapter of literary history is complicated by the subsequent development of literary consciousness (much as our access to German idealism is complicated by the subsequent linguistic and phenomenological turns). It is the modernists, not the romantics, who are our more immediate dialogue partners. It is useless to scold them for being so secularized and so skeptical about religious claims. Their sensibility and language are ours in a way that those of the romantics are not, and it is they who have set the exigent criteria for a convincing religious language today. Postmodernists who would see modernism as an elite museum product seem to me oblivious of their own epigonal status. Indeed, *postmodernism* is now a more out-of-date term than *modernism*.

Balthasarians discuss modern literature in the context of fundamental theology, but they do so under the unhelpful rubric of beauty, conceived massively as a transcendental convertible with being and truth. "The beautiful opens a world of gratuity; it is a superfluous and contingent gift. The wonder it excites reminds us of the contingency of the beautiful and the gift. This dimension of gift and gratuity is what should be retained in the contribution of the literary work to theology" (Sèbe, 410). This angle hardly opens access even to Weimar classicism and German romanticism, which were far from being fixated on beautiful forms, and still less can it embrace modernism, which may have been shaped by a fin-de-siècle cult of beauty but which also outgrew it, even in Rilke and Proust. Great writers are the product of a tradition and are located at a strategic point in its development— Rilke in the development of German lyric, for example, or Proust in the development of the novel since Balzac. The effect of beauty in their works is shaped by the ultimate literary concern of their historical moment as well as by the conventions developed to meet it and further developed by themselves. Theological insistence on "beauty" may function as a strategy for avoiding the primary impact of modernist literature, its radical questioning of existence and meaning. Modernist artists ask what can be done in the current situation of their art, so as to "make it new" (Pound), and what can be done is what must be done, an imperative of art (not of the willfully authoritarian artist, as postmodern critics of modernism allege).

Literary beauty is subtly intertwined with ethical questioning or a more general existential reflection. Schiller saw the four basic qualities of the beautiful—its universality, its disinterestedness, its inwardness, and its inexhaustible fullness of meaning—as determined by the ethical concerns of practical reason (Frank 2007:204). Philosophers of a Kantian stripe may see this as an illegitimate conflation of two distinct registers of judgment. For the theologian, the claim of modernist literature is not that of a beauty to be serenely enfolded within a capacious Christian aesthetics or subordinated to a Christian ethics. Rather, it is a great enterprise of questioning and transformation that could easily be seen as a hubristic, Promethean effort to replace the biblical vision long dominant in the West. But while theology will find much to argue with in modernist literature, nothing is more futile than the effort to discredit modernity itself or this literature as a major threshold in modern self-awareness. A new horizon or regime of truth has been established within which the biblical message must be rearticulated, and it cannot be effectively communicated as glad tidings if it finds expression only as a critical reaction against modernity. Many

Christian thinkers—G. K. Chesterton, say, or even Karl Barth—have beaten the drum of a joyful archaism over against a modern world viewed as pitifully narrow and blind. But no one is immune to the modernist alteration of the landscape or texture of spiritual awareness. It implies a new culture of judgment in which we discern anew the questionability and flimsiness of our conventional world and also the gleams of ultimacy, aesthetic, ethical, or religious, that pervade it, and in which we apply the same discernment to inherited religious representations.

Heirs of the fin de siècle ethos of art for art's sake, modernist writers are keenly conscious of the irreducibility of literary art to any nonliterary frames of understanding, be they sociological, philosophical, or theological, and they seek to affirm that irreducibility by making the substance of their art at every turn as purely literary as possible. Just as abstract painters drop representation so as to let painting explore its inherent nature and resources, so the writers court the ideal of writing "a book about nothing" (Flaubert, Mallarmé, Beckett, Blanchot). Their cult of style takes on a new seriousness as an instrument of vision and transformation. To discuss their writing under pregiven headings such as beauty is to miss their originality and radicality, their quest to realize the essence of literature, in all its strangeness, as the conditions of their place in the tradition made possible in a new way. This aesthetic ultimacy cannot be subordinated to the ethical or religious, despite its close and tense interaction with them. The theologian or moralist who seeks to "use" literature will miss its essence, its otherness. Philosophers who parse literature in terms of their own major themes, such as Spirit, Being, existence, or, in the case of Kyoto School philosophers, self-awareness, emptiness, or nothingness, risk missing the wider space of a dialogue between poet and thinker (such as Heidegger envisioned). Conversely, though literature is irreducible to philosophy and religion, it cannot set itself up either as a substitute for them, though it can offer some gleams of religion to those who have no religion. When De Botton laments: "We are by no means lacking in material which we might call into service to replace the holy texts; we are simply treating that material in the wrong way. We are unwilling to consider secular culture religiously enough, in

other words, as a source of guidance" (111), he is trying to force literature to play the role of religion. The quest for moral guidance from
literature has been carried as far as it can go, since Matthew Arnold
and F. R. Leavis, down to the more recent moralizing of feminist and
postcolonialist readings. The phrase "religion of art" is best understood as expressing the radical devotion of modernist artists to their
distinctive and irreplaceable task of transformation. If they had sought
to set up art as another religion, promising salvation, that would spoil
both art and religion.

It might be objected that the rarefied projects of modernist art are
ill suited to nourish the wider pastoral dialogue with modernity that
theology must undertake. Despite the literary excellences of the New
Testament, we do not find the apostolic authors entering into dialogue
with Virgil or Tacitus. One may deck a homily with some literary
graces, but if this is overdone, so that the homily becomes literature
rather than biblical address, there has been a failure of communication. Yet ultimately the churches cannot pass by major expressions of
the human spirit and new understandings of being and the divine, any
more than the fathers could pass by the summits of Greco-Roman
culture. In real life, believers are attending to the voices of literary
modernism, which blend with the questions of faith, and theology, especially fundamental theology, should lend this real-life dialogue a
formal and comprehensive framework.

THE SACRIFICIAL DYNAMIC OF MODERNIST ART

The great modernists, from James and Conrad on, or rather from
Flaubert and Baudelaire, enact the autonomy of art, which cannot be
set at the service of a religious ideology. Their ethos encourages a view
of past religious art as using gods as a mere pretext for the artist's creative project. Yet the modernist artist exhibits a concrete religious
stance in his or her total creative performance, which is marked by a
dynamic of sacrificial transformation. Scholars in theology, religious
studies, and philosophy of religion may pick up the sacral overtones
in modernist works such as *To the Lighthouse* or *The Rainbow*, but

they may learn more if they suspend their interpretative frameworks to let the phenomena of modernist art show themselves on their own terms, terms by no means making for an easy accommodation with inherited religious representations.

The individual who creates a work of art dies to himself or herself and is reborn as an artist, defined by the work that is being created. Mallarmé speaks of the *disparition élocutoire du poète* (1945:360), meaning that the poet as individual vanishes into the voice that utters the poem, or is transubstantiated into that voice. "I am now impersonal, and no longer Stéphane whom you have known,—but an aptitude that the Spiritual Universe has of seeing itself and developing itself, across that which was me" (1995:343). This death of the poet is associated with an experience of the death of God: Mallarmé speaks of "God, that wicked old plumage, happily overthrown" (362; ce vieux et méchant plumage, terrassé heureusement, Dieu). The crisis in self-identity and the break with conventional visions of the world characteristic of modernist creators seem naturally to entail a crisis in their idea of God as well, and a sacrifice of inherited ideas of God. This of course does not exclude the possibility that the writers become fixated in an atheistic stance, or in an unhappy consciousness torn between recognition of God and revolt against God. Indeed, the Christian reader of modernist writers is faced with a near-impossible task of sifting out the potential seeds of a renewed theological vision from the symptoms of a mere failure of faith. Theology seeks to inculturate the Gospel in modern ways of thinking, yet at the same time has a responsibility to check and heal the unruliness of the modern mind, a situation not unlike that faced by the fathers with regard to pagan philosophy.

Balthasar celebrates sacrifice in Gerard Manley Hopkins, but he means the readiness to sacrifice art and the entire aesthetic sphere (Sèbe, 274), rather than a sacrificial dynamic in his poetry itself. "The writer has no mission if not the Christian mission" (274); all that Balthasar can take from Hopkins is his theological thoughts, and he has little to say about the specificity of the poetic vocation. Adrian Grafe (quoted in Sèbe, 274) better grasps the modernist character of Hopkins's writing, which he sees as centered on "decreation": "When the man is decreated, the poet is recreated; a new poetic language can then be born." This makes Hopkins sound like Mallarmé and Rilke, sharing the same dynamic of sacrifice. The figure of Dionysus, repristinated by Nietzsche and haunting Wagner, Joyce, and Thomas Mann, inspires a modernist project of decreation, returning to an original fertile chaos, or to the depths of the unconscious, in order to let new forms emerge, to forge anew, with Stephen Dedalus, the "uncreated conscience" of the race. This sacrifice of old identities and birthing of new ones solicits theology toward a comparable self-transformation.

Rilke offers the most thorough demonstration of how an individual is transformed as he lives into his poetic identity, shedding earlier conceptions of self, world, and the divine. He was disturbed by Paula Becker-Modersohn's uncanny portrait of him, painted long before the sovereign breakthrough of the *Duino Elegies* and the *Sonnets to Orpheus* in 1922, for she caught his essential identity, the poet latent in the man, a somewhat frightening figure, dehumanized, an oracular mask (see Petzet). T. S. Eliot sees the poet as haunted by "a demon against which he feels powerless, because in its first manifestation it has no face, no name, nothing." The poem is a kind of exorcism, followed by "a moment of exhaustion, of appeasement, of absolution, and of something very near annihilation, which is in itself indescribable" (98).

In a genuine artwork, just as the human being who penned or painted it survives only as a poetic voice or a mode of seeing, the language or palette used is transmuted into a singular idiom, and the world itself emerges in an uncanny new light—"The light that never was on sea or land" (Wordsworth, "Elegiac Stanzas"). The materials of stone, paint, language, or musical sound are transmuted in function of the style that is the very signature of the artist's new being. Finally, the experienced world that is the theme of the work of art reemerges, in a scarcely recognizable form, in the vision that the work embodies, a vision taking actual shape only in the process of composition. The transformation or revelation effected by style replaces the substance of the things painted or the experiences narrated with the substance of the artwork, be it painting, poem, or novel, which simultaneously transcends the world by its singularity and perfection and lights up the world from within. The work would be spoiled by any untransformed residue of the artist's everyday identity, or of everyday speech, or of an everyday vision of the world.

Rilke's poetry attempts to establish "the pure relation" (*der reine Bezug*) or "the cognized figure" (*die gewusste Figur*) that holds the world together (see Allemann). He speaks of the *Weltinnenraum*, the world as relived and reshaped in memory and imaginative re-creation. Unlike Hölderlin, Rilke does not explore a cosmic horizon, haunted by divinities, but practices a quite secular art of transmutation of everyday things into invisible poetic essences. "We are the bees of the invisible," he wrote. One might find a similar transformation in Wordsworth, for whom external landscapes, recollected in tranquillity, become a "picture of the mind," triggering a mystical mood in which "with an eye made quiet by the power / Of harmony, and the deep power of joy, / We see into the life of things" ("Tintern Abbey"). But where Wordsworth has a vision of the cosmos, Rilke proceeds with the empirical prudence of a phenomenologist, sedulous as a lab scientist, working on the texture of experience as the matter to be clarified, transformed, interiorized. The inspiration on which he waited, and which released the *Elegies* and the *Sonnets*, is seen, not as a delivery from God or the cosmos or being, but as a crystallization of the poetic form in its total self-transparency. The "angels," like the mythical Orpheus, are ciphers of this happening of the truth of poetry, which is an end in itself. For Heidegger, this represents a falling back into the prison of a modern metaphysics of subjectivity, but perhaps it could be regarded as more like the breaking down of the opposition of self and world, subjective and objective, that Zen Buddhism aims at. Christians will wonder how the cult of poetic truth accords with Gospel concerns of justice and charity.

In the ideal modernist book "about nothing," both the author and the subject matter are sublated into an enactment of literature itself, of style, in a kind of transcendental turn. This can spell a new intimacy with the real, as the labor of form allows common words, incidents, moods to emerge in their mute undiluted presence, in a bonfire of the conventional procedures of narrative and characterization (see Chrétien, 297–98). If pushed too far, content can fail altogether, and the texts become sets of writing gestures with nothing to write about.

Something remotely analogous occurs in the radical fundamental theology of Barth and Bultmann, where the Reformation quest for the essence of faith produces a shift from theology to metatheology, highlighting so starkly the existential impact of a pure hearing of the Word that reference to any particular content comes to seem a blot on it. In this radical orthodoxy theology is disencumbered of controversies about particular theologoumena and is consumed in meditation on its own authentic essence. The idea of theological style or of "Christianity as style" (Theobald) does not necessarily spell a retreat to abstract aesthetics. Rather, it overcomes heavy-handed objectifications of the matter of faith, of the kind on which biblical and magisterial fundamentalism thrives, in order to trace the fundamental intuitions or imperatives of the believing conscience. Just as literature wins its freedom and its proper role by sacrificing author and subject matter, so faith, by radical reflection on itself, becomes a force of liberation, no longer entangled in the debts and scruples generated by a multitude of credenda. Simultaneously the object of faith, the saving event that lifts up the believer, conferring a new identity that places us outside ourselves (Luther's *extra nos*), is itself emptied of names and forms that make it an imprisoning idol. Buddhism similarly becomes a religion "about nothing" as it sacrifices the ego and its objectifications in order to let the essence of its core liberation event emerge.

It will be objected that the concrete data of the Incarnation cannot be whisked away from Christian faith. But this preliminary turn back to the essence of faith establishes the horizon in which those data can come into view as worthy of faith. Barth, Bultmann, Rahner, and the liberation theologians, in different ways and imperfectly, set up a constant critical ferment as each of the concrete elements of the Christian message is reprocessed in the style of authentic faith as established at the level of fundamental theology. Theologies in which this reflective cast is missing, replaced by a stolid insistence on points of doctrine, or on horizons of understanding not generated from faith but from ancient or recent ideologies, fail in the same way as literature that remains oblivious of the modernist revolution.

The modernist artistic vision sacrifices past representations of reality and art not by ignoring them but by consuming them in new ways of seeing and expressing, as is clear in the densely intertextual fabric of the writing of Joyce and Eliot, whose rewriting of the tradition could be paralleled with Heidegger's retelling of the history of Western philosophy or with Bultmann's revisioning of the New Testament or Barth's reprise of historical theology. For the modernists intertextual allusion was not an idle game but a struggle to appropriate and surpass what humanity had allowed itself, up to that point, to see and to say. Harold Bloom's theory of "the anxiety of influence" does little justice to this; these artists were not concerned with their own originality but, in a Nietzschean spirit, with allowing the new to emerge from the husks of the old.

TRANSFORMATION IN PROUST AND JOYCE

Sacrificing traditional securities and conventions is not just a matter of shaking them off in order to see things plain. When Proust and Joyce champion the everyday, they do so by denying that it can ever be simple and ordinary or emerge in a transparent neutral language. Their "epiphanies" are not simple data but elaborately staged phenomena; the experiential basis is thoroughly recreated as fiction, filtered through the medium of imagination, or carefully set in a context that confers maximum signifying power on it.

The phenomena at the core of Proust's and Joyce's art are not natural objects but the spectacles of modern urban culture. These can be focused only in a vast play of reference matching the historical depth and cultural breadth of the city. The modernist sacrificial dynamic comes into play in both novelists in their refusal of documentary naturalism. Both are martyrs of style, bent on transubstantiating their cities, without remainder, into linguistic monuments. Both evoke eucharistic symbolism, not only for the mutually nourishing relationships between the characters (the mother's or Albertine's kiss in Proust, the prostitute's kiss in *A Portrait of the Artist as a Young Man*), but for the way their art is nourished by the reality of experience and in turn nourishes its consumers. Proust, recalling devotions of his childhood, toyed with the title *L'adoration perpétuelle* for the contemplation of the lost time immortalized in art. Composition, in the immature imagination of Stephen Dedalus and in the mature resolution of Proust's narrator, becomes the confection of a sacred food of which the reader is welcomed to partake. (One of Proust's admiring readers compared his novel to a rich cake.)

Where Cézanne, and Rilke in his wake, feed on natural things, birthing them anew in the idealized or primordial medium of art, Proust and Joyce are involved in an enterprise of transformation that works not on the secret rhythms of nature but on the complexities of individual and group behavior. They have consumed their cities, having first been consumed by them, and after long digestion in memory they rebuild their cities, or embalm them, in the medium of style. The rhythm they take up is one not of nature but of culture, namely, the voracious dynamism of consumption that keeps the modern city ticking. Their urban novels are peopled by consumers of all kinds: the snobs and culture-vultures, sexual prowlers and mercenary lovers in Proust, and the drinkers and commercial travelers in Joyce, are part of a vast capitalist machine. Capitalism reaches its tentacles even into the intimacy of perception in Proust's dizzying analyses. For instance, in the slow Wagnerian introduction of three personages, Madame de Villeparisis, Saint-Loup, and Charlus (at Balbec, where they can be observed at leisure), each of them is, as it were, x-rayed in capitalist terms; their clothes, behavior, accent are appraised; their social value and its signs are registered, with comic errors, by the hotel staff, Françoise, and the Blochs. In both Proust and Joyce we are dealing with a remembered city, made malleable to poetic transfiguration. Like Musil's Vienna or Kafka's Prague, the vanished city, viewed across the gulf of the Great War, becomes a precious relic as it glows in its novelistic shrine. The transformation is tinged with a deathly hue, and the action of the novels proceeds as a memorial ritual. The author who writes *À la recherche du temps perdu* is no longer the living fleshly Marcel but his ghost. The Dublin of *Ulysses* is dead, and the book is its astral body.

Proust's consumption of the city is still an essentialist reduction, whereas Joyce shows that style does not constitute the essence of things but sets up a pluralism of perceptions that can never be recalled to a unitary vision. Just as Rilke explores the "pure relation," Proust embarks on a quasi-scientific quest for hidden liaisons between one thing and another, which enable the writer to translate the book of life into the book of art. In so doing, he transforms remembered time into the space of art, but not in the sense of the spatial flattening of time denounced by Bergson, for the space is structured by temporal relations, as in Rilke. In Joyce the relations that bind and order the experiences of city life are no longer pure laws but are dictated arbitrarily, like the rules of a game, rules that change from chapter to chapter of *Ulysses*. Density of significance is not brought out of the depths of the object through the magic of style but resides more in the free play of linguistic creation for its own sake. Joyce shows us Stephen in the act of willfully creating liaisons—notably in the library scene in *Ulysses*. The imposition of Homeric myth on a Dublin day is a formula for generating artificial relations rather than discovering natural ones. Joyce subverts essentialism by demonstrating that any harmonious and necessary connections between the realities of experience and the texture and structure of art are illusory. Thus the characters metamorphose before our eyes as the styles used to describe them whisk us through the whole history of English language and literature in the parodies of "Oxen of the Sun," while the frozen objective scientific language of "Ithaca" shows that the effort to get beyond the arbitrariness of style and subjective perspective results in the strangest distortions of all. The "odyssey of style" through the eighteen episodes of *Ulysses* reveals an endless variety of ways in which the data of experience can be portrayed and processed. The age of Cézanne has yielded to that of Picasso. Devotion to deepening one style has changed into virtuosity in mastering many, and in forswearing any individual style of one's own, as Joyce, more than any previous writer, succeeds in doing in the second half of *Ulysses*. This is not just the ventriloquism of the parodist but the revelation that the world is what style makes of it.

In Proust and Joyce, the web of motival connections is so thickly spun that the novel absorbs the readers' energies, or consumes them. Proust recruits our imaginations into the service of his labyrinthine rumination, and Joyce's ever-multiplying enigmas grip the resources of our minds. Readers of Proust are likely to find that their everyday life takes on a dreamlike hue as if it were an extension of his novel, and readers of Joyce will find that the conventional continuities of their everyday life have been sapped and that their perception has become more pluralistic and relativized. Thus these novels take revenge on centuries of casual novel readers by being texts of which one cannot blithely say, "Oh, I've read that." Instead, they are novels that read their readers by hijacking the reader's inner language, the constant murmur that precedes all our abstract thoughts or formed judgments, for both novelists supply a language for the most intimate movements of consciousness. The sentence "Longtemps je me suis couché de bonne heure" hypnotizes readers into making it their own, by its simplicity and familiarity, and also by the way it floats free of connection with any firm temporal or spatial coordinates; and that is only the beginning. Similar insinuating arts are deployed by Joyce, not only in the stream-of-consciousness sections but also in the way he makes the reader an ally in the linguistic creation of the novel. The change these writers effect in the relation of art to its consumers is probably only bringing out something that was implicit in the great art of the past. The communing of the reader in the work goes hand in hand with a priestly self-effacement of the author, as in a sacrificial ritual.

Dublin in 1904 offered Joyce an immense lump of material, an *objet trouvé* untouched by other artists. The barrage of techniques he brings into play are up to a point at the service of seeing this object and recreating it in the space of fiction, in which its inherent relations are clarified. Dublin is focused from the distance of exile, in the long perspective of memory. Perspective, triangulation, is also provided by the places and the traumatic historical caesura referred to in the last words of the text: "Trieste-Zürich-Paris, 1914–1921." But midway through the novel the rules of the game of mimesis have changed. The motif becomes subject to free variation, and its development is dependent less on considering the original, the historical Dublin, than on consulting the earlier pages of the novel, now become a self-consuming artifact, especially when earlier episodes are replayed, varied, and inverted in the phantasmagoria of "Circe." The imaginative digestion of the city is complete when it is offered to the world as a self-contained city of words, when the realistic mimesis of its first half is redigested in the verbal fantasia of its second. The city is first trans-figured by style and then, more radically, sacrificed to style, to a plu-ralistic display of styles.

Rather analogously to science, modernist art inspires a sense of wonder, yet in its foundation it seems to turn its back on God, of ne-cessity. The sense of wonder that art generates may put atheism to flight. Yet theism, with its confessional claims, finds little purchase in modernist art either. How does a sacral effect emerge in *Ulysses*? The "mythic method," as T. S. Eliot christened it, lends depth and mystery to the three protagonists and to the city and the mass of its denizens. It might lead the reader to exclaim, "Here too are gods!" (Heraclitus), but it is calculated to discourage the response "God is here!" (Jacob in Gen 28:16). It is the style, or styles, above all, that open up the streets of Dublin as a numinous landscape, and eventually a mind-scape, a constellation of mutually interacting motifs. The spectacle is enchanting, but it does not prompt paths of religious thought unless one brings a set of tactical (and tactful) theological questions to bear on it. Joyce and Proust are not floundering in an agnostic "cloud of unknowing" that demands a religious reading. Rather, their vision is assured and self-contained, even though its texture is one of endless exploration. Joyce plays with uncertainty, to be sure, but in order to open up room for experimental variation; reveling in the pluralism of experience and art, he does not bend his efforts to seek an ultimate unitary sense of things.

The more radically the arts and sciences develop, the less their "revelation" allows itself to be retrieved and categorized in the terms of traditional theology, including biblical theology. They present to theology above all a challenge, calling on theology to match them, if it can, in the rigor and depth of its explorations. Theology must undergo a radical self-sacrifice in order to find the place where it can speak to modern experience in depth. Yet it must retain the capacity, as it plunges into the supersubtle depths literature explores (for in-stance, in the ethical perspectivism of Henry James, with his endless shifting assessments), to make felt there the authority of conscience and of the Word of God, and to bring out those aspects of literature that can make it an ally in this task.

For deconstructionist critics, Joyce's texts, along with Mallarmé's, provide the clearest illustration of the indeterminacy and dissemination of meaning that prey on all writing and that are taken on board by a writing worthy of the name. But Joyce is not only a surfer of polylinguality and hypertext; he is also a classical artist bent on establishing order over against the forces of chaos. In *Finnegans Wake* he unleashes all the powers of Babel but also aims to dominate them, to recall them to the gathered force of a unified articulate word. The apparently infinite plasticity of sound and sense here is again governed by rules, notably the use of "nodal systems" that "may be built around or evolved from narrative sequences, descriptive tropes, clusters of words in an exotic language, song tags—indeed from anything remarkable enough to be isolated by the reader" (Hayman, 37). A series of narrative set pieces offers stable landmarks comparable to the "numbers" in traditional opera, and the surrounding leitmotival flux which threatens to engulf them is largely organized in groups or sequences that may be local (names of rivers in "Anna Livia Plurabelle" and of popes in "The Mookse and the Gripes"; motifs of space and time in "The Ondt and the Gracehoper") or spread across the entire text (HCE and ALP; Thomas Moore's song titles). Literary Wagnerism seemed to have reached saturation point in the recycling of all the leitmotifs of *Ulysses* in the "Circe" episode. Now Lord Rutherford's 1919 annihilation of the atom is matched by "the abnihilisation of the etym" of "the first lord of Hurtreford" (Joyce, 353), that is, Dublin, "town of the hurdled ford" in Gaelic. With the breakdown of individual words and the recourse to many different tongues Joyce can give his set of motival phrases an endless capacity for significant and ludic transformation, a development contemporary with the radicalization of motif and structure in the twelve-tone serialism of Schoenberg, Berg, and Webern. The more language is released into its freedom, the less it can communicate unambiguously. Its conventional textures threaten to become nightmarish, narcissistically self-absorbed. Language descends to the underworld, falling prey to dream-distortion, Freudian slips, and the peculiarities of "schizophrenic" speech. Mischievous deconstructive agencies cause would-be plain statements to tumble clownishly. But the ultimate thrust of the process is one of regeneration rather than entropy, insofar as the reader can always be surprised by the emergence of luminous form, though not as completely and satisfyingly as in Anna Akhmatova's experience with *Ulysses*: "At first I had the feeling of not understanding it, but then everything gradually oozed through, you know, like developing a photograph" (Cornwell, 60). Many readers of "The Dead" take its first half to be a freely moving account of the casual events at a social gathering. Closer inspection shows, however, that the story is tightly structured in a series of closed sections, each exhibiting a musical structure such as ternary form (A-B-A) and ending with a marked cadence that points ahead to the grand conclusion of the story and of *Dubliners* as a whole. While death pervades the entire story, the pervasive presence of musical form seems to resist dissolution, conferring a supplement of significance on the fleeting words and gestures of the characters. Yet even in these early texts the density of allusion and the clever planting of cryptic words and incidents ensure the impossibility of a definitive, exhaustive interpretation of the many-layered palimpsest.

The process of transformation at the heart of modernist creativity combines in a remarkable way the ultimate and the conventional. The freedom of style shows up the conventionality of all thoughts and of all objects, even as it labors to reveal the thusness, the *tathatā* of the experienced world. Style is emptied of extraneous content while the world is kenoticized into style, confirming the Buddhist sense that emptiness is the signature of reality.

BECKETT: THE SELF-DECONSTRUCTION OF MODERNISM

The questioning project of modernist literature is relayed from one author to another. A late modernist text such as Beckett's *Company* takes its full sense from the literary history behind it—not just that summoned up by its intertextual echoes of Dante, Shakespeare, Milton, and Wordsworth but that of the existential dramas staged in closed spaces by Mallarmé ("Igitur"), Kafka ("The Metamorphosis"), and Sartre (*Huis clos*). Beckett lies at the end of the line, closing off the entire event of literary modernism. It is this event as a whole that theology must respond to. It has produced a revolution in awareness and a framework for theological questioning that has not been surpassed or added to in subsequent literature and that can now be brought into view in a unitary fashion as historical distance lends a clearer perspective. Some modernist masterpieces, notably *Finnegans Wake*, have been judged to be fiascos or cul-de-sacs. Beckett could be seen as making the fiasco and the cul-de-sac the very principles of his art, boldly setting up his lodging in a dead end and practicing an art of failure, without the detour of Joyce's impossible ambitions.

At first sight *Company* may look like a mere piece of ingenuity, but the ciphers it deploys carry the existential weight of the entire modernist tradition, including a tacit theological dimension. A man lies on his back in the dark: among the ideas this image conjures up is the idea that "God" may lie hidden somewhere in the depth of this dark. "The proposition" (8) that is the germ of the entire textual performance—"A voice comes to one in the dark" (7)—is elaborated in a shuttling between prosaic directives and intimations of sublimity. The "voice" itself is another theologically charged image, recalling the voice of God speaking to Moses from the burning bush (Ex 3:4) or from the dark cloud (Ex 19:9). The situation could also be taken as a parody of the way prophets are addressed: "The word of the Lord came unto me, saying, Jeremiah, what seest thou?" (Jer 1:11).

The problematic that the text explicitly stages is that of the act of writing or "imagining" itself. This act is the core of Beckett's personal religion, and his interrogation of the riddles of writing and selfhood continues the broodings of Mallarmé, Proust, Kafka, and Woolf, and the general self-conscious thematization and problematization of writing in modernist authors. The penumbra of theological implications spreads out around this but is not allowed to develop an autonomous substantiality independent of the explicit puzzles of the imagined situation; this keeps direct theological utterance at a distance and installs us in a regime of the oblique, the opaque, and the ironic.

The writing stages a breakdown of the naming function of language in face of that which constantly withdraws before its advance. The comic spectacle of a man fumbling with words, baffled by the endless difficulty of getting said even the simplest thing, serves as a cipher of irresoluble metaphysical dilemmas. The text never gets written because human beings never manage to be. Through glancing allusions, Beckett puts in play the other "darks" and the other "voices" of the tradition, from Milton, Dante, Kant, all summoned to join him in the realization of the impossibility of their poetic or philosophical projects.

I find it helpful to distinguish five phases in *Company*, the five acts of the drama, each containing three of the biographical "flashbacks," spoken in the second person by the "voice" to the hearer. In the first phase the hearer attempts to verify what the voice says to him. The implication of the doubt spreads beyond its immediate context, suggesting an allegory of Western man, at the end point of an exhausted tradition, listening to the religious voices of the past and assessing them skeptically. We soon encounter a third instance besides the hearer and the voice: "in another dark or in the same another devising it all for company. Quick leave him" (8). Speculation about the deviser, "that cankerous other" (9), will increasingly pervade the text, echoing the conundrums of philosophical theology. Of course, the deviser is a projection of the author, the merely human inventor of the text. Yet his appearance within the text is analogous to the presence of God within his creation, and from the first his presence is enshrouded in mystery, as an unthinkable ultimate.

The flashbacks punctuate the text like windows opening on a dark room. But these epiphanic scenes are themselves pervaded by the doubt and questioning that has become the element in which the hearer lives. The "small boy" of the first one is already an anxious questioner: "Looking up at the blue sky and then at your mother's face you break the silence asking her if it is not in reality much more distant than it appears. The sky that is. The blue sky" (12–13). The boy's *hantise de l'azur* is an inchoate reflection on the distance of God. Human faces are an elusive emblem of this distance.

The text steps onto a treacherous path of self-emendation when it undertakes to correct the hearer's faulty reasonings: "So with what reason remains he reasons and reasons ill. . . . Were it not of him to whom it is speaking speaking but of another it would not speak in the second person but in the third" (14–15). The diction parodies that of logicians, grammarians, lawyers, or theologians and shows the deviser firmly, cockily in control of his creature, the hearer. But this assurance masks a deeper insecurity, concerning the status of the deviser himself. Pedantic expertise masks radical disorientation, and the mask keeps slipping.

In the second phase (paragraphs 11–25) a new restlessness arises as alterations are contemplated to the scenario as thus far imagined. The first such suggestion is that the hearer might respond to the voice: "What an addition to company that would be! A voice in the first person singular" (20–21). But this improvement will never be enacted. For the hearer to say "I" would be a lie. The self relates to its past personae as comforting memory-fragments, relics for elegiac musing, but does not assume them in a project of self-creation. Intervening on these cogitations, the sixth flashback, a childhood suicide attempt, speaks of the trauma underlying the inventions and revisions of the deviser.

In the next phase (paragraphs 26–33) the question of the deviser's identity is confronted: "The longer the eye dwells the obscurer it grows. Till the eye closes and freed from pore the mind inquires, What does this mean? What finally does this mean that at first sight seemed clear? Till it the mind too closes as it were. As the window might close of a dark empty room" (29–30). Here is a parody of a Platonic ascent from sense knowledge to mental insight to a dimension beyond mind. But the bliss of mystical unknowing is not granted. The deviser indeed devises himself, but that is more a mark of his arbitrary, shoddy half-existence than of any rational impregnability of a divine *causa sui*.

The deviser, up to now an authoritative narrator, becomes himself the principal character, subject to alteration and duplication in a potentially uncontrollable process. The fourth phase (paragraphs 34–48) brings a radical crisis of imagining: "Impending for some time the following. Need for company not continuous. Moments when his own unrelieved a relief. Intrusion of voice at such. Similarly image of hearer. Similarly his own. Regret then at having brought them about and problem how dispel them" (41–42). A new pitch of crisis is marked by the ensuing general collapse: "Wearied by such stretch of imagination he ceases and all ceases" (59). The literary imagination has been the last resource of modern humanity for imposing order and meaning on a world which has lost its religious, philosophical, and ideological frameworks and finds itself increasingly consumed by a technological order which itself is becoming splintered and rudderless. What if this resource fails? What if the entire modernist project is crumbling here? Panic grows as the repressed division of the deviser resurfaces: "Yet another then. Of whom nothing. Devising figments to temper his nothingness. Quick leave him. Pause and again in panic to himself, Quick leave him" (64). He turns away from the devising deviser to imagine improvements of the devised deviser.

In the last phase, the deviser, now visualized as crawling about in the dark, is unable to imagine the end of his fiction, which emblematizes the unfigurability of death. He returns to the hearer, whose various senses are considered, with theological overtones: "Some sixth sense? Inexplicable premonition of impending ill? Yes or no? No. Pure reason? Beyond experience. God is love? Yes or no? No" (73). The review of various modes of privileged cognition imagined by philosophers and theologians reduces them to suspect shortcuts. The "crawling creator crawling in the same create dark as his creature" (73) suggests a parody of God's creation of Adam. The deviser's last appearance shows him stuck in his quandary: "What visions in the dark of light! Who exclaims thus? Who asks who exclaims, What visions in the shadeless dark of light and shade! Yet another still?" (84). At first the empirical hearer was clearly distinguished from the transcendental deviser; then the deviser, ceasing to be a lofty third-person voice, became an objectified presentation of the self, increasingly physical, to the point of crawling and smelling, and the narrative presenter of this crawling deviser assumed the transcendental role; now it appears that this presenter is himself materializing as yet another empirical ego. The last flashback brings the wanderer to his final halt: "And how better in the end labour lost and silence. And you as you always were. / Alone" (88–89). Abolishing the infinite chain of devisers by accepting the identity of hearer, deviser, and voice as aspects of the fabling self, the text has whittled away some possibilities of creation which can no longer be used; at each stage in his trajectory Beckett drops some of the trappings and techniques of fiction, to start yet again with a narrower range of more elementary imaginary givens in the succeeding. Each text is an action of kenosis, of descent into vacuity, and the reader is drawn into the process, shares in the spiritual exercise.

What is the nature of the silence and darkness into which the text finally leads us? It is nothingness given a precise contour, opened up through the artful deployment of minimal form. The Beckettian self is constantly crumbling into the dust of death, yet even in the process of its dissolution the silence that deepens about it is a space of communion. The riddles of Beckett's text concern explicitly the nature of self-identity, but by parodic implication the question of God is also rehearsed. The deviser pursues elaborate logic-chopping in the manner of a philosopher, one who, instead of checking and verifying the contents of his consciousness and cautiously building up a series of deductions in the manner of Descartes, instead cautiously creates a fictional figuration of the self. The Beckettian self is the last variant of the Western individual. His quest meets defeat at every point at which Kant's seemed to succeed. The transcendental self now lacks all synthesizing power, and the fictive world it begins by positing with a show of authority collapses in aimless rearrangements, which indicate a lack of secure identity on the part of the ultimate deviser. Instead of a sovereign consciousness, we have a scriptor toiling at the impossible task of assembling a text, fiddling with opaque words which cannot attain the clarity of the concept but remain clogged in their materiality.

Adorno wished to dedicate his posthumous *Aesthetic Theory* to Beckett. Both of them can be seen as marking the end of the modernist adventure, which had run its course. But the owl of Minerva comes out at twilight. A thorough philosophical and theological reflection on the implications of modernism has now become possible. To be sure, we can no longer take the great modernists, any more than the great romantics, at face value. Beckett shows modernism deconstructing itself even before various forms of postmodernism started to dismantle the modernist tradition in parody, in social, political, and ideological critique, and in relativization and pluralization of its founding myths. This leaves theology all the more free to learn from the critical ferment and the transformative possibilities that the modernist experiments unleashed. If theology steeps Christian language and images in these turbulent waters, a long-overdue renewal may result. In any case, we can sound the hollowness of our language, measure its obsoleteness, by pitting it against the radical novelty of modernist diction. Practicing a constant awareness of the call to self-critique and self-transformation that modernist art poses to theology thus becomes one of the key disciplines for a reshaping of theological judgment today.

In terms of the dialectic of ultimate and conventional, literary modernism might seem to recognize only a single ultimate, namely literature itself, consigning everything else—religion, philosophy, ideology, and even rational argument and communicative speech—to the realm of crumbling conventions. One might even see this ultraliterariness as the cult of a false god who traps its adherents in a narrow tunnel with no exit. One might long instead for a bigger literature capable of embracing the world with Shakespearian generosity. Nonetheless, it is the merit of modernism to have created an acute sense of both ultimacy and conventionality, challenging all religious rhetoricians to examine their speech more scrupulously, never allowing conventions to claim more than their due, and letting ultimate realities emerge on their own terms, disposing language in such a way that they are not cheapened, manipulated, or replaced with simulacra. An impossible prescription perhaps, but one that gains persuasiveness from the sublime moments attained in modernist art.

Chapter Four

METAPHYSICS AND
ITS OVERCOMING

The path to God as origin and final goal of the world and humanity is no longer as short and easy as it once seemed. To invoke God in connection with the beginning of the universe, or of the individual soul, or as Providence at work in evolution or history or individual destinies, or as assuring the future of the cosmos or humanity, has become a difficult act of faith, obscure in its bearings. If one turns to sacred texts, the same withdrawal of the divine is found, for they speak the language of their times, indicating the divine to us now only obliquely, and we can use them only by subjecting them to radical reinterpretation. Jews and Muslims experience the same wound, which draws us close to them in a new way.

People continue to believe, pray, feel the divine presence, engage in work for justice and peace, but these activities have taken on a new inflection. The language of theology reflects this change when it uses expressions like "God" with implicit quotation marks, revealing their status as historical constructions with a functional purpose. Religious words, ideas, and acts have become palpably fragile tools for keeping a link to a dimension that they no longer map and regulate. Faith is intimately corroded by a nominalism that can go hand in hand with the tokenism of so much religious culture. In times of dire need or dread, prayer of petition or compunction comes near to direct expression of the real. But in general a secure and direct dwelling in the language and gestures of faith, such as might have been normal within the unbroken church culture of the recent past, has become rare. Religious gestures have become oblique and opaque, tangential to ordinary reality. Even when we suspend the unease that this obliqueness causes, by stepping back into the immediacies of a past piety, in beloved hymns or archaic liturgies, that very step is affected with a troubling tangentiality. A quiet and cumulatively reflective culture, one that is patient with opacities and voids, is what may best palliate and overcome this unsettling situation.

An implicit negative theology undercuts any too solid and affirmative reliance on the inherited coordinates. Unlike classical apophasis, this is not supported by ontological and hierarchical schemes that could give it a firm sense of direction. It cannot take up old conceptions of divine withdrawal, from Neoplatonic, Jewish, Christian, and Islamic mysticism, or from Vedānta or Buddhism, for these schemas themselves withdraw into the mist. Philosophers of religion who try to fit the modern experience of God's withdrawal into inherited schemas that see God as hidden in inaccessible majesty at the summit of an ontological ladder, or within a cloud of unknowing, miss the weight and density of secular experience for which the divine, rather than hiding itself, seems unable to impose itself.

Joseph Moingt speaks of "mourning for God," convinced that "contemporary Western culture, which has long lost all trace of God, will not find the track anew by practicing some 'metaphysical meditation,' but by following the steps of the man from Nazareth" (2002:12). This stance may miss insights into the divine in contemporary spiritual culture, which could make of it a *praeparatio evangelica* and a catalyst for a new interpretation of the biblical language. If "the most common reason of our time holds God to be unthinkable and faith unintelligible" (22), on the margins of that reason there extends a sensibility that furnishes the conditions for a new hearing of the language of faith. To treat the gods of the philosophers as mere idols is contrary to the generous recognition, extending from Acts 17 to Vatican I's *Dei*

Filius, of a knowledge of God sown in all hearts. "Modernity has lost a false God; let us return to the Gospel to find the true one"—this sharp antithesis must yield to a dialogue that gleans the religious insight harbored within modernity. The study of post-Cartesian philosophy need not be only "the reflective taking stock of unbelief." If modern reason contests biblical personalism, perhaps it is in order to liberate the true sense of this personal language, as pointing to a reality known in encounter, as in the case of Abraham or Moses. From another angle, Spinoza's joyful sense of God as the creative force of nature itself is more than a flabby pantheism; it points to the need to think largely of God, to make God coterminous with supreme reality rather than confining God to a province of the mind or the imagination. Scholasticism developed the personal language of scripture within metaphysics, in talk of the decrees of the divine will. This challenged philosophy to impose a strict rational control on such language, as when Leibniz subordinates divine actions to the principle of sufficient reason and the compossibles, or when Spinoza reduces them to the impersonal operation of *natura naturans*. The value of such metaphysical chastenings of language about God should not be underestimated, even if, paradoxically, their result is to prompt the step back from metaphysics to a more attentive espousal of the texture of biblical insight and religious experience.

THEOLOGY AND PHILOSOPHY

To orient oneself in the modern space of the withdrawal of the divine, it is necessary to traverse the controversy about the status of metaphysical tradition and its usefulness for thinking about God. Where Heidegger seeks a step back from metaphysics to the phenomena with which it has lost touch, Marion, in a manner reminiscent of Neoplatonism and dialectical theology, practices what Kant would call an *Übertritt*, a step over rather than a step back, transgression rather than retrogression, an "exodus" from metaphysics to an ineffable God of whom we can say neither that he is nor that he is not, nor both, nor neither, a God revealed as what is "impossible" for us (2012:254–61).

The danger of this is that it abandons any rational criteriology of the divine. To rely on phenomenology alone seems a feeble defense against the religious fanaticism that has wrought so much havoc in our time. The role of metaphysics in regard to God cannot be merely that of revealing its own limits and pointing beyond itself. It also serves to discipline and purify untutored ideas about divinity, subordinating them to rational control before pointing beyond what reason can master. Such rational control is not a derogation of God's majesty, since its object is not God himself but human conceptions of God. God falls under the concept of being in Scotus; but this is a semantic observation, not an idolatry of being, a promotion of being over God (see Cross, 69).

In the case of revealed theology, which is a science based on historical experience and reflective judgment rather than on the systematic conceptual mastery after which metaphysics strives, the corrective and disciplining roles that metaphysical conceptuality and argument may play have only an auxiliary status and cannot take the upper hand. Neither the exodic transmetaphysics of a God beyond being nor the phenomenology of a premetaphysical Sacred can be given the status of controlling horizons for revealed theology. They, too, have an auxiliary status at best. One of the tasks of fundamental theology is to determine the due place of philosophical reflection within theology. But this requires that it look over the border to see what is happening within philosophy itself. Can it count on the solid existence of a metaphysical natural theology, perhaps one that has taken a transcendental turn, as in Lonergan and Rahner? Or has this discipline been abandoned except in narrow rationalistic circles of analytic philosophers? Meanwhile the phenomenological discourse on God, developed so diversely by Levinas, Michel Henry, Derrida, Marion, Kearney, Caputo, confronts fundamental theology with a host of tantalizing methodological issues. Should it generously embrace this theological turn in French phenomenology, in light of its manifest apologetical value in putting faith and God back on the intellectual map?

Much of what the religious-minded phenomenologists write is a straightforward contribution to fundamental theology, or even to Christology or sacramental theology. Much else is straightforward philosophy, though inspired by theological themes. Much else again is a religious thinking blending theological wisdom and philosophical speculation, a rather tricky genre, since it risks substituting scriptural citation for well-grounded philosophical analysis on the one hand (as in Michel Henry's use of the Fourth Gospel) and precipitously imposing philosophical patterns on biblical realities on the other. An amphibian movement between theology and philosophy is perfectly legitimate, but one would scarcely expect it to contribute to a methodological renewal of either discipline. Yet the later Schelling and Kierkegaard drew on divine revelation to shake philosophy out of its rationalistic slumbers, as did Pascal before them, so that phenomenological and existentialist philosophers must confess a debt to this theological incursion, however illegitimate they may deem it and however diligently they seek to cover its traces by converting the theological terms into purely philosophical ones, as in Heidegger's *Being and Time.* Philosophy must labor to establish its insights on a strictly philosophical basis, just as theology must seek to give full theological body to whatever striking religious ideas it finds expressed by the philosophers. Indeed, theology must "heal" Pascal, Schelling, and Kierkegaard by regrounding their insights in a broader scriptural vision and integrating them into a fuller and more systematic theological reflection. Philosophy must "heal" them too by reappropriating the elements in their thought that belong to philosophy and can be further developed in strictly philosophical terms. In this way the principled autonomy and distinction of the two disciplines can be reestablished despite the tangled history of their interactions.

Emmanuel Falque appears to oppose such differentiation in his argument that the critical role of philosophy over against theology should be complemented by a *choc en retour* of theology on philosophy, since "the more one theologizes, the better one philosophizes" (2013, back cover). He believes that philosophy can only benefit from receptiveness to the impact of theology, but history shows that philosophy has benefited most from this impact when it has remained on its guard against illegitimate incursions alien to the philosophical task; for this reason Plotinus is more philosophically exemplary than Iamblichus within Platonism, Aquinas than Bonaventure within scholasticism. To be sure, the identity of philosophy alters when it engages with other disciplines, and following Derrida's logic of the treacherous supplement, what begins as a supplementary engagement ends up altering the essence of philosophy itself. Indeed, philosophy never had a pure essence to begin with, being embedded in social, religious, and literary contexts that compromise any ideal autonomy it may propose to itself. Nonetheless, even when it allows itself to be invaded by theological, sociological, and literary wisdom, philosophy aims to transmute it all into something genuinely philosophical, no matter how the definition of philosophy may change in this process. The autonomy of exegesis and the autonomy of philosophy are both, for theologians, checks on theological judgment, barring the way to convenient simplifications. Most philosophers, meanwhile, respect the differentiation of the specific concerns of philosophy and theology, and few would wish to return to Hegel's philosophical absorption of theology or Schelling's theologization of philosophy. It is true that analytical philosophers of religion have busied themselves with the logic of the Trinity, the Incarnation, and the relation of divine foreknowledge and human freedom, generally with so poor a grasp of the texture of biblical thought that their work has remained without influence on theology proper. Unwittingly, they attest to the phenomenological and hermeneutical resistance of scripture to metaphysical rationalization.

The editors of the series "Interventions" cite Maurice Blondel's denial that a "separated philosophy" that does not reach "the one thing needful" deserves to be called philosophy at all, and William Desmond's suggestion that "modernity is more an interim than a completion—an interim between a premodernity in which the porosity between philosophy and theology was granted, perhaps taken for granted, and a postmodernity where their porosity must be unclogged and enacted anew" (Kilby, ii–iii). But if such porosity undercuts the autonomy of both disciplines their critical impact on one another is enfeebled. Blondel himself insists on the necessity "to discern what is of faith or consequent to faith, from what is of reason or antecedent to and consonant with faith starting from reason. . . . What is of human knowledge must not be confused with what is of divine inspiration. More than ever this work of dissociation is urgent" (Blondel, 156). Blondel "renounces making his own convictions enter the texture of his philosophical discourse" and indeed submits them to critique "so that they are no longer prejudices" (Virgoulay, 29), resisting maximally his own religious postulates. His Catholic vision can "elicit a philosophy that is appropriate to it" (quoted in Virgoulay, 51), but this philosophy is worked out in strictly philosophical terms and "cannot fulfill its precursor role except by being impartial and free" (54). Even so, Jacques Maritain objected that Blondel was led astray by his wish "to integrate into the dynamism of the natural effort of the intelligence towards being . . . a wisdom that is in reality the wisdom of the Holy Spirit" (quoted in Virgoulay, 60). Blondel's later philosophy attempts to "give more consistency to the natural order" (184), in opposition to some of his own disciples. He excluded all explicit references to Christianity from his massive trilogy on action, thought, and being. Yves de Montcheuil and Henri Bouillard thought that for Blondel no philosophical value or truth could stand without the affirmation of the supernatural, but this was refuted by Henry Duméry, who claimed to speak on behalf of Blondel himself. For Blondel, philosophy may handle the rational content of theology but cannot enter on the "reserved domain" of theology itself, including fundamental theology and apologetics, for it does not work by the light of faith in a revelation; conversely, fundamental theology can draw on philosophy but "does not deserve its name unless it rehandles all its materials in the light of faith" (Duméry, 504). "The disciplines are less and less separated. All the more reason to distinguish the research procedures, to define the rules, the mental outlook, and the scope of each method" (594).

Blondel's attitude is close to that of Marion, who when writing as a philosopher construes the phenomena of a divine call and of revelation in general outline, leaving it to theology to fill them with concrete biblical content, which he proceeds to do in other, explicitly theological works. This confirms rather than subverts classical borders between the two disciplines, though the philosopher's choice of topics is influenced, for better or worse, by his religious interests, and though his thought may segue from philosophy proper into philosophical commentary on scriptural or patristic texts that is indistinguishable from theology. Marion is right not to throw caution to the winds, for if theologians use philosophy, they want it to be real philosophy, established by its own autonomous reasoning, just as when physicists use mathematics they want it to be real mathematics, not a mathematics tailored in light of physics. For John Milbank (47), Marion remains captive of a self-sufficient metaphysics, the foundation and hallmark of secular modernity, failing to resist secularism by a theological interpretation of being itself (since only theology has an integral understanding of being). For Milbank, theology "must entirely evacuate philosophy"; "An independent phenomenology must be given up, along with the claim, which would have seemed so bizarre to the Fathers, to be doing philosophy *as well as* theology. . . . Philosophy in fact *began* as a secularizing immanentism" (quoted in Hankey 2005:20). But to strip metaphysics of the independence, substantiality, and necessity that it retains within Aquinas's vast theological project is to effect a depletion of ontology that theological rhetoric cannot amend (see Hankey 1999b:389).

A theologian, looking at philosophy from the vantage point of revelation, may well see it as expressing a human striving toward the supernatural, an anonymous response to the "supernatural existential." But from within philosophy itself such thoughts should be rigorously excluded. Heidegger was very conscious of this, and brings out the inherent tension between philosophy and theology, a tension that the theologian likewise should refuse to erase, for it is a tension that challenges and nourishes the practice of theological judgment. The theologian should not lay down the law for philosophy. To be sure the "separationism" between theology and philosophy "favoured until recently, especially by clerics and those trained in church institutions" (Marenbon, 59), can become a stilted and sterile arrangement. But the promiscuous conflation of the two by no means ensures mutual fertilization; rather, it shrinks the intellectual space in which both disciplines are entirely free to pursue their own questions and refine their own methods, thus becoming thoroughly equipped, on occasion, to undertake a robust confrontation with one another in their challenging difference. Aquinas allowed metaphysics to have its own autonomous procedures within his capacious work as a theologian, though integrating them into the larger fresco of *sacra doctrina*. Today we may expect such collaboration between philosophy and theology, if each is doing its job right, to exhibit a much greater degree of mutual independence, so that theology is no longer able to tell us authoritatively what the ultimate upshot of philosophy is and therefore cherishes philosophy (or philosophies) all the more as a stimulating partner in dialogue.

When the status of theology in the academic world is diminished, its place tends to be taken by other disciplines, such as the philosophy of religion, often producing a hybrid discourse of uncertain methodological status. Clarification of the disciplinary status of theology, in fundamental theology, is enhanced by considering the relations of fundamental theology to that neighboring discipline. But *philosophy of religion* can mean different things: (1) it can be a philosophy that examines religious phenomena and discourses as from the outside, bringing the distances of a specifically philosophical mode of interrogation to bear on them (Kant and Bergson are among the few philosophers who cultivate this attitude in an exemplary way); (2) it can be a form of natural theology, a rational discourse on God or the divine that can be developed within philosophy, using purely philosophical resources, whether in a metaphysical style or in the more risky phenomenological style attempted by Gabriel Marcel and Heidegger; or (3) it can be a religious philosophy, inspired by a confessional tradition but elaborating its insights in a philosophical style, moving outside specifically theological discussion in the direction of a wider, nonconfessional wisdom (Schleiermacher in his *Speeches on Religion*, or Kierkegaard, Rosenzweig or Buber, H. Tanabe or K. Nishitani). Both (1) and (2) can be practiced by atheists as competently as by believers. Sometimes (1) may have the ambition to replace theology as the more rational explication of confessional religious material, as in Hegel, and theology (or a religious philosopher such as Kierkegaard) has to argue back, stressing the irreducibility of the religious realities to philosophical categories.

Is philosophy of religion what Fredric Jameson calls a "dead knowledge," as appears to be the case with the disciplines born contemporaneously with it at the close of the eighteenth century—

philosophy of history, philosophy of art, and philosophy of nature—
or has it a vital critical function such as can still be claimed by political
philosophy and the philosophy of science? Is it doomed to remain
what Duméry called "an immense lumber-room" which, "as long as it
is not in possession of its methods and laws, . . . will remain a disappointing, impure, and useless genre" (quoted in Greisch 2002:449)?

Jean Greisch argues that a philosophical reflection on the nature
and status of religion has an essential role in a triangular cooperation
with fundamental theology and the history of religions. Without it,
theology hardens into dogmatism, and the history of religions loses itself in positivism or is absorbed by sociology or psychology. A free
play of the philosophical mind over the phenomena of religion lends
space and sanity to the other two disciplines. Both theologians and
historians of religion generally ignore philosophy of religion, confident that they can supply from their own resources whatever reflection their disciplines demand as the need arises. It seems the destiny of
philosophy to be shunted aside as superfluous. Meanwhile religion can
fiercely resist becoming an object of philosophy. The condemnation of
Duméry by the Holy Office in 1957 reveals that philosophy of religion, in its claim to mediate between dogmatic faith and the scientific
study of religion, can arouse church fear as giving too much autonomy
to rational judgment. One even wonders if a cooperation between
confessional fundamental theology and nonconfessional philosophy
of religion is at all possible. They are perhaps rival perspectives that
cannot be maintained simultaneously. Philosophy of religion walks a
tightrope, for when one invests faith in a given tradition one leaves the
philosophical attitude behind, whereas if one maintains a phenomenological bracketing suspending any commitment of belief, one falls into
the positivism of a science of religions that is jealous of its autonomy
and sees theology, even in the capacious guise of a quest of the sacred
in the manner of Rudolf Otto or Mircea Eliade, as the enemy.

If Schleiermacher tended to view religions as Platonic essences,
underestimating the shadow side of their historical positivity, it was
because of his confidence that one can overcome the externals of a de-
graded religious tradition by remounting to its original wellsprings
(Greisch 2002:107). Many philosophers of religion quietly assume that

they are more capable than theologians of healing distorted traditions. Yet in his theological work Schleiermacher seeks the wellsprings within Christian tradition and subordinates the resources of philosophy of religion to providing the broad foundation of confessional faith in "the feeling of absolute dependence" (not the potentially Spinozan "intuition of the universe" in the first edition of the *Speeches*). Paul Tillich saw philosophy of religion as an exercise of autonomous reason that recognizes religion to be founded on the theonomous concept of the unconditioned. Barth dismissed this as creating "a peaceful heaven, infinitely tedious, truly worthy of Schleiermacher," and "playing hide-and-seek with the frozen monster of the unconditioned instead of speaking frankly of the good Lord" (quoted in Greisch 2002:420). Tillich fought back: "Theological method rests on a normative concept of religion, drawn from a particular religious experience. In seeking to pass off this normative concept as the essence of religion, the theologian commits an unjustified categorical transgression" (quoted in Greisch 2002:424). In the end, though, this philosophy tends to become a theology of the unconditioned, or of ultimate concern, in rivalry to positive, biblical theology.

The uneasy relationship with philosophy of religion should not be smoothed out; rather, its tensions should be acerbated in more self-conscious methodological reflection so as to provide a testing field for theological judgment. The development of method in theology should aim, not at tidy systematization, but at the fullest awareness in the exercise of flexible and subtle judgment. Theological lucidity demands that one differentiate the respective roles of various disciplines, but this does not mean compartmentalizing the disciplines so that they no longer pose a challenge to one another or give rise to friction. All such disciplinary arrangements, however hallowed or institutionally established, are contingent on a particular conjuncture and can be overturned by a change in the landscape of belief. Dogmatic theology has become much more rooted in historical awareness in the last two centuries, giving a different meaning to the project of "faith seeking understanding" (see Bouillard 1966). As for "natural theology," its relation to dogmatics has altered as the possible philosophical points of departure have multiplied. Since Blondel, a concrete logic of human existence has seemed the best propaedeutic to revealed theology and indeed accompanies this theology throughout its development. Natural theology thus yields to a religious philosophy conceived as existential quest, which in turn is hardly practicable today without consulting the diverse religious possibilities explored in human history. Philosophy of religion, or religions, roots the religious quest in concrete history, and it is in that horizon that the Christian event comes into view; this reinforces the historical texture of its self-understanding.

Fundamental theology takes notice of such questions as belonging to a level of inquiry anterior to its own project. Securely based on the standpoint of Christian faith, in its apologetic dimension it is not concerned with purely philosophical arguments about God's existence or the problem of evil. But today it cannot presuppose the positive result of those arguments as a given. The philosophical prolegomena bequeath a space of questioning and meditation rather than confirmed findings and offer theology a model for its own reflections. Mapping the fundamental orientations of faith and defending the credibility of its object, fundamental theology tries to maintain an openness and flexibility matching those practiced by philosophy of religion or religious philosophy. But is there a real distinction between fundamental theology and religious philosophy as pursued by such thinkers as Franz Rosenzweig, Gabriel Marcel, or Paul Ricoeur? Fundamental theology offers a prospective first approach to the great theological themes, envisaged from the perspective of their credibility and the manner in which they are revealed. Its aim is to lay the foundation for the exposition of Christian doctrines in their full form. In contrast, philosophers of religion approach faith either as the point of arrival of a philosophical reflection, or as a given to be surpassed and absorbed in a more integral understanding, or as a traveling companion on the path of philosophical questioning. The frontiers between the two kinds of enterprise are sometimes blurry, but the basic distinction between theological and philosophical judgment is that the former is founded on and gives primacy to the affirmations of faith.

But surely this entire attempt to define frontiers and relations between disciplines is in contradiction with a sense of the contingency of their construction and the conventionality of their texture, and with the ideal of flexible and open-ended reflection? Not so, for a wise management of conventional truth treasures all the valid distinctions that emerge within it, even though conscious that the entire arrangement of different perspectives and approaches at any given time has arisen contingently and is capable of modification as the play of judgment develops. Appeals to ultimate truth cannot override the procedures that have established themselves as fruitful and illuminating in their slow development over centuries of discussion. Indeed, it is the mutual independence of theology and philosophy that most reminds each of their limited and conventional status. Whenever one totally absorbs the other the result is an integralist or totalitarian ideology that is inimical to questioning thought. Both disciplines are tempted to claim an absolute knowledge of absolute reality, and their troubled coexistence thwarts this hubristic ambition.

THE ONTOTHEOLOGY DEBATE

Heidegger recognizes the power and truth of metaphysics and strives with it in order to find the way back to a premetaphysical thinking that metaphysics occludes. Frédéric Nef has written an eloquent polemic against the detractors of metaphysics, but much of his polemic fails to touch the project of overcoming thus conceived. Since he does not recognize the validity of any kind of thinking other than argumentative reason, he can only see Heidegger—and no doubt all other phenomenologists as well—as lapsing into irrationalism; even Hegel, accused of abolishing the law of noncontradiction, is seen as decadent. Nef's blind spots are clear in the way he quotes as manifest proof of irrationalism Heidegger's remark about reason being the most stiff-necked opponent of thought (204). The coherence of phenomenological reflection cannot be measured by the criteria of a logic that prescribes in advance the legitimate use of words.

The end of ontotheology, as Heidegger would see it, does not mean that classical metaphysical reason is false but that the ontotheological regime of truth is no longer suited to what is to be thought today—be it "the truth of being" or the reality of the divine or the encounter with God in Jesus Christ. Heidegger does not make any metaphysical criticism of ontotheology; he does not claim, for example, that it makes God dependent on being as the ground of God, as Cross (73) imagines, or that it undercuts the immanence of being by positing a transcendent superbeing (Falque, 168). Rather, his point is that metaphysical logic and conceptualization cannot attend to the phenomenological texture of being (and also of the divine). On the level of ontology being is already slighted by being treated logically, and on the level of theology the being of God is similarly curtailed. The notions of "being as such" and "the supreme being," developed in so many styles since Aristotle, may continue to stimulate philosophical thought, but their inadequacy to the phenomenality of being, and *a fortiori* of the divine, marks a limit to the reach of that tradition and invites us to think against it, to open a greater space of the thinkable. If ontotheology is the constitutive structure of metaphysics since Aristotle, it represents reason in all its force and truth—the very things that make it, according to Heidegger, so powerful an enemy of the other truth that concerns the thinking of phenomenality. The use of reason is not always innocent, for it can blind and enslave those who trust too exclusively in it. The most truly rational reason is the one that recognizes its limits, either by facing its internal aporias, as in Kant, or by taking account of external realities that elude its mastery. Like philosophy in the wake of Heidegger, theology assumes the responsibility of judging reason itself, for the kerygma it defends is precisely one of the realities that confront reason from outside and that elude its grasp. The question of the "unthought" posed by Heidegger obliges us to reread the most rational texts of classical theology to uncover a dynamic of thought that surpasses conceptual formations or is hindered by them.

The usefulness of Heidegger for revisiting classical theology is undercut by those who claim that his critique of ontotheology applies only to modern philosophy since Descartes (or perhaps Duns Scotus) and that figures such as Augustine and Aquinas, far from exhibiting the ontotheological constitution of metaphysics, have no interest in metaphysics or ontology at all, but rather map an apophatic relationship to the ineffable God who is beyond being. Theology would thus have no call to critique the metaphysical investments of these theologians but should rather show how their vision surpasses the horizons of modern and postmodern questions, bringing a response that exceeds their expectations. This line of argument, advanced by Marion and his colleagues and taken up by Radical Orthodoxy, fails to recognize the immense weight of the metaphysical tradition for the fathers and for Heidegger.

The precise topic of ontotheology does not play a controlling role in Heidegger's critical hermeneutic of the metaphysical tradition. He illustrates the notion of ontotheology by Aristotle in 1936 (*GA* 42:87–89), and even as early as 1926 (*GA* 14:50, 286–87; see Courtine 2003:195), and it resurfaces again in connection with Hegel in 1957, in what may be called "a piece of loose armchair reasoning to show why metaphysics must be onto-theological" (Marenbon, 58). It should be noted that Heidegger is far from reducing Aristotle, or even Hegel, to ontotheology. He finds within Aristotle's text both the metaphysical conceptualization of being and a phenomenological apprehension of being that resists this conceptualization; in his commentary on *Physics* 2 (*GA* 9) he brings out the concreteness of Aristotle's apprehension of the phenomena whence his thought proceeds, working against scholastic traditions that reduce these phenomena—for example, form and matter, potency and act—to pawns in a play of abstract concepts. Indeed, for Heidegger, the history of metaphysics is not merely the monochrome advance of ontotheology; at each of its turning points it enacts a new encounter with the phenomenality of being.

The God of ontotheology does not come into philosophy from outside; but if the biblical God enters philosophy, becoming identified with the God of ontotheology, this hybrid formation should be contested in the name of both theology and philosophy. A metaphysics affirming God as *ipsum esse*, on the basis of our knowledge of creatures, no doubt allows an openness to being that one does not find in a conceptualist system culminating in the idea of God as a self-grounding or self-validating concept. Nonetheless, insofar as Aquinas seeks to *explain* created being by reference to a supreme being he moves within the regime of metaphysical reason that falls short of the phenomenality of both God and creation.

"The history of philosophy tells us nothing about the truth-value of past doctrines" (Boulnois 2008:585); perhaps, but it tells us much about the ontological bearing of those doctrines. That is what Heidegger assesses; he never contests the truth of a particular metaphysical doctrine. His interest in the theological bearing of the history of metaphysics is slight: that is, he focuses not on how the metaphysical take on being provides an insufficient basis for thinking God but rather on how the metaphysical take on God as foundation occludes the phenomenological apprehension of being as ground and "unground" of beings. In a sense Heidegger overcomes metaphysics for its own benefit: "The overcoming [*Überwindung*] of metaphysics is recovery [*Verwindung*] from the oblivion of being. Overcoming does not put metaphysics aside, for the recovery is preservation [*Wahrung*]" (*GA* 76:5). Some still hope for a creative retrieval and renewal of Thomism on the basis of the perspectives opened by Heidegger. This would presuppose that Thomism had "won out" over other historical systems such as those of German idealism, in the gigantomachy staged by Joseph Maréchal and Bernard Lonergan. Historical systems can probably be "recovered" only as memory and inspiration, like the Old Masters in the world of painting. Contemporary metaphysical inquiry cannot be authentic if it carries the label "*neo-*," and indeed all the great "neos," such as Neoplatonism, Neo-Thomism, and Neo-Kantianism, have long exhausted their resources. While past metaphysical systems are "true," they are so within the limits of their historical horizon, and their importation into the contemporary context would spell the foreclosure of contemporary perspectives on truth.

The taming of Heidegger in current French phenomenology and history of philosophy means that he is used only to shed light on the turn that produced modern metaphysics, in a way that adds little to the old Gilsonian picture of an occultation of the Thomist act of being by the dominance of the univocal concept of being in Scotus or Suárez. If that is all that is meant by overcoming metaphysics, then the Heideggerian step back does not lead to another radical beginning of thought but rather throws us into the arms of Aquinas, seen as an apophatic thinker in the line of Pseudo-Dionysius, who in his turn is celebrated as having freed the Gospel from hellenistic frameworks of thinking. A string of short circuits thus disables the Heideggerian questions. Lacoste sees Suárez as the most perfect example of what Heidegger meant by *ontotheology* and suggests that Scotus's God escapes by his infinity the suspicion of ontotheology (2009:21, 27). But the suspicion Heidegger exerts applies not to one or another thinker, guilty of an "ontotheological lapsus" (14–15), but to the very nature of metaphysics as the effort to *ground* beings in being or in a supreme being, which is bound to bypass the phenomenon of being as such. To "escape" this suspicion in the relevant sense one would have to engage the *Sache* of thought, being in its phenomenality, a domain overleapt in metaphysics, and it does not seem that Scotus's conception of infinity moves in that direction; he is closer to Hegel, for whom the *Sache* of thought is thinking itself (*GA* 11:53), "being as the thinking that thinks itself" (55), not the unconcealedness of being as phenomenon.

"An ontotheology requires, to attain its strict conceptual rigor, ... first, a concept of the entity, next the univocity of that concept for God and creatures, and finally the subjection of one and the others to a foundation by principle and/or cause. If these conditions are not fulfilled, if to the contrary being remains an inconceivable *esse*, without analogy, even *penitus incognitum*, then the mere intervention of being does not suffice to establish an ontotheology" (Marion 2001:175). In aiming to exclude ancient metaphysics from the domain of ontotheology, Marion gives a rigid cast to Heidegger's suggestions and creates artificial caesuras between ancient and modern reason. No doubt metaphysics attains a new unity and conceptual rigor with Scotus, and one may even claim that the essence of metaphysics is fully determined for the first time by these thinkers. Nonetheless, the ontotheological structure of metaphysics, in Heidegger's sense, is not dependent on this modern logical streamlining but is rather the basis it presupposes. Thus Heidegger is far from excluding Aquinas from the history of ontotheology; if Aquinas is not an exemplary ontotheologist in Heidegger's eyes, it is because he could not resolve the imbalance between ontology and theology in Aristotle, for he permitted the creator God of the Creed to interfere in philosophy (see *GA* 29/30:69–77). Marion's stress on the (Scotist) "concept of the entity" goes beyond Heidegger, who speaks of metaphysics since the Greeks as "the question of the entity as such *and* in its totality" (*GA* 11:63; die Frage nach dem Seienden als solchem *und* im Ganzen), a question developed as both ontology and theology, the ontology answering the question of the entity as such, the theology answering that of the entity in its totality. The term *vorstellendes Denken* here (62), and the description of ontotheology as representing entity as entity (*GA* 9:379; "weil sie das Seiende als das Seiende zur Vorstellung bringt"), do not refer to the post-Scotist "concept of the entity" that Marion wants to see as essential to ontotheology. It is clear that for Heidegger, ontotheology is exemplified in Aristotle, even if the ontological and theological dimensions are not as strictly coordinated as they become in scholasticism and in modern systems such as Hegel's. No doubt ontotheology is not fully constituted by what Rémi Brague calls the "katholou-protological" structure of Aristotle's thought, "essentially aporematic, diaporematic, indeed dialectical" (Courtine 2003:192). It is in Platonizing Aristotle that the Greek commentators "overcame the last resistances of Aristotle's text to the ontotheological interpretation" (194). Aquinas "no doubt represents a quite unique moment in which the ontotheological is balanced with the achieved logic of analogy" (192).

Courtine seeks to show by an "historico-critical examination" (2005:364) that ontotheology is a notion with no bearing on Aristotle and thus that the Heideggerian vision of the constitution and history of metaphysics is baseless. But it does not appear that Heidegger is guilty of projecting back onto Aristotle the ontotheological structure as developed in metaphysics from Scotus to Hegel, and the simpler ontotheology he identifies in Aristotle seems to survive Courtine's philological strictures quite well. The effort to check Heidegger's account against the facts of history would be more fruitful if it espoused the first concern of Heidegger, namely the phenomenon of being— which is not an empirical pluralism but a theme of unitary meditation, *pros hen*. The phenomenological reading of Parmenides' imperative— "This is needful: to say and to think that beings are"—is an option that can go against the letter of the Parmenidean text, though less than the reductionist readings practiced by analytical philosophy. It is justified by the phenomenon that it lights up and that allows one to measure what is missing in metaphysics as the project of thinking "the entity is" according to *logic*. The precise status of the two complementary sides, the ontological and the theological, in Aristotle matters little; from very early on a synthesis between them was sought. Here, again, one may speak of a defensive synthesis, a conceptual control of the otherness of being and of God, the reduction of both to the harmony of a systematic vision. The synthesis holds also in Aquinas, though in conceiving being as act and God's being as infinite and ineffable he sets metaphysics firmly at the service of a reality beyond the concept. It is hard to agree that in Aquinas "metaphysics is doubled; for the first time in the history of this discipline there is no longer *one* but *two* metaphysics" (Boulnois 1999:466), for Aquinas labored to produce a seamless synthesis between all the resources of reason. Whatever can be established in philosophy, apart from reference to revealed data, is carried over into the sphere of theology, where it continues to fructify.

When Boulnois says that "the ontotheological structure" is found only in late medieval and modern metaphysics from Henry of Ghent up to Kant, he is using the word *ontotheological* in Kant's sense, refusing to take it "in the very general (and not very enlightening) sense of the entry of God into philosophy" (1999:515), which means that his discussion does not really engage with Heidegger. Heidegger's claim is that metaphysics can think being only according to the paths of a logic of being in general or of being as a whole (ultimately integrating both); God comes into metaphysics as the foundation of beings as a whole (not from outside, of course). Defining ontotheology more tightly so that it fits only post-Scotist metaphysics erases the point of Heidegger's observations on the structure of Aristotle's thought. It is not convincing to find in these observations a hubris that invests in the "superpotency of *Seinsgeschichte* that crushes any doctrinal or philological inquiry" (Courtine 2005:60). Heidegger derives the notion of ontotheology from examination of Aristotle and does not impose it on Aristotle from the ideology of *Seinsgeschichte*, which he had not yet formulated in any case. If anything, the notion of ontotheology does not fit Hegel, to whom Heidegger applied it in 1957, since Hegel does not explicitly think of beings, being as such, and a supreme being or beings in the way that Aristotle does.

The point of the Heideggerian critique of Hegel is missed when it is claimed that Heidegger opposes to rational thought "a mysticism (supported by negative theology) of the transcendent and ungraspable Deity" (Vieillard-Baron, 294). Heidegger's first concern is with the phenomenality of being; his remarks on the religious fallout of Hegelianism are secondary, and far from emphasizing an ungraspable transcendence seek to recall the phenomenality of the divine. Neither does Heidegger aim to "present Hegel as philosophizing in a much too pretentious way, in putting himself in the place of God and in making him speak, whereas what is required is to return to a philosophy of finitude" (292). Heidegger never caricatures metaphysical rationality in this way, and it is in the name not of the finitude but of the phenomenality of being that he pursues the overcoming of metaphysics. To say that the philosophy of Hegel "is not ontotheological for the reason that it is not an ontology" (12) is to fail to see that for Heidegger the Hegelian name of being would be the *Begriff* (or the *Idee*, rather than the earlier, relatively abstract conceptualizations of being as *Sein, Dasein, Existenz, Wirklichkeit*). If one puts the accent on the *logical* aspect of ontotheology, it is clear that in Hegel being is absorbed in the movement of reflection while God, likewise, is situated as that at which reflection arrives. Each time that Hegel meets something transcending the conceptual level, whether in Indian religions, Plotinus, Judaism, or Christian piety, he either reduces it to the conceptual or treats it as a product of an irrational or unhappy consciousness. Similarly, every phenomenal presence of the divine is reduced either to an early stage of the emergence of the Concept or to a reverie of the beautiful soul.

The Heideggerian way of "placing" Hegel is again inadequately characterized when Heidegger is seen as "poeticizing the concept" and prophesying an uncertain future overcoming of metaphysics, to which one must prefer "the prosaic, but frank overcoming effected by Hegel" (Bourgeois, 36). First, Hegel sublates metaphysics into a higher, freer mode of critical rationality—not only Cartesian and Wolffian metaphysics, as some suggest (Bourgeois, 28; Mabille, 313), but ancient Greek metaphysics as well. From Heidegger's phenomenological point of view, this is a perfecting rather than an overcoming of metaphysics, for it does not break open the concept to the phenomenon. Second, that breaking open is not a poeticizing of the concept but an attention to the phenomena that the concept occludes (and to which the poetic word can point). Third, while overcoming metaphysics may be an endless project, it is not unverifiable, for it is already afoot in rereadings of the metaphysical tradition that bring to light its occlusions and also its unrecognized or unthought phenomenological content.

Even if Thomistic thought is not ontotheological in the full sense, it needs to be shown in detail how it avoids the ontotheological subjugation that seems to threaten it. A partial surpassing of ontotheology, even before ontotheology is fully constituted, is found in principle in all the great texts of Christian metaphysical theology since Origen; but one must divine this resource of resistance in the texts, rather than claiming that they have no relation with ontotheology and are in no danger of being absorbed by its logic. Lewis Ayres holds that Christian theology was constructed according to its own inherent dynamic with only occasional interferences from Greek philosophical tradition, at points where the Gospel kerygma itself invited a metaphysical elaboration. This underestimates the degree to which the basic understanding of God and of God's relation to the cosmos in the Apologists and in Clement and Origen derives from Greek philosophy. It has often been suggested that had the kerygma been propagated in China rather than the West, quite other categories would have been developed to speak of the divine and its incarnation.

According to Heidegger, modern rationalism actualizes potentialities inscribed from the start in the project of metaphysics. To overcome triumphant rationalism one must go back to its ancient roots, discovering a forgetting of being, as phenomenon, in Aristotle and still more in Plato. If the Leibnizian principle of sufficient reason perfects ontotheology (see GA 10:43), it does so in fulfilling the rational quest of the ancients, though a long incubation period was needed before the principle could be formulated explicitly (see GA 10:80–81). If ontotheology reaches a summit in Hegel, it is because he realized integrally the rational project of the Greeks. Taking ontotheology according to Heidegger as an ahistorical structure, and seeing the primacy of the possible over the actual in Heidegger as a metaphysical thesis (missing its phenomenological sense), Adrian Pabst claims that "Christian theology took an ontotheological (or idolatrous) turn when it abandoned the conception of being as relational and privileged possible being over actual being," which happened in "the convergence of Gilbert of Poitiers' formalist and causal metaphysics and Avicenna's metaphysics of the possible" (591). Actuality in Scotus and Ockham is only the realization of the possible and no longer has any ontological significance, which is what furnishes the basis of modern nihilism. Heidegger's history of being has a dubious mythical aspect. "If the prehistory of the principle of reason can be thought as a time of incubation, it is at the very least a paradoxical incubation—or a late one, no doubt posterior to Duns Scotus" (Carraud, 100). But the principle of sufficient reason is not just a formula; it is fundamental to the exercise of reason and thus to all metaphysics. The effort of historians of philosophy to restrict the scope of Heidegger's sweeping diagnoses does not take this sufficiently into account.

Another common way of missing the point of Heidegger's critique of metaphysics is to associate it with an apophatic leap beyond metaphysics, such as one finds in Neoplatonism. Thus Werner Beierwaltes presents Heidegger as a metaphysician who feigned blindness to the fact that Plotinus had anticipated his discovery of being as other than beings: "If there is one place in the history of metaphysics (a history *not* amputated and *not* masked in many ways) where difference *as* difference was not merely sketched by thought with resolution and conceptual intensity, that place is the philosophy of *Plotinus*" (2002:38). A Heideggerian reader of Plotinus may well find some glimmers of the thinking of "difference," or the *Ereignis*, in the otherness of the One from Intellect and being, but this does not concern directly the Heideggerian theme of the being of beings as apprehended by phenomenological thought. According to Pierre Aubenque, Plotinus is "the first Greek philosopher to recall to its true place, the second place, an ontology that, as an answer to the question of the being of the entity, was content to exhibit a particular entity, albeit privileged: the Permanent, the Always-Being, of which the highest figure was the Divine." Plotinus thus reveals "what is particular, and thus limited, in what has been called the 'ontotheological structure of metaphysics,' fruit of a partly arbitrary decision of thought" (1971:104). But Plotinus surveys the ontotheological shape of Greek metaphysics from above, Heidegger from below. Beierwaltes's "conceptual intensity" is far from the kind of thinking by which Heidegger approaches this theme, namely, a meditative thinking focused on phenomenality at a level beneath conceptual constructions. Heidegger and Plotinus, in Beierwaltes's view, pursued the same idea of difference, and this "links Heidegger objectively, in many ways in a hidden and unavowed fashion, to true metaphysics (notably metaphysics of the Plotinian type) far *more closely* and with far *more consequences* than he, with his brusque rejection based on his own reconstruction of 'metaphysics' in view of an alleged 'new beginning' [*anderer Anfang*], cared to recognize" (Beierwaltes 2002:39). The myth of a Heidegger who jealously kept silent about his "hidden sources," whether biblical or Taoist or Neoplatonic, betrays incomprehension of the specificity of Heidegger's question, that of the phenomenality of being. Beierwaltes says that Heidegger propagated "clichés" about the history of metaphysics, whereas Hegel, better informed, reached "a fundamentally different evaluation of the historical significances of Neoplatonism" (39). Given that Hegel reads Plotinus in strictly intellectualist terms, playing down the dimension of the One beyond Intellect (see Halfwassen), it is hard to see how his appreciation of the speculative power of Neoplatonism, never denied by Heidegger in any case, can be adduced in an argument that Plotinus prefigures Heidegger. Had Heidegger commented on Plotinus, he would no doubt have corrected Hegel's blind spot.

MARION ON AUGUSTINE

In an astonishing exercise in "hermeneutical violence" (such as Heidegger practiced on Kant), Marion seeks to overcome metaphysics in Augustine by claiming that Augustine had left metaphysics behind from the start, and that what needs to be overcome is only the metaphysical misunderstandings of his modern interpreters. Anything that looks like metaphysics in Augustine's discourse, as Marion reads it, shows itself on closer inspection to be a phenomenological testimony to biblical truth. Thus all the appearances of metaphysical theorization can be reduced to an underlying level of discourse in which Augustine is no longer theorizing about God but addressing God in the existential situation of grace-enabled confession. Such a reading of Augustine is a drastic methodological shortcut, causing distortions that are worth correcting before an alternative path of overcoming is proposed. It plays off the witness to ultimacy in Augustine against the conventional fabric of his discourse on being and presumes that Augustine must have already implicitly overcome the latter, so that his apparently serious handling of it is really only a kind of play.

Marion claims that the philosophical thought of antiquity had little impact on Augustine's mind. It is true, of course, that Augustine sets up an autonomous intellectual operation, in which scripture and church doctrine are processed with increasingly little reference to philosophers; yet he did sustain a lifelong dialogue with Platonism, growing in knowledge of the tradition, citing Plotinus on the day of his death, and pitching his most ambitious works, the *City of God* and the *De Trinitate*, to readers versed in Platonist lore. Against the claim that Augustine does not use the fundamental concepts of Neoplatonism, "if only because God is not identified with the One, or with a Principle, or even with the Good" (Marion 2008:19), it should be noted that God is indeed identified as *ipsum bonum* or the Good in Augustine (*De Trinitate* 8); that God is as much a Principle as in Origen; that Augustine does use fundamental concepts and structures of Plotinus, with clear influence of particular Plotinian texts, in discussing God (*Conf.* 7) and the soul (*De Trinitate* 9–10); that the influence of Neoplatonism and the wider middle Platonist streams reaches Augustine not only by explicit readings but by the diffuse Platonist conceptions in the philosophical culture of the time and in the leading Christian thinkers of the early centuries (Origen and the many fathers he influenced, including Augustine's mentor Ambrose, Marius Victorinus, and the Cappadocians); and that though he rejects some Neoplatonist doctrines he embraces others, for the encounter with Plotinus—a true meeting of minds, a "transmission from mind to mind," as Zen masters say—was a central event in Augustine's intellectual and spiritual life. One is free to bypass the way in which Augustine's concepts, vocabulary, and methods and structures of argumentation are informed by frequentation of philosophical thinkers such as Cicero, Plotinus, Porphyry, and the general doxographic tradition, as well as by the Christian metaphysics of his predecessors among the fathers. But such a choice abstracts from the real-life context of Augustine and his predecessors, as intellectuals in the Roman Empire, engaged in an apologetic debate with classical thought. It produces an "ahistorical" and "utopian" reading, as Marion actually confesses.

The fact that Augustine easily modulates from philosophical lines of argument to biblical ones and finds biblical verses to warrant all of his philosophically shaped thoughts in no way entails a total overcoming of metaphysics by scriptural phenomena (or by what Augustine understands scriptural phenomena to be); rather, his approach to these phenomena is shaped by his metaphysical thought forms. His exegesis of John and the Psalms is guided and framed by his philosophical notions of God as being and as the ground of beings, of the soul and its capacities, and of the goals of human life conceived in terms of a quest for beatitude. It is thus impossible to cut Augustine off from the history of metaphysics, transporting him to an extraterritorial realm of purely Christian thought. The supreme phenomena at the heart of Augustine's writing cannot be severed from their close relationship to Neoplatonic experience of similar realities, or rather, in Augustine's own view, of the same realities.

Marion claims that Augustine cannot be categorized as a philosopher or a theologian. Augustine understands philosophy as love of wisdom, and Christianity as the true philosophy. But need this forbid a commonsense categorizing of Augustine as a theologian who uses philosophical lore and arguments when needed and whose vocabulary shows a steady presence of philosophical culture? Augustine is quite unambiguously a theologian in his sermons, scriptural commentaries, and anti-Donatist and anti-Pelagian writings, and clearly so as well in the *De Trinitate* and *City of God*, which use philosophical lines of argument within a theological project, coming back again and again to scripture as the primary authority. The *Confessions* chronicles and enacts a religious quest that draws on philosophical argument within a specifically theological overall context of grace and confession. In none of these cases are the philosophical sources, arguments, and tenets dissolved into a "love of wisdom" that is no longer recognizable as part of the culture of classical metaphysics and ethics. Augustine discusses the usual loci of classical philosophy, topics such as friendship, beauty, the origin of evils, cosmic order and providence, the being of God and the soul, the freedom of the will, and time, though his engagement with philosophy is always led by his ultimately theological purpose. The task of critical theologians is to do full justice to the power of Augustine's metaphysical thought, while at the same time recognizing the tensions between it and his scriptural vision and revisiting these tensions, with and against Augustine, in light of all that has been learned about metaphysics and scripture since his time.

Marion gives excessive weight to terminology when he claims that Augustine did not know the words *metaphysics* and *ontology* and that his thinking is thus foreign to the concerns of these disciplines. Gilson's critique of the relatively undeveloped state of Augustine's ontology is countered by the objection that Augustine "not only did not know the word (which appeared some ten centuries later), but would never have used it, since for him *Sum qui sum* does not even pertain to a questioning on beings" (413–14). But in *Confessions* 7 Augustine is involved in a questioning about beings—that is, to overcome Manichaean dualism he needs to grasp the nature of spiritual being and also the unity and goodness of being, and his reading of the *libri Platonicorum*, culminating in the revelation "*Ego sum qui sum,*" brings him this double insight. That his questioning does not proceed in the academic mode of Scotist or Wolffian ontology is not a good reason for denying that a thinking about being and beings is afoot in this text. Though obliged to concede that Augustine is an ontologist at least to the extent of identifying God as *essentia*, as *qui est* or simply as *Est*, Marion plays down the significance of this. He notes the association of divine being with immutability and suggests that the phenomenon of God as unchanging somehow surpasses or relativizes the identification of God as being. "God calls himself *Sum qui sum* because he attests himself first as immutable, and not the contrary. Whereas in the system of metaphysics eternity follows on the being of God among other properties, here the divine difference over against the world is marked in the first place by immutability, which determines originarily their difference in the manner of being entities, and in consequence their difference of being. *Aeternum* determines *esse* and not vice versa" (411). In fact the stereotyped characterization of divine being as immutable seems rather to betoken some dullness in Augustine's handling of the notion of being, held captive by the conceptual opposition of mutable and immutable. When Marion takes it up he sounds as if he is reducing discourse on God's being from the ontological to the merely ontic.

Augustine says that scripture only rarely uses words that are said properly of God ("quae proprie de Deo dicuntur") and that the key instance of such is Exodus 3:14; he adds that while bodies and souls are also said to be, only God can be said to be in the proper sense (*proprio modo*; *De Trinitate* 1.2). But Marion, convinced that Augustine has no interest in being as such, comments on this text as follows: "However, since it is a question first of all of a biblical name, even if it takes an ontological sense through resonances with Plato and Aristotle, this argument cannot suffice to impose being itself (in the sense of philosophy) as a divine name" (396). Marion seems to forget that in *De Trinitate*, the last of the great anti-Arian treatises, Augustine is making his contribution to the controversy on precisely the being (*ousia*) of God that had obsessed Christian theologians since Nicea in 325, some ninety years earlier. Nor was this discussion sealed off from metaphysics or, if that word be disallowed, from *hē theōria tōn ontōn* (Gregory of Nyssa, *Contra Eunomium* 2.572), *hē peri tōn ontōn philosophia* (*In Eccl.* 7.7).

Marion is silent about the immediate connection between that language about divine being and the comprehensive vision of the being of beings which is equally part of the yield of insight brought by the encounter with Plotinus in *Confessions* 7.16. Marion does talk about being and nothingness in connection with God's creative activity but not about such metaphysical theses as the convertibility of being and goodness and the characterization of evil as lack of being—both formulated by Augustine as a metaphysical correction of Manichaeism. The following statement takes no account of this: "It may be that St. Augustine, who does not pose the question of Being, or even that of beings, who therefore does not name God beginning from Being, or as the being par excellence, who does not speak the language of the categories of the entity, nor begin from the first of these categories, *ousia*, who does not inquire after a first foundation, nor seek it in any *subject* (whether understood as substrate or as *ego*) does not belong to metaphysics, either explicitly nor implicitly" (27). To be sure, Augustine is not an autonomous metaphysician but an "embedded" one. But this does not entail that his thought can be cleanly reduced to the categories of a theological phenomenology or that metaphysical "essence" becomes biblical "spirit" without remainder. There is a tension in such texts as the *De Trinitate* between the dynamic of metaphysical thought, focused on being and mind, and the dynamic of biblical thought; to interrogate this tension allows a more differentiated and interesting reading of the text than approaches which stress only one side.

Marion makes much of those texts in which God is called *idipsum* or "Itself." This is indeed an apophatic trait in Augustine. A homology with the Plotinian One need not be dismissed as quickly as Marion dismisses it. In the mystical ascent at Ostia (*Conf.* 9) the divine *idipsum* is touched with the summit of the mind, as in Plotinus the One is touched (*thigein*) rather than seen (in contrast to the language of light in *Conf.* 7). Marion is right to say that those who translate *idipsum* as "true Being" are blinded by metaphysical presuppositions, missing the gap that Augustine signals between the *idipsum* and the discourse of God as being. The *idipsum* is "radically and definitively apophatic, expresses no essence and attains no definition" (406).

But immediately after expressing his inability to say anything about the *idipsum* Augustine goes on to ask, "Quid est ergo 'idipsum,' nisi, quod est?" (*Enn. in Ps.* 121.5; What then is "itself" except "what is"?). When Augustine seeks words approximating it or helping to lead the mind to it, the first words he finds are those of a "metaphysics of the Exodus." Marion insists that the stress is on the otherness of immutable divine being, not on a definition of God as *ipsum esse*. "Exodus 3:14 comes into play only after the *idipsum* and following its apophasis, so that far from identifying with it or vanishing into it, it encloses and gives its meaning to the *Sum qui sum.* In consequence, one sees above all that *Sum qui sum* cannot be translated as an *ipsum esse*, which would make being the most proper name of God, and so it no longer works to establish a 'metaphysics of the Exodus,' vanishing into the *ipsum esse*" (407). This is well observed. But even if *idipsum* transcends and encloses the language of *esse*, it does not disqualify that language or cause it to vanish into the apophasis of *idipsum.* A staple account of God as true being seems to survive quite robustly despite the apophatic inflections.

A forthright attack on Augustine's ontology would be preferable to this strained special pleading, which attempts to dragoon Augustine (and also Aquinas) into an apophatic tradition that is not as central to Christian theology as Marion would wish. Marion's discourse of "God without being," suitably interpreted, can indeed appeal to the tradition going back to the *epekeina tēs ousias* of Plato and developed by Plotinus and Pseudo-Dionysius. There is truth in his association of Thomist *esse*, being as act, with Neoplatonism, for Porphyry, and the later Plotinus as read by Porphyry, may lurk beyond Thomas here. It is true, too, that Heidegger devoted little thought to how this apophatic tradition might be situated in the context of his vision of metaphysics as ontotheology, or how the phenomenon of the One beyond being might be related to the phenomenon of being or the question of being. Nonetheless, to reread Augustine and Aquinas as radically transcending and leaving behind the tradition of Christian ontology founded in the Greek translation of Exodus 3:14 is a step too far; the apophatic opening at the summit of their thought does not undo the fact that it is structured as a theory of being.

Marion's quest for an Augustinian God uncontaminated by being is of a piece with his discourse of "God without being" and with his reduction of giver, gift, and receiver to a process of giving or givenness that seems to have no anchor in being. Some will see this as a nihilistic ontophobia, and others will try to save it by correlating it with the Buddhist discourse of emptiness. Indeed, what Levinas and Marion attack as "being" can be interpreted as close to that fixed substantial identity that Buddhists call *svabhāva*, "own-being." When the emptiness of all phenomena has been demonstrated and the illusions of *svabhāva* have been put to flight, one is left, not with a barren void, but rather with the authentic empty texture of things, their *tathatā*, "thusness." In this sense "givenness" is Marion's way of naming being in its empty thusness. His thesis that God is not obliged to "be" makes little sense, except as a riposte to Heidegger's subjection of the phenomenality of God to the phenomenality of being. But if we rephrase the thesis as "God is not obliged to be given," its inappositeness comes to light. Marion would surely claim that God is given, and given in a preeminent way; there is no question of God being forced to be given. Similarly there is no implication of imposing constraints on God in the basic statement, however faltering or fumbling, that "God exists, God is." A radical purge of religious language that would disqualify such basic statements would contribute not to the refinement but to the paralysis of theological judgment.

Marion seems aware of how implausible this radical rereading of Augustine is, for he admits the force of Heidegger's diagnosis that Augustine was impeded in his phenomenological or existential thinking of the realities of faith by an attachment to Greek theoretical methods of thinking that he was not able to overcome. Marion is on a promising track in his sense that Augustine, for all his acceptance of metaphysical language and frameworks, is in the last analysis a thinker who cannot be brought within metaphysical bounds and who can therefore be appropriated for an overcoming of metaphysics. But the best way to follow up on this is frankly to enlarge the Heideggerian-cum-Lutheran project of overcoming metaphysics by applying it directly to Augustine himself rather than only to modern thinkers. The overcoming is best achieved not by radical gestures but in a patient, reflective, deconstructive reading focused on the tension between biblical and metaphysical in Augustine's texts. Some solicitation of these texts, some hermeneutical violence, might have a tactical role in such a reading, but the ultimate aim would be to let the texts themselves show the full complexity of the conflicting forces at play in them. What is persuasive in Marion's approach is the intuition that for all his talk of being, Augustine is not fully at home in ontology, in that "totality" that Levinas and Derrida have made us feel to be a straitjacket, so that when he exclaims, "*Idipsum*," he seems to yearn for a "beyond being," or an "otherwise than being," even if he falls back into explaining the *idipsum* in ontological terms.

Augustine's experience and discourse of grace can be developed autonomously without reference to philosophy, and in his writings on this topic, which express the heart of his distinctive theological vision, being seems to drop out of view. To follow up the suspicion that Augustine's metaphysics threatens to encumber or occlude his vision of grace, one should espouse and carry through more fully the partial overcoming of metaphysics operative in Augustine's texts. Impatience with metaphysics and refusal to recognize the extent of Augustine's investment in metaphysical discussion and reliance on basic metaphysical notions, such as being, mind, soul, the Good, foreclose other interesting paths to retrieving Augustine in a contemporary critical key.

The effort to rewrite Christian tradition in a key suited to the contemporary world can piggyback on the ideas of the Reformers, who declare a stark break with past structures, including the Platonism infiltrating patristic theology. But this has disadvantages. First, the Reformation imperfectly overcame those structures, which continued to resurface within its own theology. Second, the Reformation itself is a tradition in need of being rewritten in a contemporary key. All that theology can do, faced with such a massive block of tradition as Augustine represents, is to draft revisionist proposals and then to interrogate Augustine's texts patiently in light of them, letting the proposals themselves be modified and nuanced in the process. This is an infinite task of interpretation and judgment, but if the revisionist proposals have merit, they will prove themselves by the critical grip they give us on the ancient texts, which begin to cede to their pressure, and by the opening of a conversation with the texts, in this case a conversation about the merits and pitfalls of various ways of using ontological language when speaking of God.

CAUSA SUI

The name of God in ontotheology, according to Heidegger, is *causa sui*, and unlike the biblical names of God it cannot inspire joyful worship. This may underestimate the element of religious joy in Plotinus and Spinoza, who used the language of *causa sui*. In any case the idea of God as self-caused was rejected in Christian theology and in medieval metaphysics. Even in its refined Spinozan and Hegelian form, according to which God is *causa sui* in that the full-fledged concept of God entails the reality of God, it is rejected by those who follow Aquinas's dismissal of the ontological argument. Does this rejection of *causa sui* mean that Thomist metaphysics cannot be placed in the "incubation period" of the principle of sufficient reason but forestalls in advance the rationalism of Leibniz and Hegel? Heidegger is perhaps influenced by the view of Kant and Hegel that all proofs of the existence of God are in principle reducible to the ontological argument, an idea that is of a piece with their conceptualist understanding of judgment. The Thomist affirmation of being and of divine being cannot be seen as reducing either of them to the function of an explanatory ground or as making them pillars of a self-enclosed system. If there is forgetfulness of being in Thomas, it lies not in the structure of his thought but in the lack of a phenomenological dimension. Heidegger's phenomenological explication of Aristotle brings out the concrete origins of the language of being in a way that Thomas's commentaries on the Latin translations of Aristotle cannot.

Marion, in line with his effort to see Heidegger as challenging not all metaphysics but only the conceptualist metaphysics dating from Scotus, wants to make *causa sui* a late idea, an invention of Descartes (1996:143–82; Carraud, 230–35, 266–88). Historically this is again an impossible claim. Plotinus's discussion of *causa sui* anticipates Descartes, even if it does have the context of a reduction of causality to efficiency alone or an extension of the search for causes to the eternal ideas or truths or God himself. The fact that "Plotinus himself says that he should not be taken strictly literally" (Carraud, 40) only makes the resemblance with Descartes more striking, for Descartes too extends causality to God only analogically. Though there are many self-generating entities in Stoicism and Gnosticism, the idea that the Supreme Being is cause of itself is rare. Plotinus dares to speak of the One as "cause of itself" (*aition heautou; Enn.* 6.8.14), nuancing this by adding the word *hoion* ("so to speak"). The term *causa sui* evokes first the autarchy of a sovereignly free agent; the guarantee of its liberty is that it is such as it wishes to be. Even if it is impossible for something to bring itself to existence (6.8.7), nonetheless the One "gives itself existence [*hupostēsas hauton*]. . . . It is as it has awakened itself to be" (6.8.16). Plotinus met strong opposition among his interlocutors to the idea of the One as self-caused, and he himself recognizes, much as Descartes will, the malaise bound to be caused by a notion that seems to defy logic and imperil divine simplicity. His defense of the expression recalls the acrobatics of Descartes on the same topic. In his reply to Narbonne, Marion (1996) denies "the *efficient* character of Plotinus's *causa sui*," but this contradicts the letter of Plotinus's text, in which the *causa sui* is presented even more explicitly than in Descartes in the sense of efficient causality.

Marion notes that the Cartesian usage of the notion is distinguished by "its inclusion in a principle (soon that of sufficient reason)." But while it is true that Plotinus wants to defend the freedom of the One rather than subject it to a demand for radical intelligibility, this defense requires nonetheless that the One should have a necessary foundation in itself. In freeing the One from chance, Plotinus appeals to the authority of reason: "What is in accord with rational principle [*logos*] is not by chance." It is true that the One is beyond reason, since it is its root (*Enn.* 6.8.15), so that Plotinus knows that his rational speculations on self-causedness in the One cannot be taken literally and have only an indicative function, as an effort to bring out the specific sovereignty of the One.

From the negations with which Plotinus surrounds his use of *causa sui*, Marion wants to conclude that "Plotinus expounded the *causa sui* only to refute it, like all the medievals after him." But that is not how his critical Neoplatonic successors interpreted his view. That in Proclus the idea, even as applied to entities below the One (the only ones for which he accepts self-causation), is only a "relic" has no bearing on its status in *Ennead* 6.8 (Marion 1996:148–49). If the Proclean notion of self-constitution is merely a relic, its influence on Erigena and Hegel is a fine tribute to the power of relics.

Marius Victorinus presents the notion of God as self-caused without the protection of Plotinus's *hoion*. The idea is introduced by his Arian interlocutor, to underline the simplicity of God, neither engendering nor engendered: "The first cause is cause to itself, not as a different cause is cause of something different from it, but that itself, which God is, is the cause for this—that he should be" (*Candidi epistula* 1.3; Etenim prima causa et sibi causa est, non quae sit altera alterius, sed hoc ipsum, quod ipsum est, ad id, ut sit, causa est). This sounds like daring speculation but may mean only that the one cause of God's existence is the fact that God exists; whereas the doctrine of the Son's generation would seem to posit a more real causality in God. In his reply, despite apophatic warnings, Victorinus affirms: "God is the one who establishes the Logos itself. For if God is first cause, he is not only cause of all, but cause also for himself" (*Ad Candidum* 18; Ipse enim constitutivus est et ipsius tou logou. Si enim prima causa, non solum omnium causa, sed et sibi ipsa causa est). He also speaks of a self-generation of the Logos (22), which prompts the interpretation that "the *causa sui* should then rather be understood to apply to the generation of the Son" (Carraud, 41). But this restriction cannot hold for statements such as the following, on the subject of God the Father: "He is cause to himself that he should be that very thing that exists" (*Adv. Arium* 4.6.38; Sibi causa est ut hoc ipsum sit quod exsistit). There may be a Gnostic influence here, mediated by Porphyry, but the major influence is probably *Enneads* 6.8. "The highly differentiated trinitarian theory of Victorinus is the immediate effect (and also an effect mediated by Porphyry) of Plotinus's idea of the self-causation of the absolute," which Beierwaltes sees as "remarkable evidence that without philosophy there cannot be a self-aware theology capable of reflecting on its conceptual possibilities, and that philosophy can operative productively within Christian theology without worrying about hellenization" (2001b:151–52). Dismissing the questions of Harnack and Heidegger, Beierwaltes reaffirms the exclusive competence of metaphysical thinking to do justice to the phenomena of being and of revelation.

Augustine's *De Trinitate* begins with a polemic against the *causa sui* that is perhaps aimed at Victorinus's precipitous speculation but may be directed at Plotinus himself (the text echoes, with an ironic twist, a passage in the *Enneads*). Rejection of the *causa sui* becomes an apotropaic ritual in the Middle Ages. Even Scotus Eriugena limits the *causa sui* to what comes after the first principle. If "God made himself" (*Periphyseon* 3.674A; Deus se ipsum fecit), it is in the sense that God engenders or expresses himself in wishing to create: "In manifesting himself, God creates himself in a wondrous and ineffable manner in the creature" (678C). Even Eckhart, who is so keen on the language of a dynamic self-generation of God in the soul and of the soul in God, follows Aquinas (*ST* I, q. 2, a. 3) in declaring that "nothing is cause of itself" (*LW* 2:470). But the idea of *causa sui* lingers as a background to discourse on the necessary being and aseity, especially in Islamic and Jewish scholasticism. Avicenna says: "His existence, which is necessary, is due to himself," and for Gersonides, God "has his existence of himself."

When Heidegger sees *causa sui* as the name of God in ontotheology, he is probably thinking not of Descartes but of those who reduce the efficient cause to the intrinsic reason, so that a self-caused being is defined as "that whose essence implies its existence, or that whose nature cannot be conceived except as existing" (Spinoza, *Ethics* 1, def. 1; id, cuius essentia involvit existentiam, sive id, cuius natura non potest concipi, nisi existens), or is "its own reason" (*ratio sibi ipsi*; Leibniz). In metaphysics, according to Heidegger, "The being of the entity unveils itself as the ground that grounds and founds itself" (*GA* 11:65; Das Sein des Seienden entbirgt sich als der sich selbst ergründende und begründende Grund). God, to be thought in metaphysics, must show himself as being capable of radical self-foundation. "The being of the entity in the sense of the ground can fundamentally be represented only as *causa sui*" (*GA* 11:57; Das Sein des Seiendes wird im Sinne des Grundes gründlich nur als causa sui vorgestellt). All of this has only a tangential connection with Christian theology, which the doctrines of Creation and divine freedom protect against these rationalist reductions. But within theology a certain rationalism is deployed at the service of the transcendent and sovereign God. The presentation of the divine attributes, the relation between God and creatures and the logic of providence in classical theology depends on a questionable premise: the stability and transparency of the basic terms. Should these become opaque or fluid in the least degree, the entire construction totters. The human, biblical perspective, where God is spoken of in metaphorical language, offers little foothold for an account of God in himself. The one on whom we depend, before whom we live, and toward whom we advance is an ultimate referent that can be apprehended only in these perspectives. A discourse constructed outside of all perspectives invokes a doubtful argument: "If God is such as our trust and hope suppose him to be, then he must have the following attributes . . ." The notion of God is an open horizon, a mobile language permitting affirmation of ultimacy; to build a science of the divine attributes one arrests the free unfolding of this horizon by extracting elements considered to be the essence of God. It is the great merit of Schleiermacher to have restored the human perspective where we have access to the idea of God.

THE OBJECTIFICATION OF GOD

A theological overcoming of metaphysics may focus on the theme of the objectification of God that seems inevitable in metaphysical discourse, which can acknowledge the actual modalities of the divine presence only by disqualifying its own discourse or putting itself under erasure. The Plotinian metaphysics of the One, which was taken up by Augustine in his vision of an utterly simple God who is totally present in every place, *ubique totus*, and which lives on in the doctrine of divine simplicity set at the threshold of the *Summa theologiae* (I, q. 3) and in Dante's sublime image of God as a single distant luminous point (*Paradiso*), escapes from such objectifications. Some speculate that Plotinus achieved his concept of the divine and the procession of being in tacit dialogue with the doctrine of Creation introduced by Jews and Christians, pointing out that his forerunner Numenius was acquainted with Genesis and that Christian Gnostics, steeped in a cult of the hidden, unknowable, utterly transcendent God, frequented Plotinus's lectures in Rome.

It would seem temerarious to suggest that this sublime metaphysics of divine simplicity could ever come to occlude the biblical God. But note that to sustain it intense conceptual acrobatics are required, prompting the Chestertonian quip that if divine simplicity is so complex, what must divine complexity be! The thoroughness of this logical and ontological purging of the divine of any suggestion of differentiation (also pursued by Islamic theologians in polemic against trinitarianism) was seen as necessary to think through biblical faith in a cogent way, yet it threatens to pit a philosophical construct over against the God of Abraham.

Objectification sets in more palpably when God is connected to the cosmological metaphysics of the Greeks, which obliges us to rationalize the notion of Creation in terms of principles and reasons hidden within the divinity and to conceive the relation of Creator and creature in terms of philosophical oppositions between eternity and time, being and becoming, archetype and image, necessity and contingency, one and many, simplicity and composition, impassible and passible, infinite and finite. The more these schemas are developed, the less they connect with the biblical situation of humanity facing the Creator and Redeemer. Aquinas and the other scholastics develop rich anthropologies (and angelologies) situating the human in the total order of being, with a satisfying place for all the biblical data. The great machinery of Platonism is developed to sketch an encompassing order of love, *ordo amoris*, in which divine agape and human eros harmoniously intertwine. But there is biblical grit that refuses integration into this vision, notably the event of the free justification of the sinner, a theme handled by Aquinas in the inappropriate categories of the Aristotelian metaphysics of change. To understand oneself within a metaphysical order of being is already to objectify oneself, to lose the posture of hearing the Word. It is necessary to query the authority of Christian metaphysics, to bring out the subtle fault lines that recur in its successive syntheses from Origen to Rahner, in order to let the Word of God emerge untrammeled in its power to save.

But is not the New Testament itself metaphysical, and the Septuagint before it? As a document written in Greek in hellenistic times, it can hardly avoid echoing the Platonic and Stoic terminology in the air, and a text such as Hebrews is not remote from the Middle Platonist world of Philo. Yet again and again the text enacts a distancing of philosophical understandings. If Paul has traces of Stoicism, they are overrun by the centrality of Christ in his view of reality; if John has a creative Logos enlightening all minds, the nature of that light is far from the wisdom and conceptual insight cultivated in philosophy; the Philonism of Hebrews is far less marked by philosophical terms and ideas than Philo's own discourse is. In its most central themes—the Kingdom of God, faith, love, justification, sanctification, resurrection—the New Testament has an intensity of thought that is very different from philosophy and that has no need of philosophy.

Insofar as the classical metaphysical language of God is in use today, it functions best as a set of linguistic constraints, prohibitions against saying that God is temporal, changeable, dependent, contingent, multiple, passible, finite; to affirm that God is eternal, necessary being, one, simple, and so on, is then less a matter of objective knowledge than an ascesis of language and thought aiming to keep open the horizon of awareness of the divine. This ascesis has importance only for the metaphysical way of thinking. Other rules of language come into play when one seeks to awaken and cultivate the sense of the divine beyond that domain of argument.

Awareness of the obsolescence of mythic and metaphysical languages about God leads to their replacement by a regime of discretion and indirect allusion, not because faith has grown weak, but because it is adjusting to the subtlety of divine presence, bending its language to what can be known of it. If "finding-oneself-utterly-dependent is the only mode whereby God and I can be together in self-consciousness" (Schleiermacher 1:173), metaphysical discourse on God is exposed to the suspicion of keeping that consciousness at a distance.

Post-Schleiermacherian theologians tend to give a historicizing turn to the expression of their faith. "I believe in God" then means "I place much trust in the heritage of the language that speaks of 'God,' convinced that it puts me in some relation with ultimate reality." An enlightened, critical faith, or rather a canny and prudent faith, thus risks making "God" a useful cipher, like x or y in algebra, such that the capital of trust invested in it is only a provisional calculus, to be rescinded if unprofitable. God becomes a question, a possibility, a language game. The literal content of direct invocations of God, for example, a phrase such as "Thy kingdom come," is less eloquent than its performance as a gesture of hope, of taking one's stand before God. Thus read, direct language is affected with indirectness and reduced to the allusive. Accepting this withdrawal of its ultimate referent is not a failure of our religious culture but the crossing of a threshold of maturity in our way of handling the biblical heritage.

Can such a nebulous God still be the object of faith, or even of unbelief? Rereading the tradition, one finds that the notion of God in himself has always been ungraspable: "I am who I am" (Ex 3:14). Given this fluidity and obscurity, to say that "God exists" has hardly any meaning; the language of faith is more concrete, focusing on God at work in creation, in Christ, and in the church; these concrete loci procure the only possible access to the divine (cf. Jn 1:18). Such a faith is not a general affirmation that one has found the divine meaning of the world but a continual interrogation of that meaning, an interrogation within which the cosmic, Christic, and ecclesial aspects mutually illuminate and correct one another. Yet even as thus "incarnated" the notion of God remains obscure. We dwell on its mediations, hoping to find in them a place of encounter with God, but these mediations are so complex that it becomes impossible to define the God to whom they give access. Rather than forming the tight logical system that classical dogmatic treatises suggest, these mediations have the texture of an imaginative play with conventional representations. Reflective theological judgment will discern the logically binding elements in their composition while fully recognizing the role of creative invention. Theology studies the traditional discourses as so many different texts, provisional attempts to speak of God, and renounces the idea of deciding once and for all what must be taken as the correct language on the divine. A discourse on God guided by Thomist metaphysics, even when so modern in appearance as Karl Rahner's, or one guided by the Bible, like Barth's, no longer satisfies a faith and theology that have become aware of the mobility of the notion of God. It appears that we can never again form a monolithic language about God, and that plurality is to prevail.

Our thought progresses in refusing the way of essentialism, finding everywhere relativity, indetermination, contingency, and pluralism. To make of these a new logos or essence, under the sign of Buddhist emptiness, is not possible either, since emptiness is not an essence but on the contrary sends us back to the texture of our "dependently co-arising" world. The Buddhist perception that everything comes to be only when the requisite conditions are in place, and in dependence on these conditions, so that nothing has an autonomous existence, is a phenomenological perception rather than an essential definition, and it is a perception that is more negative than positive, its negativity consisting in the destruction of essentialist illusions.

Can one make of this retreat of being and essence a framework in which to insert theology? That would be an incautious move, for however one deepens the idea of this "retreat," with the help of Buddhist emptiness or Vedantist ideas of the absolute, it has little to do with the specific call of the biblical God; it is *khōra* rather than transcendence, a place of radical indeterminacy that militates against the clear perception of God. The topography of encounter with the biblical God is irreducible to the topography of an exploration of being, whether in the classical form of projections of ideas of truth, goodness, being itself, or in the postclassical form in which the relative and indeterminate prevail. The exploration of being and the encounter with God are two heterogeneous traditions of experience, formed by history, whose interaction cannot constitute a flawless synthesis. As Wittgenstein saw, we are always already caught in a multitude of language games, and it is not possible to step back to some criterion or foundation that would allow their reduction to a single luminous order. We must accept the pluralistic goings-on of language, which is perfectly in order just as it is. Projects of reducing this pluralism to a foundation in pure perceptions or in transparent logical formulations fail again and again. The same is true of their theological equivalents. Christianity came to birth in an irreducible heterogeneity of perceptions and languages, and we cannot reduce it to a foundation in some pure experience of Christ or some logically transparent dogmatic proposition. The same situation applies to monotheism as a whole.

RAHNER AND METAPHYSICS

Wittgenstein's dictum "A picture held us captive" can well be applied to Karl Rahner. A strong metaphysical thinker in his early years, he was later to become the prisoner of the metaphysical platform he had erected. It provided a basis for effective forays into theological debates that he was able to wrest free from the crippling grip of the preconciliar scholastic theology. But it remained fixated on a picture of the finite human being before the infinite God, which fused elements from existential Ignatian spirituality, negative theology, transcendental Thomism, and Heideggerian phenomenology to create a distinctive Rahner formula. The horizon Rahner worked within could process a great number of theological questions, streamlining theological discourse and making it more assured and well grounded. Where the limits of this metaphysical vision appear is in its failure to engage closely with the phenomenality of the biblical world or even the contemporary one, and especially to deal with historical, cultural, and religious pluralism in a convincing way. The two poles of Rahner's vision—the transcendental pole of the *Vorgriff*, the questioning human mind opening onto the unfathomable mystery of God, and the categorical pole of finite knowledge and concepts—might invite comparison with the Buddhist dyad of ultimate and conventional, though the complexity of both sides of that comparison will no doubt prevent it from generating more than tentative critical suggestions.

In the eight pages in *Grundkurs des Glaubens* devoted to "a meditation on the word *God*," in a chapter entitled "The Human Being before the Absolute Mystery," Rahner begins from a transcendental experience of openness to mystery that can never be adequately retrieved and thematized in reflection. Yet he accepts that the word *God* correctly names the "whither" of this openness: "The human being knows explicitly what *God* means only insofar as he allows this transcendentality of his over anything that can be given objectively to come before him, assuming and reflectively objectifying what is always already posited with transcendentality" (1976:54). God is here rather securely located and identified. But the stability of the identification depends on the stability of the horizon of transcendentality. Perhaps Rahner underestimates the degree to which that horizon is itself a conventional construction. In our culture, *God* has become a cipher that functions obliquely, opaquely, elusively as an occasionally useful way of evoking a sense of depth in things or a nostalgia for such depth. "In the epoch of discourse analysis, as we know, all directness has been put out of circulation" (Sloterdijk, 213).

"One can say that what is simplest and unavoidable in the question of God is the fact for the human being that in his spiritual existence the word *God* is given" (1976:55). This sentence circumscribes the ensuing meditation, confining it to a particular sphere of Western consciousness and undercutting its claim to transcendental universality and necessity. For in reality the word *God* is given only to those who have learned to think philosophically about God in dependence on Christian conceptions. The Bible does not contain the word *God* in the general sense intended here; rather it names God concretely as the God of Abraham or the God and Father of our Lord Jesus Christ. What God might be apart from or in abstraction from such naming is a question not broached in scripture. The chief names of God in the Hebrew Bible—*El, El-Elyon, El-Shaddai, Elohim, Yhwh, ha-Shem*—have a concrete cast, as proper names, that the word *God* in abstraction does not. The word *God* is not given in biblical Hebrew in any obvious sense. In biblical Greek we have *ho Theos*, which, as Rahner himself argued, always refers in the New Testament to God the Father; the New Testament does not have the name *God* for the Trinity or for godhead in general. In classical Greek a word corresponding to *God* is even harder to find. In Latin, it is more natural to talk of the nature of the gods (*natura deorum*, as in Cicero) than of God, *deus*. As with the Japanese word *kami*, the Greek word *theos* gravitates toward a plural usage: the gods.

When Francis Xavier asked for a Japanese translation of *God* his interpreters proposed *Dainichi*, the characters of which mean "great sun" and which is the Japanese translation of the Sanskrit *Mahā-vairocana*, the name of the supreme or quintessential Buddha, the essence of Buddhahood, in the esoteric Mikkyō (Shingon) branch of Buddhism brought to Japan by Kūkai in the ninth century. Discovering that this usage made Christianity look like a form of Buddhism, Xavier decided instead to call God *Deus* in Japanese; the missionaries in China found a better solution, calling God "Lord of Heaven." Today, Japanese Christians call God *kami-sama*, which sounds like "mister god" or "mister spirit." Clearly, the word *God* is not "given" in Japanese, but struggles to secure for itself a precarious perch.

At what point did the word *ho Theos* or *Deus* cease to translate the proper names of God in the Bible and become also a general category lending itself to philosophical analysis? Perhaps this shift took place in the mission preaching of the early church, or earlier in Alexandrian Judaism, as part of the effort to build a bridge between hellenistic and Hebraic piety. Paul's discourse on the "unknown God" in Acts 17 appeals to a vague universal sense of divinity (unless one wishes to confine it to the specifics of the local Athenian cult), offering perhaps the most plausible biblical basis for Rahner's meditation. Yet Paul goes on to confiscate the unknown God, identifying him as the biblical Creator and the God of Jesus Christ, leaving no remainder of a general concept of divinity. This is even clearer in Paul's *ipsissima verba* in Romans 1:19–25, which offers a starker, strongly judgmental view of the knowledge of God in the pagan world, now ascribed to a revelatory initiative of the biblical God. The fathers tend to see Platonism as attaining a glimpse of the true God and his Logos, but again they identify this firmly with the concrete Christian identification of Father, Son, and Spirit, which completes and surpasses whatever Platonists may have intuited. Perhaps it is only with Anselm's ontological argument, or with the "two-truths" theory that lodges at the edges of medieval scholasticism, that one first encounters a notion of God that is not absorbed and concretized in the Christian, Jewish, or Muslim naming of God.

Increasingly abstract speculation on the attributes of divinity, in increasing alienation from biblical usage, led to the Reformers' rejection of the God of nominalist theology as an idol and to Pascal's dramatic contrast of the God of Abraham with the God of the philosophers (or of Descartes). If the word *God* is still "given" for Western intellectuals in recent centuries, it designates two different things: the proper name of the biblical or Christian God, and the pallid philosophical definition of a supreme being. Catholic philosophy and theology have labored to hold the two together, but the tension in this synthesis is such that one can no longer speak simply of the givenness of the word *God.*

Rahner himself admits that to speak in such a generalizing way of the word *God* is to call up a blank, inexpressive cipher, "as if the word gazed at us like a blinded face" (1976:56). Instead of stepping immediately back to the concrete naming of the God of Abraham, Rahner feels he has to linger with and interrogate this abstract divinity:

> Nonetheless this terrifying contourlessness of this word—to which the first question would be "What at all is it, then, that this word means to say?"—is still clearly appropriate to what is intended, regardless of whether or not the word originally was already so "faceless." Whether its history commenced from another form of the word is something we need thus not go into. In any case the present form of the word mirrors what is intended by the word: the "ineffable," the "nameless," that which cannot be inserted in the named world as a moment thereof; the "silent one," which is always there, yet always overlooked, unheard and—since it expresses everything as unity and totality—can be passed over as meaningless, that which really has no word any longer, since any word acquires limit, proper resonance, and thus comprehensible meaning only within a field of words. (56)

Rahner is convinced that the empty abstraction and indeterminacy with which the word *God* confronts us is something deeper and more radical than the variety of concrete namings that the history of biblical traditions (or more widely, the history of religion) might reveal. What he is evoking here is the ultimacy toward which talk of God points, which is revealed rather than undercut when one demonstrates the conventionality of any particular language about God. But the idea of divine facelessness is an unfortunate way of indicating this. Neither scripture nor the fathers of the church ever dwell on God as such a faceless quantity. Even if we were to regard the negative theology of Gregory of Nyssa or Pseudo-Dionysius as the deepest patristic thinking about God, they still characterize God concretely, as the one revealed to Moses on Sinai, hidden in the depth of a cloud. The faceless God that Rahner sees as indicating the true nature of God is a distillation of metaphysical reasoning. It is more faceless than the God of Aquinas, for even in identifying God as pure being, Aquinas is bearing in mind the concrete revelation of God to Moses in the burning bush (Ex 3:15), and Aquinas insists that the Tetragrammaton (Yhwh) is a still higher and more concrete name of God. The ineffability of God is not divorced from the power of God's presence and the concreteness of God's identity. Rahner thinks of God as the ultimate X envisaged by the transcendental reaching out of the human spirit beyond all that is categorically graspable. He thinks that this transcendental opening up of the realm of the divine clears the ground of the limitedness of all historical namings of God, including those of scripture, allowing a deeper and more radical grasp of ultimate mystery.

Rahner's discussion of the word *God* may owe something to Heidegger's meditations on the word *being*, which first appears as the most empty and general of expressions, easily slighted by the mind that is busy with individual beings. But Heidegger does not assess this emptiness and generality as a breakthrough to a radical insight into the nature of being; on the contrary, he labors to replace this abstract notion with concrete phenomenality. The universality and emptiness of being is a first indication of the difference of being from beings (the ontological difference). Metaphysics is content to build on this universality, speculatively, and thus loses sight of the difference again, whereas a phenomenology that overcomes metaphysics can bring into view the phenomenon of being ever more concretely, while interrogating the history of being in Western metaphysics as a long series of withdrawals or concealments of being. Rahner, unfortunately, does not follow such a countermetaphysical path in regard to the notion and phenomenon of God but rather shores up metaphysical reasoning, seeking to grasp God more deeply by meditating on the ineffability, namelessness, and silence that mark God's presence. He does, to be sure, underline the conventionality of the abstract word *God*, which "can speak to us of God, in that it is the last word before that falling dumb, in which we have to do with the grounding totality as such through the vanishing of all nameable individual things" (1976:56). This overcoming of metaphysics by stepping beyond it to the ineffable is a step from conventionality to ultimacy. But it still works with a metaphysical duality between the absolute and all finite individual things, and perhaps with a Thomist opposition between finite beings and God as being itself in its fullness.

God, for Rahner, is not only the "whither" of transcendentality but also the "whence" of grace and revelation, or rather the one who is present and "communicates himself" in grace and revelation. Here God becomes phenomenological in a more attractive way, not as the ineffable and incomprehensible beyond but as a warm, loving, encompassing paternal presence. He might have explicated this in a more attentively phenomenological way, in dialogue with the full range of human experience of the divine. But he sought instead to explicate it metaphysically. His way of thinking about such themes as "uncreated grace," divine self-communication, and God's universal saving grace is in the vein more of metaphysical theorems and explanations than of phenomenological interpretation. The theme of the Spirit becomes prominent in his theology in the later 1970s, when this simpler and more biblical image of divine presence and action was put at the forefront of church life by the Charismatic movement. But the Spirit is not a major presence in *Grundkurs*. A reference to the Spirit would be too concrete and would spoil the effort at metaphysical radicality, an effort very dear to Rahner. In short, there may be an ambiguity or a tension in Rahner's language about God between a concrete sense of the divine in its ultimacy, in incarnational interaction with the human and religious phenomena pointing to it, and an abstract metaphysical concept of God that resists dialectical movement or a phenomenological step back.

Rahner's inclusivism is at the service of building a comprehensive metaphysical vision, but its effect is to deplete the phenomena subject to its embrace. Other religions are depleted when characterized in terms of anonymous Christianity. It is not entirely surprising that Rahner showed no desire to study them, or even to study the culture and theology of Protestantism. His metaphysical "picture" of God may even have blunted his sensitivity to the riches of the Bible, which are depleted by theological schemas that anticipate and forestall its meaning. The work of art, too, even though Rahner recognizes it as a *locus theologicus*, is depleted when placed within a schema of divine revelation, for the phenomenon is explained before the labor of interpretation has been undertaken.

Rahner does develop a very concrete phenomenological or existential grasp of the question of God in his meditation on modern secular experience of the absence of God from the natural world, with its un-broken chains of causal reason. But here again he seems to move too quickly from this experience to a theological explanation: "This experience is incorrectly interpreted if one thinks that only this-worldly, a-theistic experience is given to the human being. It must rather be shown how the human being always already transcends this experience, so that this experience of troubled atheism basically only indicates the growth of God in the mind of humanity" (1975:216). A more complex and flexible account of how the conventional dependently arisen world attests the silent ultimacy of the divine needs to be liberated from the rather rigid schema of finite and infinite being. This schema appears when Rahner denies that the scientific world-picture can be what is first and fundamental in human existence: "Prior to it lies the truth of religion, the knowledge of God and faith in God's historical revelation" (218). Religion in its concrete Christian form raises its head rather suddenly here. This sudden leap thwarts the possibility of teasing out more fully what the world of science might have to teach us about the presence and absence of the divine. The conventionalities of science, art, and religion point to ultimacy in a more subtle way than this. They are not simply finite representations, all indiscriminately surpassed by the unrepresentability of the infinite. When science and religion are in contradiction, Rahner urges, each should examine itself critically. "But religion is not thereby simply handed over to science and its world-picture. It is of higher, because earlier, origin, since it springs from a more original realization of human existence. All world-formation, all world-representation, all ordering conceptual grasp of the plurality of things takes place in the forward grasping toward the unrepresentable, the inconceivable, that which is not a part of the world and the world-picture, but as an inconceivable infinity stands behind all plural world-actuality" (218). *Begreifen* of the finite is carried by a *Vorgreifen* toward the infinite, which is *unbegreiflich*. In placing science, as well as history and the arts and concrete religious languages, within his inveterate epistemological schema based on the distinction of the categorical and the transcendental, does Rahner allow these finite realities to speak for themselves, and, as their conventionality becomes apparent, of the ultimacy that they attest or secrete?

Rahner notes that the articulation of the *Vorgriff* toward the transcendent in the language of scripture makes modern believers uncomfortable, but "this inhibiting sense of the 'inexactness' and 'pictoriality' of all our talk about God, even as it emerges in revelation itself, is our fate" (220). Had Rahner been a pure philosopher, he might have swept biblical imagery aside and constructed a systematic rational metaphysics of the divine. In fact he bends his thought to a constant listening to scripture and church tradition. But his listening is most eager when that tradition comes halfway to meet his speculative quest. He does not revel in scriptural languages that thwart that quest and does not bring out their intelligibility that is on another plane than metaphysics. A flexible Buddhist sense of the variety of possible "skillful means" might have allowed him to embrace the inexactness and picturality of scripture in a less inhibited way. The "fate" he speaks of could just be a hermeneutical blockage caused by an imperfectly resolved attachment to a certain picture of metaphysical intelligibility. His account of religious language stresses its awkwardness and impotence. Theology knows, he insists, that for all its efforts at interpretation and clarification "its speech about God is always and *in principle* a stammering"; and so theology is "a gaze into the clear night of divine mysteries" (220). This is a replay of a classical trope of negative theology, but it does not do justice to the concrete functioning of religious language in its interplay of ultimate and conventional.

Surprisingly the paragraph just quoted has the heading "Christianity and Religions" (219), yet it makes no mention of the religions. This suggests a vague wish to reach out to the variety of religious language, which falls short in a resigned reflection on the limits of all possible religious language. In general Rahner has a rather simplistic view of the role of language. He optimistically thinks that the demythologization of scripture has little effect on its meaning: "For one thing 'mythological' utterances retain their meaning perfectly even when the world-picture that once provided the frame for their development has fallen away. And second, that meaning is precisely that which was intended at that time" (221). The mode of the utterance changes but its content remains. A hermeneutically sophisticated theology would have to take the historical and linguistic embeddedness of religious ideas much more seriously than this. The possessor of a true metaphysical system, such as transcendental Thomism or Hegelianism, is in danger of thinking that all the deliveries of experience have been foreseen in principle so that there is no need to explore them too diligently. Rahner did not escape this danger.

The adroit dance between tradition and critique that Rahner stages in so many of his measured, sober, pithy essays, never without a twinkle of humor, is well worth studying today. On a wide range of theological questions, he has provided Catholics with the key to a sensible and rational approach, dissolving painful conundrums. If Rahner is held captive, ultimately, by his own "picture," he has liberated the rest of us from the grip of other pictures, narrow and oppressive ones, so effectively that he must no doubt be considered the foremost intellectual liberator of twentieth-century Catholicism. Rahner is able to "show the fly the way out of the fly-bottle" (Wittgenstein) precisely because he himself has internalized so deeply the claims of dogmatic tradition. As one would expect in this situation, sometimes his liberation falters halfway, and we need to use Rahner to go beyond Rahner. The faltering can often be ascribed to a recurrence of an urge for metaphysical, speculative explanation where a fuller trust in the phenomena would have been more appropriate.

A striking example of Rahner's dexterity in applying to dogma the arts of metaphysical revisionism is his treatment of another venerable Catholic dogma, scriptural inerrancy. He steps forward as a champion of the magisterial doctrine, yet navigates toward an acceptance of error throughout the Bible that seems incompatible with the claims of Leo XIII in *Providentissimus Deus*, retained in the footnotes of Vatican II's Constitution on Divine Revelation. Rahner's conclusion is that "something disordered on the inner-worldly plane, and the error connected therewith, can mediate a salvational action" (1975:234). The transcendental horizon takes such minor problems on the empirical, categorical plane in its stride. Whether this can deal satisfactorily with some of the problems Rahner himself notes, such as the divinely prescribed genocide in such texts as Numbers 31 and 1 Samuel 15, remains doubtful. A more relaxed hermeneutical phenomenology of how divine truth is enshrined in scripture alongside scandalous all-too-human perversions of it is impeded not only by the official doctrine but also by Rahner's metaphysical model of the categorical and the transcendental, which again functions here to dispense from a fuller engagement with the phenomena in their unpredictability. The categorical-transcendental distinction allows him to give full autonomy to the human Jesus on the empirical and categorical level, so that Jesus, too, can have fallen into error. On Jesus's expectation of an imminent parousia he writes: "In this 'error' he would merely have shared our lot. . . . A genuinely human consciousness *must* have an unknown future before it" (238). Note that this interplay of categorical and transcendental chimes with the relation of the humanity and divinity of Christ as clarified at the Council of Chalcedon in 451. Rahner strongly insists on Chalcedon's teaching that the humanity and divinity are "unmixed," in contrast to the neo-Chalcedonian interpretation that prevailed in slogans such as "One of the Trinity was crucified." Intent on keeping the Chalcedonian horizons open, he argues that even the expression "Jesus is God" is an indirect statement permitted by the *communicatio idiomatum*, not a massive identification. But then, once again, he becomes bogged down in metaphysical ideas on how God unites himself with humanity, how God can "become" in the other. Perhaps a due sense of divine ultimacy would rule out such language of a "theology from above," treating narratives about divine action as just poetic skillful means for articulating consciousness of breakthroughs of ultimacy in our human historical world.

Rahner's sense of grace—increasingly vivid and present throughout his career—is a theological surplus that transcends the metaphysical horizon and that is well brought into play in his vision of the hypostatic union as a high point in humanity's response to the presence of divine grace, building on Aquinas's thought on the *gratia unionis*, and further back on Origen's conception of the preexistent soul of Christ as divinized in virtue of its loving adherence to the divine Logos. But he cannot help metaphysicizing grace as divine self-communication just as the Incarnation is metaphysicized as God becoming man in the other. His slogan "Chalcedon is a beginning, not an end" begins to look suspiciously like a plea for treating Chalcedon as the launchpad for elaborate metaphysical speculation. One might oppose a counterslogan:

"Chalcedon is an end, not a beginning." That is, Chalcedon is the best that can be said about Christ within the horizons of metaphysical clarification, and now we need to step back to a fuller apprehension of the meaning of Christ at the phenomenological level. The metaphysical clarification is of the conventional order, a skillful disposition of our concepts, and becomes unskillful when it arrogates to itself an ultimate status.

The struggle between phenomenological and metaphysical leanings in Rahner's dealing with the complex doctrines we have mentioned might be charted at great length in fuller detail. Taken as a whole, Rahner's defense-cum-deconstruction of traditional doctrine is an exemplary performance. He translates implausible traditional claims into terms that make them intelligible and credible in today's horizon. His revisionist view allows biblical and Christian history to be itself, without apologetical defensiveness or suspension of critique before beautiful legend. Going beyond Rahner, we need to broaden the scope of what is understood by tradition and by critique as we pursue the interaction between them. Rahner's focus on dogmas as the principal data to be dealt with, and his heavy reliance on a number of speculative, metaphysical insights as the instruments of his rethinking of dogma, imply a narrowing of the scene of theological inquiry that can give his reasoning an archaic cast. Often he brings a line of reasoning to its climax in some ingenious rephrasing of classical doctrine in terms reminiscent of German idealism. With the passage of time, these exhibitions of speculative prowess come to seem rather fragile. A fuller reflection on the historical and linguistic texture of the doctrinal elements and of his own intellectual choices could open up his thinking to a more sophisticated interplay between the full sweep of Christian and religious history on the one hand and the broad landscape of contemporary thought on the other. Then Christian theology would be well positioned for a deeper dialogue with Judaism, Islam, Hinduism, and Buddhism, no longer locating them on metaphysical maps but eagerly debating with them on the questions and phenomena at the core of religious history, about which these traditions have so much to learn from one another.

Rahner's ineffable God, before whom we can only fall dumb, but whose loving presence is what is nearest to hand, has all the marks of ultimacy, and when he does not view the categorical world in an overly abstract way (falling into traditional rhetoric about the sad limits of finitude) he helps us to see it as a set of props or pointers, conventional skillful means which lead the mind to God or become gracious signs of God's self-communication. But his awareness of ultimacy would be still deeper if he freed it from fixed conceptions of the relation between the human finite and the divine infinite, which themselves should be assessed as conventional representations. Then his awareness of the conventional texture of the categorical world could also become more free and flexible, allowing him to taste emergences of ultimacy in many different conventional spheres, no longer seeking to resolve them in a single image of the divine. These remarks are only a fragile pointer to a vast task, that of constructing a revisionist understanding of the achievements of Western metaphysics and metaphysical theology in light of Buddhist conceptions of the status and functioning of conventional language.

Chapter Five

SCRIPTURE AND REVELATION

The withdrawal of God, or at least of God-as-origin, that is observed in modern cosmic and epistemological inquiry is mirrored also in the withdrawal of the historic origins of biblical and Christian tradition, which slip away from us uncannily. There is a parallel between how God becomes harder to find in the pages of the Bible and in the book of nature: the universe can be read as the result of an immanent process of evolution, and the Bible appears as the product of the historical evolution of religious ideas. The Bible can still address conscience, but there is a sharp gap between our current use of biblical texts and the almost magical status the Bible enjoyed in former times, which encouraged the extravagances of both literalist and allegorical readings. The moral or spiritual response to biblical words cultivated in the practice of *lectio divina* sharply contrasts with the critical scholarly analysis of their composition, just as the feelings that nature inspires seem to contradict the reductive aspect of evolutionary science. If on the cosmic level God "has created a situation in which his own involvement is so totally hidden that the process gives every appearance of operating without any guiding hand at all," in other words "a situation in which it is reasonable for us to believe that he is not involved" (Rachels, 125), it seems that *mutatis mutandis* the same is true of scripture.

The origins of Israel seem today indistinguishable from the cultures of the surrounding peoples, and the great structure of the covenantal religion seems to have been put solidly in place only by the religious leadership of postexilic Israel. The Bible's constructions are characterized not by a splendid isolation from the pagan lore of non-Israelite nations but on the contrary by a massive absorption of foreign influence. Antonius Gunneweg (211–24) points out that the patriarchal narratives point to a pre-Israelitic, pre-Yahwistic polytheism, whose gods were only retrospectively identified with Yahweh; that the story of Joseph depends on the international phenomenon of Wisdom literature; that the tales of desert wanderings go back to local stories about particular oases; that Sinai is but one of the many holy mountains of old religious lore; that the Law revealed there has close connections with common Oriental law and may be identical with the law of Canaan; that the cult of Israel exhibits many parallels with Canaanite and other Oriental religions; that the temple of Solomon followed foreign models; that the Jerusalem priesthood and monarchy derive from old Canaanite sources; that Israel's historicization of the Canaanite calendar by connecting it with particular events of salvation conversely brings salvation history back to the cyclic annual recurrence of mythical time; that the parallel between the Exodus and the cosmic mastery of chaos in the creation myth is but one example of this. The rhythms and the atmosphere of a mythic cosmos are far more present in Old Testament religion than we often realize. What distinguishes Israel is the critical discernment it brings to the traditions it has received from elsewhere (though similar efforts of discernment can be found in other Oriental religions, as Gunneweg remarks). The distinctiveness of biblical faith emerges only within a context of porousness to other traditions. Perhaps today we can bring the distinctiveness of Christian faith into new perspective only by recognizing its porousness to secular wisdom and other religions, which are reshaping the self-understanding of faith. Within that new perspective, the Bible can speak to us afresh with a different kind of authority, and with no effort to conceal its all-too-human aspects.

The composition of scripture has been demystified by source analysis, notably the documentary hypothesis of the Pentateuch, according to which a final editor or editors spliced together four documents, each with its own internal compositional history. The demise of this hypothesis has so often been proclaimed that one would imagine that there is no need to speak any longer of Yahwist, Elohist, Deuteronomist, or Priestly writers, and that teachers of "the Bible as literature" may breathe a sigh of relief that they need no longer bother their undergraduates with so complicated and annoying a matter. Yet it proves impossible to advance very far in a close reading of Genesis without noting at least that the juxtaposition and interplay of J and P are essential to what the editors of this great work of literature achieved. Meanwhile alternative theories are often either vague or farfetched. An advantage of source criticism is that it reveals collective rather than individual authorship as the scriptural norm. Bart Ehrman (2012) deplores the rampant pseudonymity of scripture as fakery, but it could be taken as marking the inspired witness of an entire community, gathering their best thought and narration around a hallowed name, be it Moses, David, Solomon, Isaiah, Paul, John, or Peter. To hear the Word of God means to hear a vast chorus of voices from our Jewish and Christian past and to be caught up in a great conversation launched in the biblical texts, with all the contradictions and mistakes that one might expect, and sustained ever since in the endless play of interpretation. That something speaks to us and claims us with divine authority out of the heart of this tradition is the reality that theology seeks to clarify. The opening of the contemporary believing mind to the full dimensions of this reality is hindered by overprotective safeguards, such as rigid doctrines of inspiration and inerrancy, worry about historicity, devotion to medieval allegorical traditions, insistence on the total canon of scripture as the framework for valid interpretation, and indeed some of the emphases in the *sola scriptura* ideology of the Reformers.

Origins are never as pure as one would wish. To probe them historically is to find that luminous words of foundation—"Let there be light!," Gabriel's annunciation to Mary, Jesus's founding of his church on the Petrine rock—may be screens behind which lurks some primal randomness and contingency. Naturalistic and materialistic philosophies see all ethical, metaphysical, and religious achievement as mere sublimation of animal instincts and refuse the rope ladder thrown down by metaphysics in its claim that the entire process of evolution is guided from afar by the Good or Truth or Reason: "Metaphysical philosophy helped us out of this quandary up to now, by denying that the higher arose from the lower and by claiming for the more highly valued things a miraculous origin, directly from the core and essence of the 'thing in itself.'. . . Humans prefer to banish questions of origin and beginnings from their mind" (Nietzsche, *Human, All Too Human*, para. 1). True, phenomena of a higher order emerge in the course of evolution or of history, and they withstand cynical reductionism. But these phenomena are elusive, receding horizons, which the aesthetic, ethical, intellectual, and religious traditions of humanity point to and reach after, and which make themselves majestically present only in rare moments. When we freeze and objectify them as securely given foundations we are no longer drawn by their elusive withdrawal (as Platonic dialogue or dialectic is drawn by the elusiveness of the Good). Just as Nietzschean genealogy can dislodge our conventional ideas of ethics and aesthetics and relaunch the questions of justice and art, so historical research into Christian origins dislodges conventional images of Christ and of God and reopens the interplay between history and transcendence.

SCRIPTURE AS A CONVENTIONAL VEHICLE OF ULTIMACY

Over against the idea that the Bible is merely a human record of past religious experiences, twentieth-century theologians have promoted the notion of revelation—not as a source of cognitive information but as a total event, a self-communication of God himself (see Eicher). As heard by the community of faith, the Bible becomes the Word of God, carrying ultimate authority and conveying the presence of the divine.

An element of mystification in this notion is betrayed by the tendency to see only the New Testament and the Christ event as revelation in the full sense; no religion matches Christianity in its emphatic claim "to have proceeded from the revelation of the living God" (Kaftan, 41); without this fulfillment the preparatory Old Testament revelation remains only "a torso"; "The outpouring of the Spirit in the community is the concluding limb of revelation" (48). Fulfillment-thinking takes its cue from John 14:9, "He who sees me has seen the Father." Yet it may be possible to read John in a way that goes back to the mediating, distancing medium of the Torah. How does Jesus reveal the Father? Through the mediation of his teachings and his works (Jn 14:10–12); to "see the Father" means to be sent back to these earthly signs. "We have seen his glory" (Jn 1:14)—in the cross and the modest, elusive Resurrection appearances—not in a naked blaze that would place the Christian revelation on a completely different plane from the Jewish. "The Torah was given through Moses, grace and truth came through Jesus Christ" (Jn 1:17); the two are not placed in stark opposition but linked as grace to grace—*kharin anti kharitos* (1:16); "grace and truth" are the *hesed wa emeth*, loving-kindness and faithfulness, that are the heart of Torah and the defining qualities of the God of Israel.

Perhaps we need to think of revelation in a more low-key way, as a quality that may attach to scripture at any point but that cannot be distilled as a pure essence of a different nature than the mundane concerns of the historical and wisdom books of the Old Testament. The cult of revelation among twentieth-century theologians glossed over the difficulties raised by critical historical scholarship by insisting in a somewhat idealizing way on the core reality underlying the words of scripture and the events they describe. Revelation was a special kind of "thing in itself," a noumenon that was also a phenomenon and could take in its stride all the complexities and inconsistencies of scripture, seen as a groping human attestation to this Word event. As a result, a demystified acceptance of the human and historical texture of scripture could become normative in the world of scriptural scholarship, while its impact on doctrine was softened. Yet even here the split between scholarship and faith, denounced by the Anti-Modernist Oath, continues in a milder form. To heal this residual tension, some attacked recourse to revelation as leading to a "revelatory positivism" (Fisher, 306–40) and as failing to recognize that "revelation and the cultural-cum-historical expression of it are not to be had separately" (Schillebeeckx, 48), while some suggested that the notion of revelation is superfluous (Downing). The embeddedness of revelational language in literary conventions, which permitted a repertory of revelation effects, invited an unmasking of the ultimacy claimed by revelation and its reduction to merely conventional status. Yet when the conventions attract the investment of faith and are acted out in adoration and praise they again and again become occasions of breakthrough to ultimacy; this experience is the empirical warrant for talk of revelation.

The deflation of such unitary categories as revelation or the Christ event, allied with a new appreciation of the historical processes by which the elements of Jewish and Christian faith were set in place, brings a new distribution of emphasis, with the weight falling more on the ethical, prophetic, and spiritual wisdom of Israel, Jesus, and the early Christians and less on miracles and revelations from above. Demythologization spells a comprehensive transmutation of the signs and wonders of ancient narrative into a searching spiritual vision persuasive to post-Enlightenment humanity. If God is at work in history, across the activities of Israel, Jesus, and the church, it is in an oblique and opaque manner. We cannot rip through the texture of history in order to grasp the divine revelation and activity in naked form. The great myths of revelation—from God's calls to Abraham and Moses to the stories of the Transfiguration and Pentecost—are pointers to the vision emergent in the centuries of struggle and debate recorded in scripture. The divine impact on history is quieter and more realistically embedded than traditional theology suggests, and it is entirely mediated by human responses. Scripture records a history of faith, and of the discernment of faith; its impact as revelation, its ultimacy, is secreted within this human history, which lies open to critical view. By reading that record from its peaks, where a transcendent light seems to shine in scripture, faith may discern something that goes beyond the naturalistic frame of understanding.

The earliest Christianity is a foreign country. Its eschatological schemas inherited from Persia, and its expectation of the imminent coming of the Kingdom, are almost incomprehensible to us. Already 1 Clement reduces the "nearness" of the Eschaton to a presence of the omniscient God who watches over our actions; the eschatological events are put off to a distant future; the resurrection of Christ as first fruits of the resurrection of the righteous is no longer lived as the irruption of the end times but can be illustrated by analogies with a seed, or the phoenix, or the alternation of day and night (1 Clem. 24). The delay of the Parousia, and the need to oppose claimed Gnostic revelations that sought to fill the hollow space left by that delay, obliged the church to define itself as an institution and to recuperate the Hebrew scriptures and the traditions of the apostolic generation within a comprehensive dogmatic vision. Protestant theology tried to revive the memory of what came before this emergence of the Great Church, reaching back to the thoroughgoing eschatology that structured the thought of Jesus and Paul, and to the pluralism of praxes and theologies that orthodoxy was to repress. But the eschatological Jesus is also an origin that withdraws. This Jesus, according to Schweitzer, seems to turn his back on the entire Christian tradition. Many recent portraits of Jesus, as one full of the Spirit or as a nomadic sage comparable to the Cynics, seem to dodge the strangeness of his eschatological attitude. The contemporary church's eschatological awareness presupposes a vision of evolution and history with no New Testament counterpart; it has been built in an oblique relation to the teaching of Jesus, which is an irrecoverable point of origin. It is only in the here and now that any religion has its meaning and coherence, and it is useless to clutch at any past landmark as defining once and for all who we are and where we stand.

Johannes Weiss hailed the transition from a theology centered on Pauline justification to one that takes the principal theme of Jesus's preaching, the proclamation of the Kingdom, as its point of departure, making possible a reintegration of dogmatics with ethics and religious experience (Weiss, 3). He noted the danger that a dogmatics using biblical concepts may lose sight of their original shape as it manipulates them in view of current goals and perspectives. The constant recollection of the differences between the original bearing of biblical ideas and what becomes of them in their current use is a condition of responsibility and transparency in the practice of theology. In doing justice to history one assumes at the same time responsibility for decisions that history cannot sanction but that new questions make necessary.

Our use of eschatology stumbles against the fact that "we no longer share the eschatological feeling that 'the figure of this world is passing away.' We no longer pray, 'May grace come and may the world perish,' but we live in joyful trust that this world will become more and more the scene of a 'humanity of God'" (Weiss, 67). Weiss retained for eschatology only an existential use—to live with the consciousness of having to die—and it seems that even Bultmann subscribes to this limitation to the individual plane. The renewal of eschatological thought in prophetic liberation theologies does not rejoin the biblical world but finds a dynamic equivalent for it, more satisfying than that of the centuries of Catholic and Protestant individualism.

Contemporary scholars accept the discontinuities between the historical Jesus and the Pauline or Johannine Christ and often seek to root faith in a better knowledge of Jesus in his Jewish context. Already fifty years ago "The new hermeneutic had in effect gone behind the kerygma's coded mythological language, which has made Jesus's decisive significance intelligible back then, but unintelligible today (Ebeling)" (Robinson, 9). If we accept the gap between the historical Jesus and the Christ of the church's faith, then dogmas appear as fragile pointers to the significance of Jesus, and no longer as the very foundation of the Christian vision. It is insufficient to recall dogmas to the "Christ event," since even this expression is a mystifying reification which at best takes us back to the varying theological visions of the significance of Christ in the New Testament rather than to the historical Jesus. We need to step back further, accepting that Jesus and the interpretations of Jesus form a history that cannot be perfectly surveyed. Jesus launched a new style of thinking of and relating to God, bringing a new richness to the Jewish traditions and releasing the power and illumination of the Spirit, a new nearness of God. In seeking to name a distinctive or unique or absolute status of Jesus, his Christhood, or his divinity, one must begin from this historical trajectory in all its humanness, contingency, and finitude. This is the "flesh" that is "the hinge of salvation" (Tertullian), and the constructions of dogma lose their weight if they are not referred back to this fleshly history. The church's faith takes the words and deeds of Jesus as an address to humankind of God's eternal Word. But that faith is falsified if it impedes in any way the study of the historical humanity of Jesus in its context, let the chips fall where they may. Serenely accepting that the traditions about the words and deeds of Jesus offer topics for reflective judgment, we relinquish the fretful quest for historical certitudes and impregnable dogmatic horizons. In all its fragile conventionality this web of traditions still functions well to convey the vision and presence of Christ and the actions they enable.

"The peace that dialectical theology thought it could seal with historicism has turned out to be illusory" (Künneth, 19). Barth had such a capacious understanding of the relationship between the Word of God and the scriptural texts that attest it that he could, in principle, allow those texts the entire freedom of their complex history, retaining as essential only their effective function, particularly when used in church, as enabling encounter with the Word. In practice his dealings with scripture are still constrained by an orthodox slant. To some extent he realized that orthodoxy is not an absolute rule but rather the indication of a general direction. It is not clearly defined but cuts out a clearing or horizon that is the best it can do at a particular moment. Barth meditated on the provisory character of dogma in a rather transcendental mode, making it illustrative of human weakness and finitude as we struggle to understand and witness to revelation, and did not focus on how every element of scriptural and of church discourse is historical through and through, and thus thoroughly revisable. But historicity has become less hard-edged as we become increasingly aware of the literary character of all our sources. Theology is no longer so prone to stumble on some hard fact to be glossed over but meets rather a skein of flimsy literary re-creations that invites imaginative flexibility. The insistent quest for a historical Jesus scarcely escaped becoming a foundationalism, an effort to put the real Jesus in his place and to view any account falling short of perfect historical accuracy as therefore secondary and negligible. Yet the alleged secondariness turns out to be the very fabric of all our traditions, perhaps the very fabric of textuality in general. Nothing ultimate can be definitively pinned down amid this play of conventions, which is best appropriated by a quiet play of reflective historical judgment. Such judgment locates historical truth less in assured positive atomistic facts than in the pluralistic texture of the discourses testifying to an event that cannot be apprehended independently of faith and imagination. The Bible's frequent blitheness about facts is not due to fuzzy spiritualizing or docetism, but rather reflects a concern more with the truth of events than with mere factual details. Sometimes when the Bible tosses out a piece of factual information, for example, that Abraham's steward was Eliezer of Damascus (Gen 15:2), it seems to mock our historical curiosity, creating the literary "reality effect" discussed by Roland Barthes. Yet concern with historical fact cannot be dropped either, for it is a control on idealizing methods of reading scripture, such as those of patristic allegory or the "biblicism" into which Barth sometimes slides.

The effort to overcome metaphysical objectifications by a turn to the subject has been afoot in theology since Schleiermacher. In this turn, the agency that animates and gives perspective to theological thought becomes faith, religious experience, the openness of mind to the infinite (Rahner's *Vorgriff*), or intellectual and religious conversion (Lonergan). Barth starts from a synthesis of object and subject, founding theology on the Word of God, not in a positivist way, for the Word is not bluntly laid down in scripture and dogma; rather, it draws a response of (ecclesial) faith, which includes the activity of critical interpretative reception of scripture and dogma as attesting the Word. Defined thus broadly, and nourishing a constant movement of reflection within the faith that embraces it, the event of revelation leaves the field wide open for the exercise of judgment. Revelation and faith become transcendental instances of judgment, critique, and even deconstruction. Barth becomes a powerful resource for theologizing today when read deconstructively as one who "demythologized dogmatics . . . without actually realizing it" (Robinson, 4). First, he subordinated dogma to the act of faith that hears the divine Word. Dogma is not revelation-truth but is oriented to it, not the divine Word but a human word (*KD* 1/2:283). "Dogmas are not *veritates a Deo formaliter revelatae*. In dogmas it is the church of the past that speaks" (281). Faith accepts the Bible as God's Word and does not subject it to any external justifying criteria (278), as Protestant liberalism is accused of doing. But deconstruction comes in when we ask what exactly is the Word of God, for it turns out to be unmasterable, uncircumventable in its ultimacy, and as such has a critical, destabilizing impact not only on the human words of dogma but on those of scripture, frail vehicles of the Word. The ultimacy of the Word goes hand in hand with the sheer conventionality of its multiple literary vehicles. Broadening Barth's perspective, we can say that the criteriology of liberal theology is out of order only when it would supplant the Word as supreme criterion or impose a dogmatic positivist conception of what really "counts" in scripture. Working on the conventional texture of scripture, the modern Enlightenment criteria can purify and enrich the reception of the Word, but they need also to register their own conventionality, as but strategic moments within the entire hermeneutical process (which does not mean, to repeat, that this process can be brought back safely into the fold of traditional scriptural interpretation; the process is more open than either the traditional imagination or its Enlightenment dismantling envisaged).

What is *given* in Christianity? If the religions are human constructions, devised to keep up human morale in face of the inclemencies of nature and the catastrophes of history, who is to say that they are not a powerhouse of legend fabrication, so that the tales about Jesus would carry no more weight than those about Elijah and Elisha? Some, such as the Anglican theologians Richard Holloway and Andrew Furlong, subordinate the figure of Jesus to a larger horizon of religious imagination and identify as the basic datum of faith not Jesus Christ but the values he incarnates. Must Christianity, having insisted on de-absolutizing all other religions, now de-absolutize itself? Christian faith embraces the space opened by the Christ event as equal in its dimensions to ultimate truth (the Logos), a space by definition unsurpassable. The historical figures of Christ rejoin that space not by their positive content but by the modesty of their withdrawal, the way they indicate what surpasses them, that which is "greater than I" (Jn 14:28). One might go so far as to say that Jesus classes himself as a skillful means for igniting awareness of the ultimate divine horizon. Yet this ultimate reality, in the New Testament vision, does not abandon Jesus as a vehicle that has served its purpose. The vision of God in Christ reconciling the world to himself (2 Cor 5:19), or of the fullness of godhead dwelling in Christ bodily (Col 2:9), or of God's Word tabernacling in the flesh and manifesting its glory (Jn 1:14), indicates that Jesus is not merely a teacher of values but in the fullness of his paschal identity the embodiment of the divine as saving process. To abstract from Jesus in order to grasp the process itself in its purity, or to universalize the reference to Jesus into one to all humanity, is to rob God's saving presence of concrete embodiment.

If earliest Christianity is difficult of access, Constantinian Christendom has become foreign to us in a different way. It is less incomprehensible, but it seems a dream, at times a nightmare, from which we have awoken. Some of its great figures can still inspire us by some aspects of their thought or spirituality, but they all belong to a radically different world from ours. The more we study that past, the more we sound its obsolescence—again a ground that trembles, an origin that withdraws. Sloterdijk takes Thomas Mann's portrayal of Joseph, "or better the Josephian position as such, which one must characterize as being doomed to success in Egypt" (198–99), as a key to three generations of Jewish dream interpreters: Freud conquered bourgeois society by analyzing the dreams of its leaders and their wives; Walter Benjamin and Ernst Bloch took the subversion further through "interpreting the signs and traces with which, according to the Messianic mode of interpretation, humanity from ancient times anticipated communism"; Derrida's "radical semiology" outbids psychoanalysis and messianic hermeneutics, showing that "the signs of being never yield the fullness of meaning that they promise to give" (200), in Heidegger's dream of the "mittences" of Being. Many thinkers apply the same demystified hermeneutic to the dreams of religion, and a few theologians, such as Michel de Certeau and Jacques Pohier, have attempted to react to this, but their effort has remained marginal.

Structuralism and poststructuralism inflict a humiliation on Christian theology comparable to those linked to the names of Copernicus, Darwin, and Freud, or to Kant and Marx. If St. Bernadette Soubirous was correct in teaching that "it takes many humiliations to create humility," the epistemological restrictions imposed on theology today may make it more deeply humble, and thus more authentically Christian. Catherine Cornille (forthcoming) associates doctrinal humility with a sense of the "perfectibility" of Christian doctrine, but perhaps this word evokes too much the accumulative and systematizing attitude to doctrinal development, rather than the chastening that is currently imposed on us.

Umberto Eco wrote: "Semiotics owes it to itself to define its limits of applicability. . . . It cannot be at the same time an operational technique and a knowledge of the Absolute. If it is an operational technique, it should refuse to say *what* occurs at the origin of communication; if it is knowledge of the absolute, it cannot say *how* communication functions" (quoted in Moingt 2004:108). As judgment, theology has a divinatory character, aiming to approach a knowledge of the absolute; but the more it invests in method, the more it becomes an operative technique, losing confidence in the power of mere reflection. Eco's question, taken up by de Certeau, is one on which "all theologians should long reflect before setting to work, if they want to make faith thinkable in the epistemic fields of our time" (Moingt 2004:108). De Certeau cast discredit on a hermeneutical theology that in its critique of tradition maintained continuity with the origins. The best method for espousing the "founding rupture" effected by Jesus would be to open up to the ruptures of the present, the time of "exploded Christianity," even being ready to see Christianity disappear if such be its fate: "It may be that Christianity or, more generally, religion is but a historical figure of the major problems of man in society, and that others are replacing it today" (Dosse, 206). What becomes of Jesus in that perspective? "Christianity is only a particular strand in the entirety of human history and cannot take credit for that history or speak in the name of the whole universe" (203). This is reductionist historicism, which hermeneutics might correct by detecting in the message of particular historical figures their universal intention and the possibility of recovering that universal relevance at least in part. The universal significance of the messages of Jesus and the Buddha is in part verified in a series of particular encounters throughout history. When the Gospel is exposed to the whirlwind of the human sciences and the kaleidoscope of religions, its irreducible identity, its divine character, appears in a new light, as it takes a more modest status, renouncing old claims of universal conquest and adopting a posture of dialogue with the other traditions that complete it.

The disquiet of de Certeau echoes the question of the Modernists thus formulated by Pierre Colin: "How can the gaze of faith accommodate the application to biblical exegesis and history of dogma of that other, scientific gaze that has its own norms, which are quite independent of religious authority?" (Dosse, 131). Can our conviction that we are engaged with ultimate truth be reconciled with this consignment of biblical and doctrinal tradition to the lowly realm of human conventions and historical contingencies? Can we draw here on the paradoxical assurance that "the foolishness of God is wiser than men" (1 Cor 1:25); "my power is made perfect in weakness" (2 Cor 12:9)? Could the weak human texture of our traditional languages be the very mark of their authenticity as bearers of divine revelation (and of their accord with Buddhist discernment of the "emptiness" of ultimate reality)? Against a propagandist outlook that wants faith to become again invulnerable, impregnable, we learn to accept that "the believer's every word bears the wound from which our Christian language suffers today" (Colin, quoted in Dosse, 125). This is not a downbeat defeatism but an active self-humbling, a relearning of Christian speech as *sermo humilis*. Direct reference to "the existence of God" or "values" or "Life" is waylaid by the poststructuralist imp and sent circulating in the dance of signifiers. Yet the two worlds here clashing are not absolute quantities, with defined and unalterable frontiers. A higher hermeneutics, something like a deconstructed Barthianism, might negotiate the conditions of their interaction, and of the underlying interaction of conventional and ultimate truth. The acuity of critical historical scholarship can be taken up by the imagination of faith, which can revel in the plurality of finite and most often obsolete religious visions, sensing that the movement of life underlying them is not discredited, but rather confirmed, by the obsolescence of its historical expressions. The alienation and indirection that structuralist exteriority inflicts on the language of faith set the context for a new spurt of belief, a practical, adult investment of religious imagination under the constraints of what is epistemologically viable today.

Archaic religious identity formations are a source of perturbation and violence in the contemporary world. For the sake of peaceful cooperation among nations, they need to be replaced with more functional conceptions of religious identity and of the role of religion in practical life. But to engineer this shift is no easy matter. Philosophical and theological arguments can contribute to conscientize believers about the need to invest more in reason and dialogue and less in primeval instincts that wrongly call themselves faith. But arguments have little power against instincts. To bring real conversion one needs to engage the instincts themselves and turn their energy in a new direction. When one recognizes that what one took to be unalloyed faith is in fact in large part compounded of fear for one's own identity and hatred of the threatening other, or when one sees this writ large in violent acts, one may learn a discernment that allows a new investment of the energy of faith. That is, faith must treat its own language more lightly, as "mere straw" (Aquinas), serving as a provisional and flexible indicator of ultimacy in the very confession of its own nonultimacy.

Control of primitive instincts by high theology is not the full therapy required by the religions today. Monotheism, once the unquestionable gold standard of religious truth, is increasingly seen by religious thinkers as a problematic construction, one that can be salvaged from association with fundamentalism and violence only by critical discernment of its buried liberative potential. It, too, must be numbered among the hallowed conventions of religious discourse, pointing to an ultimate significance that eludes its direct grasp. The word *significance* sounds reductive or evasive, but if we think of this significance as ultimate truth, as the final horizon that the biblical kerygma attests, the task is to allow this ultimacy to emerge convincingly as we wrestle with the inherited conventional languages in a double-pronged hermeneutic, which both fully opens up to the contingent, all-too-human texture of those languages and appreciates the glimmers of ultimacy that they can serve to convey. All the positive data of scripture are indeed cultural-cum-historical products, but this web of conventions can nonetheless be cherished as staging breakthroughs of ultimacy. The inerrancy and inspiration of scripture are problematic doctrines when stated bluntly; but scripture becomes inerrant and inspired when its words take on an ultimate or revelatory quality in contemplative reception by the church or the individual. This potency of scripture does not depend on an artificial spiritualization or allegorization of the texts. Rather, when one lets scripture fully manifest its conventional texture, in a kenosis of all attempts to vamp up the text in the desired theological direction, then one can tune in afresh to the use or function of the text as staging an address from the divine or to the divine. Even the naming of God can be seen as a conventional skillful means, yet one still capable of triggering a disclosure effect, a breakthrough of ultimacy.

LACK AT THE ORIGIN

Whether one is a believer or an unbeliever, the Moroccan Jewish psychoanalyst Daniel Sibony claims, religions are manifestly displaying a pathology, an anxiety about identity, which needs to be treated. He proposes that in recognizing their sickness the religions will also find a constructive and peaceful relationship to one another:

> Could these three monotheistic currents one day tolerate and forgive one another, not because they concern the same God and are "brothers" (that kind of fraternity produces more wars than agreements, more ruptures than ententes), but because they will recognize in themselves the same deficiency, the same type of infidelity to what founds them; because they will recognize themselves as children of the same original lack; each marked by a flaw at the origin, a flaw for which no one is to blame, in any case not one's neighbor, a flaw intrinsic to the human and which other humans outside the religious field face as best they can? (Sibony, 10)

This invitation to go behind the explicit debate back to the unconscious motivations that lead it, and to suspect that the very firmness of our convictions might be the symptom of an obscure lack, will be rejected by some as deriving from a Lacanian dogmatism of "original lack." Marion finds in Gregory of Nyssa, whose desire of God is "nourished by excess, not destroyed by it," a refutation of the Platonic model, "ruling all metaphysics until Lacan," of desire as lack (see Leask and Cassidy, 249). Sibony would no doubt see in this "saturated" plenitude of the divine a projection of desire as lack. In any case, the history of interreligious violence suggests that the pathogenic elements in monotheism are not merely incidental and encourages us to explore the path of this Lacanian suspicion. It may not provide the last word on our religion, but it could reveal all that has to be overcome in order to regain the original freedom to which the monotheisms, in their most enlightened expressions, bear witness. Even if Sibony's view of religion is just another form of reductionism, courtesy of a metaphysics of lack, it is good for religion to be confronted with such critical perspectives and to be chastened by them. To be sure, it is desirable that the psychoanalytical and anthropological critiques of biblical religion be raised to a specifically theological level, by being connected with the manifold critiques of religion within scripture itself.

The religions are fragile, finite constructions, rafts with which to embark trustingly on the ocean of being. That basic trust in being already gives to the religions a positive significance, whatever gaps and errors may subsequently emerge. As each religion discovers its flimsiness, a new sense of commonality with its equally flimsy fellow religions becomes possible. A flaw in the origin generates a perpetual malaise in the further career of a religion, whether it seeks to impose itself by arms or arguments or turns in on itself defensively. No doubt every historical tradition, like every individual life, has some imperfection inscribed in it from the start. A religious tradition need not be constituted at a single origin but may represent a confluence of tributaries, like the Nile. Judaism may have been constituted in the postexilic period, in a critical reception of scattered older traditions. Buddhism, too, is born as a late, reflective reform of previous traditions. Such a perfected classical religion presupposes that the defects of earlier cruder forms have been recognized and overcome. Yet a great religion must continue to work critically on itself. Triumphalism, or the sense of "having arrived" at the religious ideal, brings with it a growing, unacknowledged gap between the religious ideology and the realities of its surrounding context, and a corresponding sense of loss of inner reality. Religions work best when aware of their poverty and incompletion.

Yet none of this undermines the reality of revelation, not as a massive unchanging datum but as a history of fresh encounters with

God in his Word, in Christ, wherever scripture is heard. It may be objected that revelation of the divine is afoot everywhere and that the exceptional status granted to the collection of texts we use as scripture cannot be justified. In practice, however, only scriptural texts address us with divine authority. Even religious scriptures from other traditions, or Christian religious classics such as Augustine's *Confessions*, cannot claim the hearers as immediately and radically in the depths of their conscience; they are at best "spiritual reading." Certainly the labor of the literary artist is aligned with or bears a deep affinity with religion, but the phenomenon of revelation comes to pass on another plane, where literary excellences are forgotten. The role of scripture is inherently other than the effects literature aims at. One can appreciate the Bible as literature, but full understanding of the Bible is expressed in adoration, whereas to adore what a literary work reveals would be not only impious but inappropriate as a literary response.

Between a cool critical or literary assessment of scriptural texts and their actualization in a fully committed act of faith there lies a wide and varied field of hermeneutical engagement with scripture. Theology will not discourage those who use scripture as a repository of cultural wisdom. "So opposed have many atheists been to the content of religious belief that they have omitted to appreciate its inspiring and still valid overall object: to provide us with well-structured advice on how to lead our lives" (De Botton, 111). Torah and Talmud can be seen in this way, but they are open to a dimension that no literary work can claim to represent, namely, the authority of the Lord. Theology stands or falls by the reality of that ultimate dimension, which lies beyond literary sublimity and even ethical wisdom. Dante and Milton simulate quasi-biblical authority, pose as prophets, but readers are well aware that this is a fiction, a literary game. The sublime effects attained by these authors (and which Milton achieved more readily for Satan than for God) are not what scripture is ultimately aiming at. Rather, it aims to bring us into the presence of the living God. One who doubts or disbelieves the reality of God can find a mute replacement, an ersatz, in the sublimities of art—by listening to late Beethoven, for example. But to suppose that the Bible is a human work in just the same sense as Beethoven's quartets is to set off on the wrong track, postponing the encounter with scripture as scripture.

The study of the Bible as literature is illuminating and instructive, but it is only in the space of the theological quest that the biblical words display their full power and authority, not in the classroom but in church. Critical scriptural scholarship and even warm literary appreciation of scripture can seem counterintuitive and profane to the believer, but these levels of understanding have their methods whose integrity must be respected; to flood them with references to doctrinal underpinnings and edifying superstructures is to miss the sturdy human and historical reality of the biblical text. Here again the coolness of secular judgment helps secure the realistic anchorage of theological judgment.

Sibony sees religious traditions as monuments of a lack, mausoleums of the withdrawn origin. Their key sites are often tombs: that of Jesus in Jerusalem, the stūpas containing Buddha relics, the tomb of Imam Husayn at Karbala. To say that the churches are the graves of God corresponds to an aspect of religious consciousness itself, the sense that religious words and gestures have an elegiac character and call out to a God who has withdrawn into a silence like that of the grave. Prayer espouses the retreat of the origin in a leap of trust. Gregory of Nyssa talks of the *epektasis* or stretching of the soul that reaches out to the infinite that the understanding can never grasp. He talks also of the soul as wounded by love of the absent Spouse. The two themes are intimately linked. The negative experience of the unthinkable is transformed into ecstatic delight in the divine or Christic presence, not gratuitously, but as if the lack-of-being, the nostalgia for being, already contained in itself all the elements of the ecstatic discovery or had hollowed out the free space in which the ecstatic encounter could take place. Attention to the unfathomable silence of the ultimate passes over into a hearing of its voice. The impersonality of the silence is what lends authenticity to the personality of the voice that is heard.

What Sibony misses is the dynamic of death and resurrection in this experience. The tomb of Jesus proclaims that "he is not here; he is risen." Negative theology is liable to treat all religious rites and claims as empty tombs, failing to enclose that to which they point. It cultivates a critical consciousness of what is dead in monotheistic traditions in order to bring out more luminously what is living. The text of these traditions is always rich enough to elicit this double reading. A patriarchal God is dead—all the more do we recognize a God who is spirit and life; a tyrannical God is dead—all the more do we celebrate a God of justice and liberation; a God produced by projections and insecurities is dismantled—to clear the space for a discernment of divine depths in the undeniable phenomena of moral conscience, love, and trust in the goodness of being; cumbersome ontologies crumble— opening the possibility of rewriting that which they pointed to in the new key of emptiness.

If the figure of God disappears in Buddhism, that is not in direct opposition to the construction of this figure in the monotheisms. If monotheistic faith learns to live with finitude, allowing God to be empty and ungraspable, and accepting that there is a pluralism of our imaginings of God that demands ongoing critical assessment and creative reappropriation, then it is brought into proximity with a Buddhist critique of notions of the divine. In the monotheisms today the unity of the notion of God is being questioned as the history of its construction becomes better known, and this permits a new dialogue with the scattered Buddhist conceptions that point to the divine dimension. Some analytical philosophers of religion continue to insist on the classical attributes of God as if nothing had basically changed. But the paradigm shift in how we think of the ultimate bypasses such metaphysical regimes. Even classical metaphysics appears as but one limited historical form of witness to the ultimate, and a restorationist metaphysics may be a counterwitness, in that it refuses to follow the paths to ultimacy currently available. Can an emptiness that withdraws attract a faith more serene, open, and trusting than that which has been dedicated for millennia to the God of dogmatic religion? A religious culture that meditates on the signs given by tradition, letting them open questions that carry us to the ultimate, can perhaps reinstate the authentic firmness of faith, not as the massive affirmation of certain knowledge, but as the practice of a path that ceaselessly opens horizons of wisdom.

Chapter Six

RELIGIOUS EXPERIENCE

Mystical experience claims to be an immediate encounter with something ultimate. Does it introduce a knockdown verification that discredits all we have said about indirect methods, the risk of judgment, the retreat of origins, and the conventionality of representations, placing us squarely before the undeniable presence of the reality that grounds any religious discourse? Against those who are skeptical about language and concepts and put all their eggs in the basket of mysticism, it can be argued that mystical phenomena are historical and cultural constructions and thus subject to the same kind of reflection we have brought to bear on religious language. These phenomena are located within a vast contemplative culture that spreads through all religious literature. Placed in this wide context, the force and consistency of mystical testimonies may emerge at the same time as a critical perspective is established. This historical approach allows one to judge religious experience, interpreting it within an integral theological horizon, while at the same time exposing theological frames of thought to the judgment of experience.

There is no need to accord a central and determining authority to privileged religious experiences, since it is the entire reach of Christian experience that constitutes the ground of our knowledge of God.

When Luther declared: "*Sola experientia facit theologum*; only experience makes a theologian" (*WA TR* 1:16), he was referring to this entire stretch, a long practice of the Christian life and study of scripture. Prematurely to identify religious experience with special states is a modern temptation. Michel de Certeau notes that the experimental and systematized mysticism of the seventeenth and eighteenth centuries coincides with the rise of modern experimental science. When Luther talked of experience, it was a question not of such quasi-scientific verification but of the Aristotelian idea of experience as practical familiarity with some matter or art. Mysticism and apophatic theology both promise knowledge of the absolute, from a privileged vantage point. But they turn out to be infiltrated by conventionality and contextuality, sending us back to the incarnational economy as the center of gravity and essential key for a religious life in touch with present realities. The experiential or existential correlate of terms like *God*, *grace*, and *salvation* eludes us, and the quest for it leads some to idolize experience, changing it into an abstract notion. Religion teaches that ordinary experience is pervaded by illusion. But if one seeks to go beneath ordinary experience to find a still more experiential experience, the irony of Lao-tse lies in wait: "Experience is what a comb is to a bald man"—superfluous and without substantial content. The lofty theological terms indicate the entire horizon of the thinking of faith, and do so in very diverse ways depending on changing contexts. In fetishizing privileged experiences we risk losing from view the more subtle presence of God and grace in the entire web of human experience. The awesome authority claimed by mystical experience destabilizes theological judgment, which is unable to find the middle path between credulity and skepticism.

It may seem deflationary to reintegrate the testimonies of mystics in the wider web of common religious experience and the conventional languages of faith, but it is an essential procedure for the practice of steady theological judgment. Embedded in history and in the linguistic constructions of particular cultures, religious experiences do not license a leap outside the incarnate and historical condition of faith. Recognition of this incarnate quality may even provide a more secure defense of the reality of contemplative experience against historicist and psychological reductionism. To draw on Buddhist reflection for light on this mutual imbrication of ultimate and conventional is rather risky, since Buddhism maps the relation of the two truths with specific reference to Buddhist doctrine and to a map of spiritual experience that can even refer to the unimaginable perfection of a Buddha's own experience, in which the distinction of the two truths disappears as being itself a conventional structure that can now be left behind. In this discussion I shall focus only on the deliveries of contemplative experience that are recorded in texts of St. Augustine, who is far from being an esoteric author. I shall try to parse them in terms of ultimacy and conventionality, at a rather pedestrian level, without dragging in the full panoply of Buddhist theorizings of the two truths or imagining what a highly enlightened bodhisattva might say about Augustine's Christian mysticism.

ULTIMACY AND IMMEDIACY

To what extent is mystical experience shaped by language? To what extent does it touch on an absolute, immediately given, beyond the grasp of language? This is a tired old question, but we can perhaps renew it and make it fruitful by drawing again on the topos of the twofold truth. Can there be degrees of ultimacy? This sounds like a contradiction in terms, since the ultimate is the unsurpassable last in a series. Yet the ultimacy that one may discern in Augustine's experience on reading Plotinus in *Confessions* 7 does not stand in the way of the richer and deeper experience recalled in *Confessions* 9. Both are what Marion calls "saturated phenomena," yet they can be related to one another as having greater or lesser depth. If one says that *ultimacy* means just the immediate brunt of the real, irreducible to categorization, swamping the categorical apparatus we might set up to process it, then should we not have to say that physical pain is ultimate in this sense no less than mystical experience (an ultimacy that in the case of pain, too, admits of degrees)? I want to understand ultimacy as *revelatory*, as bringing home the true nature of reality, in a privileged way, such that no later, fuller revelation can undercut what has presented itself here.

If the ultimate nature of things is perceived in religious experience, it seems difficult to maintain that this experience is shaped in depth by the conventions of a given period. Can such an experience be a vehicle of ultimacy in its very conventionality? All experience has an immediate aspect, and accounts of religious experiences often stress their exceptional immediacy. But when we extrapolate from this to posit a religious experience that would be *purely* immediate, an utterly simple experiential absolute, it seems that an illegitimate step into impossible abstraction has occurred. Even if such an experience could be imagined, there would be no way of expressing it that was not already mediated. Even an eloquent silence can communicate only by its place within a set of conventional codes that give it its significance. Like the Lacanian Real, the immediacy of mystical experience can be seen not only as an awakening from the Imaginary and its delusions but also as cutting a hole in the Symbolic order, imposing itself in its naked intensity ungoverned by codes of reason. Mysticism, psychosis, sudden physical pain are privileged sites of such an incursion of the Real. But even the fact that an experience becomes conscious seems to imply its subjection to mediations, even before the intervention of language. Moreover, the temporal structure of all experience excludes pure immediacy, which can be envisioned only as a fleeting instant, a vanishing wraith.

It is clear that a more intense and autonomous quality of immediacy marks privileged religious experiences and that one cannot gainsay the authority of these phenomena. Even if not clinically purified of every cultural connotation, they open a luminous dimension that carries its own meaning and is irreducible to another frame of interpretation. Even if a materialist were able to show that the experience depends on the neurons and could reproduce it in a laboratory with drugs, this would not disqualify the luminous evidence of the reality manifested in it. Further, such experiences of joy and love lay claim to a reality that makes them in their ultimate significance autonomous in respect to the context of their manifestation. Negative experiences of pain and guilt, by contrast, are reduced and surpassed when inserted in a religious context:

Suffering is in every instance contingent on the entire web of relations that forms the warp and woof of the dependently originated, empty world. For the Mādhyamika this is a matter of tremendous import because it leaves open the possibility that even the experience of physical pain could be altered and invested with a radically different significance by fundamentally altering one's form of life. . . . All elements of experience are fluid, dynamic, and constantly evolving in such a way as to reflect the interaction between consciousness and its objects. And within this interaction, where every aspect of experience is deeply conditioned by a network of natural interpretations that are themselves ungrounded and totally subject to historical and circumstantial conditioning, there lies an unlimited potential for growth and transformation. (Huntington, 124)

Religious experience should bring a sense of freedom and flexibility in dealing with the conventions of religious discourse. But when means and ends, the conventional and the ultimate, are confused, the result is a sclerosis of the religious tradition. If, instead, we go all the way with pluralism, recognizing the utterly contingent and conventional status of all religious constructions, we can traverse the religious fantasy (as Slavoj Žižek [1997] might put it) and reenact more skillfully the religious disposal of words, ideas, and actions in view of ultimacy.

Religious experience provides empirical confirmation to religious systems just as the physical world confirms geometrical systems. But as Poincaré saw, the confirmation does not take away the conventional status of the system. At best it shows that the system has a useful function in favoring the occurrence of religious experience. Perhaps there is one correct "practical geometry" of the religious cosmos. Buddhism, the most methodical of spiritual paths, may have unveiled the lineaments of this realm. Or Buddhism may be one conventional map alongside others, and all the maps may have to be corrected as we close in on the true shape of religious reality. Or each of the maps may have its own distinctive and irreducible validity, and conventionalism thus have a wider scope in spiritual than in physical space.

The mystical texts of the past give ample evidence of the flimsiness of even the most privileged religious language. To read them is to visit a museum of rusty old flying machines. There is a whole collection which is built according to the Neoplatonic model and which includes Gregory of Nyssa, Augustine, Pseudo-Dionysius, Eckhart, and many other princes of Christian mysticism. That the machines flew need not be questioned, nor have the fundamental laws of aviation changed. But we no longer know how to build those contraptions. Despite the gap between the claims of ultimacy made by mystics and the manifestly culture-bound language they use, their fragile myths did function as vehicles of ultimacy for them—an ultimacy that could be expressed and experienced only in terms of those specific myths. Our present conceptions of spiritual space and of the technology for its conquest generate a very different body of conventions from those of classical mysticism, and these in turn will seem as far-fetched to people in the future as the mystical maps of the past seem to us. Yet past texts, including the biblical ones, speak to us through the core phenomena of spiritual freedom to which they attest, despite the elaborate interpretative framework in which these phenomena are enshrined.

But are the core phenomena themselves a conventional formation, arising in dependence on a congeries of contingent historical conditions? In the case of the Protestant peasant who is related to have spent days lost in contemplation on reading Romans 8:1—"There is now no condemnation for those in Christ Jesus"—should we say that, rather than appropriate the meaning of Paul in a luminous communication, the reader constructed his own contemporary vision, kindled by Paul's words, and shaped by subsequent theological development, notably the creative retrieval of Paul in the Lutheran tradition?

A common core experience cannot be distilled out of the various languages of ultimacy. Each of them is from the start a rich particular texture, and the ultimacy they secrete is the fine fruit of an entire religious culture. Like the experience of listening to a Beethoven quartet, "music heard so deeply / That it is not heard at all, but you are the music / While the music lasts" (T. S. Eliot), the interiorized appreciation of the images, truths, or presences constructed by a given religion is not an external confirmation of these but their product. Yet as a musical ecstasy confirms the greatness of a musical opus, so a religious ecstasy confirms the greatness of a religious vision. Something clicks, something chimes, and one cries: "That's it!"

To isolate the quality of ultimacy from the cultural vehicles that open access to it would entail finding a truer, more objective, more universal language of ultimacy than any concrete tradition has found. It is as if one were to seek a true, objective language of beauty that would surpass and replace the many languages of the great poets. One might trace general patterns of the emergence of ultimacy in religious traditions or of the emergence of beauty in poetry. But ultimacy and beauty are not things but "effects." An effect of beauty in poetry is on each occasion singular, unrepeatable. An effect of ultimacy in religion has a similar individual irreducibility. One can be initiated into a religious tradition and led to its vision of ultimacy, so that one "repeats" the experience of predecessors on this path. Similarly, one can come to appreciate a great poem and have the same experience of beauty as its previous readers had. There is a tradition of experience, its transmission from mind to mind. But just as the poetry is not a dispensable vehicle of the experience it transmits, neither are the conventions of a religious tradition separable from the ultimacy they convey. They are not ways of cutting a pregiven experiential cake according to culturally conditioned conceptual or linguistic schemes. The schemes are intrinsic elements of the cake, which is always already rich in intelligible patterns.

A major objection to this way of seeing things stems from the quality of deep religious experience, which proclaims its freedom from cultural or conceptual conditioning. The current popularity of ideas of change and transformation, which are imported even into the bosom of the eternal, contrasts with ancient yoga, which aims to get beyond change. Throughout Indian tradition, yogic experience claims a prereflective immediacy that is not mixed with any discursive activities, so that it differs radically from normal experience (Angot, 126). An ontology can be built on this: "It is in my mind an open question whether we have yet faced up to the sort of problem that the ancient Sāṃkhya teachers addressed," such as "the possibility of a nonrelational (nonintentional), metaempirical (or metapsychological) consciousness (*puruṣa*), the presence of which may be achieved in a nonsensuous intuition of intellect/will (*buddhi*)" (Larson and Bhattacharya, 642). To ignore this claim of yogic experience would be to jettison one of the principal bases for a dialogue with Oriental religions. Such a dialogue can hardly become a mutually reinforcing deconstruction of the alleged myths of Eastern spirituality along with Western mysticism (and the metaphysics deriving from or underpinning both traditions). Yet yoga, even in India, takes a variety of forms. The historical study of mystical or yogic traditions is quickly obliged to register an ineradicable pluralism, despite shared recurrent themes of joyful immediacy and radical transformation of vision.

Opposing talk of religious experience as culture bound and historically contextualized, Anne Klein points to the direct perception of emptiness in Tibetan Mādhyamika Buddhism. She claims that the immediate experience of ultimacy becomes independent of its conventional vehicles and in consequence attains a universality that common experience lacks. This would disqualify the parallelisms we have just sketched between religion and art. "This knowledge and its object are unconditioned by particularities of history and thus accessible in the same form, albeit through different means, to all persons regardless of cultural or psychological particularity" (270). The cultural particularity of religious paths fades into insignificance when the ultimate emerges. The conundrum of "how conceptual conditioning yields a nonconceptual experience of the unconditioned" (271) is solved by a gradualist approach in which conceptual analysis applied to the data of conventional awareness works in tandem with an abandonment of conceptuality for a nonconceptual, nondualistic experience of emptiness. This abandonment is achieved through mental calming and concentration, which allay the tensions between conceptual thought and direct perception and reduce the impact of conditioned objects on the perceiving subject. Here a path of awareness opens up that is less and less subject to the conditioning that provides the basis for historicist and constructivist epistemologies. Insight into the constructed character of mental experience is not the highest insight for Buddhism; for such constructions are seen as interfering with cognition of the unconstructed, emptiness.

In direct cognition of emptiness, emptiness is not attained by analytical discriminations, "cultural and personal conditioning become so ephemeral as to be virtually nonexistent," and "there is no sense that the observing mind is here and the observed emptiness is there" (280). Emptiness—like love or the Holy Spirit—"exists as it appears, and thus no analytical corrective is required" (283). The mind, having attained its goal, is freed of mediations. "Virtually no contemporary Western thinker would take seriously, much less agree with, the notion that conditioned persons can have an experience outside of historical, cultural, psycho-social, and other sets of conditionings. . . . From the Buddhist perspective, such a viewpoint is limited and reductionistic in its fascination with conditionality. The Buddhist position also emphasizes conditionality but does not subsume all other perspectives to it. For Buddhists, the unconditioned is epistemologically meta to the conditioned—not the other way around" (298).

Perhaps someone experiencing the unconditioned may have a clear sense that the entire realm of the conditioned has been put in its place. But such experience is rare and brief: "The unveiling of the real when the mind is in yoga is promptly followed by a veiling" (Angot, 127). One can invoke the memory of that experience, *post festum*, as a criterion of judgment, but in doing so one has already redescended to the world of linguistic and social conditioning. Even mystics may be assailed by doubt about the value of this remembered experience. Their discourse on it will be shaped and controlled by social and communal tradition.

I would argue that we must at least recognize that experience of the unconditioned is always articulated in respect to some set of conditionings which it transcends, and that its ultimacy always retains some relationship to conventionality. When, in Hegel, God or Spirit emerges as the unconditioned, as the result of a long logical development, it emerges as free from all the limitations of the finite categories that have led to its emergence. If the entire process counts as a proof of the reality of God, this does not entail that the divine reality is conditioned by the process. Proofs of divine existence always point beyond themselves, ladders cast away in the affirmation of the unconditioned. Religious experience offers access to the unconditioned as a phenomenon, transcending whatever finite vehicles lead to it or accompany it. Yet "an experience lived by an individual is never as individual as he thinks it is" (Angot, 128). Even the Buddha's enlightenment depended on his formation in ascetical traditions, and its recognition by his disciples shows that it was a response to questions these traditions had posed and that it was understood within the frameworks of understanding these traditions had provided.

This embeddedness of religious experience in a given historical, cultural, traditional, and linguistic context means that that experience cannot be treated as a pure delivery of ultimate reality. Certainly any attempt to formulate it as such is immediately compromised. Anne Klein sees "immediate" cognition as tending toward universality, but she admits that it "does not do away with objections to claims for complete universality" (276). The universality is not total, for when one seeks to articulate that immediate cognition one falls back on the language provided by the tradition. The experience lights up the texts of the tradition as the *testimonium internum Spiritus sancti* does those of the New Testament. The texts are not the source of the light but are traces of previous experiences of it, now recognized as such.

Ultimacy can only be indicated obliquely by the torsions of a manifestly nonultimate language. Even silence, situated at the end of a traversal of speech, is always located as a signifier within a given cultural context: a world separates the silence of Vimalakīrti from that of the Pseudo-Dionysius. Ultimacy is encountered situationally, as confirmation and fulfillment of a pregiven language but also as revelation of its inadequacy. At the very point where the conventional web of religious discourse is most charged with a sense of the ultimate, it is also shown up in its thinness, almost to the point of breaking. Here the text will start using the negative terminology of ineffability or incomprehensibility or will burst into poetic metaphor or nonsensical paradox, mantras, glossolalia. In the past such apophatic rhetoric was not terribly unsettling, for the writer was securely situated in prayer before the divine incomprehensibility. Today our religious metaphors are more likely to have a spectral quality, as remnants and quotations from a historical repertory.

In discussing religious experience, we are not dwelling on a fringe phenomenon, for privileged religious or mystical experiences lie at the very heart of the great religions. In the Buddha's enlightenment the conventional constructions of centuries of Indian religious exploration click into a new and luminous perspective. In the resurrection of Jesus the conventional constructions of centuries of Jewish religious exploration find a new bearing. Both events represent a happening of ultimacy amid the conventional. The same may be said of the tremendous scene of the giving of the Law on Mt. Sinai (Ex 19–20). The suspicion might arise that all such accounts project a merely literary sublimity. Yet the Buddha's enlightenment might be "verified" by subsequent Buddhist attempts to enter the same realm of experience, and the mystical depth of the apostolic witness to the Resurrection may find confirmation in subsequent church contemplation of the risen Christ present in our midst.

In the latter case, apologists are far from happy to accept the Resurrection as a disclosure founded in religious experience, always suspected of being merely subjective. A wooden apologetics confronts "naturalistic" hypotheses about the origins of the Resurrection discourse on the basis of a distinction between "hallucinations" and experiences of the risen Christ that "were caused *extra-mentally*" (Ter Ern Loke, 573), failing to consider that perception and experience shaped by faith and contemplation may have subtler modalities than this covers. The Buddha's enlightenment was neither intramental nor extramental. It was contemplative insight into the texture of reality. The Resurrection experiences and the narratives they inspired point to a similar realm. "The diversity and multitude of the resurrection experiences" is cited as proof of their extramental reality (576). Better to say that the diversity of the Resurrection narratives, most dating from more than forty years after the event, testifies to the richness of the original experience. They contrast with the laconic character of the earliest known accounts, in Paul. The state of the texts weans us away from clutching at positivist claims of a brutal "external" reality. If "the presence of guards at the tomb" (581) is a fact, then it is easy to defend the factuality of the empty tomb. But proving that the guards are not a Matthean invention, some fifty or sixty years after the event, and refuting the unlikelihoods pointed out long ago by Samuel Reimarus, is a complicated business. Surely Matthew would not commit a "credibility suicide" by inventing it (582)? But by the same argument we would have to accept the other legendary accretions to Mark,

Matthew's source, such as the earthquake at the death of Jesus, when bodies left their tombs and appeared to many (Mt 27:51–54), or the dream of Pilate's wife (27:18–19). Literary sensitivity and common sense bid one desist from seeking the objectivity of a police report in documents pictorializing a conviction of faith.

Not the letter of the Resurrection stories but their spirit is what it is needful to transmit. Letting go of the letter to embrace the spirit is an excellent education for believers in the transition from conventions to ultimacy. In breakthroughs to ultimacy, Gotama becomes Buddha, and Jesus becomes Christ, "descended from David according to the flesh, and designated Son of God in power according to the Spirit of holiness by his resurrection from the dead" (Rom 1:3–4). Ultimacy is a radical transformation of the conventional world, and it can be known only in this way, starting from this conventional basis.

MYSTICISM ON TRIAL

Religious experiences such as those Augustine recalls in *Confessions* 7 and 9 bear witness to a dimension of reality that triumphs serenely over death and meaninglessness. The authority of this witness comes from the quality of ultimacy inherent in the experience itself, rather than from the metaphysical ideas and scriptural teachings linked with it. Of course a scriptural word may be the occasion of the experience, in which case it is precisely this living word that has authority and ultimacy, not the mere text or secondary elucidations of it. The image of hearing a word may originate in the conviction that the experience is not merely subjective but is an encounter with the real. Thus in Vedānta, the nonduality of *ātman* and Brahman is not simply an insight but a revelation, something heard (*śruti*), which as in the case of the prophets and the Qu'rān refers more to the mode of encounter with the divine than to the authority of canonical texts. Phenomenologically, the deliveries of religious experience impose themselves as unmasterable (in the sense of Barth's *Unverfügbarkeit*), as phenomena that we cannot go behind or seek to subordinate to any explanatory framework. The reality encountered is to be accepted entirely on its own terms, which are those of supreme being, awareness, bliss (the Vedantic *sat-chit-ananda*). Were one to interrogate it, to seek out its hidden background, to query its legitimacy, that would be a demonstration of phenomenological ill-breeding, or what Aristotle would call *apaideusia*. In the numinous moment there is no room for doubt or questioning. The reality apprehended is more undeniable even than the reality of the everyday physical world: "Non erat prorsus unde dubitarem, faciliusque dubitarem vivere me quam non esse veritatem" (*Conf.* 7.16; There was nothing that gave a pretext for doubt, and I had more easily doubted that I lived than that this truth existed), echoed in Newman's reference to an "inward conversion of which I was conscious (and of which I still am more certain that that I have hands and feet)" (Newman 1994:25).

Nonetheless, the rights of the conventional will not be denied. Orthodoxy attempts to regulate and assess religious experience in terms of its conformity to doctrine. Mystics will have trouble honoring the constraints of doctrinal discourse, which may not fit well with their more vivid sense of the realities to which dogma points, since the entire realm of words and ideas belongs to conventional or world-ensconced truth, whereas religious experience is a breakthrough to the *paramārtha* level. The wise mystic will patiently negotiate the realm of conventional reason.

The ultimacy of religious experience is attacked from another angle by psychoanalysts. While they respect experiences that show the subject engaging in the symbolic order in a realistic give-and-take, they tend to view religious experience as a saturnalian feast of the unconscious, in which all its repressed grandiose desires are given free rein. They assume it can be nothing more than an immanent psychic process, a blind *jouissance*, an oceanic feeling linked to prenatal bliss. They might find in the *Confessions* nothing more than libido on the loose, ego inflation, masochistic self-annihilation before the superego. What a catastrophe it would be not only for religion but for civilization if these dismal diagnoses turned out to be the "truth" about Augustine!

Žižek points out that in religious ecstasy, according to St. Ignatius Loyola:

The positive figure of God comes second, after the moment of "objectless" ecstasy: first we have the experience of objectless ecstasy; subsequently this experience is attached to some historically determined representation—here we encounter an exemplary case of the Real as "that which remains the same in all possible (symbolic) universes" . . . precisely *jouissance* as that which always remains the same. Every ideology attaches itself to some kernel of *jouissance* which, however, retains the status of an ambiguous excess. The unique "religious experience" is thus to be split into its two components, as in the well-known scene from Terry Gilliam's *Brazil* in which the food on a plate is split into its symbolic frame (a colored photo of the course above the plate) and the formless slime of *jouissance* that we actually eat. (1997:50)

Studying "profane" or "natural" mysticism, Michel Hulin confirms Žižek's two-stage account: "First, there is a raw, massive, suffocating, ineffable joy. For a brief instant, the intellect is put out of circuit, no definite 'thought' is possible. Next, no doubt very quickly, there emerges the need to 'breathe,' to take some distance from the event, to understand what it happening to you. It is then that the subject links up again with his familiar world, his cultural baggage, his beliefs, his categories, and that he attempts, with 'the language of the tribe,' to integrate with them what he has just lived through" (2008:61–62).

But to speak of the *jouissance* as "formless slime" hardly does justice to the illuminative power of contemplative experience. Romain Rolland rebuts Freud's reductive explanation of his "oceanic feeling" in *Civilization and Its Discontents*: "If it can in some aspects be assimilated to 'a return to the primary stage, to the intrauterine state,' it is also an unlimited expansion, positive and self-conscious, and is accompanied by a 'sovereign well-being' that cannot be reduced to infantile quietude" (Hulin 2008:42). It is lived as an opening onto reality. The testimony of literature, in Blake, Wordsworth, Proust, to ecstatic moments of vision does not exhibit a gap between *jouissance* and an ideology that is added on; rather, the ecstasy is one with a vision of the way things really are, lighting up the totality of experience. What is called "raw" experience can be ablaze with intuitive intelligence. "That pleasure and pain do not have the structure of pure *intellectual* judgments does not entail that they should be reduced to mere data of sensation. Despite their apparent immediacy, they may well embrace a whole process of thought integrating complex data" (215).

If the core of religious experience is a blissful pneumatic illumination, in the Christian context this occurs often, perhaps normatively, in close conjunction with an illuminating or illuminated word. The "inner witness of the Holy Spirit" lights up the biblical text and charges it with radiant meaning. The immediacy of joy bears a flood of intelligent insight. Both aspects of the experience are transformative: the spiritual bliss is a liberation from chains of delusion, from psychic blockage; the word associated with it is a judgment of truth, cutting through the false or unreal positions in which one had been entangled and establishing a secure new perspective. Even if *jouissance* were always the same, the word in which it finds expression inevitably varies according to the context of the experience. The word cannot be a pure expression of ultimacy, as it invariably relies on the conventional data of the given context. But again we wonder if even the core *jouissance* itself is shaped by its context, so that the effect of ultimacy could never be disentangled immaculately from the culture-bound contingencies of its emergence.

Religious experience, as Augustine's accounts show, is also a source of metaphysical insight, yielding a renewed vision of the world and of being. Even if one calls this body of scriptural and metaphysical insight an ideological construction, the relation between the insight and the ecstasy is more integrated than Žižek recognizes. To be sure, there is an excess of the joyful sense of ultimacy over the framework of understanding which it both confirms and shows up as "mere straw" (Aquinas), a vessel of clay. "We have this treasure in earthen vessels, to show that the transcendent power belongs to God and not to us" (2 Cor 4:7). For Paul, this excess is a mark of the divine glory, not of an obscure psychic murk. The darkness of divine glory is further along the trajectory of dazzling insight that the religious experience conveys: "Dark with excessive bright thy skirts appear" (Milton). If what is touched in mystical ecstasy exceeds the grasp of the mind—"what no eye has seen, nor ear heard, nor the heart of man conceived" (1 Cor 2:9)—this is not because it is a slippery preconceptual slime but because only the Holy Spirit can investigate it: "The Spirit searches everything, even the depths of God" (2:10). Contemplation is access to the dimension of Spirit, *pneuma*, marked by an intensification of the sense of reality, as "seeing" gives way to "touching." (Here, though, I am yoking together two disparate traditions, the biblical *pneuma* and the Neoplatonic touching, *thigein*.)

This dynamic of transformative illumination in religious experience is not undermined by the discovery of a connection with erotic drives. Those places in poetic or religious texts when we perceive the dawning of the sublime often bring a surge of erotic excitement or delight: consider the blissful release in the second variation of the third movement of Beethoven's Ninth Symphony (bars 99–114) or the vaulting quasi-fugato of the final movement (bars 432–525). To be "surprised by joy" is an erotic experience. But to reduce every summit of religious or aesthetic joy to instantiations of an invariable blind animal ecstasy is a doctrinaire curtailment of the phenomena and their significance. The idea that *jouissance* is always the same scarcely applies even to physical eroticism. Just as the mood of sexual delight lights up intensely the varied beauty of the objects that elicit it, so the light and joy of the Spirit constantly reveal fresh aspects of the object of contemplation.

Given his skeptical attitude to contemplation, it is unsurprising that Žižek dismisses the idea of the Resurrection as a breakthrough to ultimacy. The most ultimate reality is that of "modern science," and what does not fit under its rubrics must be cut down to size: "In our era of modern science, one can no longer accept the fable of the miracle of Resurrection as the form of the Truth-Event. Although the Truth-Event does designate the occurrence of something which, from within the horizon of the predominant order of Knowledge, appears impossible (think of the laughter with which the Greek philosophers greeted St Paul's assertion of Christ's Resurrection on his visit to Athens), today, any location of the Truth-Event at the level of supernatural miracles necessarily entails regression into obscurantism, since the event of Science is irreducible and cannot be undone" (1999:142).

The primitive resurrection kerygma no doubt concerns a physical raising of Christ from the tomb, seen as the first fruits of the general resurrection of the dead. Demythologizers in the line of Schleiermacher and Bultmann have reinterpreted this ancient language as referring to a pneumatic eschatological event, which no longer clashes directly with science. John Keenan supplies a Buddhist twist: "The resurrected Jesus can be seen only upon the awakening of conversion that he came to preach about, not in some supernaturally perceptible coming back to show his new glorified body" (1995:394). The miracle of resurrection is not the literal raising of a corpse but the conquest over exactly the dead end beyond which Žižek believes it is impossible to go. "After Freud, one cannot directly have faith in a Truth-Event; every such Event ultimately remains a semblance obfuscating a preceding Void whose Freudian name is *death drive*" (1999:154). The resurrection, claims Žižek, obfuscates the Real manifested in Christ's death, "the lowest excremental remainder" (228). Yet in the Christian kerygma this Real is not eluded: "Ego sum vermis et non homo" (Ps 22:6). The abyss of the Triduum is the condition of the paschal dawn.

Žižek himself speaks of revolutionary acts that "miraculously" break through the constraints of a given symbolic order. Correlative with resurrection is forgiveness: "the *miracle* of Grace which retroactively 'undoes' our past sins" (331)—an idea found in Wilde's *De Profundis*. Here it is not science that objects, but a skepticism based on the feeling that this is a tired old ideology. The phenomena of forgiveness and being forgiven provide, however, an empirical basis for belief in this miracle. The impact of Christ's revolutionary act of forgiveness can be described in Žižek's own terms: "An act proper 'miraculously' changes the very standard by which we measure and value our activity; that is, it is synonymous with what Nietzsche called 'transvaluation of values.' . . . The act occurs when the choice of (what, within the situation, appears as) the Worst changes the very standards of what is good or bad" (307). Christ "becomes sin" to free us from sin, and his resurrection is perhaps the dialectical reversal brought about by this radical confrontation with sin and death. The joy of the Resurrection is not sparked off by the news of a fabulous miracle;

rather, it is correlative with a vision of the full significance of Christ's teaching and his death, the vision that "God was in Christ reconciling the world to himself" (2 Cor 5:19).

Beyond the finality of physical death lies the ultimacy of the death drive, the meaningless entropic noise at the heart of the universe. It is heard as a sublime interruption in a love lyric of Catullus: "Nobis cum semel occidit brevis lux / Nox est perpetua una dormienda" (For us when once the brief light dies / One perpetual night is to be slept). Freud and Lacan have increased the pervasiveness of this dark sublime. It, too, is unmasterable; there is no going beyond it. Yet Christ "abolished death and brought life and immortality to light through the gospel" (2 Tim 1:10). The dark places of death are entirely comprehended by the light of the Gospel word, so that their meaning changes. "The grace that is in Christ Jesus" (2 Tim 2:1) is known on a nearer acquaintance with suffering and death. It is not by eluding the phenomena of sin and death, but by surrendering entirely to their claim, that one enters the domain of the forgiveness of sins and the resurrection from the dead. This paschal paradox resonates from afar with the Buddhist discovery of nonduality between death and life, the samsaric conventional and the nirvanic ultimate.

Religious experience, then, is a miraculous breakthrough to a realm of freedom—be it conceived as enlightenment, resurrection, the Vedantic Brahman, or the Plotinian One. Is there a specific form in which this "truth event" is to be sought today? The leveling and alienating effect of global capitalism reduces all experiences to commodities. Religious vision is stymied by it, much as is artistic and political creativity. When we study the breakthroughs to ultimacy recorded in the classic religious texts of the past and attempt to discern how they related to the historical and cultural contexts in which they emerged, we may find clues for an opening up of the contemporary context to a liberating ultimacy. Thorough recognition of the historical pluralism and the contingent, conventional status of all our languages of ultimacy will be a distinctive feature of a contemporary retrieval of mystical traditions, and we may draw from Buddhism the encouraging thought that to recognize the conventional as conventional is to be already aligned to the ultimate.

CONSULTING THE CLASSICS

Very interesting to the theologian are those figures, such as Plotinus and Augustine, who after experiencing a powerful encounter with ultimate reality turn back to the realm of conventional language, which they revise in light of the encounter. Mysticism thus impresses its mark on language. The comprehensive critical labors of the Neoplatonists or the Mādhyamika thinkers are a clearing of the pathways of thought and language that lead to and from the breakthrough to ultimacy. These include the pathways of established religious tradition, hellenic or Indian, now purged of representations that have become obstacles to insight, and given a relativized and more functional status. Today the movement of history brings breakthroughs to a simpler vision of what matters in religion, and these breakthroughs, though of a more existential than mystical order, are our cues for reappropriating the radicality and clear-sightedness of the classic mystical texts. Reassessing conventions in light of ultimacy takes on today a historical depth. We measure the entire sweep of religious traditions by the orientation to ultimacy manifest in classic texts, and in doing so we gain a new sense of the radical contingency and conventionality of religions as historically constituted. This allows us to acquire a free relation to the tradition, so that instead of being a prison that blocks out all sense of ultimacy, it becomes a repertory of skillful means that can serve in varying manners to orient the religious quest to its ultimate goal.

It might be objected that this critical enterprise can proceed on the basis of modern theological common sense and that there is no need to invoke the luxuries of mysticism. But if mysticism is really nothing more than a matter of seeing things as they are, and thus filling in the central piece in the puzzle of existence, then theology at its moments of highest lucidity may find itself rejoining the insights of those contemplatives who grasped most clearly the phenomena that are religion's concern. However, there is a more serious objection to harping on ultimacy and mystical breakthroughs—namely, that it misses the point of the biblical revelation. If God has come to humanity, incarnately, in a generous outpouring of the Spirit, then mysticism and contemplation are no more than a registering of this reality, within the context of the total response to it constituted by the multifaceted life of the people of God. To talk of the ultimate or of religious experience is to cut across the breadth and wealth of biblical language and lifestyle, intruding on them an alien and narrow concern. Philosophers of religion are quite likely to project a warped theology in their preoccupation with such matters as religious experience and mysticism. The theologian cannot in any case ignore the heritage of mystical texts, but he will bring to them critical discernment, even suspicion, as, for example, Luther did in esteeming Augustine and rejecting Pseudo-Dionysius. Luther was able to read Augustine's contemplative texts as revealing an entire lifestyle, both individual and ecclesial; perhaps those of Dionysius could have been read in the same way if Luther had been attuned to the lifestyle of the Eastern Church. Perhaps one may say quite generally that mystical experience gains its meaning and validity only within the total context of the way of life that secretes it. The fleshliness of the biblical world is then not the exception but the rule. Even mystical purists such as Plotinus, if looked at closely, may be found to be engaged in wide-ranging communal praxis, within which the rare encounters with the One acquire their full significance.

To read a mystical text one has to be attuned to the contemplative wavelength of its author; that is the reason why for most of us, most of the time, mystical texts are not the most attractive reading. Of course there are countless mystical texts that fail to communicate at all, either because they merely repeat the conventional spiritual jargon of their time or because they flounder helplessly in their effort to articulate the ineffable. That is why theological consultation of mysticism confines itself to classic texts, where effective communication has been achieved. It might be objected that the cozy frequentation of approved classics is a narrow and old-fashioned approach to religious experience. Wider and more adventurous anthropological study would no doubt offer a rich field for theological judgment. Still the classical mystical texts have a distinctive strategic significance. Key contemplative breakthroughs in the history of religion, which realize in a ripe and illuminating form the spiritual potential of the tradition within which they arise, and in turn serve as the foundation for further developments of the tradition, have usually been secured by correspondingly great literary texts—such as the *Bhagavad-gītā*, the *Enneads*, the epistles of Paul, the Zen kōan collections. As objects of study these texts are more manageable than phenomena of real life, because the textual inscription reveals clearly how the mystical witness is involved with all the conventionalities of a given culture. This does not freeze the mystical moment by confining it to its historical locus but on the contrary exposes it to the various treacherous features of textuality rehearsed by Derrida: dissemination, citationality, iterability, and all the other dimensions of *la différance*.

The achievement of the religious classics is that they succeed in disposing the resources of their cultural context toward the dimension of ultimacy, allowing it to react on that context with critical and illuminative force. A mystical text empties out conventional language before the ultimate, burns the language like straw, but in such a way that it then functions as a burning bush, indicating the contours of the numinous real by its stammerings and silences. This eloquent breakdown of the conventional before the ultimate is favored by cultural crisis or by a meeting of cultures, a fusion of horizons, in which conventional frameworks are enlarged and broken open. The traumata of the twentieth century have enabled artists to approximate to the dynamic of mystical expression, nowhere more powerfully than in the poems of Paul Celan. Our meditation on the interplay of conventional and ultimate as expressed in peaceful old classics may seem far from this intense modern experience of divine withdrawal, but it does chime with it from a distance. The shattering of conventions, which reveals them in their shattered state as still reaching out to an unfathomable ultimate reality, which is near, lies at the heart of contemporary negotiations with religious tradition. Investigation of mystical and apophatic discourses of the past may show that this iconoclasm brings out something that was always inscribed in the structure of religious language, and that what looked at first like terminal alienation from the religious heritage turns out in reality to give renewed and more radical access to it.

AUGUSTINE'S PLOTINIAN ECSTASIES

Much modern philosophy has sought to be refounded in an encounter with bedrock reality, by a return to empirical sensations, or to the im-

mediate data of consciousness (Bergson), or to the "things themselves" in phenomenology. Schelling sought the mystical foundation
of philosophy, conferring on himself the bliss of intellectual intuition:
"The Self is, because it is, without any condition or limitation. Its
originary form is that of pure and eternal being; one cannot say of it:
'It was, it will be,' but only: 'It is.' . . . Eternity is the form of intellectual intuition." In the Self "there exists neither possibility, nor reality,
nor necessity; in effect all that the absolute Self posits is determined by
the pure form of being" (quoted in Philonenko, 92). Neoplatonism,
the cult of the "God-intoxicated" Spinoza (as Novalis called him), the
prizing of *Gefühl* from Pietism to Schleiermacher, and the discovery
of Vedānta reinforced a mystical climate among German romantic
thinkers. Echoes of this continue in French thinkers who bathe in the
mystery of being, such as Louis Lavelle, Gabriel Marcel, and Michel
Henry. The current "theological turn" in phenomenology, with its
cult of otherness as call, distance, saturated phenomenon, the Impossible, gives hyperbolic expression to the desire for bedrock data and
can take on the proportions of a mystical quest.

   This strange courtship of mysticism by philosophers carries great
dangers of irrationalism. The current interest in Plotinus is due in part
to the sense that he links mysticism and thought in their purest form,
unencumbered by the representations of a religion of revelation and
faith, which would have stifled the élan of his thought. His mysticism
is thus philosophically pleasing in itself, and in addition it is embedded
in a highly reflective practice of fearless rational questioning which assures philosophers that mysticism need not be the enemy of thought.
Plotinus is a purifier within the Western world and a bridge to the
world of Vedānta and Buddhism. He is both the father of mature
Christian and Islamic mysticism and the patron of free thinkers that
reject revealed faith. The question of his status is not an esoteric one
but is the obverse of another question—the one he himself puts to us
about the status of Christianity and of all religions.

   Porphyry writes: "To Plotinus 'the goal ever near was shown': for
his end and goal was to be united to, to approach the God who is over
all things. Four times while I was with him [in Rome, 263–70 CE] he
attained that goal, in an unspeakable actuality and not in potency

only." Porphyry himself "drew near and was united" only once in his sixty-eight years (Porphyry, *Life* 23). Plotinus himself attests: "I have come to that supreme actuality, setting myself above all else in the realm of Intellect. Then after that rest in the divine, when I have come down from Intellect to discursive reasoning, I am puzzled how I ever came down" (*Enn.* 4.8.1). When philosophers talk like this, are they any longer philosophers? Or can there be a specifically philosophical mysticism, to be handled by strictly philosophical methods?

The taste for mystical immediacy in philosophy may have less to do with a search for bedrock than with a thirst for freedom that the principle of sufficient reason oppresses. In Plotinus, the thought of the One is a space of intoxicating liberty and inspires the transgressive idea of the One as so supremely sovereign and free that it is cause of itself, *causa sui* (*Enn.* 6.8), which carries the demand of reason and foundation into the very heart of the absolute while revealing at the same time how the absolute subverts and overturns every conceptuality seeking to encircle it. Plotinus could unite the most exigent rational dialectic with a mystical relation to the ultimate. He is like a fisherman casting his line in an immense lake: the play of concepts can at any moment begin to vibrate and tremble, having captured some live manifestation of mystical reality. The One as space of final liberty is made accessible by all the labor of philosophical cogitation. It is also the place of highest necessity, for Plotinus opposes Gnostics who had God say: "I become what I want to" (Bréhier, 121). He seeks to grasp freedom and necessity as two aspects of the same process. Hegel's reading of Plotinus stops with the noetic integration of all that exists, the contemplation of the *Nous* as source and summit of all intelligibility, but this level is the plateau for the leap beyond: "One must leap [*aixaî*] to the One" (*Enn.* 5.5.4). As in Wittgenstein, mastery of the conventional clears the space for encounter with the ultimate. One finds a similar to-and-fro between the rational and the mystical in Plato. Rational inquiry into forms is crowned by the contemplation of the *ontōs on*, that which truly is, evoked in mythical or visionary language. Contemplation of the intelligible is surpassed, already in Plato, by the deeper movement that is drawn by the Good beyond being and the intelligible, the ultimate One that undoes all our categories. A relentless logical necessity governs the arguments of the *Parmenides*, in which Plato shows himself the heir of the dialectical prowess of Zeno and the Sophists, yet refuses to use his virtuosity to avoid difficulties. He is a Houdini who will not sneak out of his chains but lets them bind him ever more tightly until the dark night of the last hypothesis, where it is proved that nothing exists. He does escape in the end, thanks to a paradoxical reversal: the supreme principle that has no being, the One beyond being, is the ultimate recourse that saves thought. The affirmation of freedom is expressed in a leap beyond logic or in a dismantling of the concept with a view to returning to the dynamic life of the mind.

But this leap need not be mystical; the Platonic and Catholic tradition is countered by a Protestant one which renounces mysticism for faith. In Kant a philosophical faith protects freedom against the rational regime of necessity. Fichte proclaims a spiritual revolution that has no recourse to mystic givenness:

> Freedom allows finite thought to surpass its fate. If consciousness overcomes fate, it is not because it situates itself in thought in some intelligible, timeless world whereby it could overleap the facticity of events in time but on the contrary because it is linked intimately in its very being to the future, it is the power that continually revokes the present or past fact in the name of the future. Consciousness thus enacts the project that always overturns fate in recreating at every moment of time the Ideal to be realized. . . . This project that is formed before all thought is deeper in me than my own self. It is the expression of an originary freedom of which I am the means. (Philonenko, 339)

Here the leap out of the system plunges right into the heart of temporal experience, and this return to the real is born of renouncing the enchantment of mysticism. "Duty and action are the sources of happiness, and the real decadence is the refusal of time and history, taking flight to an illusory eternity, in which consciousness turns in on itself in loving self-knowledge" (92). Foremost among the antimystical thinkers are Hegel and those influenced by him. They demystify "experience," placing it in its historical contexts where it appears as a cultural construction rather than a pure given, and where it is subjected to dialectic, as the contradictions inscribed in its finitude are unfolded.

Leaps beyond the merely rational are hardly likely to enjoy a nonproblematic status in philosophy. They figure there as provocations, problematic gestures inciting debate on the status and limits of the rational, themes for questioning reflection. Whenever a philosopher enthuses about a mystical source of illumination, cooler reflection soon supervenes, pushing the mystic light to the margin or demanding that its deliveries be established on a firmly rational basis. Theologians are more likely to embrace the mystic core of a philosophy, often with scant concern for the web of complex argument in which the philosopher will have embedded it, as we see in the Christian reception of Plotinus. Augustine's reading of Plotinus substantiates what we said above about ultimacy and conventionality in religious experience and reveals how theological judgment, even when it seems to be dealing with purely spiritual realities, moves constantly in the realm of historical textuality, with its inbuilt tensions. What might be called the incarnational texture of theological thought has its own rigors, having less to do with philosophical acuity than with seasoned appraisal of its concrete sources of insight, individual and communal, mystical and kerygmatic, speculative and scriptural.

Though Augustine of Hippo was a very busy ecclesiastic and a very productive intellectual, his works are steeped in a steady contemplative awareness, which at times blossoms into direct testimony to experiential encounter with the divine. It was at the time of his conversion, in 386–87, that mystical aspirations gripped him most; his experiences of that time are written up in glowing colors in the *Confessions* (401), but the mystical does not retain this central place in his preoccupations. It had given him just enough light to illumine the great public mansion of his thought, without withdrawing him into an esoteric sphere. Plotinus's circle was a laboratory of the spirit, and in Milan Augustine frequented a circle modeled on it. But already in his own circle in Cassiciacum the wider world of the church is shaping spirituality in a more homely, communal, down-to-earth manner.

A fusion, or mutual cracking open, of cultural horizons (Gadamer's *Horizontverschmelzung*) underlies the spiritual synthesis that

Augustine wrought. The classical world and its values had entered a twilight zone of incertitude, intensified by the barbarian menace, whereas the Christian Church, having secured its basic dogmas, was crossing a new threshold of self-conscious lucidity. In Augustine's thought classical values are Christianized wholesale. Most notably, the Platonic tradition of philosophical eros, which ascends to the ecstatic vision of Beauty and, beyond that, to a mystical contact with the One, is transformed through encounter and synthesis with the New Testament mysticism of the divine agape poured forth in our hearts as a gift of grace descending to our fleshly, historical world. The mutual transformation of the two horizons is not achieved in calm philosophical reflection but lived out in contemplative experience and ethical decision. Augustine had appropriated two languages, two cultures, which were already intersecting in previous Christian tradition. Milan in the 380s was the site of a repristination of both traditions. The Latin reception of Plotinus and Porphyry revealed an unsuspected spiritual majesty in Greek thought. The Latin appropriation of the spiritualizing, Origenian approach to scripture, represented by Ambrose, made the biblical tradition equally fresh and exciting. Augustine steeped himself in these currents. His mystical experience is inconceivable apart from them and represents his internalization of them, his appropriation of the existential possibilities they opened up. The traditions prepared the ground for his breakthrough to an ultimate level, and this in turn permitted him to retrieve the traditions with a lucid mastery, which is not merely intellectual but constantly harks back to that encounter with ultimacy. It may be regretted that the Greco-Roman conventions lost much of their substance in being sublated so deftly, just as the Indian gods became shadowy when integrated into the Buddhist panoply of skillful means.

Disentangling himself from Manichaeanism, Augustine was plagued by dualistic and reified conceptions of the world of spirit. His confusion on this account had become a nagging kōan. The words of Plotinus, like those of a perceptive Zen master, cut these knots and kindled an enlightened awareness: "Et inde admonitus redire ad memet ipsum intravi in intima mea duce te et potui, quoniam factus es adiutor meus" (*Conf.* 7.16; And being thence admonished to return to myself, I entered even into my inward self, with you as my guide: and I was able, for you had become my helper [trans. Pusey, 132, modified]). The phenomenon that Augustine first names is a new intimacy with an inner depth in himself to which his access had been blocked. As Zen masters also testify, enlightenment is not merely a change in subjective vision; it is a return to the bedrock reality of one's being, from which one had been cut off by the fabric of habitual deluded thinking; hence the Japanese term for enlightenment, *kenshō*, "beholding (one's) nature." Consciousness, Sartre says, in words that resonate suggestively with Buddhist themes, is "the absolute existent by dint of inexistence" (Sartre, 26). This "nonsubstantial absolute" (25) also resonates with Plotinus: "He has nothing and is the Good by having nothing. But then if anyone adds anything at all to him, substance or intellect or beauty, he will deprive him of being the Good by the addition" (*Enn.* 5.5.13). Contemplative awareness is intrinsically empty of substantiality, empty of being. It opens up at the "absolute near side" (Keiji Nishitani). It is a joyful unfolding of the light of the phenomena such that distinctions between subject and object do not arise.

Heisig (2013) speaks of Augustine's desire of God as that of a self for an object, but this misses several overtones of Augustine's language. The desire of God expressed in the Psalms, which underlies the language of the *Confessions*, is only at a surface level the desire of an object. It rises to a disappropriation of the desirer (Luther's *nos extra nos*) and a deobjectification of the desired. The love of God poured out in our hearts (Rom 5:5) is not a matter of subject over against object, but of abiding in love (1 Jn 4:16), the divine milieu. A phenomenology of what the great Christian contemplatives meant by the love of God reveals affinities with Buddhist ideas of human and divine nonself or emptiness. Since they lived a breakthrough to ultimacy or of ultimacy, we must treat their conventional expressions of this with the utmost hermeneutical charity, not putting them back in a box of ego or object that they have in principle left behind (or at least provided the resources to overcome).

The self that clings to itself, that projects itself as a solid substance, then clings to objects, gives them substantiality too. The ego, as Freud and Lacan show, is a projection of our deep-rooted needs, an objectification of self that, by masquerading as the true subject, actually shelters us against true subjectivity and alienates us from our original empty freedom. Such an ego will cling also to fetishized objects in the world around it. But the self that has discovered its own emptiness also lets objects go, in their emptiness, and abides in a state of pure experience in which subject and object have not arisen. When Augustine speaks of God as *esse, essentia, eternitas, veritas, bonum, caritas,* he is not projecting a narrowly anthropomorphic concept of the personal God, but rather naming God as a place of spiritual freedom and enjoyment (*frui Deo*). The divine initiative in all this is not a crude arrangement whereby God imposes himself on his creatures but is named grace, an event of liberation.

For a Hegelian (as Vieillard-Baron points out), metaphysical experience is inscribed in a reflexive process. This is true in Augustine, too, even though his experience bears all the marks of authentic mysticism. Freed from the conceptions that shackled it, the mind discovers its own nature, then that of the transcendent Principle, then that of the being of all entities, following a Plotinian path of reflection. The nonreflective experience is itself a response to reflective questioning. Reflection was impotent to produce the liberating vision; rather, it imprisoned the mind in aporias, but in such a way as to intensify the thirst to be freed from them. The breakthrough, as a return to self and a return to the things themselves, was long prepared by reflection, yet it surges from a region to which reflection has no access and to which no method can furnish the key. Meditative methods in Neoplatonism, or in Buddhism, keep the mind disposed to open to forces that they do not master, whether those of the unconscious or of grace or of Buddha nature. The conventions of the discourse of their time, intelligently disposed by Plotinus and Augustine, became vehicles for a breakthrough of the real. Yet the two registers are foreign to one another; one level is mastered in thought and speech, and the other surpasses thought and speech, so that whatever is thought or said of it is seen as a falling back to the conventional level.

A phenomenologist, nervous about the invasion of philosophy by mystical ultimacy, might argue that the saturated givenness of the mystical breakthrough is but the consummation of what is already experienced in ordinary phenomena, or in wonder at "the miracle of all miracles: *that* beings *are*" (Heidegger, *GA* 9:307). Thus mystical insight in philosophy would merely serve to confirm the aim of phenomenology, to provide an intuitive fulfillment for abstract significations. But mystical breakthroughs are more than a perfecting of intuitive givenness; they are a move to another plane. If every experience as a contingent event eludes thought, so that preconceptual perception of, say, a physical pain can have an affinity with the mystical by its independence from the will of the perceiver, mystical experience is distinguished by its transformative impact, by the new situation in which it sets the subject, who becomes other than himself and no longer differentiated from the object in a dualistic way.

For Wittgenstein, the mystical is that which shows itself and of which nothing can be said. Its role is not to verify the philosopher's ideas but to insert them in a larger existential context. To tend the garden of language, either in the style of logical positivism or in exploiting the resources of ordinary language, is a labor on conventions; the ultimate lies elsewhere. In locating the ultimate in relation to the conventional, one reaches first for the vocabulary of limit: when language and concepts are lacking, or fail, or break down, the real can arise—or at least be postulated—as that very thing in face of which they fail. Philosophers trade in conventional truth, and their deepest insight is precisely the recognition of the conventional status of their discourse, all that separates it from ultimate truth. But it is perhaps a defensive move, prompted by concern to draw a reassuring border that places the mystical as the limit of philosophical thought. Plotinus and Augustine would not accept such a marginal, mute, impotent position for their mystical breakthroughs, which are rather the summit and the heart of their thought, and which bring with them a cascade of discoveries.

Augustinian *caritas* opens up at this radical level; it is not, originally at least, an objectified psychic construct: "To place interiority before one is necessarily to give it the weight of an object. It is as if it shut itself up, offering us only its external aspects . . . an interiority closed on itself" (Sartre, 66). However, it is true that *caritas* gives an interiorizing and spiritualizing inflection to biblical agape and that it is shaped and limited by a kind of Platonic self-containment. Lutheran scholars such as Anders Nygren have pointed to the task of finding the way back from this enclosure to the open horizons of agape. *Caritas*, for Augustine, was supreme reality, the inner light of love. Yet after centuries of *caritas*-thinking we can see that the regime of *caritas* is a product of cultural conditions, which could function within a medieval regime of truth as a useful convention for attunement to a gracious ultimacy, but which is less immediately functional within modern horizons of thought. Charity and grace are indeed ultimate and unconditioned realities, yet there is a specifically Augustinian staging of their emergence. Augustine's conventional world, with its notions of the human psyche, of temptation and sin, and its residual Platonist preoccupations and structures, belongs to a past epoch, so that we cannot fully assume it as coterminous with our own world. Consequently, the style in which he figured the presence of the divine as *gratia* and *caritas* is no longer ours. We must seek the ultimacy specific to our present conventional world, the specific way in which our world signals its limits, its emptiness. Here we sight a paradox of the imbrication of ultimate and conventional in religious experience: Augustine broke through to the pneumatic immediacy which is the milieu in which one can begin to apprehend the divine, yet the ultimacy of this experience comes to us now shackled by the time-bound conventions of thought and language that once were its perfectly efficacious vehicle.

Augustine's narrative is surprising in that his conversion begins with an experience of philosophical mysticism, a type of experience that has been overshadowed by religious mysticism, Jewish, Islamic, or Christian, but that we can sometimes quarry out of the latter in a rather surgical reading, showing how it is in principle independent of biblical revelation and faith. That is, one can reconstruct for some religious thinkers, at least as a virtuality of their thought, a rational philosophical procedure crowned by a mystical intuition that is not yoked to any confessional investment. Theological scruples about the necessity of revelation or grace need not keep us from seeing how such a metaphysical experience was foundational for all of Augustine's thought. Augustine's earliest references to the enlightenment he experienced in Milan on reading the *libri Platonicorum* (*Contra Academicos* 2.5; *De Beata Vita* 4) are more nakedly Plotinian than the account in *Confessions* 7 and lack the rich biblical harmonies of the later text. Thus such expressions as "Quoniam factus es adiutor meus" (Ps 29:11) may refer less to the phenomenology of the original quasi-Plotinian experience than to a retrospective recognition of divine providence and grace at work in it.

The borderline between experience and interpretation, already problematic at the heart of the experience itself, becomes more so in the case of the remembered experience. The joy and light of Milan and Ostia had their own irreducible reality, but their articulation in words, the interpretation of their theological and metaphysical implications, and their placing within the total edifice of his vision required many years of further study and reflection. At least in Augustine's case, breakthroughs to ultimacy are inseparable from the long processes of interrogation and interpretation that precede and follow them. The classic religious vision is by the same token inseparable from its classic literary expression in the text of the *Confessions* itself. Here again the intrication of ultimacy and its conventional vehicle turns out to be more intimate than one might have expected.

Despite the powerful unity and simplicity of Augustine's experience, the harmony between Plotinian and biblical sensibility in his account of it harbors tensions that lie open to deconstructive interrogation. The retrospective biblical recuperation of the Plotinian experience may be an act of hermeneutic violence, erasing the pluralism implicit in the difference between Plotinian ultimacy (book 7) and Pauline ultimacy (book 8). Augustine is constantly weaving a unitary language of the spiritual realm from his two sources, the Platonist and biblical traditions, and the seam between them, with the occasional dropped stitches, marks the conventionality and constructed quality of his vision. The Augustinian system began to unravel when Luther pulled more heavily on the Pauline thread, releasing a dynamic of agape—the divine love that justifies the unrighteous—that could not be recuperated within the regime of Platonist interiority. The scenarios of Plotinus and Paul, with their distinctive traditional terminologies, do not coincide smoothly. Augustine practices a to-and-fro between them, conjoining them in a collage on which he works incessantly (in *De Trinitate* especially). This is the usual procedure of the intellectuals among the fathers as they expound the Gospel in relation to the dominant Platonist rationality of their time. "Intravi et vidi qualicumque oculo animae meae supra eundum oculum animae meae lucem incommutabilem, non hanc vulgarem et conspicuam omni carni . . . sed aliud, aliud valde" (*Conf.* 7.10; I entered and beheld with the eye of my soul, [such as it was,] above the same eye of my soul, above my mind, the Light Unchangeable. Not this ordinary light, which all flesh may look upon . . . but other, yea, far other.) Immediately supervening on the rediscovery of the *intima mea* is a new awareness of God as spirit, imaged as the Plotinian sun (the One) that rises above Intellect itself which contemplates it: "One should not enquire whence it comes, for there is no 'whence': for it does not really come or go away anywhere, but appears or does not appear. So one must not chase after it, but wait quietly till it appears, preparing oneself to contemplate it, as the eye awaits the rising of the sun. . . . What is the horizon which he will mount above when he appears? He will be above Intellect itself which contemplates him" (*Enn.* 5.5.8). The *intima mea* are not quite identical with the eye of the mind that perceives the divine light. The spiritual freedom that allows one to be fully present to oneself is the milieu within which the eye of the mind, the purified intellect, can open. In Augustine the light and the mind that contemplates it differ as creator and created: "superior, quia ipsa fecit me, et ego inferior, quia factus sum ab ea" (above my soul, because It made me; and I below It, because I was made by It). Is this recognition of the light as creator a retrospective construction, or was Augustine's experience conditioned by his biblical formation, recently renovated by the sermons of Ambrose? A retrospective refashioning of the experience would be facilitated by the fact that Plotinus, too, speaks of the Good as making all things (through the *Nous* and the soul), so that the realization "Ipsa fecit me" could have been part of Augustine's Plotinian vision without the fully developed biblical sense of a personal Creator.

The next phenomenon noted is the sense of unworthiness that overcomes Augustine faced with the purity of the divine light:

Et cum te primum cognovi, tu assumpsisti me, ut viderem esse, quod viderem, et nondum me esse, qui viderem. Et reverberasti infirmitatem aspectus mei radians in me vehementer, et contremui amore et horrore: et inveni longe me esse a te in regione dissimilitudinis, tamquam audirem vocem tuam de excelso: "Cibus sum grandium: cresce et manducabis me." (7.10)

———

[When I first knew you, you lifted me up, that I might see there was something I might see, and that I was not yet such as to see. And you beat back the weakness of my sight, irradiating upon me most strongly, and I trembled with love and awe: and I perceived myself to be far off from you, in the region of unlikeness, as if I heard your voice from on high: "I am the food of adults; grow, and thou shalt feed upon me."]

The Platonic language here corresponds to the sense of the numinous as *fascinosum* (inspiring *amor*) and *tremendum* (inspiring *horror*), though as the coiner of these terms points out it is the *fascinosum* that prevails in Augustine (Otto, 232). The violent emotions here recall the *thambos kai ekplexis* of Plotinus, a writer of great affective as well as interrogative mobility, to whom it is wrong to ascribe a marble calm (see Sorabji, 159–60, 165, 169). The words after *tamquam* integrate, post factum, the Platonic ecstasy into biblical perspective. The sense of alienation, deficiency, lack of being, accords with the Platonic tradition that presents the rays of the Good as blinding feeble minds.

From this encounter is born an ontological vision, which confirms Vieillard-Baron's claim that metaphysical experience "gives the élan for elaborating a complete metaphysics" and is "an absolute point starting from which the entire set of speculative utterances can be rethought." The voice of God that is imagined to be speaking is a later gloss ("as if") on the gulf Augustine feels between his own want of being and the supreme reality of the spiritual realm. The gulf Augustine perceives will be interpreted in Pauline terms as bondage to sin, to be broken at the end of book 8. But the Platonic topos of how the mind is dazzled and thrown back in mystical vision has no immediate connection with the Christian topics of sin and faith. The same note of failure or incompleteness inheres in Augustine's postconversion mystical moments also, and the explanation of it in terms of moral weakness is an extrinsic, ideological interpretation. In the anti-Pelagian writings the Pauline framework dominates and references to the mystical scenario recede, so that we have a more consistent but narrower vision. Both the Platonic language of vision and the Pauline language of grace were vehicles of encounters with ultimacy for Augustine, yet the tense pluralism between them, and between the corresponding experiences, is not erased in any leveling vision. Augustine needs to narrate his spiritual voyage, since no closed systematic presentation can do justice to the variety of encounters it embraced. As in every human life and every system of human thought, Augustine knew a variety of experiences and of intellectual perspectives, all shaped by the conventions of historical traditions, and while he sought to hammer them into the unity of a single vision, he left a literary record that respects their different textures, allowing Plotinian or Ciceronian terminology or argumentation to unfold in loose harmony with biblical analogues or in tension with them. Consider the contrast between the quasi-Plotinian evocations of truth in itself and the Good in itself in *De Trinitate* 8 with the neighboring discussion of biblical faith and charity. The lack of seamless integration of the two lines of thought testifies to Augustine's pluralistic experience. Consider, similarly, the juxtaposition of the Ciceronian development on the *beata vita* in *De Trinitate* 13.6–11 with the surrounding development on Jn 1:1–4 (13.1–5; 12) and the ensuing discussion of Christ as redeemer (13.12–24). "Et inspexi cetera infra te et vidi nec omnino esse nec omnino non esse: esse quidem, quoniam abs te sunt, non esse autem, quoniam id quod es non sunt" (7.17; And I beheld the other things below you, and I perceived, that they neither altogether are, nor altogether are not, for they are, since they are from you, but are not, because they are not what you are). Compare: "All these things are the One and not the One: they are he because they come from him; they are not he, because it is in abiding by himself that he gives them" (*Enn.* 5.2.2). These theses do not seem to derive directly from the vision but rather from a labor of reflection, which is in accord with the vision, unless one wants to detect here a gap or deconstructive fault line between vision and reflection. The content of the vision can be resumed as follows: to see how things are. It freed Augustine from reasonings that had gone round in circles for want of intuitive sustenance, but it freed him for a new reasoning that was better founded— unless we see those metaphysical cogitations as already betokening an enfeeblement of the vision, become memory.

Augustine's vision affirms the goodness of being, the convertibility of being and goodness, so that evil has no real existence. Such belief is inherent in biblical praise of the Creator, but it attains a specifically philosophical articulation in Augustine. In opposition to depressive Manichaean attitudes, it is wholesome and helpful to affirm in this way the radical goodness of being. Yet many questions might be asked about the nature, function, and status of this bedrock insight of Christian metaphysics. Augustine always steps back from its metaphysical articulation to the language of the Psalms. He is more inclined to confess that "nothing of what Thou, God, hast created can be bad" than to fix the certitude in ontological argument. He develops the argument but in the end brings it back to the act of praise. It is as well that he does so, since the metaphysical assertion can seem feeble when faced with actual evils, whereas praise and trust in the spirit of Job or of Rilke's *"Ich rühme"* can confront the scandal in authentic faith. Salvation lies not in metaphysics, however deep and true, but in the act of trust in the biblical God.

Note that the vision of book 7 freed Augustine's mind but not yet his will. For the latter we must wait for the encounter with Paul in book 8. This other pole of Augustine's inner world signals a limit of philosophy even when it takes on a mystical dimension. In a Protestant reading, this shows the secondariness or the impotence of mysticism, its uselessness for salvation, in comparison with faith. Disappointingly, Augustine, having well prepared this second major breakthrough by a dense presentation of the dialectic of the enchained will, gives no description of the moral liberation that the Pauline verses restored to him. The action of grace is more powerful here than in the encounter with Plotinus, and it concerns the heart of Augustinian thought, yet we find no equivalent of the hymn of joy that burst forth at the comparable moment in Romans (chapter 8).

The vision of book 7 is personalized by a Psalm quotation: "Mihi autem inhaerere deo bonum est" (Ps 72:28; In my want of being I can truly be only by dwelling in the one who is). The biblical quotations serve throughout to Christianize the Plotinian experience. From there he expounds his ontological vision of the convertibility of being and goodness, with the corollary that evil has no real existence, which overcomes Manichaeanism at its root (7.18–22). Are these ontological considerations seamlessly derived from the religious experience, or is Augustine reading back the fruits of years of thought into a single dawning of fresh insight?

Does ontological speculation already begin to project a space of thought that is in tension with the space opened up by the vision, and tend to screen it out? Is the vital immediacy of consciousness being replaced by a reflective objectification? Is speculative interest thwarting the unfolding of the phenomenological insight lying at the root of such convictions as the convertibility of being and goodness? If so, this process is carried further in the *De Trinitate*, where the experience of God as Spirit cohabits uneasily with the analysis of God as substance, and where analysis of triadic structures of an objectified "soul" is in tension with evocations of its preobjective consciousness.

Augustine tells how he sought to recapture the visionary moment by the practice of a Platonic ascent (as opposed to the complete gratuity of the initial enlightenment), passing by degrees (*gradatim*) from the beauty of bodies to that of the soul, and thence to the inner sense that even animals have, and to the reasoning faculty which judges the deliveries of that sense, until he reaches the level of intelligence, of *nous*, and above it the light whereby the intelligence judges. The ascent culminates in another ecstatic encounter with what truly is: "Et pervenit ad id quod est in ictu trepidantis aspectus" (7.23; and thus with the flash of one trembling glance it arrived at That Which Is). Augustine again falls back, more quickly this time: "Sed aciem figere non evalui et repercussa infirmitate redditus solitis non mecum ferebam nisi amantem memoriam et quasi olefacta desiderantem, quae comedere nondum possem" (But I could not fix my gaze thereon; and my infirmity being struck back, I was thrown again on my wonted habits, carrying along with me only a loving memory thereof, and a longing for what I had, as it were, perceived the odor of, but was not yet able to feed on).

Here the labor of deliberate cogitation precedes the mystical moment rather than subsequently reaping its harvest of insight. This intrusion of intellectual reflection into the sphere of infused contemplation has led one author to suppose that there is nothing mystical about the Milan experiences at all. Even the first experience (7.16) would represent, "not a mystical intuition of God, but an implicitly reasoned ascent of the mind to the height of truth which is God. . . . God is pictured as engaged in a brief I-Thou dialogue in which he tells Augustine that he is 'I am who am.' But this utterance is essentially an intellectual or quasi-theological locution, not a mystical deliverance" (Quinn 1994:258). This is a flat and literalistic paraphrase of Augustine's sublime words "Et clamasti de longinquo: immo vero ego sum qui sum. Et audivi, sicut auditur in corde" As Quinn describes it, "The analytical invocation of God's self-given name does not affectively move him or set his spirit afire; rather, it fills his mind with light . . . the satisfaction consequent upon a perception or experience characterized by expressions such as 'Aha!' or 'Eureka!' . . . He achieved intellectual fulfillment with an intense delight that Catholics born into the faith can abstractly conceive, but never concretely imagine" (1994:258–59). "Arrival at the apex of his reasoning process is accompanied by an undeniable intellectual pleasure as well as a peripheral affective satisfaction; still, neither of these affective modes even approaches full-flowered mystical experience. Significantly, the decisive factor of passivity is missing" (265). The intellectual and the affective are dissociated here in a way that cannot do justice to such thinkers as Plotinus and Augustine, in whom intellect and passion worked together in constant mutual illumination and stimulation. To see mysticism as a matter of "affectivity" and to suppose that because Augustine, following Plotinus, describes a mystical enlightenment of the mind, which also stuns the mind and exceeds its grasp, he must therefore be talking about something "merely intellectual" (though his language is charged with wonder and joy) is to bypass the phenomenon the text presents through reliance on cut-and-dried binary oppositions. (For the vibrant, indeed violent affectivity of Plotinian mysticism, taken up by Augustine, see Sorabji, 159–60, 165, 169.) Later Quinn modified this: "He was afforded a kind of vision, in this instance a short glimpse of the divine being . . . a quasi-intuition of God as spiritual light" (2002:367), though whether it was mystical remains a "disputed question" since there were "no indicators of strict passivity"; still, "he was the beneficiary of a mystical encounter in the broad sense, along quasi-Plotinian lines" (371).

Quinn (1994) finds genuine mystical passivity in the Ostia experience and ascribes it to the grace of the sacraments Augustine received and the spiritual life he practiced after his conversion. The idea that Augustine could have enjoyed mystical experience while in his unconverted state seems to Quinn to presuppose a special miracle, one God was unlikely to work. This is a surprisingly high-handed dismissal of the testimony of those who have had mystical experience in quite unchurched modes, behind whom lie legions of "mute inglorious Wordsworths." Augustine does underline the greater perfection of the joy of Ostia, firmly rooted in the practice of agape, and of friendship, and the communion of saints. "Whereas the earlier ascensions culminate not in mystic illumination but in a heightened lucid understanding of God or vision, only tenuously achieved, the Ostia event does not border on but is nothing less than a genuine mystical encounter" (Quinn 2002:506). But the Milan experience, at least in 7.16, has the notes of passivity and grace as well, as the phrases *duce te* and *tu assumpsisti me* indicate. It is of Milan not Ostia that Augustine writes that he touched *id ipsum, id quod est* in a moment of pure ecstasy, *in ictu trepidantis aspectus*. And *Ego sum qui sum* is no abstract proposition, as Quinn thinks, but *auditur in corde*—it is a homecoming to the maternal breast of being and to the paternal abode. The presence of God is with Augustine as a holy sweetness—*dulcedo mea sancta* (1.4), an inner light, food, strength, and the breast on which his thought reposes: "lumen cordis mei et panis oris intus animae meae et virtus maritans mentem meam et sinum cogitationis meae" (1.21). Perhaps the immediacy of the first encounter with the dazzling light is already waning when he hears the voice: "As he slips away from the relation that he longs to enter, God cries out to him from afar" (Vaught, 43).

The imagery of ascent can be translated into the more "passive" imagery of stripping away, Plotinian *aphairesis*. Like the Zen suppression of thought and images (*munen musō*), it allows the mind to be receptive to phenomena. The ascent is inward, away from the tumult of sense involvement, thus in the direction of noninvolvement in external activities, and of passivity before the higher light that enlightens the mind. Eckhart, reading this passage, refers to a *pati divina*: "quando scilicet lux divina per effectum suum aliquem specialem irradiat super potentias cognoscentes et super medium in cognitione, elevans intellectum ipsum ad id quod naturaliter non potest" (*LW* 5:93–94, quoted in Lossky, 180–81; when the divine light through one of its special effects irradiates upon the cognitive powers and the cognitive medium, elevating the intellect itself to that of which it is naturally incapable). The language of elevation is perhaps misleading, as well as archaic. The One of Plotinus is not only "above"; it is the reality nearest to hand. The negations of apophatic theology do not build a ladder to a remote beyond but remove illusions that prevent God from speaking to us here and now. In Mādhyamika and in Vedānta this is clearer; the dialectical negations serve not to take us beyond the world but to reveal emptiness or supreme reality in the here and now.

Both Milan and Ostia are breakthroughs to ultimacy, but the Ostia experience is richer and more integrated. Between them lies the moral conversion made possible through the impact of the words of St. Paul (8.29), another breakthrough to ultimacy, which allowed Augustine to be serenely at one with himself and with his fellow Christians. A crisis of Platonic eros is enacted in the "drop" Augustine feels after his first experience at Milan; the crisis is resolved when his eros or striving is inserted in the context of communal agape, *caritas*, and at Ostia Monica and Augustine taste the delights of this more securely rooted contemplation. Augustine is now on a spiritual plateau, in daily enjoyment of the *internum aeternum* (9.10). Though the language of the Ostia experience is still that of Platonic ascent, and in fact is close to the willed *tentative mystique* of Milan (see Courcelle, 157–67), the affective tonality is very different. The subject of the experience is not an isolated philosophical seeker but two friends united in serene praise of God in his creation.

> Erigentes nos ardentiore affectu in id ipsum perambulavimus gradatim cuncta corporalia . . . et venimus in mentes nostras et transcendimus eas, ut attingeremus regionem ubertatis indeficientis, ubi pascis Israhel in aeternum veritate pabulo. . . . Et dum loquimur et inhiamus illi, attingimus eam modice toto ictu cordis; et suspiravimus et relinquimus ibi religatas primitias spiritus et remeavimus ad strepitum oris nostri. (9.24)

[Raising ourselves up with a more glowing affection toward the "Self-Same," we passed by degrees through all things bodily . . . and we came to our own minds, and went beyond them, that we might arrive at that region of never-failing plenty, where you feed Israel for ever with the food of truth. . . . And while we were discoursing and panting after her [Wisdom], we slightly touched on her with the whole effort of our heart; and we sighed, and there we leave bound the first fruits of the Spirit; and returned to vocal expressions of our mouth.] (trans. Pusey, 194–95, modified)

Here again Augustine shows mastery of the conventional techniques of contemplation, of metaphysical analysis, of a rhetoric of eros mounting to meet the descending manna of agape (*ubi pascis Israhel*), and of the arts of fictional and dramatic presentation. Ostia might be seen as a synthesis or a dialectical result of the metaphysical vision of Milan and the moral liberation of the *tolle lege* scene, producing yet another way of experiencing ultimacy. Can we contrast Milan as "visual . . . , a vision of *God*," with Ostia as "tactile" and its "object" as "*Wisdom* rather than God as he is in himself" (Vaught, 128)? The same vocabulary (*ictus, idipsum*) underlines the immediacy of the breakthrough to ultimacy in both cases, yet the color of the experience is different.

Perhaps we might call this a Johannine ultimacy, given the key role of interpersonal love and the eloquence with which Augustine will discourse on this theme in his homilies on 1 John. The whole of scripture becomes a set of occasions for breaking through to the ultimate level of vision, and the hearers are urged to knock constantly until the light of *intellectus* dawns for them: "Surge, quaere, anhela desideria, et ad clausa pulsa" (*Tractatus in Iohannem* 18.7; Arise, seek, breathe your longing, and knock on what is closed). The taste of ultimacy gives Augustine great freedom in imaginative penetration of the biblical text, handled as a functional skillful means for evoking contemplative vision.

All of this work with conventions circles around the vividly experienced truth event, the encounter with *id ipsum*, an intimacy with the divine in conjunction with a privileged moment of intimacy with a beloved human being or in communion with the quest of the praying pilgrim community. Fragile and elusive as the moments of *intellectus* are, their value as clues to the ultimately gracious nature of reality spurs us to work on the conventions of our religious discourse to make them more effective antennae for picking up such signals. Augustine's entire theological oeuvre is an effort to render the conventional transparent to the ultimate. He joyfully disposed the linguistic and intellectual resources of his culture into alignment with this contemplative ultimacy. The equivalent achievement for theology today would be to explore the horizon of ultimacy onto which the questions, the lack, the unease of modern civilization open out, and to revamp religious discourse so that it no longer obstructs access to this realm but kindles experiences of ultimacy through recognition of its own thorough conventionality.

Chapter Seven

NEGATIVE THEOLOGY

When we try to approach the absolute origin of all being, we find that this origin eludes our grasp and takes on a nonfoundational, nonsubstantial character, indicated in Neoplatonism as the One beyond being, or as the Ineffable beyond even the One (Damascius); in Thomism as the infinite ocean of being, conceived as pure act, which can be grasped as a nothingness in regard to finite substances; in Buddhism as an ungraspable emptiness that is the ultimate truth emerging each time one subjects entities, or would-be entities, to a thorough critical analysis; and for Eckhart as utter darkness and unknowing, which prepares the soul for the divine infusion that inevitably comes (*Predigt* 59). In "praying God to deliver him from God," Eckhart transcends limited figures of God—such ideas as that God is good or wise or merciful—toward the unlimited realm of the divinity, just as Vedantins move from the creator (Iśvara) or the qualified Brahman (*saguṇa*) to the unqualified (*nirguṇa*) Brahman. The Islamic mystic Ibn Arabi (1165–1240) similarly moves from Allah to the unity of being, and Schelling moves from the positive identity of God to a prior original divine freedom. This step back to originary simplicity—the simplicity of the divine, the simplicity of being—unites religious paths in a basic orientation, even if speculative systems that build too confidently on

217

such mystical foundations should be discouraged (see Izutsu, 45–46). The importance of Eckhart as the one in whom this orientation emerges most clearly in Christian tradition is boosted not only by his rich retrieval of Neoplatonic apophatism and his influence on subsequent German thought about ultimate reality, down to Heidegger, but by the sense of immediate recognition he inspires in those steeped in the traditions of Buddhism, Taoism, and Vedānta. He is the one who cut the Gordian knot and who broke the sound barrier between East and West, releasing the fundamental religious sense from a misplaced evaluation of logic, doctrinal niceties, and objectifications, just as Nāgārjuna, Śaṃkara, and Chuang-tzu play that role in Asian traditions. All of these figures embrace emptiness, radically deconstructing the illusions that attach to religious belief, yet all of them express a deep trust in the goodness of reality.

Religious and theological language cannot remain permanently on these lofty heights, contemplating a silent ultimacy beyond the play of conventions. At a time when theological language, and faith itself, are exposed to incertitude, indecision, and instability, negative theology can have a therapeutic function. Much of the interest in negative theology among philosophers and religious thinkers today treats negative theology as an end in itself or as the summit of wisdom. But unless reinvested in a concrete therapeutic handling of religious language negative theology is no more than a speculative luxury. It can even become an ersatz for the critical modesty with which the traditional languages of faith need to be handled, for one can cultivate flights of apophasis and in the very next breath return to unreconstructed metaphysical dogma and speculation, as if the apophasis had made no effective difference to the actual fabric of Christian speech. Negative theology should subserve the task of articulating the truths of faith, preserving a due sense of the finite, human, incarnate condition of all theologies and all expressions of faith; that is, it is a critical auxiliary and should not take on an autonomous role as launching an ecstatic leap beyond all formulable utterance, into a mystical embrace of a divine night. As Nāgārjuna insisted, ultimacy can be communicated only by recourse to convention. Every reflection on ultimate simplicity should send us back with new appreciation to the complex conventions that have functioned effectively over the centuries as vehicles of religious communication.

A difference between the present situation and that presupposed in classic apophatic theology is that whereas the latter is in a sense parasitical on a stable basic language of faith, our basic language itself is infected with mobility and pluralism to such an extent that one might say the apophasis has begun as soon as we open our mouths. We understand very well that God is ineffable, because all the words we summon to speak of God fall pitiably flat and are soon shown up as the products of a particular culture and history marked by much fumbling. In contrast, classical negative theology develops in a regulated and systematic way, referring at every step to the well-defined base language. Today negative theology may highlight the intrinsically aporetic character of language about God and seek in this linguistic malaise itself a cipher of divine mystery. This homeopathic remedy risks worsening the malady it would heal, yet by remaining close to the incarnate condition of the language of faith it can correct both the crassness of an unreflectingly cataphatic language and the unreality of the apophatic languages of the past.

That unreality has largely to do with the Platonic origins of the apophatic tradition, which are mismatched both to biblical realities and to the changed epistemic conditions of today. To retrieve the apophatic tradition critically means to see clearly what its limits are and thus to overcome the excessive claims of this form of metaphysics within Christian tradition. At the same time this tradition can be appreciated as a labor of faith, especially when it ends up bringing Christian thought back to the humble fare of the incarnational economy. It is a resource for sharpening theological judgment but must itself be "vetted" in all its forms by that judgment. Recognition of the conventional fabric of Christian discourse can perhaps integrate and replace apophatic theology; in any case it provides a platform for revisiting the apophatic tradition and recovering its potential usefulness for today.

The apophatic tradition also opens doors of dialogue to Vedantic and Buddhist counterparts. Both in their critical awareness of the limits of language and conceptuality and in their cultivation of a spiritual awareness that curbs the babble and busyness of everyday thinking, these traditions challenge us to bring our language into new focus and to learn to use it more freely as an efficacious skillful means. Here again apophatic impulses double back on themselves and issue in a sense of the functionality and conventionality of language. Even the ultimate silence enacted by the legendary bodhisattva Vimalakīrti immediately sends us back to speech as skillful means.

NEGATIVE THEOLOGY AS PLATONIC

One feature that might seem to limit the usefulness of classical apophatic theology is that it is, to speak like Harnack, "a product of the Greek mind on the soil of the Gospel." If biblical language has come to seem insecure, there is no reason to expect that the language of Platonism, on which classical negative theology heavily relies, will be any less so. For Franz Rosenzweig, "All those who find here [in Ex 3:14] notions of 'being,' of 'the-one-who-is,' of 'the eternal,' are all Platonizing. . . . God calls himself not 'the-one-who-is' but 'the-one-who-is-there,' i.e. there for you" (quoted in Soskice, 493). By the same token, those who greet such Platonic expressions as "infinite," "ineffable," "beyond being," or "nonbeing" as clues to the reality of the biblical God are running athwart the texture of biblical revelation. If the Greek vocabulary of being makes God "merely metaphysically mysterious—no more mysterious, that is to say, than Plato's divine Architect or Aristotle's Prime Mover, indeed their kinsman" (493), recourse to the Greek vocabulary of "beyond being" merely ensures that one remains longer within the Greek language game, allowing a mystique of nonbeing to replace the distinct countenance of the God of Israel just as the promotion of being since the Septuagint translation of Exodus 3:14 masked it for two millennia. If the Platonist apophatic discourse steps aside from the concern with redemption to develop a theoretical epistemology of the divine, its legitimacy will be put in question in a theology that has recovered its biblical roots. Of course one can aim to shake up apophaticism and dislodge it from its Platonic framework, with help from the Oriental versions of apophasis. But it is worth dwelling carefully on the Platonic regime of apophatic theology predominant in the West, to show that it is not as radical and universal as was thought but rather represents a set of strategic moves within a particular metaphysical framework or language game.

Janet Soskice accepts that Rosenzweig's critique is "substantially true of a great many accounts of the divine attributes after Descartes and Locke" (493), metaphysical abstractions that have lost the dynamic and concrete character of the divine names in older theology. This reflects a suggestion of Marion that pre-Cartesian philosophical theology was concerned with the divine names rather than with "attributes" that God possesses; but while the confessional context of medieval theology works against an objectifying approach to the divine attributes, it would be hard to deny that the metaphysical quest to define God (as *ens a se*, *esse subsistens*, etc.) and to focus logically on such divine characteristics as simplicity, omnipresence, omniscience, and omnipotence was not fully subjected, even in Augustine and Aquinas, to the confession of the divine names. Rosenzweig's quarrel, then, is not with modern metaphysics; rather, it renews an ancient unease with the language of the Septuagint and Philo. It was Christian hands that saved these texts when the Jews were massacred or expelled from Alexandria in 115–17 CE, and subsequent Jewish thought has disregarded them (Mélèze Modrzejewski, 231). "Too Greek, too metaphysical by half!" is an ancient Jewish reaction to what the Septuagint and Philo make of the Hebrew Bible.

Philo "strains every Jewish fibre to say that this 'one-who-is' is always already 'the-one-who-is-there,' the one who is present to Israel. . . . It is indeed his heightened and distinctly Jewish sense of the holiness and otherness of God that precipitates in Philo the crisis of language for the divine—that propels him to say—the first as far as we know to formulate it thus—that God is unnameable and unknowable" (Mélèze Modrzejewski, 231). Even if this were so, it would not render unnecessary the task of a critical assessment of the massive importation of hellenistic metaphysics in Philo. John Dillon confirms that the terms *arrhētos*, *akatonomastos*, and *alataleptos* are first found in Philo (*Somn.* 1.67); but this is no indicator of a sturdy biblical sensibility resisting Platonism, since Plato himself said that the One is not *rhēton* (*Ep.* 7.341C) and has no *onoma* (*Parmenides* 142A), and

Platonists generally found it natural to say that God is *arrhēton* (Alcinoos, *Didaskalikos* 10.1 and 4) and unnamable (Maximus of Tyre, *Diss.* 17.9). That they were influenced by Philo in this is unlikely: "There is no indication that any of the school Platonists read Philo" (Dillon 1996b:155). The exegesis of the *Parmenides* sufficiently accounts for the preponderant sense of the ineffability, transcendence, and simplicity of the divine in Neoplatonism.

It is true that Philo's sense of divine holiness, shaped by the Pentateuch, led him to heighten these themes (notably in *De posteritate Caini* 13–22 and *De mutatione nominum* 7–17). Though Philo is the first major exponent of the Platonic hermeneutic of scripture, his biblical stress on creation—"The cosmos is totally dependent on God and God in no sense dependent on the cosmos" (Soskice, 495)—brings a more radical realization that "we *cannot class* God or insert God into any category appropriate to our created kind" (495), along with a sense of God as intimate and near. Thus from the start of the tradition of metaphysical theology the biblical vision works to resist and subvert the Platonic framework. But Philo is far from consciously problematizing his use of Platonic language. He evokes divine ineffability in terms of the Platonic structuring of reality, which can be at odds with the perspectives of biblical faith, even—or perhaps especially— when the phenomenological immediacy of the Platonic encounter with the One is brought out. Philo's concern with the divine names is indeed very Jewish, yet his stress on divine unnamability is rather unbiblical (despite Gen 32:29; Ex 3:14; Judges 13:18; Prov 30:4), even if "naming, in the philosophy known to Philo, involves classification and God cannot be classed" (Soskice, 503). It may be linked to the absence of the name YHWH in the Septuagint (Starobinski-Safran, 50). Unbiblical, too, are the rational explanations Philo gives of such titles as *Lord* and *God*. The seven to nine proper names of God in Judaism (see Dupuy, 105–6, 118–19) are unlike ordinary names; they cannot be manipulated, and they guard the divine transcendence. This sense of the divine names as themselves the shield of divine transcendence is lacking in Philo. Or it has become confused with a hellenistic sense that the purity of the One is preserved by consigning involvement with lower cosmic levels to subordinate entities such as the Powers (a

Platonic expression; Dillon 1996b:161) or angels (the equivalent of Plato's mediating *daimones*).

At some point the Platonically shaped tradition of divine ineffability may become an ersatz for articulating the biblical sense of transcendence. As a convention of theistic discourse it may lose its cutting edge and become merely a received piety. Of course the same can be said of biblicist reactions to it. Even the most finely calibrated frameworks are only a means toward enunciating questions and answers that engage with the matter itself. The task of theological judgment is to identify the points where an ancient discourse effectively connects with living concerns and to take these points as guides for an evaluative rereading. Platonism is based on powerful experiences, reflected on in the most refined concepts, and undoubtedly it catches in its net a great amount of metaphysical and religious truth. But modern thought has woven a different fabric, with which theology must engage. That engagement is ill conceived if it takes the form of defending a heritage of Platonic wisdom from a modernity assumed to be culturally inferior. Rather, Platonic thought forms must be detected and translated or overcome wherever they lodge in our tradition, in order to bring it into living dialogue with the present.

Philo holds that one can attain a real knowledge of the God who truly *is*: "But the being that in reality IS can be perceived and known, not only through the ears, but with the eyes of the understanding [*dianoia*], from the powers that range the universe, and from the constant and ceaseless motion of His ineffable works. Wherefore in the great Song there come these words as from the lips of God, 'See, see that I AM' (Deut 32:39), showing that He that actually IS is apprehended by clear intuition rather than demonstrated by arguments carried on in words" (*Post.*, 167; trans. Colson and Whitaker). But this knowledge offered by the biblical text consists not in seeing God but only in seeing that he exists; or—in a slightly contradictory interpretation, when we say that God is visible, the word is used in an irregular way, to refer only to the two Powers of God, "for it is impossible that the God who IS should be perceived at all by created beings." Thus the meaning of the text is "Behold my subsistence [*hyparxis*]." "For it is quite enough for a man's reasoning faculty to advance as far as to learn that the Cause of the Universe is and subsists. To be anxious to continue his course yet further, and inquire about essence [*ousia*] or quality in God, is a folly fit for the world's childhood" (168). What comes "after God" (Ex 33:23) can be grasped by the wise, but God himself is *akatalēptos* by a direct approach, even if he is "brought within ken by the powers that follow and attend Him; for these make evident not His essence but His subsistence from the things which He accomplishes" (169). The statement that we can know that God is but not what God is had a long life in apophatic rhetoric but hardly proved a fertile source of theological insight; it is a rather irritating schema, tied to a summary ontology.

This Philonic tradition lends weight to the apophatic touches in Basil and Gregory of Nyssa. Among the themes that echo Philo are the following: (1) one can know *that* God is but not *what* God is; (2) his powers (*dunameis*), but not his essence, can be known; (3) God is known by his activities (*energeiai*); (4) the divine essence is indefinable, infinite. Gregory differs from Philo in rejecting any being midway between God and the creation (*Her.* 45.205–6; *Somn.* 2.188–89; *QE* 2.94; Daniélou, 125–28), an idea that makes Philo the father of neo-Judaism, that is, Arianism (*CE* 3.7, 8–9). Again it is not clear how these themes connect with the question of how God is known and how God is hidden today. A secure knowledge of God on the basis of contemplating the cosmos or the saving acts recorded in scripture is less accessible than in the time of the Cappadocians, and it often seems as if knowledge of God reduces to fragments, to hints and guesses, pointers found in ethical concern, aesthetic perception, in religious or ecclesial experience, and only in a much enfeebled sense in metaphysical speculation. The Christocentrism or Christomonism of some theologians is a refuge from this elusiveness of the divine, and it tends to invest in the figure of Christ the absoluteness and fixed identity that can no longer be securely upheld in regard to God. The new version of apophasis would then be "We cannot know God, but only God as revealed in Christ," which, despite its echo of John 1:18, actually foreshortens the scope of biblical revelation and produces a double distortion, generating a monophysite image of Christ and subjecting the divine to anthropomorphic projections (Balthasar, Moltmann). Jesus, like the other biblical figures in whose lineage he stands, lived *coram Deo* in the openness of a horizon of ultimate trust. The Johannine language of a nonduality between Christ and the Father should not be used to close off this horizon.

If classical negative theology from Philo on takes as starting point the questions of Platonism about the knowledge of God, the effects of this cannot be mitigated by some subsequent adjustments. A metaphysical captivity of the biblical God is already afoot when the authority of Platonic vocabulary is recognized, even with some show of resistance. Platonizing theology reflects biblical realities, but in a distorting mirror. If we still lived in a Platonic world, these distortions would go unnoticed, but the course of history has removed us so far from that world that if we notice a Platonic structure in a theologian we realize that we are dealing with an older inculturation of the biblical vision that must now be surpassed. An erudite imagination may delight in recreating an archaic world of thought and in living in it, but theology, responsible to the present canons of intelligibility, cannot rest content with this, still less make it a prescribed virtue. Patristic scholars are wont to declare that Harnack's "hellenization thesis" is long discredited, and in doing so they often unwittingly subscribe to a restorationist attitude that impedes attention to the play of intellectual forces in the ancient texts and the hermeneutic challenge they present for the articulation of faith today. To be sure, the critical assessment of governing horizons of thought can seem an unbearable complication of the task of historical scholarship. Yet if it is neglected, systematic theologians, relying on the findings of the historical scholars, are left without a compass in their appropriation of the past and will be weakened in their effort to negotiate between a frozen heritage and the anarchic dismissals of it by postmodern philosophers.

Though the apophatic elements in Platonism were not purely the result of philosophical epistemological analysis but were rooted in a particular style of Greek religious piety, they tended to set off a critical ferment within the religious *Lebenswelt* when brought to bear on terms such as *God*, which have a pragmatic sense as used within a religious lifestyle (Dalferth, 118). The result can be dissolution of concrete God-language into empty metaphysical abstraction, in which

God becomes an unknowable X. Rosenzweig admits that we know nothing of God but then goes on to stress, paradoxically, that "this not-knowing is a not-knowing of God. As such it is the beginning of our knowing him"; negative theology has too often "understood this not-knowing as the end and result of our knowledge" of God (quoted in Dalferth, 120). Naturally, theologians in the three Abrahamic religions seek to bind apophatic methods to the positivity of the scriptural revelations. As they seek to accommodate these methods to the particular constraints of the practical religion, they may find it difficult to close the gap between the Platonic procedures and the concrete needs of Jewish, Christian, and Islamic discourse on a personal God. Too philosophical, apophatic thinking remains on the margin and is not harmoniously integrated into the tissue of theology. Perhaps that is the real reason why, despite the enthusiasm of its adherents, its historical destiny has been rather ghostly.

A MODEL: GREGORY OF NYSSA

Since Pseudo-Dionysius (sixth century), apophasis in theology is marked by the use of dizzying paradox and hyperbole. Let us step back behind this author to a more elementary stage of its development, where it remains more fully at the service of the ordinary language of faith, by looking at a minitreatise on negative theology inserted by Gregory of Nyssa into his second book against Eunomius, shortly after the Council of Constantinople of 381 (*CE* 2.67–127). According to the Cappadocians, the radical Arian bishop Eunomius had excessive confidence in the capacity of human thought and language to define the divine essence. Correcting this, they stressed the impossibility of grasping that essence. This apophasis was thus a weapon in controversy before it became, in Gregory's later writings, a source of spiritual nourishment.

A more generous interpretation might have recognized in Eunomius himself an apophatic theologian. He taught that divine names are all synonymous and that when a name such as "light" is shared by God and a creature (such as the Son, first of creatures and creator of the others), it can be only in a purely equivocal sense. To confess God as "ingenerate" would thus not be a hubristic attempt to define his essence but would rather be comparable to the Jewish use of the Tetragrammaton to indicate what lies beyond all ordinary naming. "For Eunomius insistence on *agennētos* as characterizing the divine *ousia* is a way of spelling out what is implicit in the fact that God's name is *ōn* [who is]" (Wiles, 166). Origen, too, had spoken of the divine essence as having a single name, "He who is" (Ex 3:14), with which all the other names are synonymous (*De Orat.* 14.2), whereas the Son, since he lacks the absolute simplicity of God, possesses many distinct *epinoiai*. The Eunomian slogan "God is *agennētos ousia*" could be read with the accent on *ousia*, as an assurance "that the God whom we claim to know is real, or better *the* real, and not a figment of the imaginative power of human words" (Wiles, 168). Eunomian cataphasis is minimal, limited to naming God as he is and as he commands us to name him, without any play of human considerations brought in from outside. Stressing the simplicity of the divine essence, Eunomius gives the plurality of divine attributes a nominalist status; they can serve only to express the essence again and again, and the variety of their significations is illusory.

Across the centuries, William of Ockham seems to connect with Eunomius when he rejects the Thomist and Scotist view that we can name aspects of God that differ in reason yet communicate objective knowledge of the simple divine essence: "Thus nothing is said absolutely of God, except 'God,' for, speaking absolutely, God is only God. Beneath connotative names, there must be a name that is absolute, that is, one that does not signify one thing at a first level and another at a second," for example, " 'God,' which alone allows us to say absolutely 'God is God' " (Muralt, 183). This causes us to fall back into a radical apophasis: " 'God is in everything in every way one and indistinct' is all one can say distinctly about God. . . . An attribute is said of God only in virtue of the effect that God produces in the creature according to that attribute. . . . Nothing is said of God, for the tautology 'God is God' is vain, as long as nothing else is said of God" (184). But Ockham does not teach the synonymity of the attributes (*In Sent.*, dist. 3, qu. 2).

For Basil and his brother, the attributes do not name the essence but represent our conceptions (*epinoiai*) about it; or rather, as Andrew Radde-Gallwitz has clarified, they represent intrinsic properties of God, which believers instinctively ascribe to God, such as goodness, justice, mercy. But Basil's scriptural good sense cannot suffice to ward off Eunomius's logical questions or to make unnecessary the tighter account of divine attributes developed in later theology, which stresses the *fundamentum in re* of the attributes, and the identity of each attribute with the essence. Basil and Gregory themselves recognize from time to time that they are in agreement with Eunomius on this point, an agreement that would have been easier to see if Eunomius had chosen to illustrate his view of theological language by an attribute other than the ambiguous "ingenerability" (*agennēsia*), which can mean "without a Father" or "without a cause" (*agenētos* with one *n*). The negative character of this attribute prompts a hasty reaction from Gregory: "How can something purely negative name the divine essence?" In its trinitarian sense (*agennētos*) the term signifies that the Father is not generated; the status of this idea remained obscure for the Cappadocians.

Gregory teaches that our *epinoiai* grasp only what is around the divine essence, whereas the *hypokeimenon* remains ungraspable (*CE* 1.181–82), and that God's being, "what he is by essence, flees every attempt at comprehension and every investigation. For us, as the word of Wisdom somewhere says, 'From the greatness and beauty of created things comes an analogous perception of their creator' (Wisd 13:5), by his operations [*energeiai*], conferring only faith, not knowledge of what he is" (*CE* 2.12–13). Philo is clearly the ancestor of these ideas.

In the systematic exposition of this negative theology in *Contra Eunomium* 2.67–129, Gregory speaks at length in his own voice, interrupting his commentary on Basil's *Against Eunomius* and Eunomius's riposte to it. This minitreatise is marked by high-flying rhetorical passages. He enunciates a thesis: "There is no capacity in human nature for the exact apprehension of the nature of God" (2.67), supported by three proofs. "Gregory deploys three proofs, metaphysical, mystical, and epistemological, of divine incognoscibility. The second is entirely his own. The other two, though developing insights of Basil's, receive a quite new systematic character" (Pottier, 36). But perhaps it is an undue leveling to speak of three proofs. One finds rather (a) an exposition on divine unknowability, based on the difference between finite and infinite (*CE* 2.67–83); (b) a discussion of faith as the only path to knowledge of God, illustrated by Abraham (2.84–96); (c) practical, biblical counsels on the right use of knowledge, against the idle speculation of Eunomius (2.97–129).

(a) The Ontological Gulf between Finite and Infinite Makes God Unknowable

Not only humans, but all creatures, are incapable of grasping God. Gregory evokes rhetorically the diversity of creatures, bringing out the exalted status of angels and the failure of even their understanding before the divine majesty: "The barrier which separates uncreated nature from created being is great and impenetrable. One is finite, the other infinite" (*CE* 2.69; trans. Hall, 74). The proof continues with an argument *a fortiori*: We do not know the essence of finite things, how much less that of the infinite. First Gregory signals the analogy between the two kinds of knowing: we see that cosmic phenomena *exist*, but we do not grasp their *essence*. Similarly, of God, "We know that he Is, but admit we are unable to understand his Being" (2.71; trans. Hall, 75), an echo of Philo.

With almost Kantian glee, Gregory shows the dilemmas of cosmological inquiry, driven by quenchless curiosity yet at the same time obliged to respect logical coherence (*to akolouthon*; 2.75). The argument reaches a dizzy summit: "If one were to speculate mentally and suppose that this too has a frame which ensures that it stays firmly in place, then surely the argument must logically go on to postulate a framework for that framework, and for that another, and for the next yet another, so that the inquiry repeats itself and goes on in an infinite regress, ending up in perplexity" (2.75; trans. Hall, 76). An alternative theory, based on the idea of the void, falls victim to antinomies exposed in a string of quick-fire questions (2.76). Larger questions show how cosmic phenomena elude explanation in many ways (2.77).

The conclusion: "He who made all things by wisdom alone knows how to account for the universe; and for our part, 'By faith we perceive that the worlds were made by the word of God,' as the Apostle says (Heb 11:3)" (2.78; trans. Hall, 77). Thus fideism infiltrates scientific cosmology.

An *a fortiori* argument follows:

> If then the lower creation, which is within range of our perceptive faculties, lies beyond the limits of human knowledge, how can the one who by his mere will constituted the universe be within the grasp of our mind? . . . It is like infants. . . . Often, when a sunbeam streams in upon them through a window, they are delighted by its beauty and pounce on what they see, and try to take the sunbeam in their hand . . . , but when the clasped fingers are opened, the handful of sunbeam makes the children laugh and clap because it has slipped from their hands. So too the children of our generation (Mt 10:11) . . . clutch with logical tricks at the intangible to catch it, and suppose that they can get hold of it with syllogisms. . . . They toy vainly with the impossible, and with childish hand lock up the incomprehensible nature of God in the few syllables of "unbegottenness." (*CE* 2.79–82; trans. Hall, 77–78)

The sunbeam image indicates that the divine nature offers no hold to the mind that would grasp it. Elsewhere Gregory speaks of seizing the ocean with one's hands, an image that might allow one to think of some drops of knowledge remaining in the hand. The present polemic context pushes to a more purely negative conclusion. It is noteworthy that he does not refer to the divine simplicity as what frustrates the intellect, but only to infinity. Simplicity was a theme that attracted Eunomius, but Gregory is more inclined to think of infinity, perhaps to correct a meager and reductionist quality in Eunomius's cult of simplicity.

Note that the upshot of the argument is purely negative. "The concept of infinity plays a key role in his explanations of the distance separating Creator and creation as well as the way they come together through participation. These two uses of the concept have given rise to different interpretations depending on which one is emphasized" (Harrison, 25). In a first emphasis, "God, whose existence is not structured by *diastēma*, eludes our comprehension. In him there is no discernible sequence for us to grasp, measure and analyze, as is the case with created things" (26). In its completely apophatic sense, infinity "is not a boundless ocean of being or a fullness of positive perfections but a simple absence of limit or boundaries. It says nothing about what God is; only that time, space and *aiōn*, which structure boundaries as we know them, are not present in him. There is a radical ontological discontinuity between God and us, which nothing can bridge" (29). In contrast, the second emphasis envisages "the infinity of positive perfections" and "leads directly to the infinity of unending growth in our knowledge of God" (33). "For Mühlenberg, God is the infinite horizon toward which we move in an unending series of steps" (33–34). There is some talk of God as the infinite fullness of perfect life elsewhere in *Contra Eunomium*, but the mystical or contemplative aspect of this is in evidence only in the section that now follows.

Gregory, in this discussion, has not contented himself with building a biblical fence around divine holiness and transcendence; nor has he remained content with Platonic or Philonic clichés. Rather, he has put forth a strong rethinking of the nature of God in terms of infinity. The precedents for this positive sense of infinity in philosophy and in previous Christian tradition are obscure and disputed. Even if we take the dominance assumed by the notion in Gregory's mind as an effect of biblical contemplation, we note that the construction of the notion and the arguments supporting it are dependent on philosophic tradition. This new image of God is again a product of the Greek mind on biblical soil, and we may expect to find it in tension or even rivalry with a more strongly biblical thinking about God.

(b) The Knowledge of Faith, Illustrated by Abraham

So far negative theology has been presented as discouraging speculation, and not at all as providing a launching pad for a hyperknowledge of the divine beyond conceptuality, even if Gregory has quietly or unwittingly slipped in a quite strong speculative vision of God as infinite.

Apophasis has sent us back to the created domain, to an indirect knowledge of God by his works. Now Gregory turns to a more positive and biblical aspect of divine incomprehensibility, which allows a higher relation to God by faith. The scriptural references, especially the figure of Abraham, again take us into Philonic territory. In later works it will be Moses who exemplifies Gregory's apophasis in its fullest development, again clearly under Philo's influence. But in *Contra Eunomium* 2 the apophatic attitude is more modestly represented by Abraham, who, as also in Philo, has a simpler experience of the unknown God: "Abraham . . . so far as possible lifted his mind above its ordinary material limits. . . . 'Walking by faith and not by sight' (2 Cor 5:7), he rose up so far in his breadth of knowledge as to be reckoned the measure of human perfection, knowing God as far as was possible for this little, mortal power to reach out to and achieve" (*CE* 2.85–86). The traditional interpretation of Abraham's migration from the sensible to the intelligible receives a Pauline inflection through the words "walking by faith," which is what distinguishes Gregory's image of Abraham from Philo's.

The ascending movement of apophasis, as a dialectical progression from stage to stage, which will later intoxicate Gregory and still more Dionysius, begins to appear in the following text, which expounds the basic apophatic dynamic:

> In thinking about God he was led to an understanding by nothing material. . . . From the beauty of things observed and the harmony of the heavenly wonders he yearned to see the original model of beauty. In the same manner, all the rest of what he grasped as his reasoning advanced,—whether power, or goodness, or existence without beginning, or being bounded by no end, or whatever similar idea we may have for the divine nature,—using all these as means and staircase for his upward journey, always stepping upon what he had discovered and reaching out to what lay ahead, "setting up in his heart," as the prophet says, the beautiful "rising stairs" (Ps 84:6). . . . Having cleansed his mind of such notions, he resorted to faith . . . , and he took as his indicator, infallible and manifest, of the knowledge of God just this—that he believed God to be greater and higher than any epistemological indicator. (*CE* 2.88–89)

Abraham here quite properly approaches the divine through creatures. But far from remaining in a modest epistemological situation, as the earlier discussion might have led us to expect, he undertakes a Platonic ascent that brings the higher noetic satisfaction of grasping the ideal model of sensible things. Then he moves beyond the level of ideas to the unknowable, as the very mark of God's character. Philo did not develop the idea that knowledge of God is beyond concepts, nor did he conceive Jacob's ladder in terms of a perpetual movement of ascension, nor did he retain the erotic and aesthetic associations of Plato's ladder image (*Symposium*). Gregory's account is quite dramatic and might recall the majestic progress of Plotinus's great tetralogy (*Enn.* 3.8; 5.8; 5.5; 2.9). At the top of the ladder, however, Abraham switches from intellection to faith, leaving behind all the notions acquired in the ascent. The epistemic content of this faith without ratiocination is a "knowledge of God," but one with a negative cast, consisting in the realization that God surpasses "any epistemological indicator." Plotinus might say the same about the union with the One; even in foregrounding the faith of Abraham, Gregory is shadowed by the Platonist model. But he is not entirely reabsorbed by it, for the eschatological character of Abraham's faith, his reaching out to a future that lies ahead, gives an irreducible biblical inflection to the Platonic movement of transcendence.

Abraham here learns the divine attributes by *epinoia*, a relatively modest intellectual activity. "It is not clear from the text to what extent this involves philosophical inference and to what extent it is direct noetic perception" (Harrison, 65). As he advances in insight, "he puts aside what he can guess about the divine nature from its presence and activity in creation and seeks a greater knowledge of that nature itself. What he finds is that the greatest possible knowledge of God is an awareness that he is greater than all we can know of his presence and activity, hence that he is incomprehensible and ineffable. Abraham arrives at his awareness of divine incomprehensibility by a kind of ecstasy" (65). With regard to "the relation between the patriarch's shocking encounter with the Unknowable and the bride's intimate union with it through faith," Harrison suggests that "an initial shock is gradually transformed through experience and familiarity into loving intimacy" (71). Perhaps this supplies Abraham with a more detailed psychology than the text warrants. Suffice it to say that the ultimate apophatic posture has passed from nescience before infinity to blind faith in God as the greatest and highest. One can surely not say that "there is no explicit apophasis in Gregory" (Williams, 35). Rather, a variety of apophatic models jostle one another. It is true that even in *The Life of Moses* and *The Homilies on the Song of Songs* Gregory does not develop an apophatic method as systematic as that of Dionysius. His concern with the equilibrium between apophasis and cataphasis gives his thought a practical character that impedes such systematization (as is still more the case for Basil and Gregory Nazianzen). "Cataphatic and apophatic theology are of equal value. Neither of them assures participation in God nor describes the essence of God as such. Both are at best approximations with limited validity. On this point Gregory differs from the author of the *Corpus Areopagiticum*, who accords to apophasis a clear precedence over against cataphasis" (Alexopoulos, 414–15). It is striking that this movement of transcendence does not lead to a dark night of the pure ineffable or to a touching of the One in its absolute simplicity but is rooted in a basic posture of faith, which includes a relation to a personal God and a temporal progress guided by eschatological hope. "There is no way to come near to God, unless faith interposes and of itself joins the enquiring mind to the incomprehensible nature. . . . What eludes our understanding, faith makes ours, by its own assurance guaranteeing the unseen. . . . It is safer and at the same time more reverent to believe that the divine majesty is more than can be thought of, than to restrict his glory by certain ideas and think there is nothing beyond that" (*CE* 2.91–96).

Gregory does not transform the faith of Abraham into something purely spiritual, an ecstatic transcendence abandoning concepts for utter simplicity. The life of faith is not an epistemological condition only but an existence in time, striving forward to things hoped for. Whereas Philo's Abraham progresses in the one direction of Platonic ascent, Gregory's rejoins the path of the ordinary faithful. Like Basil, Gregory bases faith on the words of scripture and creed and sees heretics as estranged from the obedience of faith and captivated by a speculative attitude poorly accorded to our relationship to the God who gives himself to be known in human words and a fleshly economy.

This rootedness in the positivity of the kerygma is a virtue essential to any apophasis that calls itself Christian, a virtue often lost in later tradition. In Gregory himself there is a tension in the way his writing moves back and forth between Platonic epistemology and biblical eschatology. With Basil (*CE* 1.1), Gregory sees theology as circumscribed by the biblical word, so that apophasis serves to cut off speculative flights and bring us back to where we already are. This sober return causes J. P. Williams to underestimate the status of Gregory as apophatic theologian; she sees him as a stage toward Dionysius rather than a precious corrective to the latter's excesses. We can see, however, that Gregory could have gone much further along the Platonist path of transcendence and that he labors instead to subordinate it to the biblical path of faith and hope, showing a firmer grasp of the latter than Dionysius does.

One may say of both Plotinus and Gregory that "the negations refer indeed to the absolute, but can only circle it from outside, without reaching It itself" (Alexopoulos, 415). But even at the level of divine being the ontology of Gregory remains realistic. He advances an affirmative discourse on God based on five justifications: the orientation of the mind to knowledge and contemplation; the attraction of God as the goal of an unceasing quest, which awakens the soul and calls it to a participation in God as the source of all good; the affinity (*syngeneia*) of the soul with God, expressed in the doctrine of the Image, dear to the Greek fathers; the traces of God in creation that stimulate the mind to an analogical reflection on the God who exceeds our conceptual grasp; the incarnational economy that opens a path leading up toward God. The *epinoiai* continue to play a constructive role in Gregory's thought throughout his career. They are linked to the kinetic and diastematic character of creation. Their use in speech about God is necessary but awkward, and Gregory has a modest sense of the untrustworthy side of these tools of thought. He has no ambition, then, to form a complete and transparent system. Theology is at the service of the concrete language of faith, which it defends and elucidates in response to circumstantial needs. To see this reflection as a relatively primitive stage, at which theology had not yet mastered its methods, would be to underestimate Gregory. At a time when old theological fortresses find themselves poorly defended against the assault of new questions it would be a good idea to study this classical instance of a theology forming itself in relation to its concrete context. "The status of *epinoetic* theological discourse . . . is that every truth about God is also a lie about God and that every theological utterance aimed at accurately 'hitting' the truth of God unavoidably also contains fragments of the very same stones hurled at God by the heretics. . . . Truth 'from above' always appears, as it were, 'from below.' . . . Truth takes a detour, a detour always marked by a type of *kenōsis* that denies itself a complete noetic return to its absolute source" (Douglass, 466). If Gregory was indeed conscious of the impurity and the makeshift character of theological language long before it became streamlined in seamless scholastic syntheses, then he is a model for a theology once again facing its fragmented state and learning to be constantly self-critical.

(c) Biblical Wisdom and the Right Use of Knowledge

The third argument against speculation on the divine nature points to its unhappy epistemological effects. This is less an argument than a parenesis drawing practical consequences from what preceded: "Speculating about the obscure . . . allows admission and currency also to false ideas. . . . If all curiosity is stilled, then surely the inevitability of error is excluded with it" (*CE* 2.97–99).

The biblical authors identify God in a practical style. In the case of created things, "What each of them is, and how and whence, they did not say. So also with God, 'that he is, and is a rewarder of those who seek him' (Heb 11:6), they urge us to believe, but his nature itself, as being above every name, they neither named it nor were likely to" (*CE* 2.103). The ignorance in which scripture leaves us about the divine essence is then set in the context of a more general ignorance: "We humans live in total ignorance: in the first place about ourselves, and then about everything else" (2.106). This is even more unsettling than cosmological ignorance, for it concerns what is nearest to us. In neither case does scripture fill the void of our ignorance. The lesson to be drawn is that one ignorant of his own nature should not "meddle with the hidden things which lie outside him" (2.117). Science is left with a purely pragmatic status: "We learn by the senses just enough about the elements of the world to be able to make use of each for our life, but as to a definition of their being, we have not understood it, nor do we regard our ignorance as a disadvantage" (2.117). Scripture is the guide and model for the practical use of knowledge of things created and divine. Eunomius sins against common sense; in contrast with the wise Basil, he is paralyzed by infatuation with speculative arguments. "We have a faint and slight apprehension of the divine Nature through reasoning, but we still gather knowledge enough for our slight capacity through the words which are reverently used of it" (2.130).

We may take Gregory's negative theology as a landmark. It never goes beyond common sense or yields to inflationary tendencies, and its use of hellenistic rhetoric remains in subordination to biblical and ecclesial concerns. The course of history will take us far from this starting point. But in light of the testimonies to incarnational realism in Eckhart and Luther, and the critiques of negative theology from linguistic and phenomenological philosophers, and above all thanks to encounters with Asian thought, we shall rediscover Gregory with new appreciation as we delve into the roots of apophasis in this-worldly experience.

To be sure, Gregory is not as exciting in terms of speculative prowess as the medieval scholastics or the German idealists. But theological judgment can benefit from lingering with the fathers, for several reasons. Historical proximity to the origins of the Christian tradition gives their interpretations and misinterpretations of the biblical data a firsthand quality no longer to be found when theologians begin to build self-consciously on each other's work, taking up debates that have reached such a pitch of elaboration that the original point is lost from view. Even negative theology, from Pseudo-Dionysius on, becomes an abstruse and arcane scholarly game, whereas in Gregory it remains very close to the common sense of the believer engaging directly with the biblical word. In the past, theologians would often skip over the patristic sources so essential to the genealogy of any theme they discussed, for they believed that the march of scientific speculation had left the gropings of the fathers far behind. A sober historical self-critique of the Christian tradition was far from their minds. The authority of the fathers was put in question by the theologians of the Reformation, who often aimed to start afresh from the biblical text, though they, too, became entangled in an opaque scholasticism in the seventeenth century. In the same century, a critical retrieval of the fathers began within Roman Catholicism and Anglicanism. Study of the fathers was a spiritual formation (Quantin, 249–51), yet it had a desacralizing effect (583) as it undercut the standing of scholasticism (107), undermined the Tridentine ideal of the *consensus patrum* (566–67), and exposed the historical roots of dogma. Thus it had both a steadying and a subtly subversive effect on theological culture, as can be seen again in the role played by patristic scholarship in the preparation of Vatican II. Today we are likely to view the fathers from a critical distance, appraising their work as an inculturation of the Christian Gospel within the thought forms of antiquity and seeing also the limits of the now archaic conventions that it depended on. In their negative theology the fathers could be seen as measuring the limits of their own thought, but in such a way as to shore up the conventions of Platonism, failing to overcome them (though Gregory might be invoked as pointing the way to such overcoming). The kind of apophasis that the present situation of theological thought makes necessary is very different from the classical patristic (and medieval) models. A renegotiation of the terms on which the fathers addressed the problems of speaking about God can serve not only to break the hold of past conventions but also to clarify and put in historical perspective our present strategies for speaking the unspeakable.

OVERCOMING CLASSICAL NEGATIVE THEOLOGY

More than in the case of Origen or Augustine, the flaws in the synthesis between biblical faith and Greek philosophy in the work of Pseudo-Dionysius made themselves keenly felt in its reception across the centuries. Today some still invoke the Dionysian tradition as a panacea enabling a renewal or radicalization of theological method. It might be more fruitful to focus on the disturbance this tradition creates within theology, where it acts as a deconstructive ferment but also as a dissolvent of the concrete bases of biblical faith. To deploy the resources of apophasis so that they increase the clarity and vitality of the articulation of faith, we must bear in mind that apophasis is always led by concern for a concrete phenomenon. Its work is like that of a sculptor removing—*aphairesis*—whatever blocks the emergence of the form in its splendor. A rhetoric of the aporetic, the impassible, the impossible, inspired by Derrida, risks losing this concrete function of negative theology. Heidegger sometimes has apophatic locutions, as when he says of being, "It is Itself." But these clearly subserve attention to the phenomenon of being and are phenomenological translations of Parmenides' *Esti gar einai* ("for there is being"). Likewise, Buddhist ultimate truth (*paramārtha-satya*) refers to the phenomenality, the thusness, of what is near to hand, not to some remote transcendence.

In Dionysius, too, apophasis, by the sequence of its negations, delimits the contours of a presence, permitting one to "adhere without speech or cognition to the ineffable and unknowable realities, according to the union that surpasses the capacity and strength of our intellect" (*Divine Names* 1.1; [PG 3] 585b–588a). He tends, however, to make ineffability do too much work, as if this ineffability were the principal defining feature of godhead. This strategy is in tension with his stress on biblical words as the sole legitimate language on God (*DN* 1.2; 588c). The God who is unknowable in himself lets himself be known in his names and effects. These show him as supreme being, as the source of all being, yet in himself he lies beyond being. Cataphasis even at its most exalted, in a meditation on Exodus 3:14, is subordinate to and surpassed by apophasis. Only with Dionysius do we see a full Christian reception of the structures of Neoplatonic apophasis, which was nourished by meditation on Plato's *Parmenides*, in contrast to the more modest apophatism of the *Timaeus*, the favored text of the Middle Platonism that provided the context for Philo and the earlier Greek fathers.

That God eludes conceptual grasp but is given in intuition is a fundamental Neoplatonic tenet: "The One as most intensive actuality is not to be spoken of with categories that may apply to the realm of the many" (Proclus, quoted in Beierwaltes 2001a:53). Indeed, everything that Dionysius says about cataphatic and apophatic language comes from Proclus, even up to the fine point that the negative dialectic of "hyper" ends in the negation of negations themselves, so that one falls silent before the ultimate, which is beyond affirmation and negation: "Ipsas negationes removit ab uno" (*In Parm.* 7.72.1). Dionysius agrees with Proclus that "the negation of negation frees thinking from being and nonbeing. . . . One must transcend even the thinking that negates, so as to become as like as possible to the origin" (Beierwaltes 1979:361). What lies beyond affirmation and negation is not their synthesis. Rather, the two paths clear a space for the emergence of something quite independent of them: the intuition of the One in its pure simplicity (Proclus), or the Cause that is "above all privations and above all negating and positing [*aphairesin kai thesin*]" (*MTh* 1.2; [PG 3] 1000B). The indebtedness to Proclus extends throughout the Dionysian oeuvre, as shown by the ubiquity of the triad *monē-proodos-epistrophē* (remaining-procession-return), though of course his Christian belief in an intelligent Creator generates a constant resistance to the Neoplatonic projection of a silent absolute untainted by noetic activity.

Even the issuance of negative theology in an act of prayer is Proclean: "We are always praying in the substance of our soul, beneath the fluctuations of our consciousness. There is a prayer inscribed in the very spontaneity of our being . . . an indissoluble communication with the divine" (Trouillard 1972:178). This is not Aristotle's *euchē* (*Peri hermeneias*), a demand that grammatically is neither affirmation nor negation: it has an affirmative thrust that lies deeper than verbal affirmation or negation. Dionysius's development of the idea of divinization according to the measure of one's hierarchical capacities is also derived from Proclus (and is not as connected with the Incarnation as in 2 Pet 1:4, Irenaeus, and Athanasius). Of course, as a post-Nicene Christian, Dionysius "telescopes" all Proclus's divine entities into the one God, who utterly transcends all the created triads and hierarchies. Yet he manages more than any other Christian thinker to introduce the Plotinian sense of "God without being," not only at the level of rhetoric, but in the theory that God is essentially above being and is called the One Who Is only because "the before being and the above being prepossesses and superlatively possesses all being, that is, being in itself" (*DN* 5.5; 820B; see also 11.6).

Did Dionysius then force Christian revelation into the mold pròvided by Greek ontotheology, or can one argue that he powerfully reshaped the Neoplatonic vision, putting it at the service of the biblical God? To all such questions, whether addressed to Philo, Origen, or any of the Greek fathers, the answer cannot be a simple yes or no. In each case there is a mutual deconstruction of the hellenistic and biblical elements, and the results call for nuanced critical appreciation. Patristic texts embody subtle and complex accommodations of Platonist thought, each working out a different synthesis of Greek and biblical elements. It often happens that where some see an occultation of the essence of the Gospel, others see a triumph of scripture over Platonism. Both the historical assessment of how elements of Platonism infiltrate the text and the theological assessment of the resultant hybrid or synthesis provide matter for endless hermeneutical debate.

The controversy around Dionysius is loaded with denominational investments. Championed by Greek Orthodoxy, and respected by the Western Church in his medieval scholastic reception, Dionysus became a target of frontal attack in the founding texts of the Reformation. The most influential reception of Dionysius in the Latin West was that of Thomas Aquinas. The apophatic note is struck early in the *Summa*: "Since we cannot know of God what he is, but only what he is not, we cannot consider the manner in which God is, but rather the manner in which he is not" (*ST* I, q. 3, prol.). Thomas skates on thin ice here, since he rejects the view of Maimonides that the divine names are "created rather to remove something from God than to posit something in God." His gesture of negation does not abolish the use of arguments and analogies beginning from the created world, marshaled along three paths: *per causalitatem, per remotionem, per eminentiam* (I *Sent.*, d. 3, q. 1, a. 3). It is constructive negation, negation by excess rather than by defect, and it becomes a negation of the limits of language, its enlargement by the way of eminence, reversing the strategy of Dionysius. "Aquinas does not aim to plunge the believer into a nescience that would be at the same time the best knowledge possible before entering the brilliant illumination of the divine darkness. Reason and intellect ought, on the contrary, to fathom their limits to better judge their autonomy, an autonomy based on the truths of faith and respecting its mysteries. That is why Thomas cannot respect as they stand the extreme expressions of Dionysian agnosticism. To accommodate them to his project of scientific theology, he makes them pass anew through the filter of conceptual distinctions that blunt their sharpness" (Miernowski, 29–30). As in Plotinus, removal has a sculptural meaning, allowing the divine form to emerge as that which is marked by its nonsubordination to the schemas of thought that befit the finite. "In contrast to the simplicity and immediacy of *negatio*, the process of *remotio* more and more appears complex and progressive, a multiple process including a plurality of separating acts: the *depuratio* of the mind takes place gradually; the divine essence is only gradually *denudata* of all matter" (Andia 2001:53). In Gerson, even more, "having removed the imperfections of potentiality, dependence, privation, and mutability, the Gersonian sculptor can at last contemplate the 'statue of God' (*agalma Dei*), in other words the knowledge (*notitia*) of the divinity" (Miernowski, 36).

"We come nearer to knowledge of him in proportion as we are able through our intellect to remove more from him. For we know a thing more perfectly the more fully we perceive its difference from other things" (*Contra Gentiles* 1.14). The distinctive difference or otherness of God that progressively comes to light in the course of the removal does not dissolve the idea of God in an ever cloudier abstraction but on the contrary secures for God progressively more defined lineaments. Through a set of negative differences—as opposed to the positive differences by which an essence is defined—God is known in his otherness from all things, in a gap or a distance that must be guarded and deepened. However precise it may become, this quasi-knowledge of the divine leaves us in a fragile and instable position. It must not congeal in formulas; rather, it needs to be sustained by a constantly renewed attention, for it is a dynamic knowledge, which subsists only in the act of *aphairesis*.

Even this domesticated apophatic scenario is too dependent on philosophical frameworks to be able to espouse in their specific texture the phenomena of religious thought and speech. The results of apophasis are perhaps not as concrete and luminous as Thomas claims. They bring out a particular figure of the divine, but one that still depends on the framework from which the apophasis began. Today, the inaccessible transcendence of God is less a philosophical thesis than an experience of loss and lack, and it is not by abstract pyrotechnics that this loss can become a new relation to the divine; the concreteness of the cross offers a better promise of such transformation.

Luther, who had rediscovered the forgiveness of sins as the core of the Gospel, was particularly sensitive to the way that classical Christian texts tended to occlude this founding event. His assessment of the *Corpus Dionysiacum* in *The Babylonian Captivity of the Church* should not be shrugged off:

> Dionysius is also most pernicious in his Mystical Theology, which certain ignorant theologists make so much of. He Platonizes rather than Christianizes, so much so that I would wish the faithful mind to give no attention to these books. Rather than helping you to know Christ they are likely to make you lose what knowledge you have. I speak from experience. Let us listen rather to Paul, that we may come to know Jesus Christ and him crucified. For this is the way, the truth and the life, this the ladder by which one comes to the Father. (*WA* 6:562)

Luther casts aside the Dionysian ladder, just as John replaces Jacob's ladder with the figure of the incarnate Christ (Jn 1:51). Luther's reference to John 14:6 recalls Christ's dismantling of the disciples' demands for mystical maps—"Lord, we do not know where you are going; how can we know the way?" (Jn 14:5)—and for a vision of God—"Lord, show us the Father" (14:8). Many Protestant theologians believe that this recall to the sole sufficiency of the incarnate economy delegitimizes mysticism, which can only be a presumptuous human effort to lift oneself by the bootstraps, bypassing the revealed path of faith. Thus Eberhard Jüngel takes up the Lutheran critique, insisting that God is concretely known in the justification of the sinner and that this knowledge is enunciated in the kerygma (1992:307–57). Ralf

Stolina accuses Jüngel of missing "the mystagogic dimension of the Areopagite's conception and the distinction between preserving silence and remaining dumb" (2000:74). But a mystagogy leading to a silence charged with prayer is not specifically Christian. Stolina sees negative theology as registering God's self-concealment in his revelation itself (2000:179). But in thus bringing apophasis back to its biblical basis one is leaving behind the Dionysian world and its Neoplatonic structures.

Anders Nygren, following in Luther's footsteps, formulates a severe and plausible critique of the Dionysian vision. "If Augustine's Caritas is a new conception based on both Eros and Agape, we can hardly say there is anything but simple *confusion* in Dionysius: the Eros motif has inundated Christianity, and Christianity is literally absorbed in Neoplatonic Eros theory" (563). Proclus had already introduced the idea that "Eros descends from above, from the intelligible sphere down to the cosmic, and turns all things towards the divine beauty" (*Alcibiades Commentary*, ed. Cousin, 2:141), a statement Nygren finds "almost incredible in a Platonist": "That Eros should stream down from above as a divine gift is an idea of which the original Eros theory was totally ignorant" and which may be due to influence from Christianity (570). However, the "agapeic" elements in Platonic eros may be more extensive than Nygren admits. When the lover ascends "as on the rungs of a ladder" (*Symposium* 211C) to the vision of the ever-existent, is he not also passing to increasingly less self-seeking forms of love? And is there not a touch of grace in the way the supernal realm gives itself to be known? Eros is characterized as a great *daimon* "interpreting and transporting human things to the gods and divine things to men" (202E). It is on this Platonic economy of grace that Proclus builds as he makes eros a cosmic ladder, the bond of the universe. This makes luminous sense to Dionysius, whereas the biblical vocabulary of agape has become opaque to him and he supposes the biblical authors avoided the proper name of love out of fear that foolish people would think of the vulgar rather than the heavenly eros. *Eros* and *agape* are synonymous; indeed, "it has seemed to some of our sacred authors that the name of eros is more divine than that of agape" (*DN* 4.12).

The chief difference from Proclus is that Dionysius's ultimate is the biblical God, whose active concern for his creatures, as individuals, is of a different fiber from the descent of eros in Proclus, and elicits a response of prayer, praise, and trust that goes beyond Neoplatonic piety. "Not only does the soul love God and wish to return to him, but God, in turn, loves the soul and urges its return. This may reasonably be regarded as a distinctively Christian feature of his thought, since the most that can be attributed to the Neoplatonic One is a general, impersonal benevolence towards all creation" (Wear and Dillon, 123). Dionysius effects a Christian sublation or overcoming of Neoplatonic structures insofar as he confers a personal face and name on the impersonal absolute, but this process is incomplete and threatened in his writings. A thorough evangelical reduction of his vision would build on this element and complete it, sacrificing Dionysius's more piquant Neoplatonic tenets.

REWRITING DIONYSIUS

This process of saving Dionysius from himself has been going on since John of Scythopolis and Maximus the Confessor. Today Jean-Luc Marion presents an image of Dionysius that even Luther and Barth might find acceptable. Indeed, he transforms the hyperexalted God of Dionysius into the sovereign God of Calvin. The hierarchical structures are reduced to the figure of Christ crucified before the divine distance, along with a somewhat archaic insistence on the hierarchical status of the bishop within the church. The vitalism of the Dionysian universe—"où la vie afflue et s'agite sans cesse" (see *DN* 4.2; 6.3)—yields to a biblical, almost desertic, drama of call and gift. The pervasive light imagery is replaced with a sober iconography of transcendence. The figure of Christ crucified, which fits so awkwardly into Dionysius's world, becomes its very center in Marion's creative retrieval. The energies of eros that circulate in the Dionysian system are brought back within the circle of Johannine agape and communion. Dionysius's language of eros now serves "to designate the coming to us of a withdrawal" (Marion 1991:178). Such a free rehandling of classic texts, with a view to their ultimate upshot, can be a creative and liberative theological intervention. So can an iconoclastic critique of them that highlights what is archaic in their conventional

language. But preferable to either tactic is a comprehensive hermeneutics that attempts to gauge the foreignness of the ancient horizon
and to assess the ancient texts as a skillful disposition of the conventions of that horizon.

Marion identifies the transcendence of the biblical God and his
agapeic gift of himself in his names, rather than the Proclean theory of
cosmic eros, as the ground structure of the Dionysian universe. The
infinite withdrawal or ungraspability of the ultimate is identified with
the freedom of the biblical God, who graciously makes himself known
in his creations, in his names, and in the *logia* of scripture. Marion
biblicizes the Dionysian Cause (*aitia*) when he speaks of it as "summoning" beings to participate in it. But even this could be extremely
hellenistic, for oracles and *logia* play a great role in Neoplatonism
too. We can see Marion's reading as an imaginative *Wesensschau* of an
irreducible biblical scenario enacted by Dionysius, which makes him,
as no doubt mystics have implicitly grasped across the ages, not a pil-
lar of hellenization but on the contrary a powerful agent of dehell-
enization and deconstruction within theology. I would say that such
an aspect can be elicited or solicited in all major Christian thinkers,
but that it is normally in a tense and complex relation with their metaphysical investments, which are not so easily cast off, and that this is
so with a vengeance in the case of Dionysius.

Marion has the Dionysian divine names chime with the Jewish
theme of the Name as a fence around the divine holiness. But is Dionysius really responding to this strain in biblical thought? "In reality,
if most of the attributes expounded are biblical, they are philosophical
too, and in any case the manner in which they are philosophically expounded is more philosophical than biblical" (Roques, xxv). Classical
theologians were more ready to recognize the conventionality, the
nonultimacy, of biblical language, so malleable because so often narrative or poetic, than to see the metaphysical framework as conventional, since the latter had the authority of reason itself, transparently
expressed. Adopting the perspective of the Eastern Church, Marion
declares that "the work of the Greek fathers consisted precisely in
liberating the Christian theological concepts from the Greek (and
perhaps the metaphysical) horizon, in which they originally arose"

(Marion 2001:187). But critical theology cannot simply adopt this monolithic conception of the "Greek fathers," which levels the differences between sturdily biblical thinkers such as Irenaeus and Athanasius, who resist hellenistic thought forms, and intensive hellenizers such as Clement and Origen, who positively reshape originally non-Greek, nonmetaphysical theological topics in a more Greek manner (though of course they, too, practice critical vigilance over against Greek philosophy). The blanket approbation of the Greek fathers as liberators of the Gospel from a Greek horizon is overgenerous. Melanchthon's critical stance inaugurates a tradition of discernment which should not be annulled: he has high praise for Irenaeus and Athanasius, who resisted the Platonic horizon in which the Gospel was enveloped—"statim post ecclesiae auspicia per Platonicam philosophiam christiana doctrina labefactata est" (*Loci Communes* [1521], 1:6)—but he views Origen as diluting the Gospel in Pelagian moralism and John Damascene as too given to abstract philosophy (see Meijering). Such discernment brings out the interesting tensions in the texts and makes them more instructive for the articulation of Christian faith today. Dionysius is at the far end of the hellenizing spectrum, "the most extreme example of a hellenization of Christianity," according to Werner Beierwaltes (2001a:49), who nonetheless sees Dionysius as representing a "successful symbiosis" of Platonism and Christianity (20).

Marion accepts Dionysius's self-presentation as one who is not engaged in polemics with the Greeks but is merely pointing to the phenomena, the *Sache selbst.* "The mere unshakable presence of authentic truth" (*Ep.* 10.1; [PG] 1080A) renders opposition futile and defense unnecessary. Someone accused him of parricide, in that he used Greek ideas to fight the Greeks. But Dionysius sees himself as realizing the true vocation of Greek philosophy—which Paul, he tells us, called "the wisdom of God" (10.2)! Dionysius thus sees no need to overcome metaphysics, since its basic thrust, as a God-given wisdom, is in perfect accord with scripture. Unsurprisingly, the basics of Dionysian apophasis are couched in perfectly Platonic terms: God is by his essence ungraspable; the limits of our time-bound reason accentuate this; God is too great to be grasped in terms of being and is rather a not-being (*mē on*)—all of this is a direct transcription of Neoplatonist language about the One. Rather than overcoming Greek horizons, it frees Christian language from one Greek horizon to insert it in another, transferring it from a Middle Platonic to a Neoplatonic regime, and in the process losing the critical vigilance over against Greek philosophical language that characterized earlier theologians such as the Cappadocian fathers. While Walther Völker is sensitive to the echoes of Proclus but generous in admitting other, ecclesiastical and biblical supports for Dionysius's writing, Bernhard Brons is more intently critical, in the Lutheran tradition, and sees Dionysius as a "replatonizer" of Christian tradition (15). Though sometimes conscious of a need to resist and modify his Neoplatonic framework of thought in dealing with the Incarnation, Dionysius fails to follow through on this for fear of the catastrophic impact it would have on his system (276–79) and ends up, in *Epistula* 4, "ranking the individual concrete statements about the incarnate among the relatively low-placed symbolic concepts that can also be drawn from the rest of creation" (285). Correct assessment of the role of Greek metaphysical conceptions in the Dionysian corpus is of imponderable significance for theological judgment in the widest sense, not only because of the impact on medieval Christendom but even more because of the high standing of Dionysius in Greek and Russian Orthodoxy, where flamboyant speculation such as that of Sergii Bulgakov is often interfused with biblical language in a very questionable style (with a ricochet effect on Catholic theology in the speculations of von Balthasar, for example). Generous embrace of all edifying traditions, often in the name of ecumenism, should not impede critical judgment, especially given the urgency of expressing the Christian message more credibly and more adequately even today.

The tense interplay between biblical and metaphysical conventions should not be diluted but sustained in a theological questioning that seeks to grasp all conventional truth as a skillful means for intimating ultimate truth. For Marion, phenomenology provides a key for rewriting both conventional languages. The experienced ultimate of the "saturated phenomenon" provides a basis from which elements from both scripture and metaphysics are summoned to speak in a new way. Yet this appeal to phenomenality itself may be more shadowed by conventions than at first appears—conventional moves of meta-physical reasoning (as in the elaborated systematization of varieties of "givenness") or conventional representations of biblical or ecclesiastical piety. Very hellenistic is the language in which Marion evokes the encounter with God: "Terror attests, in the mode of the forbidden, the insistent and unbearable excess of the intuition of God" (2001:194). There may be such tremors in the text of Dionysius, though they are more evident in Gregory of Nyssa, who borrows from *Enneads* 1.6.4 the phrase *thambos kai ekplexis*, "stupor and panic" (*In Canticum*), which seems to evoke an archaic Greek world. Commenting on the vocabulary of terror in Gregory and Chrysostom, Jean Daniélou observes: "It is an elementary reaction of religious feeling in its still primitive form" (31). Rudolf Otto observes that in Augustine's *Confessions* the uncanny otherness of God is *mysterium fascinans*, whereas in Chrysostom's Homilies it is *mysterium tremendum*: "The irrational in the feeling of God strives here against the rational and rationalizable and threatens almost to break free" (232–33). Scripture does have awesome cosmic theophanies that inspire fear and trembling (e.g., Job 38–41), but usually it inflects this primordial basis in an ethical and eschatological sense. The "terror of the Lord" is paralleled with "the glory of his majesty" (Isa 2:10, 19) in scenes of divine judgment. In the hellenistically tinged cult of mystical vertigo there is a risk that the dynamic whereby scripture subjects the primeval sacred terror to a sober, covenantal "fear of the Lord" will become undone. The assessment of Dionysian metaphysics must be seconded by a treatment and therapy of its emotive connotations. Even if it could be stripped of this hellenistic atmosphere, the Dionysian posture of reverence for the divine distance has a narrow and archaic cast. The biblical revelation of God as we understand it today is far more dynamic and far-reaching than this cult of one or two figures of the divine. As a theologian, Dionysius is less capacious than the Cappadocians, and indeed may be suspected of the age-old ploy of using apophaticism as a pretext for signing off from theological discussions, as when he says of the Trinity: "In what manner these things are, it is possible neither to say nor to know" (*DN* 2.7; 645B). Raoul Mortley no doubt exaggerates the dissolution of dogma in Dionysius's ecumenical use of apophasis, even suggesting that Dionysius is not a Christian thinker at all (254). Nonetheless, a discerning reading of the Dionysian corpus will seek to measure how the powerful dynamic of its Platonist traditions threatens to override the concrete contours of biblical and ecclesial faith, on the level of primary affective attitudes as much as on that of categories.

Such fussing about the tensions between different strands in Dionysius, or in his modern interpreters, may seem to block the emergence of his voice in the free and bold chorus of Christian witness, dimming his place in the communion of saints. That is probably the price that has to be paid if we are to attain a lucid and demystified vision of the play of conventions whereby religious truth is transmitted. Voices from the past speak to us, and move us, but they always come from another place, from a distance, and a just measurement of that distance is part of the process of authentic listening.

The suspicion of Dionysius's hellenism concerns not only his treatment of biblical language but his fidelity to the integral vision of Christian doctrine. On the ultimate level dogmatic language falls silent, but on the level of conventional cataphasis we may expect Dionysius to uphold it as he upholds the divine names, and indeed he does so in Christological passages (*EH* 3.440C–444D; *Ep.* 4) of a subtle monophysite hue (see Wear and Dillon, 4–6). Trinitarian teaching is respectfully received from its scriptural source, but it does not become a living strand in his thought (see *DN* 2.2; 640A–B). Following a tradition of bolstering trinitarian and incarnational suggestions in the Dionysian text, Marion reads into it a Balthasarian theodrama that has little relation to biblical realities: "The Son is He who loses ceaselessly and from all eternity his life for the Father, and who, by the very fact, saves it ceaselessly and from all eternity, in receiving himself from the Father as his eldest Son" (1991:214). He stretches the incarnational reading to implausible lengths: "With the *logia* the Logos in person delivers himself. . . . The privilege of the *logia* . . . depends on the kenosis of the Son and attests it in its way" (220). Dionysius already received such biblical and doctrinal injections from his earliest annotator, John of Scythopolis (see Rorem and Lamoreaux, 67–70, 79). Even if one consistently translates *thearchy* as "Trinity," the role

of the Trinity in the economy of salvation is rather blurred in Dionysius. Otto Semmelroth points out Dionysius's discomfort with trinitarian thinking, especially with regard to the trinitarian structure
of the economy of salvation (1950:213–15). Defenders of Dionysius's
trinitarianism unwittingly confirm this. Thus Jean Trouillard, a die-
hard Neoplatonist, criticizes Augustinian trinitarianism for "redoubling, on the pretext of grounding them in the Absolute, the distinctions inherent in the created mind. One of the weaknesses of the
Augustinian tradition is that it falls short of the Plotinian exegesis of
the *Parmenides*, failing to see that therein the demands of critique and
of religious life converge to liberate Transcendence from all that belongs to the intelligible" (1961:23). Beierwaltes likewise lauds the
speculative trinitarianism of Dionysius and Eriugena but fails to assess its relation to the economic Trinity (1994). The situation is similar
with those who ascribe a vibrant incarnationalism to Dionysius. Thus
Ysabel de Andia claims that Jesus is at the heart of Dionysian ecstasy
as self-surpassing and self-dispossession (1996:442). But the suspicion
remains that this is a Jesus who is shaped by the requirements of a
system. One might say that just as Dionysius can always find scriptural texts to bolster his insights, so the pattern of the mystical dynamic finds confirmation in a particular vision of the cross but does
not essentially derive from the New Testament kerygma. "The person
of Christ is not missing in his system, but doesn't at all have the significance that the name Christianity indicates and that in fact is as-
signed to him in revelation"; his role as Redeemer is limited, since sin
is merely "a disturbance of the order of the hierarchically built
world" (Semmelroth 1949:374).

In Dionysius the divine distance is respected when we each abide
in our place in the hierarchy of beings: that is, when we remain authentically where we are, neither falling through inattention nor rising in delusion. Identification with the incarnate Christ should then
be our best access to divine transcendence. But it would take a lot of
stretching to make Dionysius rejoin Luther here; Christ crucified is
marginal in the Dionysian universe. The existential, Pauline dynamic
of grace and redemption is singularly diluted in this theology or is
even perfectly foreign to it. Spiritual ascent is enabled by God's call,

by the indwelling eros in all creatures that responds to it, and by Christ the photagogue. Christ leads us to the light by identifying us with himself; it is in this context that Dionysius quotes Ignatius of Antioch, "My Eros has been crucified" (*Ad Rom.* 7.2; *DN* 4.12, 709B). The Incarnate economy fills out the Platonist structures but does not attain sufficient autonomy to overcome them. The biblical inflection that differentiates Dionysius as specifically Christian has a smaller scope and in addition is affirmed less strongly than in Marion's interpretation.

Rather than impose our conventional notions of doctrinal orthodoxy on Dionysius's text, we should bring out the aspects that strain against orthodoxy or that are incapable of reaching it. Orthodoxy itself, of course, is always mobile and conventional in its formulations, and such inquisitorial quizzing of theological classics may seem highhanded. But every major site in the history of theology carries with it a buzz of unease, for there is no theological authority that has not been found defective in one way or another. Both the importance and the impossibility of being orthodox underline the conventionality of theological discourse. It can never securely become what it intends to be. Indeed, the constant fraying and failure of the conventional language reveal that its alleged ultimate goal, orthodoxy, is not a substantial reality, a *svabhāva*, but an art of judgment that is constantly alert and sensitive in its investment in conventions, whether scripture or metaphysical.

The conventionality of language itself, and of literary style, should be a matter of major concern in theological hermeneutics. One of the most exhausting features of the style of the Pseudo-Dionysius is his rhetoric of elevation: "Let us raise ourselves then by our prayers to the exalted summit of those divine and good rays" as if grasping "a multiluminous chain hanging from the height of heaven" whereby "we will raise ourselves to the highest shinings of the exalted and multiluminous rays" (*DN* 3.1; 680C). What is the phenomenological correlative of this diction? One thinks of the Platonic bedazzlement before the sun of the Good, echoed in Augustine and many other writers. Yet the relative simplicity and directness of these sources are lacking here, replaced by a ritual elaborateness: "His speech is like a solemn liturgy in which the celebrant makes visible the greatness of the all-holiest, by again and again making himself small in genuflections and prostrations" (Semmelroth 1950:218). This speech expresses a hierarchical imagination that piles range on range of ascending orders of being and locates God as ever beyond and above them, to be reached by an excessus of mystical transport. To be sure, the celestial and ecclesiastical hierarchies are also a ladder of divine agape reaching down from heaven to earth, but here again the language seems to fail of concreteness in bringing this home. Drawing on the Protestant critique, one might sound the hollowness of this language, as a literary critic, contrasting it with the effective impact of scripture and preaching, and even silencing it in order to let the kerygma be more authentically heard.

A phenomenological reduction of Dionysius's language of elevation to a more immanentist language of rejoining one's reality in the here and now only goes halfway to meet the dissatisfaction contemporary Christians feel with these texts. What is needed in addition is an evangelical reduction which will bring Dionysius into clearer accord with Christ crucified. "For Paul and many orthodox interpreters, such as John Chrysostom and John of Scythopolis, negative language about God is not itself a means of ascent, but is meant rather to turn one's sights from the divine transcendence 'down' to the revelation of God as incarnate in Christ, indeed, in Christ crucified" (Rorem and Lamoreaux, 82). We have seen that this is true of Gregory of Nyssa, who remains engaged in the thickets of scriptural exegesis and doctrinal clarification, so that the apophatic elements in his thought reflect the concrete experience of theology running up against the limits of articulation. Gregory aims less at Plotinian *henōsis*, union, than at *homoiōsis*, likeness, with God, in imitation of Christ, and he is not tempted to develop an economy which goes beyond or behind that of scripture. The three theophanies in Exodus allow him to indicate the place of the negative in the quest for God: the burning bush shows—in very Platonic terms—that God alone truly *is*, and that earthly passions and cogitations are to be stripped away: "Knowledge of being is purification from opinions about nonbeing" (*Life of Moses* 2.22); the vision of God in a dark cloud (Ex 20:21) shows that "the more the mind draws near to this knowledge, the more it sees the unknowability of the divine nature" (2.162), in ongoing negation of the limits of its previous understanding; the vision of God's back (Ex 33:23) suggests a development on the ladder of eros (2.227–32) with the conclusion (directed against Origen) that desire of God is never sated, for its object is infinite; here negation of limits is a positive mark of the depth of divine being. What characterizes Gregory's uses of apophasis is a sober, realistic view of human finitude; it goes together with a strong incarnational emphasis and a positive evaluation of signs and words as pointers to the infinite when used in metaphoric or symbolic style.

In Neoplatonism the embarrassment of language before the simplicity of the One is borne with as intrinsic to the travail of articulation: "We do indeed say something about it, but we certainly do not speak it, and we have neither knowledge nor thought of it. . . . We say what it is not; what it is we do not say" (*Enn.* 5.3.14); "But we speak and we write, *alla legomen kai graphomen*" (*Enn.* 6.9.4). One is reminded of Beckett: "I can't go on, I'll go on" (*The Unnamable*). This linguistic oscillation around the One is left behind at a higher stage for "the strain toward the One," and this in turn is eliminated when the soul finally abides in silence with the One (Morrow and Dillon, 603). Christian theology is less concerned with uttering the unutterable than with preserving the full resonance of the biblical language against a dry positivity on the one hand and dissolution in mystical evocations on the other. Dionysius is ill protected against the latter danger, whereas Gregory of Nyssa can serve (in the context of his times) as a model of vigilance against both.

NEGATIVE THEOLOGY AND GOSPEL KERYGMA

Christianity, even before the encounter with Platonism, inherits from Jewish visionary sources the idea of an ascent to God: Paul is "caught up to the third heaven" (2 Cor 12:2). The ascent is always enabled by divine grace, often spoken of as elevating nature to the supernatural level. So deeply was the idea that "God is above" ingrained in the Christian imagination that when liberal theologians redefined God as "the beyond in our midst" (Robinson) or "the ground of our being" (Tillich) it seemed a daring, liberating move. Yet Christian incarnationalism roots all mystical aspirations in the here and now, and even more than Buddhism sends one back to the realm of words and forms. God is present in the Holy Spirit, active in the immediacy of the here and now, and this presence is always associated with the incarnational economy, in which words and forms are instruments of salvation.

Christian spirituality has been characterized in terms of an opposition or synthesis between the Platonic ascent of eros to the world of the Forms, or to the Form of Forms, the Good, identified with the One "beyond mind and beyond being" (*epekeina nou kai ousias*), and the biblical descent of divine agape into our fleshly and sinful world, where it is received as forgiveness and grace. The Oriental conception of contemplation as simply awakening to reality, right where we are, seems at first to contradict both the Platonic and the biblical approaches, for it neither ascends to an ideal realm with Plato nor embraces the saving grace of God with Paul. But the One of Plotinus need not be thought of as "up there"; it is the simplicity of what is most immediate, and one puts aside language and thought only in order to be freed to apprehend its nearness. Likewise, divine transcendence in Christianity need not imply the image of some quasi-spatial gulf needing to be bridged by ladders up and down. God is the reality that is simplest and that is nearest to hand. Luke has Paul quote Epimenides: "In him we live and move and have our being" (Acts 17:28). If grace elevates, its more fundamental operation is to free us from bondage to sin and the Law, and this is an event in the here and now which in Paul seems to be a topic of contemplative deepening. The indwelling of God, Christ, or the Spirit in the believer is evoked in terms that recall the realization of the identity of ātman and Brahman or of immanent Buddha nature (Gal 2:20, and the Johannine language of mutual indwelling).

In Luther the terror of death and judgment belongs to the *opus alienum Dei*, which is overcome in the *opus proprium Dei*, the forgiveness of sin. Barth has a milder version of Luther's dialectic: "Between God and us stands God's hiddenness, in which he is remote and strange to us, insofar as he does not of his own accord found and create fellowship between himself and us—and that happens not in actualization of our capacity but in the miracle of his gracious acceptance" (*KD* 2/1:204). Barth criticizes the residue in Luther of an "unknown God," a God hidden behind his revelation, to be feared and revered over and above our relation to God as revealed (236–37). In the revealed economy, it is not in virtue of infinity or aseity but as the God of grace that God is incomprehensible. Wonder, not terror, is the keynote in this awareness of a God who lovingly and preveniently encompasses us in a manner for which the best analogy is perhaps to be found in a Parmenidean awareness of how the ocean of being encompasses all beings: "Ubique es tota praesens et non te video. In te moveor et in te sum et ad te non possum accedere" (Anselm, *Proslogion* 16)—words which attest "not just any hiddenness, but that of the merciful and holy God" (*KD* 2/1:215). "While the traditional idea of the incomprehensible God, still at work to some extent in Luther, signified first the inaccessible transcendence of God, even in his revelation, the Barthian idea of the hidden God absorbs the transcendence of the Ineffable in the act of grace and revelation, accomplished in Jesus Christ" (Bouillard 1957, 3:185). Barth cools toward his earlier talk of the Totally Other, which now seems to him more a metaphysical projection than a revealed datum. The incomprehensibility of revelation is of a different order from the acrobatics of natural theology and negative theology in the Platonic line. Now "the idea of grace has absorbed that of infinite qualitative difference, by which formerly it tended to be absorbed" (186). Bouillard regrets this: "The idea of the ineffable God recedes too much before the idea of the hidden God, and the latter has not the same high profile as in Luther" (188). Did the biblicist positivism of the later Barth betoken a forgetfulness of the apophatic principle that applies to all knowledge of God, even within revelation itself? Or did Barth simply find his way back to the true face of the God who is "light" and in whom "there is no darkness at all" (1 Jn 1:5), correcting the predestinarian nightmares of Luther and Calvin, based on anxiety, a bad, deterministic metaphysics, and ancient Manichaean strains?

Plotinus, Proclus, Damascius, Dionysius, and Eckhart developed styles of acting out the situation of humanity before God or before ultimate reality which served well as skillful means within certain historical cultures of religious practice. But their discourses now seem rather labored or mannered, especially to the degree that they sought to assemble their thought in a system and to outbid one another in the radicality of their conceptions of the ineffable ultimate. It is on these points also that they come most into conflict with the concreteness of biblical, incarnational faith. What is most living and useful in their work is the phenomenological element, when negation serves as a critical tool for cutting through obstructive language to rejoin present reality. This is also the element that provides a ground for dialogue with Vedantic and Buddhist apophasis. The concrete perplexities we face when we try to think religiously in a pluralistic age will sometimes give relevance to negative theology as an arsenal of vigilant critical strategies and positive contemplative insight but may also increase our sense of distance from this heritage which comes to us across such a great hermeneutic gulf. The classic discourses do not rejoin what is perhaps the most widespread form of negation in our thinking of God today: a sense of the obscurity and intangibility of whatever it is to which our overabundant inherited discourses about God intended to allude, a sense—laced with diffuse anxiety and guilt—of being "at sea" where God is concerned. Perhaps the best antidote to this is the one the Reformers urged: "And the great and good God clothed the Son with flesh, that he might draw us from the contemplation of his majesty to the contemplation of our flesh and fragility" (Melanchthon, *Loci Communes* [1521], prol.). Murky broodings about God are assuaged, not by further doses of negative theology, but by a return to the fragility of our own flesh as assumed by Jesus Christ. The perplexed explorer of humankind's religious history will find there more the mire of Calvary than the simplicity of the One. Perhaps it is time for the religions to practice a new kind of negative theology by lying down, with Yeats, "where all the ladders start, / In the foul rag and bone shop of the heart."

PHENOMENOLOGICAL RETRIEVALS OF NEGATIVE THEOLOGY

To reread Plotinus or Eckhart in a phenomenological key, bringing out the existential, liberative sense of their apophatic and aphairetic moves, is to bring that tradition into critical engagement with the complexities of ordinary life and language, making it more attractive to contemporary intellectuals and even to *l'homme moyen sensuel*. The point of negative theology then appears as the removal of blockages to spiritual freedom, enabling release of energies stifled by our bondage to conventional ways of thinking. To play its role well, negative theology has to be a flexible skill, adapting its strategies to the crude or subtle obstacles that lie in its path. The word *aphairesis* catches the spirit of this better than the word *apophasis*. More fundamental than negating language or falling silent is the shedding of delusive attachments. Plotinus forged the best slogan for negative theology in his cry "Take away everything!" (*Enn.* 5.3.17; *aphele panta*). But like Buddhist emptiness this aphairesis must not be absolutized into some kind of hypostasis or sweeping simplification of all problems; just as emptiness itself is emptied, so aphairesis itself is a critical tool to be handled critically, skillfully. At one moment we shatter the conventional to plunge toward ultimacy; at the next we reintegrate this iconoclastic gesture within the ongoing dialectic of our critical use of conventional language.

Plotinus's response when invited to a feast of the gods—"They ought to come to me, not I to them" (Porphyry, *Life of Plotinus* 10)—shows the foremost Platonist casting away ladders to claim that the divine makes itself present right where we are. Perhaps Plotinus is merely deprecating inferior daemons and their cult, as Porphyry does in *De abstinentia* 2.37–43. Compare Śaṃkara: "The one who knows Brahman becomes all; even the gods cannot prevail against him. . . . The gods depend on men for ritual support, etc., and fearing that by liberation they would lose that support they may try to hinder liberation" (Potter, 188). The disciples surmise a deeper meaning in Plotinus's retort: "What he meant by this exalted utterance we could not understand and did not dare to ask." Prophets and mystics are always shattering conventions in this way, yet it is necessary that the conventions first be in place in order for them to be shattered, and after the shattering it remains necessary for the disciples to pick up the pieces and integrate the prophetic gesture into their repertory of conventional skillful means.

Phenomenology encourages us to think of ultimacy as near at hand rather than "beyond," more accessible to a step back than to a leap. Even the One, though we tend to think of it as "pinnacled dim in the intense inane" (Shelley), can be conceived as a present phenomenon. The One is present negatively in the discontent we feel with the complexity and dispersal of conceptual thought, which betokens a thirst for the One (*Enn.* 6.9.4). Compare Proclus: "In our speculations about the first principle we should especially stimulate the common intuitions, since everything is naturally and unaffectedly related to it" (*In Parm.* 1092; trans. Morrow and Dillon, 440). The One is also phenomenologically accessible in the "traces" offered by the beings it unifies, as it confers on them "the form of the Good" (*Enn.* 6.7.18; see also 3.8.11), or, somewhat less vividly, in the "marks" (*synthēmata*) of itself that it has sown in all things (Proclus, *Platonic Theology* 2.8) and which include "the one of the soul," "the summit of the soul," "the center of the soul," and "the flower of our substance." "These figures intend to celebrate our rootedness in the universal center, bringing the mind back to the nocturnal source of its clarity" (Trouillard 1982:100). All these phenomena are but shadows of the One.

One might reduce the Platonic and Plotinian language of contemplative ascent and descent by thinking of the One as actuality itself, the very quick of the real, and union with it as coincidence with the true nature of things—to be reached then not by climbing a hierarchical ladder but by putting away limiting modes of thought and perception and letting the nature of reality manifest itself in the here and now. We encounter the One beyond being in the very midst of being as the sustainer of its being. Union with the One is the coincidence of our center with the center of reality: *hōsper kentrō kentron synapsas* (*Enn.* 6.9.10). The ascents of Platonism become metaphors for a more immanentist understanding of the spiritual quest, in which the *superior summo meo* is shown to be identical with the *interior intimo meo* (*Conf.* 3.11). But there is a limit to such readings, posed by Plotinus himself in his insistence on the transcendent identity of the One. Buddhism more radically identifies ultimacy with the as-it-is-ness (*tathatā*) of reality here and now.

Bergson sought a "dynamic schema" sympathetic to his own thought in Plotinus, his "favorite philosopher" (1626), for the cosmos unfolded in Plotinus (and in Proclus and Damascius) is a mobile one, made up of events rather than static entities. For instance, of the

Nous Plotinus tells us that "its seeing is its substance" (*Enn.* 5.3.10); likewise, the activity of the One is its hypostasis (*Enn.* 6.8.7 [line 47]; 8.13.7–8). In Neoplatonism, "Philosophy is nothing other than knowledge of the soul with all the functions that make it up and the presences they imply" (Trouillard 1972:3). Yet there is a solid backbone of fixed ontological status as well, which Bergson denounced as the basic error of the metaphysical tradition, its failure to perceive the difference between the sequential nature of intelligence and the eminently fluid character of reality, thus falling into a frozen and distorted representation of life and movement. Wayne Hankey says that Bergson "reverses Plotinus, placing him on his feet!" (1999a:136). "With Trouillard we arrive at Neoplatonism developed within an anti-metaphysical and essentially postmodern position" (144). The term *postmodern* is rather inapposite: Trouillard does not seek to subvert Plotinus in the direction of a decentering and an endless errance.

As Jean-Marc Narbonne points out, against Reiner Schürmann, Plotinus's thought does not culminate in "some absence or withdrawal of the foundation, but much rather in the representation of an absolute foundation, since the One is for him the infinite foundation of all possible finites" (1999:120). The One—unlike Heidegger's being—is not a merely phenomenological datum but an autonomous hypostasis that is other than and radically transcends all the entities that depend on it. However, it is a hypostasis without substance (*ousia*), and building on this, several scholars have striven to make the One purely phenomenological. E. Vacherot is an early example: "Hypostasis, in Plotinus and Proclus, signifies simply the act, the determination of the state, the mode and degree of manifestation of any principle. The first principle being superior to every act, every essence, every determined form, is not a hypostasis but the principle of hypostases. That is why Proclus habitually designates it by the words *to anupostatikon, to huperupostatikon*" (quoted in Aubin, 15).

Phenomenologists let loose on Neoplatonic texts often use Erl-King hermeneutics: "Und bist du nicht willig, so brauch ich Gewalt" (And if you're not willing, then I'll use force")! Plotinus sounds temptingly phenomenological when he states that the One is not conceived but given: "Awareness of the One is neither by way of reasoned knowledge [*epistēmē*] nor by way of intellection [*noēsis*] like the other intelligibles, but by a presence superior to knowledge [*kata parousian epistēmēs kreittona*]" (*Enn.* 6.9.4). Does this not recall what Heidegger says about the granting of the presence of being, the *Ereignis* in which *Es gibt Sein*? But again Plotinus's sturdy metaphysics gets in the way of a phenomenological reduction of his thought: the One is unambiguously identified as a hypostasis other than the beings that depend on it, and Plotinus formally rejected nonhypostatic understandings (*Enn.* 5.6.3). Reiner Schürmann's effort to interpret the One as a non-substantive donative process that can be correlated with the *Ereignis* runs aground on this objection. An alluring possibility is held out by Damascius's theory of the Ineffable; for this lies beyond the One and is not to be thought of as foundation, nor indeed in any way at all, yet is the object of a mute sensibility. John Dillon tentatively proposes that something like Heidegger's *Es gibt* is emerging here (Dillon 1996a). Can one say of the *Ereignis* as of this ineffable ultimate that it is, as Damascius says, "the end in itself and the ultimate in itself, the enclosing wall, so to speak, of everything"? (ed. Westerink and Combès, 5). No, because the space of the *Ereignis* is that of the world as it opens up on the level of lived phenomenality, not that of a transcendent cosmological cause such as metaphysics asks after. Can one say that the Ineffable surpasses the One as that which gives it, just as the *Ereignis* "gives" being? But Heidegger's *Ereignis* is not "unknowable." It gives itself to be perceived and thought. It is the essence of the process of unconcealment (*a-lētheia*) that takes place in the being-given of being (*GA* 14:29).

If language is problematic and inadequate, that can also allow us greater freedom in our use of it. Thus A. H. Armstrong suggests that the ultimate reality in Neoplatonism need not always be rigorously designated as "beyond being"—that is only one manner of speaking, in a given context:

In studying Plotinus, and all authentic Neoplatonic thought, one needs to remember continually that the two great negations of Being and Thought (which, as the later Neoplatonists make clear, must themselves be negated) are not designed to project the mind into void and unconsciousness but to liberate it, in the end, from its own theology (a liberation which must sometimes be sought by violent and paradoxical means) and wake it to the presence of God. Once this has been understood, then Being for a Neoplatonist can take its place as an iconic name, a signpost on the way, alongside One, the Good, and Nothing, and the Unsayable, or that variant of the last to which Patricia Cox Miller has rightly drawn our attention, the Sayable-only-in-Gibberish. (121)

The ultimate can equally be identified as the pure act of being, as in Porphyry, and it may be that Plotinus himself went along with this. When Plotinus says of the One that "one allows him his 'existence' (*to 'estin'*) without attributing to him anything which is not there" (*Enn.* 5.5.13 [13–14]), this may merely echo the old idea, attested in Philo, that we can know that God is (*hoti estin*) but not what God is (*ho estin*), without any marked emphasis on being as such. There is more in Philo: God is the one "to whom alone belongs *to einai*" (*De Vita Mosis* 1.75). Porphyry innovates in "identifying the activity of being, the 'verb' to be, with the pure essence, taken in its most absolute indetermination," and constructing an opposition between being, "an action without subject," and the entity, "which is the first subject, the first form, resulting from being" (Hadot, 490). That Plotinus would be willing to conceive of the One as being itself, the complete act of being, is also argued by Narbonne (1993:23, 27).

Armstrong's reduction of all this to a play between alternative languages might bring Neoplatonism close to Buddhism and a phenomenology of emptiness. From Heidegger's point of view it could compound the forgetfulness of being, precisely because of its focus on ultimacy and its reduction of finite beings and words to traces of that ultimacy. In practice, Neoplatonism pays little attention to the presence of common beings and is far from being "faithful to the earth," as Heidegger, following Nietzsche, wishes to remain. Even if one can salvage the treasures of Neoplatonic thought by investing them in an aporetic closer to the phenomena, it is a misprision, or at least a short circuit, to salute Plotinus as a thinker of being in a Heideggerian sense. A similar misprision is incurred by Neo-Thomists who are too eager to interpret *Sein* in light of *esse*.

Meister Eckhart might be a bridge between the Neoplatonic and Heideggerian worlds of thought. He transcends the concrete manifestations of God to plunge into the ocean of a purely indeterminate divinity, which he sometimes speaks of as pure being. This might seem alien to Heideggerian concerns. The pure act of being had a glorious career in medieval scholasticism, but with little yield for Heideggerian phenomenology of being. Even if it eludes conceptual idolatry, since it is *penitus incognitum*, and even if it constitutes a "truth of being" that is lost in "ontotheology" from Scotus to Suárez, this *actus essendi* does not set Heidegger's divining rod aquiver. It lacks phenomenological pregnancy.

But this language of pure, indeterminate being might be read in another way, as transcending names and forms to come closer to the phenomena, to what is nearest to hand. Set in the context of a Christian life centered on humble, biblical *imitatio Christi*, this radical *aphairesis* of God-language could be an expression of down-to-earth realism. The quest for the naked essence of divinity could be a hyperbole bespeaking impatience with abstractions that block access to the living God here and now. Eckhart's apophatic language would thus be that of *Lebemeister* rather than a *Lesemeister*. He becomes a thinker of being in a sense close to Heidegger's when he makes the intimate *esse* of things a theme of contemplation, seeking to "transform into mysticism the natural theology of St. Thomas" (Lossky, 31). His Augustinian "interiorization of the apophatic plunge towards the ineffable" (29) brings further phenomenological enhancement. Other Augustinian thinkers would interest Heidegger less, since their phenomenology lacks specifically ontological resonance.

Apophatic theology is not a matter of worrying about the credentials of our religious language. It is a very active kind of theology, in which the apophatic reflections are accompanied by aphairetic gestures, by removals, divestments, renunciations, affecting the actual existence of the theologian. He negates truth and knowledge, the Good and the will, being and the name "God," by a *conatus* that controls the energies of his life as of his speech, hard as it is for us to imagine this: "Every veil is removed . . . including the veil of the good, under which the will accepts, the veil of the true, with which the intellect accepts, and universally the veil of being itself" (*LW* 4:114). The ebullition of the divine being, of which Eckhart so surprisingly speaks, was reflected in his own cheerful energy as he combined action and contemplation.

Despite, or perhaps rather because of its mystical aspirations, Neoplatonism provides the most perfectly constituted metaphysical systems of antiquity. For the vision of ultimate reality does not exclude engagement with words and forms, whether as a preparatory gymnastic, a pedagogic device, a contemplative elevation—the coursing of eros through all the living beautiful forms of the universe until it reaches the summit—or simply a celebration of the abundance that has come into being through the infinite potency of the One, defined as *dynamis pantōn* (*Enn.* 5.3.13 [line 33]). And as this play is developed it yields increasingly comprehensive visions of the whole chain of being, built around the structure of the nine hypotheses in the *Parmenides*, which are fleshed out with the cosmology and psychology of the *Timaeus*. The structure of negative theology as founded by Plato and perfected by Plotinus can be regarded as an ontotheology, as can its Jewish and Christian derivatives insofar as they place the encounter with the God of Exodus atop a hierarchical chain of being. The ultimate pole in this system, the One, lies beyond all finite structures of being, which nonetheless depend on it. The grounding and integrating role of a supreme being is largely taken over by the second level of reality, the level of the Ideas or the *Nous*, leaving the One utterly transcendent in its inviolable simplicity. The flagrant exception constituted by Plotinus's discourse on the One as *causa sui* (*aition heautou*, *Enn.* 6.8.14 [line 41]) is relativized by the way Plotinus uses the expression *hoion* (as it were) to put his bold speculation "under erasure." Proclus firmly rejects talk of a self-grounding of the One (*Elements of Theology*, para. 40).

To what extent is the Plotinian One a release from cosmic structures rather than their pinnacle and foundation? Those structures originate in contemplation of the One, and one is completely released from them, and from the metaphysical language that maps them, when one is converted back to union with the One which is beyond difference or form. One might argue that the One represents a space of freedom that lies beyond the ratiocinations of ontotheology. The ascent to the One could be seen as giving metaphysics the slip, and as a leap to the "groundless ground" of which Heidegger speaks (*GA* 10:93, 183–88). But this phenomenological virtuality of Plotinian thought requires a hermeneutical and archaeological effort for its convincing thematization, unless one resorts to violent interpretations to hasten the Plotinus-Heidegger encounter.

"How does the god come into philosophy?" is answered at the second level, where the god figures as the self-thinking Mind of Aristotle, or at the third level, Soul, to which its demiurgic functions are delegated (*Enn.* 5.1.2). The One does not come into philosophy but frustrates and dislodges all philosophical speech and can be spoken of positively only in a broken language of "so to say" (*hoion*). The One overcomes metaphysics, as a reality too powerful for the feeble instruments of metaphysical reason. Yet the One is still envisaged and located from within the ontotheological horizon. It is the rational, philosophical quest for founding principles that permits the sighting of an ultimate principle that transcends the horizon of philosophical reason. In Plotinus at least, the link of the One with the Intellect that contemplates it and depends on it is too intimate to be dissolved. If that link is broken, the One becomes totally indeterminate, and we are back at square one—which does not amount to a Heideggerian return to *die Sache selbst*. One might say that the One is the figure that nirvanic ultimacy assumes when apprehended by the Greek mind, as that which eludes its grasp.

It seems that before the decisive rationalism of Descartes, Spinoza, and Leibniz, metaphysical thinking about the supreme principle oscillated between a desire for full rational grounding and a willingness to abide with the ineffable, sometimes erring in one direction, sometimes in the other. (Even Descartes is still torn, Marion argues, between rational control of God as *causa sui* and the loss of such control when God is conceived as infinite.) Our later experience of achieved metaphysical rationalism, and of the many movements that have sought to overcome metaphysics in the name of the empirical data or the phenomenological given, opens rich critical and hermeneutical perspectives on the ancient texts, which so far have been only timidly exploited by historical scholarship in theology and philosophy.

NEGATIVE THEOLOGY AND DECONSTRUCTION

The once-popular exercises of reading Plotinus as a philosopher of mind anticipating Hegel (Bréhier) or as one who overcomes metaphysics in advance of Heidegger (Aubenque, Schürmann) have yielded more recently to the idea that Neoplatonism is a form of deconstruction, an exploration of *différance* (with Derrida, accordingly, featured as the leading negative theologian of our time). Going beyond his earlier dismissal of negative theology as ontotheology in disguise, Derrida connects the apophatic tradition, in all its historical many-layeredness and inbuilt aporias, with the pluralist openness of contemporary philosophical and religious thought. Unmoored from its stable place in the classical Neoplatonist dispensation, negative theology can accompany a wide variety of religious languages, while relativizing them by insight into their finitude, their historical and cultural contingency. Derrida sees negative theology as freeing us up for a politics of hospitality that overcomes the fixations leading to hatred and violence (see Bradley, 193–215). Here theological judgment is relayed by a wider philosophical and political judgment, which itself reacts back on theology and forces it to consider the wider or secular implication of its procedures.

Within the tradition of classical negative theology, the author who most opens it up to a deconstructive development is surely Damascius, whose radical pursuit of negation can be contrasted with the way Proclus controls the functioning of negation so as to ensure it has a positive upshot. Opposing Porphyry, who saw negative theology merely as reflecting the weakness of our intelligence before the plenitude of divine being, Proclus stated that even the highest *Nous* knows the One only by negations, not by a deficient knowledge, but in a movement of thought that corresponds to the true nature of the One (*In Parm.* 1080; ed. Morrow and Dillon, 431–32). Negations come first; they are "the causes of the corresponding affirmations" (1075), even their "mothers" (1133). But Proclus insists that negations positively manifest the One and in addition found the lower realm of assertions. His *aphairesis* is what Michel de Certeau would call *une rupture instauratrice*. Damascius, in contrast, interprets apophasis as registering only the impotence of language before the ultimate, which can be intuited only in silence. The rupture of apophasis here becomes a perpetual rupture, never converted into an instauration. The ways of affirmation and negation do not determine the nature of the ultimate silence in Damascius; at best they prepare it by clearing away all speech as an irrelevance. One scholar dramatically sees Damascius, along with Pseudo-Dionysius, as representing an unwholesome extreme in the Platonic tradition, as the end point of a decline of the Greek Logos into silence (Mortley, 119–27).

It is true that Proclus, too, ends with a radical *aphairesis* of all language as one falls silent before the One, yet in his writing the One retains a more determinate identity than Damascius's Ineffable. In Proclus, "The negation of negation is sublation as consummation, not elimination of the striving of thought toward the One" (Beierwaltes 1979:363), so that the One is "ground and origin of word and silence" (365). In Damascius, apophatism turns in on itself, becoming thoroughly aporetic. The solid identity of the One is corroded by this dialectic of ineffability. The One cannot be conceived, but only aimed at by a mute sensibility. "Our soul divines that of everything, however conceived, there is a principle beyond everything and uncoordinated to everything. Consequently, one must not call it principle, nor cause, nor first, nor before everything, nor beyond everything, still less proclaim it everything; in short it must not be proclaimed, nor conceived, nor conjectured" (Westerink and Combès, 4).

Damascius exploits ingeniously a distinction between the One and the Ineffable: "Plato, by the mediation of the One, made us rise ineffably toward the ineffable of which we now treat, the Ineffable beyond the One, precisely by the very suppression of the One" (9). "The One is the last knowable," but "what is beyond the One is that which is eminently and totally unknowable, which is to say, so unknowable that it does not even have the unknowable as its nature, and indeed that we do not even know that it is unknowable" (18). Damascius seems to cut the branch he is sitting on when he plunges into talk of "that unique and ineffable that englobes all things together, so ineffable that it is not even unique, or even englobing, and that it is not even ineffable at all" (61). The Ineffable is not really other than the

One but is a deepening of the mode of being of the One. Narbonne, giving Damascius a taste of his own medicine, claims that "this Ineffable lifted beyond the One does not escape the contradictions affecting the One. . . . The Ineffable, just like the One, is basically a relative term, because it is tied, as Damascius himself avows, to the capacity for divination of the soul that aims at it" (1993:20). Hence he drops the Ineffable in turn, to remain in silence before the supreme unknowable, of which we can say nothing at all unless it somehow makes its presence felt. The One is a conjectural projection of our mind as it grapples with the unknown, but all our panting cannot liberate the One from the aporias that prey on it. What is envisaged in our desperate talk of the One and the Ineffable nonetheless remains the ultimate condition of metaphysical reason, even if it can no longer be named as Principle or One or even Ineffable.

The suspicion presses that this aporetic merely shows up a sterility in the formalism of the Platonic model of negative theology. Can one be nourished by such tenuous abstractions, taking the frustration of knowledge as a privileged contact with the Unknowable? These games do resonate from afar with a Buddhist experience of the "flight of the ultimate." Damascius might appeal to Buddhists, for his thought "treads the void" of the Ineffable, whereas Proclus finally comes to rest in the presence of the One, comparable to the Vedantic Brahman; alternatively, Buddhists might see Proclus's care for language and thought as a responsible concern for conventionalities over against Damascius's negative extreme. Some will judge, however, that the tracking of ineffable ultimacy in classic texts of Mahāyāna Buddhism and Vedānta is firmer and more authoritative than the apophatic gestures of Damascius and Pseudo-Dionysius. The Indian sources draw near to us even as the Neoplatonists seem to become terminally remote. The exception is Plotinus, who still fascinates, and perhaps the best way to "save" Proclus and Damascius is to retrieve them as subtle commentators on Plotinus.

To judge the merits of the different apophatic methods, one would have to measure their accord with phenomenological attention to the presence of the ultimate. Without such a phenomenological turn, the reasonings of Damascius would only show how ontotheology is undone by its incapacity to fix the place of its supreme principle, thrown back on a groping and divinatory nescience. Neither as systematic failure nor as mystical leap does such an overcoming of metaphysical reason rejoin the Heideggerian step back to the *Ereignis*, which concerns not aporias met at the summit of speculation but the prior blindness to phenomena that lies at the base of metaphysical construction. However, the huge leap of historical sympathy required to relive Damascius's experience and then to grasp concretely how his apophatic moves connect with it may make secure judgment forever elusive here. If we do find a phenomenologically satisfying version of Neoplatonism, we may never be able to verify that it is not a projection on the texts of a modern vision.

Despite the vitality of Damascius's rhetoric and the aura it emanates, an apophasis concerned with the paradoxes of transcendent being does not meet the primary needs of contemporary critical theology, which seeks rather to question the most elementary cataphatic utterances. While apophatic awareness is dispersed in a plurality of styles in contemporary philosophy, focusing above all on the ineffability of singulars (see Alféri 1989), the aporias of the gift and of justice, or the indetermination of linguistic reference, theology in turn is invited to practice the arts of apophasis by taking stock of the fragile and heteroclite quality of every religious language. The groaning of Damascius is no longer limited to the higher levels of reflection on the absolute but affects the task of articulation from the start. Modernist literature and art, attentive to the unfathomable enigmas of the everyday, show theology the path of this new incarnated apophasis.

Insofar as language becomes a field of aporetic research for Damascius rather than the means for the orderly unfolding of an ontotheological system as in Proclus, he is the negative theologian closest to Derrida. But there is a big difference: Damascius can leave language aside and turn to the unknown God in prayerful abandon, whereas Derrida wants to insist that even prayer is caught up in the aporetic structure of language: "Thus, at the moment when the question 'How to avoid speaking?' arises, it is already too late. There was no longer any question of not speaking. Language has started without us, in us and before us. This is what theology calls God" (1992a:99). The language to which Derrida makes a veiled allusion here is the Jewish heritage that carries him and inspires an agnostic piety. Against any *logos* anchored in an extralinguistic signified, Derrida proclaims the reabsorption of God into language—not a language harnessed to the values of knowledge and truth but one that entrusts itself to the space of a distance, which the theologians may designate as divine. The experience of "transcendence" is rooted in the reaching of the signifier after the signified that constantly withdraws in the play of dissemination. That aporetic milieu is not unfamiliar to contemporary theologians, as they mull over the conflicted repertory of God-language, finding in it more an endless play of signifiers than a sure closure on the Signified. They interpret this in a positive sense, as labor on the data of revelation, an effort to give faith intelligible form. A skeptic would see it as the autonomous development of language itself, weaving its polysemic fabrications tirelessly. Derrida situates himself in the undecidable, between these two interpretative possibilities, praying to a virtual God. Perhaps the undecidable is the medium in which theology today must immerse itself, as its essential apophatic dimension, a night more radically denuded and disorienting that comes before the night of faith. The traversal of the undecidable is an apophasis that introduces a crack in speech about God. Living with this intimate lesion, theology can perhaps find an incarnational authenticity unknown to Dionysius.

Apophatic theology aims to bring us into the presence of ultimate reality, or of the divine distance, whereas *différance* works to problematize any such quest or discovery. Recalling Derrida's 1967 titles, *Speech and Phenomena* and *Writing and Difference*, we may say that the sacred speech which brings the divine phenomena to presence is undercut by the writing that consigns all talk of the divine to endless difference, deferral, dissemination. As John Caputo points out, if classical negative theology seeks something "so really real that we are never satisfied simply to say that it is merely real," *différance* "is less than real, not quite real, never gets as far as being or entity or presence, which is why it is emblematized by insubstantial quasi-beings like ashes and ghosts which flutter between existence and nonexistence, or with humble khōra, say, rather than with the prestigious Platonic sun" (2); it is "but a quasi-transcendental anteriority, not a supereminent, transcendent ulteriority" (3). Derrida takes up a theme in Plato that the Neoplatonists could make little of, the *khōra*, which is neither beyond being nor beneath being, and he uses it to relativize and problematize metaphysical constructions of the absolute and the void: "As the very opening of the space in which ontotheology—philosophy—produces its system and its history, it includes onto-theology, inscribing it and exceeding it without return" (Derrida 1982:6). The realm of *différance* or *khōra* is not itself a sacral one, but Derrida's language tempts many interpreters to slip into talking as if it were. "Derrida seems to acknowledge the possibility of certain crossings between what he terms the abyssal 'khora' of deconstruction and the abyssal 'God' of mysticism" (Kearney 2014:203). In his reading of Angelus Silesius, Derrida states: "'God' 'is' the name of this bottomless collapse, of this endless desertification of language" (1992b:300). "It remains to be known (beyond knowing) if the place is opened by appeal (response, the event that calls for the response, revelation, history, etc.) or if it remains impassibly foreign, like *Khōra*, to everything that takes its place and replaces itself and plays within this place, including what is named God" (314). *Khōra* is that "neutral, indifferent, impassible spacing—that enables me to pray" (Derrida, quoted in Kearney 2004:5). *Khōra* imposes an ordeal on religious language, much as the Madhyamaka demonstrations of conventionality and emptiness do, and the result is to make that language more broken, modest, kenotic, desertic, and perhaps thereby more reflective of the nature of divine presence—better imaged as the quasi-feminine dissemination of the Spirit than as resuming all meaning in a single authoritative founding instance. In this regime of *différance*, the play of religious signifiers is shown to be a self-unraveling text. Religious speech survives this ordeal only as the adroit pragmatic deployment of skillful means that attest ultimate reality by confessing their own provisoriness and flimsiness. The very texture of religious speech thus throws us back on our finitude, and its inherent incompletion keeps open the eschatological horizon, pointing forward to what has not yet been grasped. Is this an eschatology without an eschaton, no more than an indeterminate hope, an open question? Or has eschatology degenerated into idle imaginings, as religious language sinks into the babbling night of *Finnegans Wake* which no clear, authoritative Word can enlighten?

Our trust in and use of the inherited concrete namings of God and Christ places our language in the specific tradition of biblical hope, as a tried and trusted skillful means for orienting ourselves toward ultimate reality. In the Middle Ages divine incomprehensibility had a fixed place—at the ultimate summit of reality—but today this metaphysical location no longer offers secure bearings; rather, we locate it eschatologically as the "whither" of our trusting use of the hallowed conventions. There is a sense that our language about God has become spectral, a matter of remnants and remains, and that tuning in to this altered status is the key to a new style of tactful and persuasive religious eloquence. But our critical appropriation and repristination of the tradition as a concrete historical vehicle of contact with the self-revealing God need not be a mere "retro" performance. Where the past language serves to articulate living present conviction, let it be preserved; where it falls short of that reality, let it fall away.

The heritage of apophatic theology, then, is solicited in two directions today—toward the plane of immediate experience and the givenness of phenomena on the one hand and toward the realm of the aporetic and plural on the other. The old apophatic structures cannot be reappropriated in any direct way; they are relics of a lost Platonic world. Retrieving this tradition as proto-phenomenological or proto-deconstructive is a creative, revisionist way of picking its bones. The critique of ontotheology as one epoch of historical reason, one regime of truth that Christian tradition has traversed, frees us to forge the paths of thought that current conditions call for, and this involves a total conversion of the apophatic tradition into currently persuasive phenomenological and deconstructive terms. The classical apophatic texts retain a lateral suggestiveness and can be revisited with profit in a local and occasional way, but their frameworks are undone and their resources redistributed in the contemporary regime of understanding. Our relationship to apophatic tradition is further inflected, or deflected, by the gravitational pull of another factor, the presence of Asian philosophies and religions, with their own highly developed apophatic traditions.

VEDANTIC APOPHASIS

We have noted a deep desire, among both phenomenologists and evangelical thinkers, to translate the dynamics of apophatic thought into a method for getting back to the things themselves, the firsthand phenomena of spiritual and biblical experience. We have also noted that negative theology can be taken up as a general deconstructive approach to religious language. Eastern analytic methods and their associated spiritual wisdom equally lend themselves to phenomenological and deconstructive solicitation. As our relationship to Western traditions becomes more oblique and critical, Eastern traditions come unexpectedly near and offer themselves to our understanding. We prize their apophatic strategies because they do not send us mounting ladders to the beyond but bring us back to the here and now.

It is said that Beethoven had placed above his desk the great saying (*mahāvākya*) uttered nine times by the sage Uddālaka Āruni to his son Svetaketu in the *Chāndogya Upaniṣad* (6.8–16): *Tat tvam asi*—"That art thou." This anecdote is pleasing in the same way as Porphyry's one about Plotinus's refusal to go to worship the gods. Deeper than reasons of cultural or religious interaction lies the revolutionary implication of the choice of slogan. The immanentist turn among German religious thinkers of that time prepared the ground for a fecund reception of Indian nonduality. Breaking with the Platonic image of mystical or contemplative attainment as mounting a ladder to a transcendent goal (*Symposium* 211C), these thinkers proclaimed that the ultimate is found in the here and now. Spiritual insight is less a matter of climbing ladders, be they even the *scala humilitatis* of medieval piety, than of casting them away. According to the teaching of Śaṃkara's disciple Sureśvara, liberation "is not a fresh thing to be brought about somehow, rather, it is the removal of error. When a person's disease is cured we do not say he has obtained something new, but merely that he has been restored to his natural healthy state. Scripture need not enjoin liberation, but it merely wakes a person up to the realization of his actual nature" (Potter, 422). Negative theology, then, is nothing more than letting go of the numberless illusions at which our minds clutch, and which narrow and enslave.

Another pleasing aspect of the Beethoven anecdote is its suggestion that awareness of ultimacy can go together with creative engagement in the world of forms and expression, not merely in a grudging concession but as actually releasing and enriching that engagement. Placing negative theology in that context of contemplative creativity, we can infer that it does not necessarily entail an austere stifling of imagination, but may actually lead creative fantasy to a new depth of penetration. This cataphatic-apophatic alliance is not a grudging concession, for contemplative awareness frees and enriches creative engagement; awareness of the *unsayable* enables a better *saying*—so that Beethoven's last works become, even in their complexity and violence, a prayer issuing from a deep recollection. Negative theology is misunderstood as an effort to go beyond language, for its true function is to create a more relaxed relationship to words and concepts so that the Spirit may traverse them and use them freely. Its vitality is not that of verbal acrobatics dodging the traps of naive religious language but that of obedience to the movement of the Spirit that sheds linguistic encumbrances, with the stale forms of life they represent, as a snake sheds a dead skin.

An apophatism that locates the ultimate in the midst of the everyday shows that mysticism and contemplation are not luxury items but furnish the central piece in the puzzle of our intellectual and sensual lives, the key to the riddle of existence: "To such a man who then asks 'who am I' (*ko'smi*) scripture answers compassionately 'that art thou'" (Sureśvara, quoted in Potter, 543). Everything converges on this center, as a place of final simplicity. Even while living distracted and deluded lives we remain in contact with this center. This immanentist message, even if we have trouble finding a hermeneutic method for its appropriation, is what most speaks to us in the Indian texts, alerting us also to what is still living in the Neoplatonic tradition, a concern for the *Sache selbst* of our existence in its openness to being or to the divine. This emphasis provides a guiding thread for a more down-to-earth, phenomenological interpretation of the problematic heritage of negative theology (as represented by Plotinus, Proclus, Damascius, Pseudo-Dionysius, Eckhart).

Vedantists claim that "all of ordinary experience is false" and must be negated in view of "the most immediate thing of all, the inner Self" (Sureśvara, quoted in Potter, 426). Common experience continues to present us with a world of distinct entities: "Indeed, this experience, though false, is found alike in those who believe that those things do not exist as different from Brahman and those who do not believe so. But those who believe in the highest truth . . . are confident that Brahman is one alone, without a second, free from all experiencings" (Śaṃkara, quoted in Potter, 197). Here we see how the contrast between conventional and ultimate provides endless resources for *aphairesis* and apophasis. When the surface, world-ensconced realities have been thoroughly undermined, the highest truth becomes manifest. But then it turns out that all our language about the latter is conventional also, which lets us in for another round of *aphairesis*.

Brahman, being without characteristics (*nirguṇa*), is impossible to describe; the only reality, it allows no point of view that could embrace it from outside; never an object but always the Self, with no object outside it, any description of it could be only a false and limiting objectification. Yet we know Brahman in all our experiences, under the form of limitation. We attribute to it all the characteristics of being, but this positive attribution is closely followed by negation, so that it does not congeal into a distorting superimposition. The entire process of affirmations and negations is led by concern for the supreme reality of Brahman. In the end an exclusively negative method prevails, which serves to free the mind for a realization of Brahman (see Sharma, 88–96).

Śaṃkara's negation denies all distinctions in regard to the absolute. The world of distinctions (*bheda*) is illusory, and the one true reality is utterly simple. Mandana Miśra, "one of the strongest intellectual personalities of classical brahmanism" (Biardeau, 1), perhaps a contemporary of Śaṃkara, shows that even on the level of empirical perception distinctions do not really occur. Thus it is not only the scriptural word of the Upaniṣads that obliges us to subscribe to this denial of distinctions; the evidence of our senses teaches the same thing. Perception is a momentary experience, in which the thing itself is grasped without any "difference" whatever. The thought of difference is secondary, adventitious, an abstract imposition that obscures the immediately given and its unity. In a dialectical confutation, Mandana shows that if difference were real the consequence would be either the self-abolition of difference or the reduction of everything to nothingness, rendering worldly transactions impossible, or the loss of all individuality or own-nature of things, or their dependence one on the other for their existence. This abolition of differences is hard to swallow for Westerners, but if we look more closely we see that on the conventional plane differences are always respected. They retain a conventional function. As Śrīharsa explains, the existence of *bheda*, due to ignorance, and making possible cause-effect relations, is not denied, but it is not recognized as having ultimate status (Mehta, 89). This perpetual parsing of the world of appearances in terms of conventionality and ultimacy is perhaps the chief locus of the play of judgment in Indian metaphysical traditions.

One might think that the Vedantic language about the ineffability of Brahman represents just the dogmatic slumbers from which Buddhism would awaken us. But perhaps this language, too, has an immediate existential force. "Now therefore there is the teaching, not this, not this [*neti, neti*], for there is nothing higher than this, that he is not this. Now the designation for him is the truth of truth [*satyasya satyam*]" (*Brhad-āranyaka Upanisad* 2.3.6, trans. Radhakrishnan). Here it looks as if apophasis issues in the positing of a massive hyper-essential reality, "the truth of truth." But perhaps the phrase indicates the elusiveness of the ultimate rather than its massive presence, just as "the emptiness of emptiness" does, and perhaps that very withdrawal of the ultimate throws us back on our own existence as the locus of contact with it: "That art thou."

Samkara comments on the text just quoted: "Words convey their meanings by relating to adjuncts such as name, form, action, genus, species, quality, etc. Brahman has none of these, so it cannot be described as a cow can be. To be sure, Brahman is sometimes described by expressions such as 'knowledge, bliss, Brahman, Ātman,' etc., but if we wish to describe its true nature it is impossible. Thus we are reduced to 'not this, not this,' eliminating all positive characteristics that might be thought to apply to it" (Potter, 193). Moreover, there is a subtle suggestion that *neti, neti* indicates not only the impotence of our language but, more positively, the serene self-sameness of eternal being, beyond all limiting qualifications. This is a recurrent feature of apophatic thought: the failure of language is not mere frustration but something sensed to have momentous significance. The suppression of words has an indicative function, arousing the joyful suspicion of the presence of ultimate reality. In devotional mysticism this presence may be "the Bridegroom," but even when it is described as "being" we must suppose that the pallid term carries the same associations of delight. It is as if the withdrawal of the ultimate from our grasp were the very mode of its joyful approach.

For Śaṃkara, "The Self is revealed in the very movement by which it eludes (even 'inner') perception as well as inference, etc." (Hulin 1978:117). This idea that the ultimate makes itself known in withdrawing from our grasp is perhaps the key link between the apophatic tradition and the phenomenological concern with the given. It could be claimed that in Heidegger's thinking being makes itself known in its withdrawal, *der Ent-zug des Seins*. In Christianity the divine "distance" (Marion) is a withdrawal that unites, a phenomenological mode of presence of the divine: "And when I was enveloped in the divine night, seeking what was hidden in the dark, then though I possessed love for what was longed for, the beloved itself fled the grasp of my thoughts" (Gregory of Nyssa, *In Canticum* 6.4). P. B. Fenton (2002) shows that a similar sense of divine presence in the mode of withdrawal runs through Jewish and Islamic tradition. The cataphatic theology of Aquinas is reconcilable with his claim that the divine essence is *penitus incognitum* only if it enacts again and again the withdrawal of God from the grasp of reason—not by tossing in the towel from the start but by pursuing the possibilities of reason until they come to the end of their tether. The withdrawal of the ultimate is inscribed within its manifestation; the two are in direct, not inverse, proportion. Only the one who has fully traversed all the possibilities of cataphasis can enter that "condition of complete simplicity" (T. S. Eliot) where God is known as unknown, is revealed as hidden, is intimately present in the majesty of distance, or speaks in silence.

Vedantists speak intriguingly of the unsleeping, unchanging witness (*sākṣin*) at the heart of all consciousness. The "witness" is neither the empirical subject nor the absolute Self but a concretization of the latter as observing the objects of the illusory world without engaging with them. It is described as a subjectivity that witnesses our empirical subjectivity as its object. As Sureśvara states: "One who sees a jug distinguishes himself both from his representation of the jug and from the object itself; likewise, Apperception distinguishes itself both from the notion of I and from the subject of suffering revealed by that notion" (Hulin 1978:203). Sureśvara points out that from the ultimate point of view the Self does not change into the witness: "Witnesshood is itself imagined (*parikalpita*) through *avidyā* [ignorance]" (Potter, 539). Similarly Brahman's presence within the illusory world is concretized as the illusory Iśvara, much as Eckhart's essential divinity is concretized in the limited figure of God the Creator. This act of knowing is the presence of the ultimate Self, which cannot be objectified; when we try to make the Knower an object of knowledge it has already slipped our grasp.

Aphairesis in both Vedānta and Buddhism affects the everyday ego, considered as a delusive construct: "When the idea of the ego sense is negated, since it is the only root of our relation with duality, all duality ceases" (Sureśvara, quoted in Potter, 538). Sureśvara's strategy is to "draw from the very failure of every attempt to withdraw the ego from contradiction a method of realizing *ātman*" (Hulin 1978:200). For Buddhism the contradictions of the ego affect also the absolute Self. The Buddhist position "consists basically in identifying the idea of the Self and that of the ego, but in such a way as to reduce the first to the level of the second. . . . In a remarkable reversal, the reputedly 'natural' phenomenon of the ego is presented as an artifact, as the psychical sub-product of a gratuitous speculative construction. Buddhism will not fail, in turn, to identify the 'speculative' *ātman* with the unduly hypostatized psychological ego" (43). In its turn the nonself doctrine is found to be riddled with contradictions, from which one escapes, in Madhyamaka thought, by consigning any discourse on the self to the realm of the conventional. "The only coherent response, from a Buddhist point of view, seems to be that of the Madhyamaka school. It consists in considering the entire problem as one of those dilemmas characteristic of the domain of worldly experience and insoluble at its level" (59).

This is still a stumbling block to the Western mind, despite Plotinus's suggestions that union with the One entails a loss of ego (*Enn.*

6.7.35 [ll. 42–45]; 6.9.10), and despite the way Freud and Lacan unmask the ego as a delusive object projected from our needs—an object masquerading as subject. Henry Corbin protests against the Indian dissolution of the ego and of a personal God. He argues that the oppressiveness of substantial conceptions of a personal God is due to forgetfulness of the apophatic background that should underpin them: "If the *absolvens* absolves the *absolute* of every determination, it remains to absolve the absolute of that very indetermination" by the "self-generation of the personal God, engendering himself from the Absolute, absolving himself of the indetermination of this Absolute" (192–93). Perhaps this scheme might be applied *mutatis mutandis* to the identity of the human person, reborn after the dissolution of ego just as God is reborn after the "death of God." Corbin admits that the false everyday ego is dissolved, but only in favor of "the integral Ego, the integral person" (204). That would not quite satisfy Vedantists or Buddhists; they too could be seen as striving to release authentic subjectivity from the carapace of the ego, but they would see that subjectivity as devoid of fixed identity.

Corbin contrasts Eckhart's view of the personal God as merely a provisional construct arising together with the created world, to be surpassed in the quest for the formless deity, the God beyond God, with Boehme's intradivine process whereby the indeterminate absolute gives birth to himself as the fully realized personal God (Corbin, 198–99). Buddhists (D. T. Suzuki, K. Nishitani, S. Ueda) accordingly see Eckhart as the exemplary Christian thinker. Some process theologians have made much of Eckhart's and Boehme's bipolar vision of deity, working it out as a formal metaphysical system. But the metaphysics of a self-birthing of the divine essence are highly problematic. We had best remain on the phenomenological plane: God is known as ultimate indeterminate reality and, more definitively, as the distinct personal presence most fully identified through the figure of Jesus Christ. We are scarcely in a position to overleap the phenomenological horizons so as to construct an objective presentation of God *an sich*, but if reason urges us to do so, its findings on the nature of God are likely to have a disappointingly negative cast, as in Aquinas.

BUDDHIST APOPHASIS

Though Neoplatonist involvement in the world of form has to do with spiritual liberation, it is also motivated by metaphysical ambition of the most thorough and classical kind, as it seeks to ground cosmic phenomena in their supreme noetic principles. Buddhist concern with forms and words is more disinterestedly soteriological, guided by a principle of therapeutic compassion. Both traditions are concerned to uphold the validity of the conventional world, in full awareness of its flimsy status. Nāgārjuna upholds the provisional validity of conventionalities that have no ultimate reality, including the teachings of Buddhism, for the reason that they are the means by which emptiness is known and taught, and that to scrap them would be to fall into nihilism and to hypostasize emptiness itself as an object of clinging. As Buddhists worried about an absolutism of emptiness, Neoplatonists worried about an absolutism of the One that would foster a nihilistic contempt for the world of form and language. That was part of the threat represented by the Gnostics, to whom Plotinus says: "It does no good at all to say, 'Look to God,' unless one also teaches how one is to look" (*Enn.* 2.9.15).

The Madhyamaka philosophy of Nāgārjuna shaped Śaṃkara's thought so markedly as to draw on him the charge of being a crypto-Buddhist. His predecessor Gauḍapāda had built a bridge between the traditions, importing such terms as *paramārtha-satya*. Gauḍapāda was intoxicated by the Madhyamaka and Yogācāra philosophies, though his Vedantic commentators seek to conceal this fact. He repeats Nāgārjuna's arguments about the impossibility of causality, which dismantles the four limbs of the tetralemma: that things are self-caused; caused by another; both self-caused and caused by another; neither self-caused nor caused by another. However, whereas Advaita cuts away words and ratiocinations in order to bring us to an intuition of ultimate being (*sat*), Buddhism goes further, practicing a thoroughgoing emptiness that leaves the mind no final entity to which to attach itself. Śaṃkara believed that every negation is implicitly the affirmation of something else—"Whenever we deny something unreal, we do so with reference to something real" (Thibaut, 2:168)—and even the ultimate negation of all terms applied to Brahman testifies to its supreme ineffable reality. In contrast, Buddhist negation does not posit anything at all. Yet this very nonpositing has a positive sense, attuning us to the freedom of *nirvāṇa*. In the negating itself emptiness is realized, and there is no further ultimate to be sought. Conversely, emptiness exists only as the negation of samsaric delusion. It cannot be set up as an ineffable absolute; rather the "emptiness of emptiness" signifies that emptiness is always correlated with the dependently arising phenomena of which it is the emptiness. Thus questers after ultimacy always find themselves referred back to the world of dependently arising phenomena. Buddhist apophaticism does not project an ever more hyperessential absolute but rather goes in the opposite direction, allowing one to taste the freedom of emptiness but giving one no foothold in anything absolute.

For Buddhism, born in a nontheist milieu, ultimate reality is ineffable not because it is above, beyond, or far from the world of language but because it is nearer, more concrete and intimate. The absence of God seems to make little difference to the mystical landscape, and perhaps it could be seen as just an extra apophatic twist, a critique of objectifying or mythic language, rather than the skeptical or materialist atheism of other Indian philosophies (including Sāṃkhya and Nyāya-Vaiśeṣika). When Nāgārjuna develops a radical dialectic that reduces every category to the absurd, it is not to take us to some hidden place far from this world but to show us how the reality under our eyes eludes the abstractions by which we think to grasp it (though these retain a conventional validity and usefulness). His critique of language is a therapy to break the chains of habitual thought, the captivity to oppositions, fixations, discriminations, and abstractions that makes a mind-forged prison of the world. The "quiescence of fabrications" or "halting of hypostatizing" (*MK* 25.24) restores us to our present and allows us to experience the world of *saṃsāra* as being already *nirvāṇa*; to be sure, only the enlightened eye of a Buddha can see this fully.

Ma-tsu (709–788 CE), the grandfather of Rinzai Zen, would say, "This very mind is Buddha." *Buddha*, etymologically, means "awakened one," and Buddhist awakening consists simply in seeing oneself and the world as they really are. On another day, Ma-tsu or a disciple of his might say, "No mind, no Buddha"—for all this language about "mind" and "Buddha" is but a skillful means to prompt awakening, a ladder to be thrown away when this purpose has been served. Another day he might add, in a still more radical *aphairesis*: "There is nothing at all." The point is not to explode the everyday world in order to break through to another world but rather to put aside dualistic conceptions that prevent one from living in the immediacy of each moment as it arises, to break out of the linguistic fabrications (*prapañca*) and discriminating conceptuality (*vikalpa*) that stand between us and the splendor of reality as it is.

In its analysis of the emptiness of emptiness itself Madhyamaka turns the discourse of ultimacy back on its own conventionality. Thus no object of clinging is provided. Yet the upshot is not that emptiness is doubly vacuous but that it is the fullness of all, which is tasted when one comes alive in the dependently co-arising world. Illustration of this structure can be found in the famous silence of Vimalakīrti. A series of bodhisattvas offer their accounts of nonduality, culminating in Mañjuśrī's declaration that "to exclude all words and to say nothing, to express nothing, to pronounce nothing, to teach nothing, to indicate nothing, is to enter into nonduality." Asked for his account, Vimalakīrti remains silent and is applauded by Mañjuśrī: "That is the bodhisattvas' entry into nonduality!" (Lamotte, 317). As the Indian party argued against their "subitist" Chinese opponents at the Council of Lhasa (792–94), "Philosophical silence must be preceded by a long correct analysis without which knowledge of emptiness is impossible" (Lamotte, 318). The silence that betokens ultimacy can be attained only by the traversal of a constantly renewed effort of speech. In the second chapter of the *Lotus Sūtra*, on skillful means, we hear that "the Dharma cannot be expressed; the forms of words are eliminated"; nonetheless, the Buddha expounds the Dharma in parables and other skillful expressions. The sutra offers no new teaching but "a controversial new style for understanding the existing teaching" (Pye, 21), as it signals the provisionality and conventionality and pragmatic function of any doctrine that can be put into words. Such a return to words from silence is a way of sustaining the emptiness of emptiness itself, keeping it from becoming a supreme logocentric or sigecentric referent. Silence signifies wisdom only when words have preceded and is compassionate only when words follow. Silence is deep only when rooted in an authentic existence: Vimalakīrti's silence would have had no power if he had not lived a bodhisattva life of wisdom and compassion.

When Mandana Miśra shows that if the distinctions between things were real it would follow logically that they had no self-nature but were mutually dependent for their being, he no doubt wants to dismiss these Buddhist consequences as absurd. "Buddhism is instantaneist and links perception to difference alone, reserving continuities, rapports, identities to the labor of imaginative thinking. The position of Mandana turns out to be symmetrical to that of Buddhism: if it is *abheda* that is true, then one must in some way find it also in perception" (Biardeau, 41). Contrary to Mandana, Śaṃkara, "instead of putting the emphasis on the *bheda-abheda* opposition, which would be in a sense a step toward an encounter with Buddhism, . . . leaves *māyā* to its inessentiality and adheres to the *ātman-Brahman* identity." For Mandana, "Difference cannot be real since it is obligatorily linked to mental formations (*vikalpa*), and to the use of language. . . . For the Buddhist, however, language is the place of identities and continuities, for they alone make language possible" (49–50). The Buddhism that Mandana opposes conceives the real as absolute distinction (*bheda*). However, Nāgārjuna too, in opposition to views such as the insistence of the Sautrāntika on pure instantaneity, refutes difference (*MK* 14.6–7). But when he defends the teaching of the Perfection of Wisdom sutras on the sameness (*samatā*) of dharmas, in view of their shared emptiness, it is not in order to grasp beings in their proper nature but to exhibit their dependent arising, their lack of self-nature.

Surpassing differences is a central strategy of Buddhism too. The ultimate breakthrough in Buddhism occurs when one overcomes discriminations between high and low, good and bad. Cosmological hierarchies, in correlation with levels of spiritual attainment, permit movement from low to high more easily than in the West, for the ontological status of the different beings is in accordance with their karmic merit. *Nirvāṇa* is not above and beyond the samsaric world structured by karma but is simply emancipation from the illusions and attachments that keep *saṃsāra* going. "There is *nirvāṇa* for the one who imagines a *saṃsāra*, and vice versa" (Viévard, 210, referring to the *Laṅkāvatāra Sūtra*). But all this is true in part also, *mutatis mutandis*, of Plotinus's ontological speculations, if taken as an analysis of the texture of our real existence, which progresses from superficial levels of phenomenality to deeper ones.

A Buddhist might consider the language of the personal God as a skillful means, permitting us to connect with ineffable ultimacy. This approach will never be completely satisfying to biblical faith, but it should be allowed to play temptingly around the margins of faith and to "solicit" its certitude, for it could be a salutary corrective to naively cataphatic approaches. Corbin might say that the Religions of the Book do not need to be dogged by the alternative perspectives of Buddhism, since they have developed their own apophatic correctives. But a Buddhist might reply that the dialectical mobility of the mind oriented to emptiness, as it progressively relinquishes attachment to being, to nothingness, and to any dualism, is thwarted in biblically based negative theology by the authority and fixity of the divine names, as it is thwarted in Śaṃkara by a residual attachment to being. Even if those names signify that God is finally unnamable, they impose a limit on the mind's movement. Should one go beyond the Bible and place the tradition of the divine names in a wider context where the apophatic dialectic goes all the way, stopping at nothing so that emptiness can be seen, or should one on the contrary impose on this movement respect for the ultimate mystery of God? This is the sort of question that it is impossible to resolve, that remains undecidable, thus giving theological judgment a lot of work to do as it negotiates between the pressure of emptiness and boundless critique on one side and the certitude of faith on the other. Again, on the level of the ego, should one abandon it to the dialectic that shows it up as illusory, or should one affirm the irreducible mystery of the person? This, too, is an open question, and reflection is buffeted between the two perspectives.

Like the status of God, the status of the self in Buddhism is diminished by the denial of any substantial or permanent entities. But a more dynamic way of thinking of both might come halfway to meeting the Buddhist perceptions. Luther's *simul iustus et peccator* implies a decentering of the self, which is no longer a substance with attributes but is displaced, transferred into a new relationship. "Therefore our theology is certain, since it places us outside ourselves (*nos extra nos*): I do not depend on my conscience, sensual person, work, but on the divine promise, the truth, that cannot deceive" (*WA* 40/1:589). Luther had an "enclitic" notion of personal being, where one is defined in relation to one's situation (see Joest). Thus instead of saying that sins are taken away from the person and that righteousness is attributed to him or her, one says that the person is transported from the condition of sinner to that of the justified. "The way of speaking of the Apostle and the metaphysical or moral way are opposites. For the Apostle speaks to indicate that the human being is taken away, the sin remaining, as if it were left behind and the human being were purged out of the sin, rather than the other way round. In contrast, the human way of thinking speaks of sin being taken away while the human being remains, so that it is rather the human being that is purified" (*WA* 56:135). This theme of the reversal of existence by the divine action shows us our vulnerability in refusing us the cocoon of a self-sufficient identity. Luther's formulas are hyperbolical, but they may acquire a more credible meaning if we correlate them with Buddhist ideas. For Buddhism the self is decentered not only in relation to God but even in its claim to substantiality on the worldly plane. If one is no longer the subject of one's acts, it is because the alleged subject lacks substantial existence. In Luther the subject, author of his or her acts, dies, to leave room for the action of God in him or her; in Buddhism nonself permits the Buddha nature in us to function fully. The decentering of the person in Luther is here generalized into a universal ontological principle, dependent co-arising.

Buddha nature is characterized by emptiness. Luther's God, too, in principle at least, is no longer a subject bearing attributes but makes himself known in his actions toward the creature, the sinner, and the justified. To posit a God-in-himself behind the God thus encountered is to suffer the same illusion that has us posit an ego-in-itself as the substrate of all the events and situations we experience. A Buddhist might accept the language of a personal God as a skillful means serving to convey contact with ineffable ultimacy. This may not satisfy biblical faith, but one may nonetheless allow it to play in the margin of biblical discourse to solicit its certitude. Buddhist ontology is perhaps just as likely as Greek metaphysics to occlude the event-quality of biblical revelation and salvation. If Catholic and Anglican theology has been marked by a chronic tone-deafness to Luther (see Hampson), a Buddhist-Christian theology is unlikely to remedy this, perhaps least of all when it invokes the Pure Land gospel of Amida's boundless grace, which tempts one into pat parallels between the two religions. Inculturation of Christianity into Buddhist conceptuality will be unsuccessful unless it encourages the irreducible distinctiveness of the biblical kerygma to emerge, albeit seen in a new light. But handled skillfully Buddhist categories may provide a foil for the Gospel, allowing the distinctive character of its revelation to be discerned both in its harmony with and in its opposition to the Buddhist horizon of understanding. The complex dealing of the Gospel with Western metaphysics should provide us with a high degree of sophisticated freedom and vigilance in entering the Buddhist world of thought. Unfortunately, much "dialogue," even when presenting itself as theological, has looked like a trading in of an unpopular classical metaphysics for a fresh Buddhist model, usually laced with Western input from processism or quantum philosophy. Perhaps it would be better, both in the philosophical encounter with Buddhism and in the theological encounter, to pool the elements of crisis or overcoming or deconstruction on both sides. The meeting of the two traditions will form not a comprehensive supertheory but rather a relativization of the theoretical horizons on both sides, leaving the two traditions more exposed, more denuded, as they take up the task of thinking or the quest of faith side by side.

Theology "lets itself be persuaded" by Buddhist arguments, which chime with modern skepticism, while at the same time preserving a distance, since it uses Buddhist theories as resources for a better understanding of its own theme. At another time it may let itself be persuaded by Vedantic arguments. It may take the same distance toward classical creational and incarnational ontology and its Thomistic elaboration, using it as a possibility of thinking yet registering the limits of its present persuasive force. To use any such resource well one must dwell in it for a long time and espouse it at least in imaginative sympathy. But the disinterested delight and curiosity of a historian of philosophy or religion cannot be a substitute for the awakening of theological judgment, which weighs every frame of thought in view of the necessities of a contemporary faith.

NEGATIVE THEOLOGY IN A PLURALIST KEY

Today apophasis is liable to a swerve in which the very word *God* is taken away, as in Buddhism. Indeed, negative theology could be seen as always flirting with the frank negation of God. Making God totally other, it risks rendering him inexistent in practice; constantly repeating that God is infinite and incomprehensible, the posture of *docta ignorantia* cannot provide the intellectual basis of a people's religion (see Jaeschke, 309). Or if it names him the "non-other" (see Cusanus, *De Non-aliud*), since no otherness can attach to him, it risks reducing him to being in the most colorless sense. If it aims at a silence that brings us into the divine presence, it risks finding only a weary resignation that prefers mutism to the headaches of having to talk about such a difficult subject. Thus instead of raising theology to high dignity, apophasis would only immerse it in a chronic malaise. Meanwhile skeptics can delight in an apophatic rhetoric that allows one to talk of God without claiming to believe in him, or deconstructionists can spread the sauce of apophatism over all other topics that may have a puzzling aspect—gift, forgiveness, justice, friendship, hospitality. Indeed, anything at all can become a topic for apophatic bemusement and bewilderment. Religion breathes its last in a play of reflections, one taking away the other, and the mystery all this is supposed to respect by avoiding positive dogmatic utterance becomes the most meager of specters, fearing exposure to the sunlight of speech. Theology is a critical science, no stranger to the power of the negative, yet theological judgment must keep negation in check, not tampering with it censoriously but ensuring that it is true to itself, not carried away by a precipitous momentum. Negation is always a conventional move within the web of our conventional language; when it takes itself for a breakthrough of the absolute it has become in reality entangled in narrowness or violent bias.

Faced with the plurality of apophatic traditions, contemporary theology can take none of them as self-evident, These methods cannot be extracted from the historical niches in which they developed, and when those niches become obsolete so do the apophatic methods, so that their direct use would only encumber theological reflection today and impede its attempts to tackle its real questions. Historical consciousness imposes its own specific apophasis, putting every discourse on God under the sign of the relative and provisional. Such discourse begins to collapse in its very formation, along with all the old discourses that theology subjects to critical examination. Registering the fragility of its discourse, theology rereads apophatic traditions with a view to their contextuality, seeking their link to the bedrock phenomena of faith—phenomena that are accessible only in a "textual" pluralism enveloping even the most acute personal experiences. Asking how negative theologies direct us to the phenomena, we correct them in view of a contemporary and more biblical apprehension of these phenomena.

Janet Williams claims foundational status for apophasis today, seeing it as a plateau on which Buddhism and Christianity may meet. But in reality apophasis, or a contemporary dynamic equivalent of it, is only one instrument of theological judgment among others and cannot be used independently of the others, nor can it give birth to the concrete structures of doctrinal truth. Rather than restore apophasis, we need to set up a new jurisdiction in theology that will do justice to apophasis by freeing it from the archaic structures in which it has been transmitted, but that will still more establish cataphatic theology on more flexible foundations, permitting it to float or swim in the element of reflective judgment.

Williams underestimates the pluralism of apophasis—"There are as many 'ineffabilities' as there are negative theologies" (Lossky, 13)—and in particular the gap between Buddhist nonduality, which concerns the here and now, and Christian apophasis bearing on a transcendent personal God. Thus she remarks: "How similar all this sounds to the 'unsupported thought' and the 'absence of thought-coverings' in the *Prajñāpāramitā* literature!" in reference to Gregory of Nyssa on Abraham's faith "that was unmixed and pure of any concept" (Williams, 29). Gregory is again nudged in the direction of Buddhism when she talks of "the inchoate undermining of the realist ontology he inherited from Plato and Aristotle" (32–33) and suggests that "the hesitation between ontology and 'disontology,' if it were a little more developed, would become the kind of recoil from ontological views which we see as characteristic of apophasis" (36). As a very cataphatic theologian in dogmatic debate, Gregory has no aversion to views; his apophasis applies only to certain views of the divine, especially heretical ones that he sees as hubristic. In Mādhyamika Buddhism, one transcends "views" about anything, but in the Greek fathers it is only views concerning God that are problematized (though it is true, as we have seen, that Gregory tends to give science a merely pragmatic status). The Buddhist transcending of views is oriented to a nondual experience of everyday reality, but in the fathers it concerns only the divine simplicity, infinity, and transcendence, and the mysteries of the eternal generation of the Son and the Incarnation. Similarly, when Williams speaks of a "shocking activity of emptiness" (141) in Dōgen she hints at a parallel with the divine *ekstasis* in Dionysius. But the latter is merely a variant of the Neoplatonic theme of the self-diffusion of the Good, and the former seems overstated too. To say that "emptiness is something whose self-emptying creates forms and beings" (144) nudges Dōgen toward Masao Abe's version of (Christian) kenosis. The tensions between Christian theism and Buddhist emptiness (in which "there is nothing which is not encompassed within dependent co-arising") are resolved through reference to "the self-emptying of divinity (the *kenōsis* which in Maximus still refers most clearly to the Incarnation of the Second Person of the Trinity, but which has intriguing parallels with Dionysius' concept of the ecstasy of the divine)" (187). From Nishitani she draws the idea of a Nothing that "does not *stand* in opposition to 'Being' but empties itself constantly into beings," which again sounds more like Abe; this is paralleled with an unconvincing image of the divine as "pouring unknowably" into the incarnate Word (203). All such language needs to be pulled down to earth by consideration of the homely function of emptiness in Buddhist practice, as a medicine against clinging to delusions.

Williams brings the apophatic structures in Dōgen close to those of Dionysius: the negation of the "Buddha nature" in a well-known kōan—"Has the dog Buddha nature?" "NO!"—undercuts substantialism and dualism but "points beyond itself to a deeper understanding of 'emptiness-Buddha-nature' in which both of the prior statements are denied but no third position is imaginable" (141), as happens with the cataphatic and apophatic paths in Dionysius. This common structure cannot however conceal a radical difference of content, which renders problematic the idea of a "rapprochement between the God who is *hyperousios*, beyond both being and non-being, and the Buddha-nature which is equally 'insulted' by being called Buddha-nature and no-Buddha-nature" (187). Both traditions "have made negation self-reflexive and used it to condition discourse about what is of ultimate concern" (184), forming a "philosophy of non-dualism," which in the case of Maximus includes an "apophatic oscillation between the poles of mixture (monism) and separation (dualism) in the paradigmatic relation of divinity to humanity in Christ," betokening a "refusal to accept the logic of contradiction" (186); note how the latter phrase again orients Chalcedonian paradox toward Nāgārjunian nonduality. Can the potential fruitfulness of a parallel between Christological perichoresis of human and divine and Buddhist nonduality be realized if we remain in the grooves of classic apophasis and dogmatic speculation? There is a need to go beyond classic discourses, using both traditions to open up new horizons.

It is unwise to give too great a role to apophasis in theology, for it can swallow any absurdity on the pretext that all language is inadequate. It is too flattering to the apophatic ideas of postmodern thinkers to call them "products of the discriminative mind," which "will in their turn require negation" (205), for these ideas do not automatically possess merit comparable to that of classical apophasis. Against the primacy of apophasis, recall that theologians cannot speak of God without wishing to say something concrete. If they denounce a given discourse as inadequate, it is to indicate a more adequate vision. Negation as an end in itself would be a false mythology without real theological content. On the other hand, it does not suffice to harness apophasis to the task of a critique of religious language. If apophasis does not make one feel the vertiginous abyss of the transcendent, the groundlessness of our existence when comforting idols are taken away, then it is merely professional prudence and lacks the élan and audacity of its use by mystical theologians.

Theological judgment is an art of modesty, born of long experience of the limits, quirks, and paradoxes of religious language. Most religious utterance is a kind of babbling to be viewed with a sense of the comic, as one might applaud a baby's first glossolalia. What learned critical reflection may build thereon does not escape the limits and paradoxes of the basic linguistic situation but must seek rather to measure their bearing. The aim is not to find the security of a finally impeccable protocol, allowing one to speak of things religious with indefectible *justesse.* On the contrary, if religious speech does not stumble on difficulties of articulation and does not fall into the excesses of risky or impossible statements, one will suspect it of having lost touch with its theme. To address the transcendent, which exceeds the bounds of everyday thinking and of science, one should run up against the limits of the sayable and discover a need of metaphors, symbols, syntactic violence, and the whole arsenal of the poetic. Poetry takes one back to the lived concrete, but religious use of poetic strategies may seem to take us away from it, creating a poetry diverted from its vocation of "being faithful to the earth," using metaphors that exploit and denature the earthly nourishments, *les nourritures terrestres,* to substitute for them illusory celestial equivalents. The danger that religious discourse may be but a flight into the unreal can be increased by an apophatism that immunizes it by testing it only against the criterion of the ineffable that it claims to serve. Critical vigilance should recall religious discourse to its real empirical conditions; negative theology can be a false substitute for this, opening the door to a second level of imaginary projections, withdrawn from real critical control.

To retrieve the apophatic heritage critically, giving it a new orientation to the concrete contexts of religion and its languages, means resisting the appeal of an ever more remote beyond and affirming the

dignity of our here and now in all its poverty. The apophatic traditions need to be reinvested in a therapy taking away the error or false
knowledge that prevents people from living here and now. When
apophasis takes us away from this, it becomes itself the error it would
remove. This angle can provide a critical reading of Plotinus, Proclus,
Damascius, Dionysius, and Eckhart with its bearings. Their apophatic
machinery finds its proper function in leading us back to the real,
and it is in light of this that we can correct its malfunctioning. This
critical rereading will take account of the present epistemological
context, marked by successive turns—Kantian, historicist, linguistic, phenomenological, existential, deconstructionist—that have done
much to return thought to its finitude.

From the interreligious vantage that allows a comparative survey
of apophatic currents in different traditions, "the Christian preference
for the rhetoric of transcendent divinity and the Zen preference for
the rhetoric of immanent reality" are seen as "tactical and cultural-
situational preferences and therefore in principle changeable" (Williams, 195). The need is felt to go beyond these classic discourses, using
both to open up new horizons. Yet to treat them as mere models or
strategies makes the step beyond them too easy, allowing one to set
up a new apophatic model implicitly seen to represent the truth or the
fulfillment of both traditions. Resemblances on the level of rhetoric
do not necessarily entail that the difference between "immanence" and
"transcendence" is a mere preference. Two worlds meet here, and they
cannot be reduced to two slogans. The undeniable affinities between
the traditions do not call for a *philosophia perennis* that would make
them converge on a single referent. Rather, each tradition of contemplative apophasis has immediate relevance to the others. The impact or
solicitation of the other tradition is most powerfully realized when it
enables a phenomenological clarification of our own, an *aphairesis* of
archaic images and structures that have encumbered it and blocked
access to its core phenomena.

Chapter Eight

INTERRELIGIOUS DIALOGUE

Religious pluralism is no longer a merely incidental "locus" for fundamental theology, or a problem to be dispatched before one gets down to the work of clarifying the Christian basis. Rather, it is increasingly becoming the governing horizon within which the Christian theological project must locate itself. A theology exposed to the questions coming from other religions can no longer reconstitute itself as a pure discipline immune to destabilization by these questions. They remain permanently on its agenda, constraining it to become an inherently dialogal practice.

Today, if theology agrees to be placed in an interreligious perspective, this entails accepting the other religions as a control on what one allows oneself to say. In particular, it means altering the terms of the ancient fraught relationships with Judaism and Islam, now accepted as prophetically challenging Christian identity, rather than dismissed as dead ends in religious development. A review of past errors brings Christianity to eat humble pie, to the point that whereas formerly the New Testament was the fulfillment and surpassal of the Old, it is now to Judaism that we look for a renewed understanding of the Christian kerygma. Some argue that Christianity is essentially anti-Jewish, because of Paul's polemic against the Law; yet Romans

9–11 has been the charter of a new reconciliation between Christians and Jews (Vatican II, *Nostra Aetate* #4; Flannery, 740–42), and a critical rereading of Paul can focus on his fundamental Jewishness as a Pharisee wrestling with the Law's demands, though tempted in the process to project his inner tensions on external enemies, be they Judaizers or pagans. We must overcome all the apparently insuperable gulfs between Christianity and Judaism found in the New Testament and bring them within the ambit of friendly ecumenical exchange by rereading the New Testament with Jewish eyes and by correlating it with its sources in the Hebrew Bible in a new style, emphasizing the continuities and playing down the language of "fulfillment." As to the further gulfs created by church doctrine on God and Christ, surely theology today must do all in its power to recover the Jewish roots of Christian dogma, no longer emphasizing the differences so massively stated in the early church or boasting of access to insights that have surpassed "mere" monotheism, but rather seeking to learn from Judaism a fresh understanding of what is meant by "God" and "Christ."

Theologies of religion that attempt to place Buddhism and Hinduism on a Christian map fall far short of the constraints of dialogue. Rather, dialogue moves between two worlds and experiences the "between" as a space of open questioning. Heidegger's dialogue with a Japanese is a text that allows this experience of genuine pluralism to shine through. The interlocutor recounts that during the experience of translating Kleist into Japanese "it often seemed to me that I was wandering hither and thither between different essences of language, and that from time to time something shone forth that allowed me to apprehend that the essential source of the two fundamentally different languages was the same" (*GA* 12:109). That common source may be somewhat mythical: better to say that one experiences in the tension between the two languages something of the nature of language itself, just as one experiences in the tension of two religions something of the texture of religion as such.

Today theology often cohabits with the discipline of religious studies, an arrangement that is highly problematical, given the secularizing thrust of the latter discipline, born of the Enlightenment. Religious studies (or history of religions) approaches religion neutrally, non-confessionally, as a human, historical construct, and does not share theology's prevailing concern with truth claims and the value of religions in terms of revelation and salvation. Sometimes scandalous religious events, such as the Jonestown mass suicide of 1978, the Aum Shinrikyo sarin gas incident in Tokyo in 1995, or the destruction of the Twin Towers in New York in 2001, will force religionists to practice ethical and human judgment on the traditions and practices they study, but the criteria for such judgment are likely to be drawn only from secular Enlightenment humanism. To be sure, some religionists seem close to theological concerns; Paul Tillich sustained a dialogue with Mircea Eliade in Chicago, and René Girard has had a wide influence on theologians. But these scholars are likely to be denounced as crypto-theologians, and the grand narratives they constructed are increasingly undercut as the radically pluralistic texture of religious traditions and practices is more fully appreciated.

Though religious studies no longer provide theology with secure models of the sacred or of sacrifice that it can integrate into its own constructions, it remains salutary for theology to steep itself in the alien element represented by religious studies. The conventionality of Christian ideas and practices comes very graphically to light when each of them is linked to similar items having a close or remote historical connection with them. It becomes clear that no Christian idea or ritual drops from heaven fully formed, but that each is constructed, piecemeal, drawing on the available repertory of anthropological and religious possibilities, though shaping them in a distinctive fashion. The effect of estrangement produced by this recontextualization shifts the focus of faith from the security of hallowed conventions to the creative project behind them, which frees faith to adjust old conventions and adopt new ones as the current and future realization of that project prescribes. What continues to distinguish theology from religious studies is the experience of the believer, who retains the certitude of faith amid all the experience of contingency and change, a faith now more self-consciously aware of its finitude and situatedness, but nevertheless confident of constituting a secure compass and a solid foothold in a bond with gracious ultimate reality.

IN THE KEY OF PLURALISM AND CONVENTIONALITY

A genealogy of religious traditions reveals that, like scientific or philo-sophical ones, they have survived in a Darwinian battle of ideas in which they had to prove their merit without any prior guarantee or magical protection. They are fragile language games, expedients, al-ways threatened with obsolescence, yet in favorable circumstances able to transmit the shock of ultimacy, even of "divine revelation," and to lead to spiritual liberation. Faced with religious pluralism, the hermeneutics of religious traditions begins to grasp the *contingency* of all religious constructions, which are always rooted in the particular circumstances of old historical contexts with their prejudices, blind spots, and limited horizons.

Interreligious dialogue may enrich its participants' sense of being somehow in touch with ultimate meaning, but it also brings a keener insight into the historical fabric of the religions. No longer a single centering system of representations, each religion comes to know it-self as one construction among others. Unchanging truth takes on a new face or faces as we recognize the contingency, historicity, and pluralism of any articulation or interpretation of it that can be pro-posed. Then the elaborate fine-tuning of theological thought over the centuries can be recuperated in a different key, as a kind of literary criticism of the founding myths, or as already a demythologization, a first step in raising the fantasies of religious imagination to the realm of philosophical reflection. But this demystified reflective reappropri-ation of religious traditions should proceed within the general per-spective of religious trust, avoiding the Hegelian temptation to sub-late that trust into a rational mastery that makes the traditions merely ciphers of philosophical insight. Hegel fearlessly recasts the biblical message in the form of a comprehensive philosophical realization of the nature and structure of consciousness and being. The scandals and tragedies of religious history come into view, in this horizon, as the birth throes of the human mind coming to mature self-awareness and overcoming the fixations and limitations of mythic or dogmatic liter-alism. The *letter* of religion kills, but from this experience of death there emerges a life-giving force, the *spirit* of religion, embodied in a community of free, enlightened minds, which can draw skillfully on the repertory of old traditions as it grows in sophisticated understanding of human and divine reality. This Hegelian vision needs to be supplemented and corrected by that of Schleiermacher. He, too, readjusts the heritage of religion to the conditions of modern consciousness. But in his revisionist stocktaking of the religious heritage he stresses that modern consciousness has not overcome the condition of absolute dependence that religion expresses but is rather learning to live that condition in a mature and reflective style.

"So much depends, of course, on what we mean by God. If transcendence is indeed a surplus of meaning, it requires a process of endless interpretation. The more strange God is to our familiar ways, the more multiple our readings of this strangeness. If divinity is unknowable, humanity must imagine it in many ways. The absolute requires pluralism to avoid absolutism" (Kearney 2011:xiv). The word *unknowable* here should not be taken to mean that our creative imagining and reimagining of God has no cognitive component. Imagining God is not some idle utopianism but the adventure of the mind that knows God because God has made Godself known—known in and across a pluralistic play of conventions, many of which figure successfully, at least for a time, as epiphanic loci, where faith allied with reason touches not an image or representation of God but divine reality itself. This fragmentary and analogical knowledge is not a fund of freely disposable metaphors but rather a stable conviction prompting certain utterances and propositions—such as that God is one, eternal, omnipotent, omniscient, just, good, wise—and hedged around with negative constraints concerning what must not be said. Religious pluralism would be a sad and tedious matter indeed if it just meant that we could revel in imaginings, and in practice that kind of pluralism ends in a new metaphysics in which God is posited as a void, an impersonal X, or an endless process—a new creed that pictures God as "the figure constructed to hide the originary abyss from which everything emerges and to which all returns" and eternal life as "the endless restlessness of a creative process that is the Infinite" (Taylor, 345). It is true that for Aquinas, "Hoc illud est ultimum cognitionis humanae de Deo quod sciat se Deum nescire, in quantum cognoscit, illud quod

Deus est, omne ipsum quae de eo intelligimus, excedere" (*De potentia* q. 7, a. 5, ad 14; The utmost point of human knowledge of God is to know that we do not know God, insofar as we realize that what God is exceeds all that we grasp of it). But this paradoxical formulation clearly refers to a concrete and certain but infinitely inadequate knowledge of God. Similarly, divine "incomprehensibility" does not mean that any and every idea of God is equally valid but that our most careful and well-grounded conventions of speaking of God cannot comprehend the divine essence. The dialectical stress implied in knowing the unknown and comprehending the incomprehensible can stimulate thought only if the mind is indeed held and grasped by a concrete knowledge of God, which Paul roots in the experience of being known by the ungraspable God (Gal 4:9; 1 Cor 8:3).

The dogmatic or skeptical sifting of religious utterances in view of their cognitive truth can distract from the task of an integral reflection on the life of faith. Knowledge of truth is presupposed in religious activities, but most of them are not primarily concerned with cognitive attainment. Even what sounds like a creedal claim can be an expression of moral, emotional, or spiritual experience or purpose, so that the question "true or false" is somehow "ungrammatical." The claim may be as much a performative as a constative utterance or may involve the investment of the subject to such an extent that its conversion into the mode of objectivity loses something essential. "Jesus is the Savior of the world—true or false?": the believer will answer "true" but with a sense of falling beside the point. The proposition seems to wither up when wrenched from the total vital context of narration, worship, praxis, within which it is used only at the proper time and place, as a skillful means attended by reflection that assesses the healing (or "salvific") function of any particular use.

When Jesus Christ is made the object of detached theoretical statements, one has slipped into a secondary, rather ghostly realm. His identity, beyond talk of natures and hypostases, is that of a decisive event, divine as much as human, in which God makes Godself known and felt to human beings as Spirit. That event is renewed wherever his commandment of love is enacted. What makes him "ontologically unique" is that he is the one, in his full fleshly historical context, in whom the face of God has become manifest in so fully gracious a form that we speak of it as eschatological, that is, as proleptic of the ultimate vision of God face to face. Doxology is an appropriate response to this: "Jesus Christ yesterday and today the same, and unto the ages" (Heb 13:8). We have relied too long on a thumbnail transcription of our doxological convictions into objective ontological propositions that can be manipulated without doxological investment. Today we can rethink those convictions, from their basis in experience and practice, in light of the new pluralistic experience brought by traditions in dialogue.

This nondefensive opening up to the actual texture of religious traditions as historically constituted does not undercut the possibility of affirming religious truth but clarifies the actual conditions of this possibility. Deconstructionists might say that these conditions of possibility are so restrictive that they become conditions of impossibility. The Buddhist twofold truth can take deconstruction on board, along with the extra twist that the conditions of impossibility are conditions of authentic possibility: conventional language is intrinsically self-deconstructive, yet can be assumed nonetheless in its very impossibility as a skillful means for orientation to the ultimate. All the creedal terms become placeholders or conventional ciphers for something supremely real that eludes direct expression or objectification. The rational justification of religion has less to do with its capacity to inform us about the way things really are than with its power to orient us to deeper levels of experience and of reality and to help us live better lives. This power must imply its correspondence to the way things really are; yet when its propositions are presented bluntly as direct statements of ontological fact their power is not in evidence. The discernment that underpins the naming of a Creator or a Savior or of grace is a rich and comprehensive apprehension of the nature of reality, not one item added to the sum of knowledge. The modality of such utterances is transcendental, and dispute about them gives the false impression that they are merely categorical. Analogously, the question "Being is good—true or false?" militates against the insight that gives rise to that metaphysical conviction, for it equiparates it with categorical questions that can be appropriately managed in such terms, such as "The box is on the table—true or false?"

In dialogue, religions learn to take a critical distance from their inherited structures and views, and are even jolted, sometimes, into recognizing them to be obsolete. Of course religion does not modernize itself automatically, with a businesslike rhythm, and even in settings of dialogue very archaic ideas may be affirmed. To make Bultmannian liberalism a mandatory requirement for dialogue would be to confine it to a narrow Western academic circle. Unlike the language of science, that of religion can survive in virtue of its very archaism, its irrational aspects becoming useful ciphers of transcendent mystery. Since there is a necessary gap between religious language and what it points to, its very inadequacy becomes a mark of success and authenticity. Moreover, modernity is not a single, univocal process of enlightenment, determining unambiguously what is living and what is dead in a given tradition. Religions often advance by stepping back, either in movements of restoration that end up losing conviction or in a deep *ressourcement* that can rejuvenate the tradition from its origins. Against the danger of a skeptical and materialist reduction of religion to a mere by-product of evolution that has outlived its usefulness, modern religious thinkers have performed a "step back" (Heidegger) to the foundational realities of their traditions—to faith or revelation, or to mystical awakening, or to prophetic engagement. They have turned a critical gaze on the historical formations that objectified or distorted that original inspiration, sometimes in a way that underestimates the wisdom of their traditions and posits unrealistically a pure, unspoiled origin. A line from Luther through Schleiermacher to Rudolf Otto's meditation on the "religious a priori" extends this "phenomenological turn" from the specific Christian case to religion in general.

Even scientific concepts can be quite slippery and elusive, and this is even more the case with religion. So the demand for lucidity includes a demand for insight into the limits of lucidity in this realm. Religious thinking is an art of dealing with the mysterious and ineffable, and it is critically opposed to the crude slogans of religious propaganda. Such slogans may be scriptural catch-phrases such as "God is love," torn from their original rich literary or contemplative context. Between a helpless floundering in the ineffable and the crudity of such false clarities, religion at its best focuses the inscrutable in gripping symbols and effective rituals. It provides a map of existence within which one can orient oneself to the ultimate: the system of covenant and Torah in Judaism; the profiling of a path through death to new life in the story of Jesus and the sacraments that encapsulate it; the various maps of transition from *saṃsāra* to *nirvāṇa* in Buddhism. In these maps everything fits satisfactorily into place; but that very smoothness suggests that the maps are products of the imaginary, in which the opacities and rough edges of real life are smoothed away. The historical and prophetic books of the Old Testament show how powerfully such a map can deal with the tangles of history—but not without occasional adjustments of the map when the historical material shows itself resistant to idealization. It is not that the maps are false; but their truth is of necessity communicated in poetic, metaphorical, symbolic terms, and the effort to squeeze out a bluntly literal statement repeatedly falls flat.

According to the classical logic of religion each such map would seem obliged to claim to be the only true map, or the map that integrates all other maps. Today such confident mapping of the other has become less and less feasible, and we are not even confident that our religious map remains entirely valid for the tradition that produced it. Religious maps are vulnerable to correction in light of scientific findings and in light of alternative maps that in one point or other are more satisfactory. The maps have to be reimagined. Their value lies in the experience and practice they enable and from which they have been projected. This experience and practice will change as the maps undergo imaginative revision, or conversely revision of the maps may be prompted by new developments in experience and practice. Religious conceptions share the pervasive mobility or instability of human historical thought. The fixity of mythic and dogmatic maps often blocks awareness of this, and they are kept in place until the day when it is realized that they have long lost their enlightening and convincing power. We seem now to be passing from a religious culture of allegedly unchanging maps to one in which the maps are constantly being revised or expanded, and in which they are admitted to have only approximate and provisional validity.

Within the culture of religious dialogue as here sketched, it would seem that Buddhism has a crucial role to play, for it combines critical reason and phenomenological awareness in a free and flexible style such as Christianity has not known since the Middle Ages. Buddhist insight into the limits of language and conceptuality offers a basis for reconciling the two faces of religion: its human face as a set of contingent culture-bound constructions, fragile imaginative strategies for arousing spiritual awareness; and its transhuman face as a vehicle of contact with (or revelation by) some absolute or transcendent reality. Yes, pluralism, open-endedness, and even a certain epistemological inconclusiveness are inherent in the nature of religion, rather than unhappy accidents to be overcome. In their very brokenness and inadequacy the religious paths that humanity has furrowed throughout the millennia enable or have enabled contact with realities perceived as ultimate. This inherent doubleness in religion, between flimsy convention and awareness of ultimacy, allows us a double freedom: the freedom to pursue a demystified critique of the various religious systems in historical perspective and the freedom to appreciate the irreducible claims of religious reality as they make themselves felt across these systems and their interplay.

One of the reasons why theology today should favor the open play of reflection over the labor of systematic control is precisely the impossibility of taming the pluralism of religious conceptions both as they emerge in dialogue and as they are uncovered by historical scholarship. Theology seeks to discover traces of ultimate truth in religious traditions, while becoming more and more aware that, whatever is divine in them, they must be seen also as thoroughly human, as historical constructions of the human mind, for which it must now assume full responsibility in a critical stocktaking. The justification and rethinking of religious belief in this key demand a perspicuous restructuring of the religious world from its roots. But this will not entail the reduction of the great variety of religious creativity throughout history to any single explanation, whether anthropological or theological. Rather, the irreducible plurality of religious formations ensures that the conversation between them and the play of critical judgment about them will continue indefinitely. One may wager that whatever divine truth is enshrined in religions will best emerge in this conversation.

Here we must step back behind Karl Barth, who attempted to preserve the purity of biblical and ecclesial faith by consigning the religions to a lower realm. The ultimacy of biblical faith coexists with an endless pluralism within the conventions of that faith itself, and it is solicited by the ultimacy attested in other traditions, in their own pluralistic conventional fabric. Śaṃkara could invoke the two truths to classify Buddhism as falling short of the ultimate insight yielded only by the Vedas (see Todd, 50), and within Mahāyāna Buddhism different schools could claim ultimacy for their own favored sutra as the definitive teaching of the Buddha. Such fulfillment or supersessionist models will have increasingly less place in interreligious dialogue, as we realize that, however powerful and central and true the claims of our own tradition, the other religions attest realities no less ultimate, while no religion conveys the ultimate in its pure ultimacy but always in the play of mutually jostling conventions. That is, ultimacy attaches to any religion worthy of the name, but no religion can be the ultimate embodiment of it; all are summoned to recognize that ultimate reality is not in their grasp and that they offer at best a secure foothold or path or bridge connecting them with it.

IDENTITY RESHAPED IN DIALOGUE

If religions enter into dialogue, they must set aside the dogmatic certitudes that divide them and foreground instead a reflective questioning in which all can share. The dogmas can still be recollected as identity markers, but the experience of dialogue itself, becoming intrinsic to one's religious practice, is a no less powerful shaper of faith-identity. An insistence on unalterable identity, without consideration of the relation of that identity to the wider family of religious identities, yields to a relativization or pluralization of one's religious identity. It is not merely a matter of fashion, but rather one of theological necessity, that the practice of "multiple belonging" has become a salient feature of our religious culture. The person who subscribes to two traditions relativizes the mental frames of both and acquires a stereoscopic vision that can give firmer orientation toward the truth of both traditions. The eventual contradictions between them are of little importance given the rich shared terrain. The Zen slogan "Great faith, great doubt, great effort" can be applied here. Great faith is rooted in the initial investment in one's own tradition and extends to embrace the new perspectives of the other tradition. Faith is not narrow affirmation of identity but hospitality to what is worthy of faith, from whatever quarter it comes. Great doubt is actuated in the reciprocal testing and purification of the two traditions. The great effort that results is that of a spiritual quest no longer limited to the familiar ruts but opening to the enlarged dimensions of religious space and the new questions it harbors. As an illustration of these virtues, I think of a missionary couple, Winston and Jocelyn King, he a Buddhist Christian, she a Christian Buddhist, who conjoined their faiths in their morning meditation. Some might cite T. S. Eliot as illustrating the opposite attitude, if he is seen as having chosen secure sectarian identity over ecumenical relativization, despite being equipped as few people were to explore and embrace the spirituality of Hinduism and Buddhism (see Spurr); but Eliot's use of the *Bhagavad-gītā* in *Four Quartets* and of Buddhism in *The Cocktail Party*, as well as his enthusiastic reception of Tillich's *Systematic Theology*, suggests that his mind was more porous to religious pluralism than is yet appreciated and that his deep-rooted Anglo-Catholic faith was carried lightly, as a skillful means.

To enter into the milieu of reflective, questioning dialogue, each tradition must first recognize its own woundedness and its need of the others. Interreligious dialogue as an intellectual luxury or a supplement to an otherwise perfectly self-sufficient faith will lack the urgency of a genuine inquiry. When born of pressing need, however, this dialogue will not only acquire intellectual bite but constitute a religious activity in its own right. Dialogue requires, not suspension of belief in the basics of one's faith, but awareness of the problematic aspects of how this faith is thought and lived, the unresolved questions that cluster about the act of faith even though it remains intact. Interreligious dialogue will not get under way without a sense of lack, a need to consult the other in view of felt deficiencies in one's own tradition. When religions realize how they are situated in history and culture, so that their ultimate element cannot be detached in a pure form, and when they realize the provisional and patchwork fabric of any language at their disposal, then a space opens up for the meeting of religions on the basis of a shared need. United by awareness of their contingency and poverty, each tradition can say to the others: "Your long duration, your vitality, the fruits you have borne, show that you, like us, are vehicles of access to a gracious and life-giving ultimate reality that has been communicating itself to the human mind since the beginning. Just as we see you as fragile and myth-laden constructions, so you have the right to see us in the same way. Help us, as we help you, to refashion our language so that it can be more functional and credible in pointing to the ultimate in our shared contemporary context."

Modern questions push the religions to give an account of themselves, not only by offering apologetical arguments or a demonstration of their internal rational coherence, but by showing their reality and efficacy. Dialogue is a help to this difficult self-articulation because it renews each religion's sense of what it is at, as it seeks alongside its dialogue partners for ultimate truth and meaning. Shared contemplation will focus the central concern of each religion at an intuitive level, and shared articulation in the give-and-take of dialogue will produce a more public demonstration of the reality of this concern. Informed by this experience, teaching and preaching in both traditions will be steadied by awareness of the wider picture that the dialogue has opened out and will become more steadily anchored in contemplative attention to ultimate truth and meaning as well. If the dialogue brings to the partners a deeper insight into ultimate meaning, new possibilities of coming to grips with it, then the dialogue will become an unmissable part of their religious quest; to drop it would be a loss of contact with the object of their ultimate concern. Superficial motivations such as curiosity or negative motivations such as a shared sense of lack or of crisis will be increasingly replaced by a positive motivation inherent in the core of each of the religions, and the dialogue will become a positive, magnetized religious expression for both religions. The identity of each of the traditions in dialogue will no longer be a static heritage, maintained aggressively against a skeptical world, but a posture of engagement with others, which renews itself through collaboration in a shared project.

All of this might sound as if a flat, banalizing, half-thought-out notion of "dialogue" were being imposed on the religions, which would inhibit their full expression and lead to a desultory show of mutual interest from which little intellectual excitement would be likely to emerge. The conversation between religions must have some pressing motive, above and beyond the urgent topical issues that may prompt them to pool their insights in a given conjuncture. This motive should be a theological imperative coming from within each of the religions in dialogue. In the past such a motive was hard to find, except in cases where dialogue was conceived as an instrument of mission, evangelization, or inculturation of the Gospel. The idea that dialogue with the other was something that a religion needed for its own good has emerged in the Christian world only recently. Dialogue, or comparative theology, could enrich the conceptual arsenal of Christianity, or could bring a clearer Christian self-awareness, according to a dictum of Ninian Smart (in a 1971 lecture at Maynooth College): "They know naught of Christianity who only Christianity know." This is a rather narcissistic motivation and leads to dialogue in which the other is a mere mirror, to be tilted this way and that. The logic of dialogue impels one further—to the recognition that the religious other has concerns and insights that are as important as our own, and that dialogue with the other cannot be primarily for my sake but must unite both our perspectives in a shared study of the matter itself, a matter that will be very variously envisaged depending on one's confessional starting point. The goal is not to clarify the meaning or reinforce the truth of my religion but to follow up the hints given by my religion on more expansive premises, while the dialogue partner similarly follows up those given by his or her religion.

The hints in question concern ultimate truth or meaning, nothing less. Does this mean that the dialogue partners overleap the singularities of their respective traditions in order to embark on philosophical questioning? No, the dialogue does not pass into the cool realm of philosophy of religion but keeps the urgency of specifically theological questions. Supposing the partners discuss the question "What is salvation?" This is a good theme, because in its transcendental sweep it is coterminous with the religion as a whole, if we may presume that all religions are concerned, in varying degree, with a positive outcome that may be described vaguely as salvific, whether in a "locative" or "utopian" style, that is, as shoring up settled order or as striving for radical transformation (see Smith, xi–xv). To fix their minds steadily on such a question the dialogue partners would have to work through the foreground level of their divergent theologoumena about salvation in order to bring into view the nub of the question. But since each of the religions will no doubt have a rich and well-defined doctrine of salvation (in some sense) already, the motivation for their pooling of wisdom initially seems weak.

Religions project a universal vision of the cosmos and of history. But this vision belongs to the register of myth. Each religious tradition sketches its role in the great scheme of things, but that is a speculative exercise, subject to revision. The intended universality of the utterances runs aground on the culturally specific resources they bring into play. Since the apocalyptic and eschatological self-understanding of earliest Christianity, across the various grand worldviews of Christendom, the Christian mythic vision of history has been revised many times. The new image that is now imposing itself is one of all the religions acting together for the future of the planet, building together the spiritual development of humankind. Within this vision, Christians will continue to assert that Jesus Christ is "the Savior of the world" (Jn 4:42) but may forgo the attempt to determine the concrete relationship of this salvation to the spiritual paths opened up in other religions. The idea of salvation becomes itself a topic for decipherment in a milieu of comparativist discernment. Inclusivist or exclusivist claims about the status of one's founding revelation are a kind of apotropaic gesture to shore up one's identity, and they proceed in the mode of "It must be something like this"—the mode of speculative mythmaking. To implement the inclusivist or exclusivist thesis in an apologetic critique of all other traditions would be a premature and counterproductive strategy, for the religions, acting together, are still at the stage of getting to know each other, and the conflicts between their mythic understandings of their place in history indicate a task of self-reappraisal rather than critique of the other.

The interaction between two religions may confirm and make concrete the sense of sharing a journey toward ultimate meaning, but at the same time it may make that meaning itself more indeterminate and elusive, so that "God" or "resurrection" or "*nirvāṇa*" or "emptiness" comes to seem an unsatisfying local perspective falling short of genuine ultimacy. The two religions may feel that they are enveloped by a characteristic modern feeling that the divine origin or ultimate goal toward which they beckon has withdrawn, becoming elusive and unmasterable, consigning the religions to a chastened sense of their finitude and fragility.

While the transcendent realm may become more mysterious, the human dimension of religion becomes more palpable as we approach other communities to reflect with them on our shared condition of wrestling with the questions of religious existence. A beginning of wisdom would be the capacity to recognize in the distortions of other religions a mirror image of distortions or capacities for distortion in our own religion or ideology. The vices the West casually deplores in Islam are vices that characterized Western Christendom in the past. Unquestioning absolutism also characterizes Western ideologies in the present, as is seen in the facility with which the defense of "democracy" against "terrorism" quickly assumed the rhetoric of a religious crusade of "good against evil." The necessity of building a self-critical reflex into belief systems should become evident as we realize how murderous they are when they lack that reflex. Nothing keeps a religion self-critical so well as constant cohabitation with other religions. Religious argument that advances within the confines of a sect is intrinsically distorted. Only the open horizon opened up by the variety of human religious perspectives provides a wholesome setting for religious discussion. Theological judgment has its tried and tested rules of procedure as it moves within the space of a single confessional discourse. But these must be enriched and enlarged, as comprehensively as possible, in ecumenical and interreligious dialogue. The panoply of theological methods for handling scripture, for instance, can be extended to sympathy with other traditions' methods of exegesis and interpretation, and then perhaps to a Christian participation in reading and learning from non-Christian sacred texts. Again, the refined Christian sensibility to the sovereignty of grace can find affinities in other traditions or can prompt original readings of aspects of these traditions.

THE PARITY OF RELIGIONS

We have, then, come a long way from the self-confidence with which the Holy Office declared in 1949: "No one who knows that the Church has been divinely established by Christ and, nevertheless, refuses to be a subject of the Church or refuses to obey the Roman Pontiff, the vicar of Christ on earth, will be saved" (quoted in McBrien, 128). This language is retained by Vatican II: "He himself explicitly asserted the necessity of faith and baptism (cf. Mk 16:16; Jn 3:5), and thereby affirmed at the same time the necessity of the Church which men enter through baptism as through a door. Hence they could not be saved who, knowing that the Catholic Church was founded as necessary by God through Christ, would refuse either to enter it, or to remain in it" (*Lumen Gentium* #14; Flannery, 365–66). A number of theologians today diligently discuss the conditions under which nonbelievers can be saved. But such a question is alien from another image of the church, also found in Vatican II, which sees it as a pilgrim people whose journey points forward to the Kingdom of God. The church exists not for itself, Paul VI insisted, but for the Kingdom, or for the world. Its mission then is dialogal witness, in which it learns as well as teaches. If it confronted Jews, Muslims, Buddhists with the message "We want you all to obey the Roman Pontiff," it would be heard as speaking the language of a ghetto. Recognition that the Spirit is at work in the other great religions has brought increasingly more subtle accounts, or suppositions, about the ways in which the Christian revelation connects with those other religions.

This recontextualization does not threaten the central vision of Christian faith but rather renews it. Faith perceives a phenomenon that imposes itself as ultimate truth: "God was in Christ reconciling the world to himself" (2 Cor 5:19); the divine Word tabernacles in our history, and "we have seen his glory" (Jn 1:14). This phenomenon overcomes the drab relativism that would say that Jesus is only one religious founder among others and that other founder figures are just as divine, just as saving, for those who follow them, as well as the dreary agnosticism that would say that all religious paths are only human projections to be cherished equally for their moral insights and intuitions of ultimacy. But what must be respected equally is the ultimacy that Muslims and Buddhists find in their founding phenomena.

An interreligious covenant would vow to respect the encounters with ultimacy that lie at the heart of all religions that have been tried and tested in long tradition. On that basis a vast ecumenical dialogue could proceed, in which sharing of insights would go hand in hand with debate about contradictions. The ultimacy at the heart of a great tradition does not entail that it has no need of dialogue with others. Since the vehicle of that ultimacy is always finite, time bound, and culture bound, it must be constantly critiqued and developed to remain adequate—or eloquently inadequate—to the vision it attests. The ecumenical outreach allows for a complementation or completion of one's religion, as well as a transformation of the religion's self-consciousness through the experience of dialogue. This does not relativize the core of ultimacy but rather frees it from over-rigid identification with its conventional vehicle. There is mutual recognition between the Muslim and the Hindu, the Christian and the Buddhist, when they engage in the action and contemplation at the heart of their religion. The joy of agapeic action and of silent contemplation is a human and spiritual reality so deep and solid that it cannot be dealt with in arguments about theological categories. The arguments belong to a lower level, which should never be allowed to weaken the level of insight and encounter.

Over against identity fixations a secular ethics focuses on the universal: universal ethics, universal rights, a parity of religious traditions based on a sense of the equality of all human beings and all human cultures. Indeed, this universality is set up as an ultimate over against the merely conventional diversity of the different religions and cultures. It is salutary to correct this by reflecting on the conventionality of the universal itself. Note first of all its historicity: this universality is the product of Europe, rooted in Stoicism, Paul, the scientific revolution, the Enlightenment, and Kant. Authentic universality and equality are not a dogmatic prescription that deadens intercultural or interreligious encounter by confusing equality with uniformity. Rather, they know themselves to be conventionally formulated aspirations, revisable in unforeseeable ways in each concrete encounter. A dialogue that bathes in "soft humanism" must be replaced by one that "systematically makes the mountain crests for discussion re-emerge" (Jullien, 10).

The parity of religions receives a deep theological justification from Karl Rahner's distinction between the transcendental revelation of God that is always pressing on the human mind and the categorical mediations of this in the course of history. The self-revelation of the divine is "*coexistent with the spiritual history of humanity as such*. This is not at all a modernist error but a Christian truth. It can be confirmed very simply from the fact that supernatural salvation is effected everywhere in history, something that the declarations of Vatican II have placed still more clearly in the light of the believing awareness of the church. Salvation cannot exist without faith, and faith cannot exist without real revelation" (Rahner and Ratzinger, 16–17). Faith, grace, revelation, and salvation are universal realities, coextensive with human history. In Rahner this background is expressed in abstract metaphysical terms, but we can discern it in its concrete richness if we interrogate the witness of the great religions, all of which speak of the miracle of grace. Christ is a sign for "the nations" (Lk 2:32), for he is in deep accord with what they have contemplated of the divine glory, and he signals the future that this universal revelation promises.

When the Johannine Jesus promises that the Spirit will lead the disciples into all truth (Jn 16:12–13), one locus of this ongoing illumination is the witness of humanity, including "secular" humanity. If the Word incarnate is the fullness of truth, the discovery of that fullness in the words and signs of Christ and his church is the fruit of an unending labor in which all humanity participates. If grace is at work in the religions, and wherever people seek truth, nothing prevents us from recognizing that grace can work in a distinctive manner in certain historical events, however difficult it is to interpret these events and to place them in a convincing perspective of faith. Today, a basic trust in the salutariness of all religious traditions provides the broad horizon of generous hospitality on the basis of which one can proceed to partake in their dialogical and critical interplay.

The parity of religions, in this perspective, is not the parity of human cultural achievements but a divinely based parity, the impossibility of denying that God is always granting his light and grace to those who open up to God, so that no religion can remain barren. A mature religion will have undergone a dialectical process of deepening and purification in the course of centuries, in polemic against travesties of religion, "false gods," that threaten its integrity. However, this parity does not suspend judgment about the quality and authenticity of a given religious message, including rejection of the shoddy cults that litter the history of religion; analogously, a parity of artistic traditions would not mean equality between masterpieces and inferior work. Parity is only the beginning of encounter, clearing away the obstacle of assumed superiority on one side. What happens in actual debate cannot be predicted. It may confidently be anticipated that real dialogue will bring unexpected inflections of one's own point of departure, even as one presents them as challengingly as possible to the other. The startling developments in Jewish-Christian dialogue are an instance of this process. Once embarked on dialogue the church is no longer in a position to define on its own where it stands and where it is going. The old self-understanding of its mission—"Preach the Gospel to all nations" (Mt 28:19)—alters in texture as the nations respond with their own questions. Still condescendingly, we speak of accommodating the Gospel to the cultures and thought forms of the nations, in inculturation or acculturation. The slogan of "mission as dialogue" more promisingly envisages a two-way process in which the message itself will undergo strange transformations. Of course this is true of any sort of dialogue, and it becomes remarkable in the case of interreligious dialogue only because of the claim to absolute truth that religions put forward. For a religion to accept the normal conditions of dialogue entails that it recognizes the conventional status of its own self-definition and the need to shake it up in dialogue with the other precisely in order to renew it and make it reflect more effectively the element of ultimacy at the heart of the religion.

Rahner's name stands for the inclusivistic vision of Vatican II, which recognizes elements of truth and grace in other religions and sees them as reflecting the light of the divine Word and the power of the Spirit moving in all hearts. Despite the vast amount of ink spilled on his notion of anonymous Christianity, the idea does not reveal much capacity for fertile development. Indeed, it has always been rather irritating. Hans Küng declared: "It would be impossible to find anywhere in the world a sincere Jew, Muslim or atheist who would not regard the assertion that he is an 'anonymous Christian' as presumptuous" (98). A world peopled with "anonymous Christians" is a surrealistic world in which no one is what they appear to be. Even the self-declared apostate will be hailed as really a Christian in disguise. Rahner's theory is grounded in an elaborate philosophical anthropology and comes clad in a stupendous armor of metaphysical jargon. He strives to give phenomenological body to his theory, but he has trouble getting beyond very general evocations of the situation of the human being before the divine mystery: "the experience of infinite nostalgia, of radical optimism, of unquenchable dissatisfaction; the torment arising from the insufficiency of all tangible things; the deeply felt protest against death; the experience of encountering an absolute love even where it appears in utter incomprehensibility and seems to shroud itself in silence; the sense of a radical guilt paired, nevertheless, with a firm hope, and so on" (Röper, 163–64). This is a very selective list of experiences, centered on the consciousness of the isolated individual, and immediately translatable into the terms of a metaphysics of finite and infinite. A more concrete phenomenology of the function and status of churches and religions is required.

BEYOND *DOMINUS IESUS*

The following passage from *Dominus Iesus* (Congregation for the Doctrine of the Faith, 2000) ascribes to other religions a more crucial salvific role than Vatican II did and avoids the aura of pseudolegitimacy suggested by the idea of anonymous Christianity:

> Nevertheless, God, who desires to call all peoples to himself in Christ and to communicate to them the fullness of his revelation and love, "does not fail to make himself present in many ways, not only to individuals, but also to entire peoples through their spiritual riches, of which their religions are the main and essential expression even when they contain 'gaps, insufficiencies and errors' (Paul VI)"

(John Paul II, *Redemptoris missio*, #55). Therefore, the sacred books of other religions, which in actual fact direct and nourish the existence of their followers, receive from the mystery of Christ the elements of goodness and grace which they contain. (#8)

The "therefore" here has the air of a non sequitur, and the sentence it introduces seems anxious to limit the role ascribed to religions in the quotation from John Paul II. It is clear, in any case, that in current church teaching it is not only in the depths of their spirit that people are open to the mystery of Christ: it is above all their religious traditions that foster this openness and give it concrete embodiment, whether this role is seen as de jure or merely de facto (a problematic distinction introduced in *Dominus Iesus*).

The religions themselves are the chief link of humanity to the Christian Gospel; we are to see them as converging on Christ or at least as oriented to the Kingdom Jesus preached. There is then no need to imagine that, in addition to their deepest religious wisdom, non-Christians also have some arcane connection with Christ of which they are unaware or which must be sought in the twilight region of their unconscious. When the CDF document denies to the religions "a divine origin or an *ex opere operato* efficacy, which is proper to the Christian sacraments" (#21), a suspicion of inconsistency arises, as if the authors are torn "between the conciliar (Vatican II) and post-conciliar inclusivistic affirmation of positive salvific elements in other religions and the pre-conciliar ecclesiological exclusivism of the *extra ecclesiam nulla salus* which obviously dominates over a number of statements in *DI*" (Schmidt-Leukel 2008:278). The tension adverted to here lies at the heart of Christian self-understanding, but it should be taken as a stimulating kōan rather than as a barrier to dialogue. The tension is usually resolved by simply saying that other religions have a partial and imperfect grasp of the fullness of divine revelation but can serve as preparations for the Christian Gospel. But this implies that we have such mastery of our own and other traditions that we can securely identify what God is doing in all of them as well as the limits of what he has done. Better to assume that at the core of every great religious tradition lies a knowledge of ultimate truth, a knowledge every bit as authoritative and convincing as the Christian knowledge of Christ. Measuring the degrees of such saving knowledge in the respective traditions and fretting about distortions or deficiencies is a worry that is tangential to the core realities in each religion. All religious traditions are fraught with deficiencies, yet they can still function as channels of ultimacy. Vatican II's recognition of a ray of divine light in other religions was a positive vision, a platform for opening dialogue and mutual appreciation, but when it is erected into an explanatory principle whereby the other religions can be categorized and graded, or a criterion for a schoolmasterly checking of their alleged distortions of the divine light, then the trustful pastoral opening of the council has been overtaken by a crippling anxiety. Augustine's embrace and critique of Neoplatonism could serve as a model here, insofar as it remained a living engagement to the end, never an effort to put the non-Christian tradition in a box and to defuse its challenge to the Christian quest for understanding.

The specific Christian conviction about the salvific role of Jesus of Nazareth cannot be in fundamental contradiction with the positive knowledge of ultimate realities in Islam, Buddhism, Hinduism. The ultimate character of Jesus best comes into clear perspective when he goes to meet the other traditions that reflect a ray of the eternal Logos. That the eternal Logos is uniquely incarnated in the Christ event is a claim to be renewed by attention to the present modalities of that event, notably the interreligious encounter in which Christ's presence is known anew as dynamic event. Theologians of religion tend to speak as if handling such abstract counters as "Logos" and "Trinity" gave them a god's-eye view on other religions, scolded for being ignorant that God is Trinity or praised for having grasped one or another dimension of the trinitarian mystery. Sophisticated historical awareness of how the conventions of trinitarian discourse were set in place would be a valuable check on such sweeping judgments.

Despite the advances made by Paul VI and John Paul II toward a richer, more phenomenological and pluralistic awareness of the religions and their cultures, their inclusivist insistence that the religions receive their goodness and grace from the mystery of Christ is often met with a hostility similar to that which Küng showed to Rahner's idea. For Vatican II and Paul VI it was not a barren logic of identity but a warm conviction of faith that led them to see all religions converging on Christ. However, when *Dominus Iesus* postulates that Christ and his church are at work invisibly in the background of the other religions, this is presented as wrapping up the problem of the de facto elements of salvific truth and grace in the religions. An intuition that is obscure and that is a puzzling theme for further reflection is transformed into a cut-and-dried solution, becoming a constraining rule in our dealings with the religions. We should know when to put such questions and suppositions aside, when they have ceased to be a help, and in fact are becoming a hindrance, to the really fruitful pursuit of interreligious thought and engagement. Theologies of religion are merely makeshift guides to understanding the stakes of interreligious dialogue and should not be imposed as dogmatic straitjackets or bloated speculative syntheses. Suffice it to recognize the deep truths in the world's religions and cultures and to bring those of the Gospel into keen debate with them. By all means let us draw on the Christocentric, theocentric, and regnocentric pictures of how the religions relate to our faith. But these paradigms should not become "views" to which we cling. Rather they are somewhat vague ways of thinking that should be brought into play only where they are useful and illuminating. Moreover, we should beware of words ending in "centric," since they suggest a narrowing of perspective (another reason why Buddhism is so suspicious of "views").

Theological judgment needs to be inserted in the context of a wider human quest of spiritual wisdom, treating the spiritual explorers in other religions and cultures not as "anonymous Christians" but as godsends, as "resource persons" from whom we have everything to learn. In this dialogal openness to each other the religions best fulfill their mission and realize their identity. To rediscover the explosive impact of Rahner's vision of the human mind as a *Vorgriff* (fore-grasp) toward divine mystery we must allow it to cleanse us of parochial obsessions and to redirect us to the divine revelation at work in all the cultures and religions of humanity. *Dominus Iesus* resists this by trying to set up an unambiguous border between Christian faith and the religions. The document refuses to recognize a parity of religions on the phenomenological plane, while on the transcendental plane it insists that salvation, revelation, and grace are mediated only by Jesus Christ and his church. "The Church's constant missionary proclamation is endangered today by relativistic theories which seek to justify religious pluralism, not only de facto but also de iure" (#4). Certainly, such a danger exists, but may it not be placed in the category of "salutary danger," imposing a necessary inflection on the way the church understands and practices its missionary task? To play down religious pluralism is no less dangerous: "By not engaging the question of religious pluralism, by ignoring its vital importance, religious thinkers and leaders render moot any restated apologetics they may offer for their faith" (Keenan 2009:44). It is a paradoxical and forced reinterpretation of Vatican II that would deny de jure dignity to the religions, products of the Spirit at work in all hearts and sharing in the light of the divine Word that illumines all minds.

On the phenomenological front it is clear that the relation of mutual illumination formed in interreligious encounter is one of complementarity and that it would be fatuous of a Christian to tell a Buddhist, "I see you have some elements of truth, but I have its fullness, so your religion is just a preparation for mine." Once the purity of an exclusively Christian or Catholic theology has been breached, through dialogue with other religions, or for that matter with secular voices of philosophy, literature, and the social sciences, it proves impossible to keep this "dangerous supplement" in its place so that the purity of theological identity remains inviolate. Dialogue reveals that Christianity has always been dialogal, never able to define its essence in abstraction from its concrete relations with the religious, philosophical, literary, and social realities of its successive contexts. The project of articulating Christian identity and the Christian message proceeds in a perpetual give-and-take interplay with its environment. Even if Christianity were to define itself in negative condemnation of all other sources of religious wisdom, this would still constitute a relationship to those sources. *Dominus Iesus* wants to have dialogue without contamination of identity. When this proves impossible, the recommendation is to have no dialogue at all, but just a mute collaboration in good works. The transformations of Christianity in the

New Testament alone, through encounters with Gentiles of various kinds, beginning with Jesus's conversation with the Syro-Phoenician woman, indicate the futility of policing the borders of Christian identity too strictly. Fidelity to tradition cannot be a matter of imposing peremptory limits on dialogue and questioning; rather, the truth of the tradition must be allowed to breathe in new climates, where it can show its durable vigor in unexpected ways.

Theologians will ponder the Vatican warnings about "the difficulty in understanding and accepting the presence of definitive and eschatological events in history; the metaphysical emptying of the historical incarnation of the Eternal Logos, reduced to a mere appearing of God in history; the eclecticism of those who, in theological research, uncritically absorb ideas from a variety of philosophical and theological contexts without regard for consistency, systematic connection, or compatibility with Christian truth; finally, the tendency to read and to interpret Sacred Scripture outside the Tradition and Magisterium of the Church" (#4). However, the encounter of Christianity and Buddhism of its very nature puts a question mark against definitive eschatological events, demands a less substantialist ontology of the Incarnation, sets up a play of ideas which cannot be reduced to systematic connections, and uncovers meanings in scripture which are thinly represented in traditional church teaching. This play of judgment eludes tight bureaucratic control. To be sure, we set up creeds as landmarks to define the essential meaning enshrined in the tradition, and theology still labors to maintain the definitive character of what God has done in Christ, including a view of the Incarnation that can claim fidelity to the truth of Nicea and Chalcedon. But the pressure of Buddhist questions on theology and Christology is not thereby dissipated. There is a set of *quaestiones disputatae* between the two traditions, and their resolution lies far in the future. These questions are often very difficult to formulate correctly. To say, for instance, that Buddhism denies God and the soul while Christianity affirms them is to miss the immense plurality of reflection on these topics in both traditions. In the meantime the Christian way of seeing and the Buddhist way of seeing must live with their apparent disaccords, while each side respectfully ponders the other's claims. These issues need not impede access to the core experience of ultimacy at the heart of the other tradition. Accepting that basic situation, one can work toward loosening up the appearance of black-and-white opposition, in view of the capacity of the central claims of both traditions to be rethought in depth. The difficulty of recognizing eschatological events in history, for example, which concerns in particular the paschal mystery, can be allayed by noting the parallels between this mystery and the breakthroughs of ultimacy in Buddhist contexts, as in the enlightenment of Buddhas; against the background of such commonality one can then refocus what differentiates the Christ event and gives it its specifically eschatological significance.

The figure of Christ can be read against the background of creation, the first and fundamental work of grace. All great religions attest to divine grace at work in creation, and it is only in dialogue with this that the teachings and destiny of Jesus take on their full meaning. To invert this sequence, to see Jesus Christ invisibly at work in all the spiritual forces that present themselves as his interlocutors, seems to distort the real process of revelation, coterminous with the religious evolution of humanity. One could say that God, or God's Word, or God's Spirit is at work in this evolution, which transcends the limits of Israel and the Christian community. To plant the figure of the Nazarene everywhere, on the pretext of avoiding a Nestorian separation between the Logos and the human Jesus, cuts violently athwart our actual experience of the cosmos and the religions and of the place of Jesus in it.

If God is ungraspable, ineffable, then a divine action in history must remain something highly mysterious. The imprint of the divine amid the political and ideological complexities that fill the Bible is a theme for prophetic discernment, including Jesus's prophetic interpretation of his own role and of his death. When dogmatic claims grow away from that prophetic matrix, the divine presence is conceived as an invisible metaphysical process at the expense of its phenomenality in the events revealing it. Linking the prophetic discernment of God at work amid historical events to the general presence of God in creation, as in Second Isaiah and the preaching of Jesus, one reads scripture in light of the first book of revelation, the book of nature, perhaps interpreting the unique role of Israel and of Jesus as lighting up the nature of creation, restoring humanity to the grace of its created condition. A breakthrough of the Creator God within history, the death and exaltation of the beloved Son would be the exemplary realization of human destiny. Thence one might go on to take up the notion of the divinity of Christ, taking care not to replace the first perspective by a new one built on that dogma.

The great advance in understanding of the cosmos in recent centuries must inflect our reception of the prophetic revelation of God the Creator as well as the eschatological framework of that revelation in the message of Jesus. A theology from below will integrate into its initial survey of the data an awareness of cosmic, evolutionary, and historical reality as we know it. Religious narrations that begin from above come under siege from the ever more authoritative empirical worldview of modernity. Their myths must be justified at the bar of reality as we know it and cannot impose their own authority in a rejection or alleged overcoming of modernity. The interreligious horizon redoubles the necessity of an approach from below, an effort to discern the true nature of the reality that empowers the religious constructions of humankind. Any claims made for a revelation of God in Jesus Christ lose credibility if they cut themselves off from that enlarged context, for they are cutting themselves off from reality. So to every religious doctrine now an implicit metadoctrine attaches, namely, "This doctrine does not contradict reality." Reality cannot be accused of heresy.

To say that "God intervenes in history" is to signal a profound truth, but in a manifestly impoverished conventional diction, in which each word has to be seen as an algebraic cipher, a pointer to an encounter with ultimacy in connection with the biblical events and their remembrance. The Gospel topics connected with that encounter—eschatological call, freedom of grace, illumination of the Spirit—associate the ultimate with a concrete movement within history, its orientation toward the Kingdom. But this movement can be indicated only in conventional terms. The word *Kingdom* points to the ultimate meaning of history, before which Israel, Christ, and the church figure as privileged vehicles; but we do not have an ultimate grasp of the ultimate significance of these vehicles. Faith trusts that here, in a definitive way, the ultimate meaning of history is breaking through, and that in linking to this one is on the way to the final consummation of creation. But to give a concrete content to that truth one must go back to the here and now, discerning the working of the Gospel values, which carry in themselves, phenomenologically, the mark of the ultimate. Salvation history as projected in imagination is but a conventional representation of the meaning of Christ. Likewise, impressive dogmatic constructions must be expressed in empirical references. To speak of "grace" at work everywhere means simply that one gives oneself the freedom to study other religious cultures and to draw from them what really addresses our present condition, finding the grace in them in this sense.

It may be logical to insist that the scriptures of other religions "receive from the mystery of Christ the elements of goodness and grace which they contain" (*DI*, #8), in that the eternal Word (God) is the source of all goodness and grace, and this Word is most fully and definitively incarnate in the Christ event and the Christ process. But this logical claim has had deleterious effects on Christian understanding of Judaism, in the two millennia when the Hebrew scriptures were read as testimonies to Christ that the Jewish people, because of their blindness, were unable to read correctly. In Origen, only a Christian, endowed with the Spirit, can grasp the full sense of the Hebrew scriptures. If we must now say that only a Christian can grasp the true theological bearing of the sacred books of India, we are stretching theological imperialism beyond the bounds of credibility. The theological claim does not convincingly tie up with the facts of history and pluralism.

"The theory of the limited, incomplete, or imperfect character of the revelation of Jesus Christ, which would be complementary to that found in other religions, is contrary to the Church's faith. Such a position would claim to be based on the notion that the truth about God cannot be grasped and manifested in its globality and completeness by any historical religion, neither by Christianity nor by Jesus Christ" (*DI*, #6). The phrase "the theory" seems to lump together many different possible positions and to consign them all to the dustbin of heresy. While Christ no doubt grasps, manifests, indeed embodies the complete truth about God, this does not justify Christians in bluntly declaring, "We have the full truth about God." Faith that embraces Christ embraces that full truth, but this faith is always in search of a fuller understanding of what it has grasped in principle, and it is on this plane of the quest for understanding that the complementary give-and-take of interreligious dialogue becomes not only rewarding but necessary—in the way the fathers' recourse to Platonism or the scholastics' use of Aristotle was necessary. "Theological faith (the acceptance of the truth revealed by the One and Triune God) is often identified with belief in other religions, which is religious experience still in search of the absolute truth and still lacking assent to God who reveals himself" (#7). Here again an important nuance risks hardening into a black-and-white opposition. All religions have faith in the sense of generosity of vision and existential trust that goes beyond rational calculation. Assent to scriptural revelation happens against this background, and it would dry up and become a narrow fanaticism if it lost touch with that background.

Theological claims need not blind us to empirical reality. The claim that Christ and the church are universal needs to be qualified by recognition of the historical and culture-bound limitations of Christian discourse as it has actually existed. Only at the end of time will the universality of Christ be an actually realized phenomenon. For now it is a projected perspective of faith, a regulative idea guiding the dialogue between Christian tradition and other traditions. In that dialogue Christianity is in quest of its own universality. The historical unfolding of the movement of faith centered on the memory of the paschal Christ is an open project that is far from a complete grasp of its own significance, and still further from being able to make a comprehensive judgment on the ultimate meaning of the other religions, surveying them from above. What is definitive and normative in the Christian confession remains open to evolution and to an enrichment brought by its alliances with the projects and the definitive and normative "revelations" proposed in other traditions. Many new things are to be learned from Judaism, Islam, Buddhism, and Hinduism, things not precontained even implicitly in the treasury of Christian

truth that the church effectively possesses, though they are precontained in the fullness of the Incarnate Word. Christian truth is not in
any case primarily a set of knowledges but the living memory of an
event, the death and glorification of Christ. Our interpretations of this
event, including the labor of dogma that produced the Nicene Creed
and Chalcedon, remain very imperfect. Christianity, viewed in its history, is best seen as a dynamic and open project that is far from being
able to grasp its own significance completely; still less can it grasp
completely the significance of other religions, judging them from a superior vantage point. The normativeness of the Christian project is an
open-ended and fluid thing, as is the normativeness of the project of
Western reason or of the Western quest for human rights. This normativeness is enriched if it can ally itself with kindred projects in other
traditions.

"The theory which would attribute, after the incarnation as well,
a salvific activity to the Logos as such in his divinity, exercised 'in addition to' or 'beyond' the humanity of Christ, is not compatible with
the Catholic faith" (*DI*, #10). Nor is there any "economy of the Holy
Spirit with a more universal breadth than that of the Incarnate Word,
crucified and risen" (#12). According to theologians such as Karl
Barth even the creation of the world is mediated by the humanity of
Christ, and the idea of Christ's descent into hell implies that Abraham, Isaac, and Jacob were saved not simply by their faith in God but
by their prophetic faith in the humanity of Christ. An inflated Christocentrism, even Christomonism, had a debilitating effect on much of
Barth's and von Balthasar's thought. Hasty insistence on stamping
Christ and the church on every phenomenon of creation and history
leads to a counterintuitive vision of reality and leaves no breathing
space for the diversity of humanity and the transcendence of the divine. That is why missionaries were mistrusted; they were often too
quick to stamp Christ on local cultures or even to stamp out these
cultures to make room for Christ.

At an abstruse, transcendental level the claim that adherents of
non-Christian religions mysteriously participate in Christ's paschal
mystery, and not merely in the universal light of the Logos, may belong to the logic of Christian faith, but an equally plausible case could

be made to the effect that the *logos spermatikos* of which Justin Martyr found traces in Greek philosophy and religion is the *logos asarkos*, the non-incarnate Logos, and that this provides a secure universal basis for interreligious thought. It may often be indiscreet and positively distorting to introduce the humanity of Christ as an explicit theme. Again, it should suffice to say that "the Spirit" is moving in all hearts, even though Christians, if pressed, will add that this Spirit is none other than that breathed forth in the fullness of its power by the dying and risen Jesus. The paschal mystery is universal because it touches the essence of human living and dying; this universality is not imposed from without, by preaching Christ, but discovered from within, in every human destiny, as a horizon of hope, given a certain definitiveness in the cross. Modesty is de rigueur in making such claims, since we are dealing with realities of faith, not of final vision. An eschatological proviso, a *docta ignorantia*, must qualify all our affirmations. We grasp only dimly and from within a human historical perspective what the Spirit is saying to the religions and to us through the religions. This stress on limitations need not signify a modernist Neo-Kantian agnosticism; what the Vatican document understresses is the degree to which this theological modesty can draw on sources deep within Christian tradition itself.

The church itself is a conventional construction, a contingent movement. Its divisions that seem scandalous are perhaps but a natural consequence of that historical contingency. The Reformers, in defining the church as the community who hear the Word of salvation, prompt us to see the plurality of the churches not as a tragedy but as a situation in which they can help one another in the quest of the Kingdom, and this is already a quite satisfying fulfillment of the Johannine Christ's wish "that they may all be one" (Jn 17:21). We need not make an imperialist slogan of the saying "There will be one flock and one shepherd" (Jn 10:16), for the unity of love between the churches realizes that vision more radically than would a doctrinal uniformity. The church has lost its temporal power and believes itself freed to affirm itself in the purity of its spiritual power. But the latter, as most often understood, even during the ecclesial enthusiasm of the times of Vatican II (Congar, de Lubac), is perhaps still a shadow of the vanished temporal power. If the real power of the people of God is the power of a "lack," the prophetic thirst for the Kingdom, then the unity between churches in dialogue better exhibits that dynamism of hope than would a church that had become a single massive body. Likewise, the plurality of religions is not a scandal but a situation permitting them to assist one another within the spiritual quest of humanity, which in the Christian perspective is part of the path of the Kingdom. The religions are open ways that go in the same direction as the Christian path, even if their relationship to this path is bound to remain in many respects obscure. The opening of religious paths onto a future that surpasses them all forbids us to put them in opposition to each other as fixed quantities. When we offer to share some Christian truth with them—for example. the claim that Jesus is the universal Savior—it is in the expectation of learning in return how better to understand that truth, rendered less opaque in the dialogal sharing.

Chapter Nine

DOGMA

One of the tasks of fundamental theology is to assess the function and status of dogma. In order to illustrate what a systematic theology in the key of reflective judgment, conscious of the distinction between the conventional and the ultimate, would look like, I shall venture here into discussion of the Trinity and the Incarnation. I do so not to make substantive doctrinal points but to show the kind of trajectories that theological judgment might follow when let loose on the massive corpus of theological tradition. To be sure, what is presented here is one model of theological judgment in action, and other approaches and trajectories could be developed as the play of critical reflection finds other themes for the critical reappropriation and overcoming of tradition. The exercises in theological judgment sketched below fit into a general quasi-Heideggerian paradigm of the "step back," a paradigm that might be complemented, relativized, or contested from other perspectives that could do better justice to the questions raised here and bring the tradition into view in a more luminous and liberating style.

The first question for theological judgment in addressing such topics is "Why bother?" It is discouraging to note that the disagreements among divines about the Trinity that drew Anthony Collins's sarcasm in *A Discourse of Free-Thinking* (1713) bear a close resemblance to those dividing theologians today. Goethe deplored the treasures of ingenuity lavished on the paradoxes of classical dogma, which he saw as an expensive impoverishment of the European mind. That the puzzles of the past continue to haunt the present, as Bethune-Baker stressed (viii), is hardly reason enough to keep worrying about them. Many a theologian has proposed to "show the fly the way out of the fly-bottle," as Wittgenstein attempted in the philosophical sphere, but so great is the danger of oneself becoming stuck in the bottle in turn that it may seem wiser simply to stop bothering about these doctrines at all. Theology should clear the language of faith of all that obscures its liberating and saving character, and it is this motivation that should govern our reprise of trinitarian and Christological controversies. A concrete point of departure is needed to launch such a foray. The most concrete *Sitz im Leben* I can offer for critical revision of the history of trinitarian and Christological thought concerns how these doctrines help or hinder interreligious dialogue, notably with Judaism. The doctrinal tradition also offers a point of application of the healing wisdom of Buddhism, and this can begin with what might be characterized as two extremes in modern theology—an extreme fixated on delusory substance, in speculative Christologies and social trinitarianism, and an extreme of negation, in reductive and agnostic treatments of the dogmatic heritage. To find the middle path between these extremes might involve not only recovering the true sense of classical dogma today but also shifting to a different kind of discourse in which dogma is more vigilantly assessed for its practical liberative bearing, as a valid convention and a skillful means, or as a "trace" that always quietly points beyond itself.

THE METHOD OF THE STEP BACK

Even critical theologians do not always keep in mind the problematic status of classical language, falling back on references to the inner life of the Trinity, for example, as if this were as solid a datum today as it was for Aquinas. Preachers, of course, enjoy a wide license to use biblical stories and dogmatic shorthand without critical probing, but theologians should rigorously renounce such convenience and should vet each of the terms they use, identifying its exact current status and bearing. Karen Kilby (165) cites some lines from Barth as illustrating his apophatic modesty, but in what they take for granted they still fall far short of the apophatic awareness required today: "We, too, are unable to say how an essence's relation of origin can also be its permanent mode of being and how, beyond this, the same essence, standing in two other different and opposed relations of origin, can subsist simultaneously and with equal truth and reality in the corresponding two further modes of being" (*KD* 1/1:387, correcting the English translation quoted by Kilby). That such language needs to be demystified seems apparent. But can one simply cut short the apparent logical conundrums raised by the biblical experience of God as Father, Son, and Spirit, each fully divine with no prejudice to divine unity, by refusing to construct any objectifying discourse of divine essence and relations? Can one simply declare that it is epistemologically impossible to speak of "the divine essence" and its "relations" above and behind what is manifest of God in scripture? A phenomenological, biblical, indeed Jewish reduction of God-talk to what is self-authenticating can set forth the core of the tradition in a manner that encourages meditation and reflection on it and dialogue about it, in contrast to the classical metaphysical extrapolations that have become as mystifying to believers as to those to whom they would address the Gospel.

However, such a step back from dogmatic construction to scriptural phenomenon, and from secure objectifications of doctrine to a sense of the conventionality of all dogmatic language in face of divine ultimacy, is best performed in a detailed and ongoing historical hermeneutic that attempts to assess critically and to do full justice to every formation met along the way, abiding patiently with each in turn. While prophetic iconoclasticism has a place in theology, theological judgment cannot be at ease with a brusque dismissal of scholastic theology, or of classical dogma, or of scriptural representations, or of language itself. In revisiting these classical sites it registers anew what Barth calls "the necessary brokenness of all theological thought and utterance" (quoted in Kilby, 166), while attempting to determine precisely where in each case the brokenness lies. First it detects the brokenness of the magnificent structures of speculative theology, and the need to return to the sobriety of classical doctrine; then it queries doctrine itself, showing its limited role and its inherent instability as a fragile pointer to the scriptural realities it attests; the language of scripture is in turn sifted as a repertory of skillful means for evoking divine presence and action in history. It is only when all these historical articulations have been grasped in their necessity and validity, as well as in their inherently problematic character, that theological judgment can give a concrete profile to the insight that all of them represent valid conventional truth, serving as flimsy vehicles of an ultimate truth not otherwise expressible. Such a historical hermeneutic may redistribute the degrees of importance attached to different moments and styles in the unfolding of the tradition. The relative simplicity of scriptural utterance may be appreciated anew, for the very fact that unlike full-fledged dogma it does not prompt intellectual puzzlement, in itself no more exalted than a troublesome crossword, but rather relaunches theology on a path of meditative reflection very different from the logical and conceptual exercises of scholasticism or of post-Hegelian speculation.

The construction of trinitarian and Christological orthodoxy was a skillful theological performance within an intellectual framework that we increasingly see to have been ill matched to the world of the scriptural texts on which it worked, and to sit ill also with today's conditions, no longer providing a secure basis for creative development. Dogma, and the puzzles it raised, developed according to a rational metaphysical logic up to the fourteenth century, with the result that scholastic brilliance increasingly replaced authentic clarification of the biblical phenomena. From the Reformation on, creative theology has focused on tracing dogma back to its biblical roots. Systematic theologies in all Christian confessions today will normally adopt a biblical pattern of exposition, as in Melanchthon's *Loci* and Calvin's *Institutes*. This biblical refashioning of dogmatic thought has revitalized basic dogmatic claims, recontextualized others, and cast others into the shade. It has exposed as inadequate the classical frameworks of dogmatic thought, shaped by canons of rationality deriving from metaphysics. Of course all theological language is inadequate in one way or another, and the precise measurement of the inadequacy in each case does not constitute a devaluation or refutation but simply a clearing of historical perspectives.

Against naive theologies that speak of grace or the Trinity as if those terms could be taken for granted, or as if dogmatic science could be constituted independently of the more basic underlying and ongoing quest for understanding, theological judgment recalls all dogmatic and theoretical constructions to the movement that underpins them. If one were to reduce Christology, for example, to a theoretical battle between Chalcedonian orthodoxy and various positions opposed to it, one would fail to see that these theoretical constructions are the product of a larger movement of theological rationality. Even this concrete context underlying Chalcedonian and anti-Chalcedonian theories—the depth-encounter of a line of thought inspired by scripture and another inspired by metaphysics—must yield place to a new site of judgment, in which all this past faces the pressures of contemporary questioning. Neither the ancient site nor the contemporary one can be reduced to the terms of a theory or a method. Rather, the constitutive rationality of dogmatic reflection is sited in the dimension of judgment, so that every theological thesis must be seen as a product of the activity of judging and must be plunged back into the dynamic activity of reflection that gave birth to it.

Fundamental theology should enact this basic movement of questioning faith, this predogmatic process of discernment, which is more persuasive than natural theology or philosophy of religion in making a Christian vision credible in a skeptical culture. In an older regime of rationality we constructed proofs of the existence of God. It would be unjust to dismiss this project, with Kant, as an intellectual pathology. Yet it does require therapy; retrieving it today from its basis in the movement of theological judgment, one may free it from the objectification that posits God as an object to be proved, set over against the questing intellect. One can give a dialectical twist to the old way of constructing the idea of God, not by denouncing its antinomies or paralogisms, but by giving it the mobility of reflective judgment that precedes metaphysical arguments.

The topic of dogma stands at the threshold between fundamental theology and dogmatic theology. Karl Barth discusses dogma at the

end of his fundamental theology, revising its status in light of the way
he has grounded fundamental theology in hearing the Word of God.
"Dogmatics tests the church discourse about God, asking about its ap-
propriateness, as a human word, for the service of the Word of God"
(*KD* 1/2:874). It is thus an exercise of critical reflection on a prior language, with a view to purifying it; but this critique is itself guided by
the hearing of the divine Word and cannot claim any independent
basis for its judgments. Metaphysical reason has been supposed to
provide such a basis, purifying and correcting the raw utterances of
scripture, or even subsuming them into the purity of a philosophical
system. Within theological reflection metaphysical reason has to be
kept in a merely ancillary role, which requires constant reflection on
the status, function, and inherent limits of such reason. When the
whole of theology attains the appearance of an imposing metaphysical system, the question of the validity of that development becomes
ever more pressing. Thus medieval scholasticism toppled over into
the open biblical horizons opened up by the Reformation, and the
Tridentine castle of canons and anathemas yielded to the dialogal and
pastoral discourse of Vatican II.

For Barth the divine Word is not identical with scripture, though
scripture is its privileged attestation. The divine Word can be invoked
for a critique of scripture itself. The conventional limits of the canon
could in theory be revised in such a critique. Going further than Barth,
but in a logical continuation of his insights, one can locate inspiration
and inerrancy not in the fixed letter of scripture but in its effectivity
when it is heard as a divine Word in its use by the praying church
community. One can build in similar style on Barth's openings to a critique of dogma, a revision of its status and function, in light of the divine Word. Since dogmas are born of the church's encounter with the
Word, Barth cannot accept the way liberal theologians such as Harnack downplay their significance. Nonetheless, the general tendency
of Barth's thinking is to approach dogmas, and the letter of scripture as
well, reflectively and evaluatively, seeing them as responses to or attes-
tations of an event that they cannot encompass or systematize; or at
least a reading of Barth along these lines could claim to be faithful to
what is best in him and to overcome the residual fixations in his reception of scripture and doctrinal tradition.

"Until Nicea confessing [*Bekennen*] was the presupposition of confession [*Bekenntnis*]. Since Nicea confession has been the presupposition of confessing" (Beyschlag, 90). Dogma was the point of arrival for the earliest Christian thought but became the point of departure in the epoch of the great dogmatic constructions. In the past, dogma seemed the principal link between human discourse and divine truth. To query it was to cut the cord tying earth to heaven. It took on a life of its own, and a sacral aura, which made it immune to challenge from scripture, experience, or critical reason. Protestant theology and history, at least in their general tendency, reinsert dogmas in a dynamic process of believing and reflection. This contextualization of dogma helps close the gap between faith and reason that has been felt so painfully in recent centuries, when post-Cartesian thinkers saw dogma as an arbitrary limit imposed on the mind, "an express prohibition of thinking" that obliged the mind to be untrue to itself: "Dogma contradicts the notion and the essence of truth. No dogma, *qua* dogma, is true" (Feuerbach, 144). Dogma becomes witness. For Schleiermacher it is in the horizon of piety, of the feeling of utter dependence, that dogmas emerge; for Barth it is from the situation of believers addressed by the Word; for both a critique of dogma is requisite. "The church formulas on the person of Christ need a continual critical treatment" (Schleiermacher 2:48).

For Harnack dogma is a product of the metaphysical theology that was formed by Christian thinkers exposed to the intellectual styles of the hellenistic world. This does not do justice to the original nature of dogma as witness and confession. Dogma emerged in the early church first of all as a means of proclaiming the story of salvation, in a normative form that secured unity and identity. Only at a later stage did it acquire the appearance of advancing quasi-metaphysical theses. As an instrument of unity, dogma took shape in the *regulae fidei* of the second century, and the old Roman Creed, which offer lapidary résumés of the essential facts about Christ. These formulas do not enact a Greek metaphysical inculturation of the faith; it is misleading to say that the vision they convey is "immediately incorporated into a knowledge of the world and the ground of the world that was already attained without regard to it" (Harnack 1980, 1:19). They may be marked by a Roman concern with discipline, over against the threat of pullulating heresy, the same concern that concurrently presided over the formation of the canon of scripture and of the monarchical episcopate. No doubt dogma will always retain this aspect of a practical intervention to defend the identity and borders of the ecclesial body. In this sense it is not against the authentic nature of dogma to be used as a shibboleth. However, in modern culture, with its complex historical awareness and its practice of open dialogue, this use of dogma is likely to be increasingly more difficult to stage and increasingly rare. Reflective calls to fidelity in confessing are likely to be more common than summary recalls to the letter of a confession or catechism.

"At the moment that the product of theology has become dogma the way that led to it must be obscured; for according to church thinking dogma can be nothing other than the revealed faith itself—dogma enjoys validity not as the exponent but as the basis of theology" (Harnack 1980, 1:12). Feuerbach, well versed in historical theology, had shown how dogma covers its tracks in this way in *The Essence of Christianity*. Harnack's own account of the Gospel is low-key and nondogmatic, and he regards the identification of faith and dogma as an usurpation, an overshadowing of the biblical truths by metaphysics. Theologians are much concerned with the origins of dogmas, and these origins are invariably murky. The divinity of Christ, the Resurrection, the founding of the church and the "institution" of ministries and sacraments, are among the points on which the New Testament offers little satisfaction to those in search of a clear blueprint, a kind of constitution to be consulted on all disputed points. The reason for this is not that the New Testament is deliberately tantalizing its readers by holding information back. Rather, it emerges from a context and a regime of truth within which dogmatic formalization of the confession of faith in Christ did not or could not arise. Dogma is no longer able to mask the obscurity of its origins or impose its clarities on the texture of scripture. This does not entail that we are left with a diluted liberal Gospel. Rather, the truths emerging so powerfully in the New Testament are too large to be contained within the dogmatic framework. Their depth grammar is subtler and richer than that of dogma.

Hegel presented Christian truths as engendered by the historical dialectic of mind, leaving little place for the submission of the mind to an external authority. Between such immanentism and the extrinsicism of a faith that merely irritated the intellect or that set itself up as a fideist paradox claiming to have vanquished the intellect, Catholic theories of development justified dogmas as expressions of a community living in history and seeking to appropriate in a dynamic thinking a datum that surpassed mere reason. The early Joseph Ratzinger, conscious that "a satisfactory positive understanding of the meaning and task of the history of dogmas has not yet been attained" (12), embraces much of the Protestant critique of dogma; "It seems to me incontestable that the dismantling of the eschatological *Naherwartung* had considerable significance for the construction of church doctrine; here M. Werner has undoubtedly had correct insights" (33). He rejects the ahistorical view of which one could say, "The purpose of Catholic historiography was in some degree to prove that no history had happened" (11). Now we grasp the history of dogma as "the ongoing appropriation by the faith of the church of what is attested in Sacred Scripture" (21). If "the history of dogma is that of the gradual explication of a total originary experience," which affirms that experience but risks making it rigid, so that this history "can become a crust that stifles and finally extinguishes life" (23), in contrast a critical hermeneutics brings a new awareness of "the double face of the phenomenon of tradition" (40). A dialectic between the dynamism of the Spirit and the conservative habits of the human mind makes the development of dogma, even from the Catholic point of view, an adventure full of tensions and movement. "Christian history is the result of the confrontation between the dynamism of the Spirit and the tendencies to decline coming from human existence" (40). "In every dogma there is necessarily a certain incongruence between the speech, the language in which it is said, and the reality it seeks to say and which it can never completely rejoin" (25).

Dogmas are traces of an event of truth, a present event, consisting in the opening of the human mind to a self-revealing God. This means that their development cannot be confined to propositional elaboration of a past deposit but should rather entail revolutions or paradigm

shifts in the manner in which this opening to revelation is appropriated and lived. In the past, the Creed, as elaborated metaphysically,
was a comprehensive framework into which were fitted not only the
set of revealed truths but human existence and the universe itself. The
place of God was itself firmly defined in this framework. Enveloping
biblical revelation and explaining its essence, the Creed itself acquired
the status of a revelation come down from heaven. "Whereas dogma
in Roman Catholic understanding is in its substance *identical* with
revelation (hence infallible, irreversible, an imperative mandate), the
Protestant confession is merely *linked* to revelation, namely to scripture (hence temporally conditioned, reversible, without an imperative
mandate)" (Beyschlag, 18). This sharp contrast is beginning to soften
as the core of what is considered irreformable and irreversible in
dogma is found to be increasingly difficult to isolate, while the historical texture of the language of dogma becomes increasingly well understood. It is no longer possible to accept the condemnation of the
proposition that "the dogmas presented by the Church as revealed are
not truths that have fallen from heaven. They are an interpretation of
religious facts that the human mind has acquired by a laborious effort" (*Lamentabili*, prop. 22; Denzinger, 566). According to Ratzinger, *Lamentabili* condemns radical evolutionism or historicism,
but "individual theses, taken in themselves, can have an entirely good
sense"; the document of Pius X adds nothing to Vatican I, but in practice it has led to "a dismissal of the question itself" concerning the historicity of dogmas (10). *Lamentabili*, as the archives now show, was
composed as an "emergency solution" and "would later precisely not
be taken as the last word of the Magisterium, useful in all circumstances" (ed. Arnold and Losito, 32). In short, the rhetoric of dogmatic absolutism characteristic of official Catholicism from Trent to
the eve of Vatican II could not repress the growth of a modern consciousness of history and development, which now shapes all mature
Catholic reflective judgment, rendering any dogmatic utterances that
do not reflect it unconvincing and ineffective. An example of the latter
would be Christological censures that invoke the language of Athanasius as if it were immediately and transparently transferrable from the
fourth century to the twenty-first.

To formulate questions in the horizon of a metaphysics oriented to substantial identity impedes thinking of revelation in terms of events and processes. Speculative construction fails to see the impossibility of extracting the revelation from its narrative sheath and suppresses the pluralistic texture of historical languages. The dogmatic criteria that orient faith toward the encounter with the biblical God are less central than the guiding criteria found in the Gospel, such as the primacy of love, the triumph of the life-giving Spirit over the letter that kills, the abundance of divine grace and mercy, justification by faith in Christ, joyful hope in the eschatological Kingdom. These criteria are not tidy propositions but require a feel for prophetic or spiritual truth.

A TRINITARIAN TRAJECTORY

(i) From Bad Metaphysics to Good

To bring the play of theological judgment to bear on the legacy of trinitarian thought, a strategic first step back could tackle modern speculative theologies which often err by forgetting the cautious restraint of classical dogma. The juiciest current target is the "social" doctrines of the Trinity that have swamped systematic theology in recent decades, under the name of a "trinitarian renaissance" (see the critiques of Mackey; Holmes; Freyer; Kilby, 103–5). The social trinitarians object that the austerity of classical trinitarian logic is the result of thinking of God in Neoplatonic terms as an absolutely simple being, whereas the Bible encourages us to think of being as relational, loving, and personal, and thus introduces an ontological revolution that shakes Western philosophy at its foundations. Since the values that social trinitarians stress can be fully handled under the rubric of the incarnational economy, as they were by the fathers, it is hard to see what is gained by the additional claim that God is suffering, changing, historical, and kenotic in his eternal nature as well. The classical doctrine on the divine nature and the trinitarian distinctions determines in a sober and minimal way what God must be understood to be if the concrete biblical and incarnational language about God is to make sense. To object that this minimal language is not incarnational enough is to miss the point in much the same way as if one were to protest against the rules of grammar because they cannot do justice to the eloquence of Shakespeare.

While social trinitarians claim to surpass the Neoplatonist metaphysics of Rahner and Barth, unfairly described as "modalists," and even of Augustine and Aquinas, their own thought often reflects the huge impact of Hegel and Schelling on German theology, a legacy that is far from having been overcome or assessed with due critical acumen. The social theory may begin in a sub-Hegelian manner by seeking to explain the constitution of the Trinity. "The divinity thought of as a field can be conceived as coming to appearance in all three trinitarian persons" (Pannenberg, 464). "A far more apt analogy is offered to the contrary by the reality of *play*. A game is a network of relations that does not arise without persons and ordering to distinct persons and that is yet 'played' in such a way that it is present as a whole in a highly specific way in each of the players" (Greshake, 190). The doctrine of the Trinity teaches that the Son is from the Father and the Spirit from the Father and the Son, which clashes with these democratic images. Greshake roundly declares that this teaching of intratrinitarian processions was never solemnly defined by the church (192). No matter that it is found in the most solemn creed of the church, "Ex patre natum ante omnia saecula; ex patre filioque procedit"—the Son is "born of the Father before all ages," the Spirit "proceeds from the Father and the Son." Greshake stresses that the generation of the Son has only a negative sense in the Creed—it means that the Son was not created but came from God in a different way (302). It is true that the image of "eternal generation" is only a metaphor. But then Greshake goes on to characterize the Father-Son relationship as essentially a social one, between equals; and though he correctly characterizes *perichōresis* not as a dance between three separate persons but as the inhering of the three persons in one another in virtue of their consubstantiality (199), he uses this to erase any order of procession between Father and Son; their complete mutual indwelling is the only reality to be considered. The difference between the three persons is cut off from its sole basis, the order of procession, and becomes the difference between social others. The identity of the Father, for Greshake, lies in his being-for-the-others, which sets up from the start what Balthasar calls "a distance between God and God" (quoted in Greshake, 242). Thus the Father gives the whole *communio* its "basis and stability," so that "the two other persons see in him their center [*Mitte*]," which does not mean "the ontological principle of a genetic process," for this center is unthinkable without relations to and from the others. The Father becomes something like a community facilitator, "the point of crystallization of the entire community" (Greshake, 207–8). Critique of such proliferant speculation should go back to its ancient sources, such as the theologoumenon of *perichōresis*, which is already a speculative extrapolation, a superfluous "meta" construction, from the seventh century, when trinitarian language had succumbed to formalism (see Prestige, 265–301).

(ii) From Speculative Metaphysics to Sober Dogma

A further step back could then save classical metaphysical theology, such as that of Aquinas, by bringing it back to its roots in the very restrained language of the creeds. To do so, it could seek to reinforce the negative aspect of Aquinas's development of the logic of the one divine nature, two processions, three persons, four relations, and five notions, so that this immense edifice is brought into view as adding nothing substantial to the simple propositions of the Athanasian Creed. Aquinas's extremely abstract logic "squares" the absolute unity and simplicity of God with the plurality of processions and persons taught by the Creed. At first sight it looks as if the biblical data are now brought into a higher and more powerful integration than earlier generations could have conceived. But the argumentation could be seen as primarily a negative process of ruling out all the wrong things which one might be tempted to say were one to lose sight of the divine unity, and which would make the doctrine positively irrational.

Even when recast in a negative key, this classical metaphysical theology still requires critical reassessment. Does the intellectual paradise of trinitarian speculation effectively witness to the God of scripture? Can the trinitarian systems of Aquinas and Scotus survive historical

research into the genealogy of their doctrinal basis? Basically the answer to both of these questions seems to be negative. Delightful as
philosophical construction, as a chamber music of the mind, this speculation nonetheless remains tangential to the questions of biblical theology. Perhaps only those who really love metaphysics are qualified to
undertake its overcoming, and likewise a love of the refinements of
this theological metaphysics allows one to grasp in depth how it falls
short of biblical witness. As one bids farewell to the scholastic paradise again and again, one learns ever afresh to appreciate the existential
task of incarnate faith. To climb back down from what must be
counted the greatest triumph of metaphysical reason within Christian
theology is thus not a mere confession of failure. The detour through
metaphysical abstraction brings the biblical phenomena into view with
a new depth and stability of focus. The dominance of dogma was a
Law that provided a pedagogy in the use of believing reason, but now
this regime of Law can be seen as ceding to a rediscovery of Gospel, a
regrounding of believing reason in an event of communication, which
entails a consequent change of style, a subtler idea of what counts as
theological rationality. Just as Heidegger sees the tragic obscuration of
the *being* of things in a technological world as the prelude to its possible rediscovery and deeper appreciation, so the obscuration of the
biblical Trinity throughout the centuries in which it was processed in
the technology of scholastic analysis prepares a new kind of thinking
in which the metaphysical representations are overcome one by one to
let the original phenomena emerge as something to be encountered
rather than conceived. Quasi-metaphysical questions may again arise,
naturally enough, but we will be cautious about pursuing them, knowing how easily they distort the concerns and perspectives opened by
scripture.

Theology has to face the hermeneutical task, an ongoing one, of
assessing the status and function of this trinitarian logic and referring it
back to the biblical basis. Thomistic trinitarian speculation does attest
an important aspect of biblical trinitarian discourse, albeit via an elaborate detour. Thomas insists that every movement of differentiation in
the trinitarian process is at the same time a return to unity: "Procedere
ut intimum et absque diversitate, per modum intelligibilem, includitur

in ratione primi principii" (q. 27, a. 1, ad 3; To proceed as intimate and without diversity through the mode of intelligence is included in the notion of first principle). The Trinity does not compromise divine unity but presents the living sense of that unity. "There is procession only according to an action that does not tend to something external but remains in the agent itself" (a. 3). Already John 1:1 presents the Logos as existing *pros ton Theon*, toward God, returning to God. But Thomas is led to this insight less by scripture than by the pathways of Neoplatonic speculation. If we step back from the trinitarian dogma to its phenomenological foundation in the New Testament, we see that the discussion in the *Summa* is based on the dogma, with no examination of its genealogy starting from the biblical sources. The intelligibility cultivated in Thomas's discussion only sporadically reflects any biblical emphasis, and sometimes biblical proof texts only show up the gap between the original phenomena and the speculative edifice into which they are dragooned.

Robert Magliola (85–89) finds deconstructive and Nāgārjunian resonances in the trinitarian logic of the Council of Florence, notably in the decree it addressed to the Copts in 1442. The Copts were given an extra dose of the logic that had caused profound unease among the Greek delegates three years earlier (Gill, 227–32, 235). How much of this later logic did the Latins read back into the patristic texts they cited? Though unbeatable in the fifteenth century, how convincing is it today? Can it really be invoked as pointing forward to a new, sophisticated thinking of the Trinity that would hold its own in dialogue with Buddhism and postmodern thought? The chief issue for theological judgment is how effectively the medieval discourse serves to transmit the biblical realities. A direct dialogue between it and Buddhism would give excessive prominence to what now appears as a secondary or tertiary construction at the expense of the primary language of faith, which that construction must subserve.

Starting from scholasticism, Rahner tried to get back to the scriptural and phenomenological basis of trinitarian theology with his axiom that "the 'economic' Trinity is the immanent Trinity and vice versa" (1967:115), as did Barth in his effort to think the Trinity in reference to the event of revelation, in terms of a triad of the revealer, the revealed, and the revealing (compare Hasidic founder Salman Schneur, "He is the knower, the known, and the knowing," quoted in Lapide and Moltmann, 23). But Rahner's outlook was not grounded in a thorough phenomenological overcoming of metaphysics, so that discussion of his axiom was caught up in speculative wrestling with the problems of the relation between the economic and the immanent Trinity, which went over ground examined long before by theologians such as Urlsperger, Twesten, Lücke, and Nitzsch from 1777 to 1841 (see Stolina 2008). Rahner argued that in addition to the works that the Trinity perform inseparably, and that may at best be "attributed" to one Person or another, there are others in which the Son and the Spirit relate to the faithful in their distinct identities. Ralf Stolina, following Yves Congar and Erich Przywara, objects that the mystery of God cannot be totally exposed in the economy. This underestimates the solid biblical and patristic basis for the view that "in the self-communication of the one God, Father, Son, and Spirit have genuine relations to the believing human being, which are not appropriated and which correspond to their personal individuality" (2008:206). Even Augustine, following Origen, showed awareness of this in a short discussion toward the end of book 4 of his *De Trinitate*, which suggests that the invisible and visible missions of the Son and the Spirit are identical with their eternal processions now made known in history.

Of course this encounter with Word and Spirit does not constitute a complete grasp of their nature. But if one separates the "mystery of the Trinity" and the "mystery of the economy of salvation," one remains bound to a scholastic metaphysical approach that sees God presenting himself in a simplified way in scripture, whereas only metaphysical deduction can establish the reality of divine relations and processions. Newman saw more clearly in his *Essay in Aid of a Grammar of Assent*, where he presents the doctrine of the Trinity in nine simple propositions which serve as a grammar preserving the integrity of scriptural revelation. The nine propositions state the unity of God, the divinity and distinct identity of each of the three persons (the Father is God, the Father is not the Son, etc.), and their relations (the Son is from the Father, the Spirit from the Father and the Son). Stolina shows himself bound to a two-tier view of Trinity when he writes, in italics: "It is not a deficit, but to the contrary it is of decisive disclosive force, that the trinitarian witness of the New Testament can forgo an ontology oriented to categories of essence, an ontology expressed in the categories of essence, nature, person, hypostasis, substance, and can rather, in reverent holding back, point to intratrinitarian processions and relations instead of 'defining' them" (2008:213–14). If we postulate intratrinitarian processions in this way, are we not bound to advance to an effort to grasp them in metaphysical reasoning?

In Augustine, the dogma is still rooted in a vision of the historical missions of the Son and the Spirit, even if that link is fraying. We can see how the dogma detaches itself from this context as fascination with the immanent Trinity throws the revealed Trinity into the shade, and how the effort not to lose sight of the latter is increasingly felt as a tax paid grudgingly to the scriptural world that one has in reality left behind for a world of more luminous ideas. "Theology from below" was made necessary by the abyss between the scholastic Trinity and scriptural language. Deeper study of the latter in recent centuries made it all-absorbing, and the idea that theology could be anything else than "from below" came to seem otiose. This courts dogmatic agnosticism, for instance in the school of Albrecht Ritschl, where those who could still keep essential elements of dogma were now the ones suspected of paying a grudging tax (see Welch, 18–23).

(iii) Overcoming the Metaphysical Horizon of the Councils

The overcoming of scholasticism vindicates the simple language of the Councils and creeds as attesting the realities of biblical revelation. But a further step will seek to overcome the horizons of Nicea (325) and Constantinople (381) insofar as these Councils still subscribe to the project of a metaphysical overview of God and the world, creation and redemption. Metaphysics is no longer the cement that gives dogma its most comprehensive form, allowing it to embrace divine, cosmic, and human reality as its definitive explanation. If we see dogma, instead, as a pragmatic adjustment to an ancient culture that required such formal articulations of belief, then we may calmly assess the successes and failures of this enterprise of inculturation, and its residual merit for today, while also asking what other adjustments of kerygma to culture are now required. Investment in dogma and metaphysics is no longer uncritically celebrated as a deep act of faith but is queried as to its possible dark side, as a repression of awareness or even its violent suppression.

A "theology from below" goes back over the ground covered in the slow formation of trinitarian dogma from the Old Testament to the fourth-century Councils, and it does so with a critical eye to the limits and problematic aspects of this history. The very fact of erecting as first principles, *archai*, the three divine hypostases, as was done from Origen on, took theology away from biblical vision, in which the word and breath of God are first manifest as activities of a "God who comes." If one begins to think of God using concepts such as existence, nature, being, one has trouble rejoining the biblical experience of the passage of God as creative power, call to justice, numinous presence. The doctrine of the Trinity was articulated in terms of *ousia* (essence, being, substance) and *hypostasis* (subsistence). But in light of the priority of emptiness over substance in Buddhism, we might renew a question asked by Emil Brunner: "What place has the concept of *substantia* in a Christian theology?" The leap beyond substance is carried out by Brunner with no help from Heideggerian phenomenology or from Buddhism, both of which articulate a reflective critique of the genesis of notions of substance. For Brunner the Trinity is a defensive doctrine (*Schutzlehre*)—not a New Testament theme but the product of ulterior reflection (Welch, 66). The same could be said of the divine attributes, named in the Bible as they are encountered, without metaphysical elaboration. The latter does not add a complementary knowledge of God but explores the conditions of possibility of our language by pointing out above all the things it is prohibited to say. Discourse on the attributes is secondary, parasitic, in relation to the openness of trust, and the ancient forms of such discourse are no longer adequate even for this secondary function.

The effort to maintain Nicea and Chalcedon in the position of final framework, giving the essential key to all facts about and interpretations of Jesus, finds little support in exegesis. The dogmatic tradition slides toward a secondary, problematic, marginalized position. A perpetual tension between history and dogma offers a field of exercise for hermeneutic and spiritual discernment. A gulf appears between the concepts of dogma and their alleged biblical correlates. The biblical metaphors of Logos and Spirit, particularly in John, reveal irreducible dimensions of the divine and an order among them. But to found these irreducible phenomena in the divine essence or substance and its relations to itself has come to seem a superfluous speculative enterprise that would take away from the phenomena even if it were successful. Mapping their experience in terms of God, Logos, and Spirit, the biblical writers were not aware of any tensions or contradictions of an ontological order. Only with the emergence of theology, fashioned after the Greek philosophical model by Philo, the second-century Apologists, and the Alexandrians, did questions about the ontological conditions and foundations of the biblical language begin to take a sharper character.

The New Testament maps a "divine milieu" that cannot be transcended toward its ontological foundations. Hymnic passages that seem to enact such a speculation on origins (Phil 2:6–11; Col 1:13–20; Eph 1:3–13; Heb 1; Jn 1:1–18; Jn 17) concern the phenomenon of the divine as discerned in centuries of contemplation and do not provide new details on the inner structure of the divine essence. Scripture shows how to taste the divine presence, but it does not give any ontological knowledge beyond the simplest convictions about divine power and goodness. The metaphysical explanations that seemed indispensable in the past can now appear as a distraction and an encumbrance. The ultimacy attaching to convictions of the presence of an all-powerful, all-knowing God is lost when the conventions of metaphysical analysis generate theorems about omnipotence and omniscience that waylay the movement of believing thought. Theology should perhaps now study these constructions only in the key of critical overcoming, as a ghost that must be "laid" so that it can no longer haunt and distort our thinking.

This means that dogma itself, as the product of a thinking that asks for explanations, may have to be seen as a premature and inappropriate response to the data of experience and faith. These call for a subtler and more capacious kind of thinking. As Pinchas Lapide shows in his conversation with Jürgen Moltmann, Jews have a certain sympathy with trinitarianism, since such formulas as "the God of Abraham, the God of Isaac, and the God of Jacob" highlight a distinction of aspects in the one God as experienced by different human subjects (Lapide and Moltmann, 21). Rare is the determination of Talmudist Saadia Gaon (ninth century) to refute the subtlest form of trinitarianism (19), whereas some Islamic philosophers are ready to pursue any suggestion of distinction in God to its last hiding places. This insistence on unity would be seen as coldly metaphysical by Moltmann (35), just as La-pide sees the fourth-century construction of an immanent Trinity as the work of Greek philosophers (28, 55). Here the step back from metaphysics does seem to leave us with anthropomorphic language about the God encountered in scripture, with no possibility of con-structing his being as in the past, either in a philosophical monotheism or in a trinitarian refinement thereof. Could we say that the effort to interpret scripture metaphysically leads either to the cold monotheism of Maimonides and Spinoza or to the awkward trinitarianism of the Cappadocians, the latter, like the whole anti-Arian reaction, being an effort to retain some sense of the divine vitality menaced with absorp-tion by metaphysical monotheism? That would give a new sense to the characterization of the Trinity as *Schutzlehre*. It would become a doc-trine arising only within the context of metaphysical debate that seeks to avoid the modalist and subordinationist theories of divine life. But a more thorough understanding of scripture might prevent that meta-physical perspective from arising at all.

(iv) Querying Scriptural Horizons

At each of the steps back effected in this trajectory, an apparently solid framework of understanding has been shown up as a time-bound con-vention, which, while perfectly valid on its own terms, is discovered to be inadequate to answer the nagging question as to the ultimate sense of the trinitarian tradition. When we come to the New Testament basis, the play of judgment does not stop. It treats the symbolic repre-sentations of the status of Christ in the New Testament no longer as the last objects of faith but as the terms of the language of an ancient judgment of faith. The reality signified by the notions of resurrection, ascension, coming of the Kingdom is simply the horizon of New Testament vision.

A step back to the Jewish context of New Testament language can produce a radical demystification of Christian doctrine. While it has become common in Christian thought to see Jesus as "revealing the mystery of the Blessed Trinity," which already in Tertullian (at the end of his treatise against Praxeas, ca. 214 CE) is seen as the major point differentiating Christians from Jews, a reading of the New Testament with Jewish eyes shows that the Logos and Spirit there referred to are already found in the Hebrew Bible and that the authors of the New Testament had no intention of bringing in a new account of the being of God in itself. That later difference emerged out of an initial difference over the status attributed to Jesus Christ, acclaimed by Christians as Messiah and worshipped as Lord. But perhaps if we apply the method of the step back to Christology, in another critical historical trajectory, we may find a way of apprehending the link between the divine Logos and the human Jesus that no longer obliges us to posit the distinction between God and the divine Logos in a manner that makes it utterly incompatible with Jewish monotheism.

Room for a still greater openness in the dialogue between Jews and Christians is created by the realization that the biblical material cannot all be seamlessly integrated into a trinitarian schema. It provides a vast chronicle of encounters with the divine and the numinous, and of postures of prayer in response to the splendor of creation and the ups and downs of life under divine protection. Moreover, beyond the limits of scripture lies the vast experience of religious humanity, a huge repertory of encounters with gracious ultimacy, healing and enlightening all hearts. The trinitarian patterning that theologians have attempted to impose on scriptural data cannot be extended to these other traditions as an authoritative schema of clarification or integration. This need not pitch us to a trinitarian agnosticism that jettisons the objectivity of the distinctions within the divine unity, but it nonetheless instills a chastened sense of how fragile and tentative the historical establishment of the valid conventions of trinitarian discourse remains, how oblique its relationship to the ultimate reality it seeks to attest.

A CHRISTOLOGICAL TRAJECTORY

(i) Chalcedon Corrects Metaphysical Christologies

As Nicea corrects this bad trinitarian metaphysics, so the Council of Chalcedon (451 CE) corrects bad metaphysical Christologies. A glance at some Christological episodes of the past reveals the blind spots and distortions produced by losing from view the Chalcedonian *horos* (formula, definition), which "placed an insurmountable barrier, at least in theory, against any mutilation of the humanity of Jesus, thereby setting up a permanent summons to deepen our grasp of what that humanity of Jesus was." That task takes on new depth since we are now "in a better position than the people of late antiquity to measure the power and fragility of humanity in its individual, personal being" (G.-M. de Durand 2002b:383), and also in its social, historical, evolutionary, and cosmic contexts.

The twelfth-century "nihilianists" thought that Christ's humanity had no reality in itself; that insofar as he was man he was nothing; that his human nature was less real than his divine (Colish 1994; 1996). Some Thomists (Capreolus, Cajetan, Billot) taught that the human nature had its being in the nature of the Logos, with no existence of its own (see Gutwenger, 178–84; Nieden). In Aquinas himself there is a development toward a fully Chalcedonian view that respects the integrity and autonomy of the humanity: "Christ has no human personality not because he lacks something positive but on the contrary because something positive has been added to his human nature," namely the personality of the Logos (Gutwenger, 177).

The schools of Laon and St. Victor, misled by a pseudo-Ambrosian slogan, "The soul of Christ has by grace everything that God has by nature," attributed divine knowledge to the soul of Christ, and some went so far as to say that "the soul of Christ is equal to the Father" (Santiago-Otero, 46). Aquinas corrects this in Chalcedonian style, distinguishing between the divine, uncreated knowledge of Christ and his human, created knowledge, which is twofold: a natural knowledge based on the senses and receptive knowing and a supernaturally infused vision of things in the divine Word and of the Word itself; the latter is not immediate but is conferred by a superadded habit whereby a created intellect is raised to what is above it (*De veritate*, q. 20, a. 2).

If Chalcedon, in principle, corrects later metaphysical distortions, it also corrects imperfections in the relatively untutored language of earlier Christology. The task of articulating the relation between the two dimensions of the phenomenon of Christ was carried out in early Christianity by paradoxical juxtapositions: "One physician, fleshly and spiritual, generate and ingenerate, become God in the flesh, eternal life in death, born of Mary and of God, suffering first and then beyond suffering, Jesus Christ our Lord" (Ignatius of Antioch, *To the Ephesians* 7.2). This takes up the Pauline dynamic of Jesus crucified and risen but freezes it in formal antitheses. In Tertullian, paradox has a doctrinal edge, underlining that the union of divine and human in Christ remains unfathomable for the human intellect: "The Son of God is crucified; it is boasted of because it is shameful. The Son of God died; it is believed because it is absurd; and buried, he rose again; it is certain because it is impossible" (*De carne Christi* 5.4). These brilliant antitheses can block the way to a truly salutary understanding of the Incarnation. "Thus from the start the duality between the humanity and the divinity in Christ is strongly emphasized in Latin theology. . . . However, it should be noted that this Christology remains a Christology for theologians," reaching its apex in the beautiful antitheses of the Tome of St. Leo, received at Chalcedon (G.-M. de Durand, 2002b:373): "Invisible in what is his, he was made visible in what is ours; unlimited, he wished to be limited; existing before time, he began to be in time; the Lord of the universe, concealing his majesty, took on a servile form; the impassible God did not disdain to be a passible human being; the immortal to be subject to the laws of death."

Chalcedon also corrects the "Nestorian" extreme that divorces the human Jesus from the eternal Word. It summons us to take seriously the Johannine witness to the Word pitching its tent in our fleshly history in and across the figure of Jesus, even as we seek to overcome crude images of God walking around in human disguise. Some speculative Christologists try to correct such docetism by falling into an even more bizarre kenoticism, again running up against the Chalcedonian ban on mixing the natures. C. S. Evans proposes that the

Word loses its omniscience and omnipotence, at least for a time, in becoming man, and even loses all memory of them, so as to be a God
who suffers with humans. One can criticize this on its own terms,
pointing to its Apollinarian presupposition that the consciousness of
the Word is identical to that of Jesus, or its vision of the Incarnation as
degradation of the divine nature, or its lurking tritheism. But it is the
basic horizon of such theorizing that needs to be overcome. An orthodox reply that uses the same categories sounds as eccentric as what
it refutes, as when Gerald O'Collins says that "the person of the
Word (through his divine mind) knew the human mind (of Jesus) as
his own human mind, but not vice versa" (14). This horizon itself is an
obstacle to grasping the meaning of Christ. It needs to be overcome
by a Christology from below that scrupulously refrains from leaping
to such "God's eye" horizons. Thus the process whereby we invoke
Chalcedon to correct speculative distortions may eventually extend
to a critique of the Chalcedonian horizon itself.

(ii) Refocusing Chalcedon

Within the metaphysical discourse the formula of Chalcedon holds
the two extremes of monophysitism and Nestorianism at bay, but its
own positive content is less substantial than the rhetoric of Leo might
suggest. Some claim that the meaning of Chalcedon is so transparent
that theology is left only with the task of building on its achievement,
enriching it with supplementary knowledge coming from exegesis,
for example. But rather than fetishize and absolutize the dogma in
this way, we should re-place it in the flux of history, showing not
only how it illuminates and judges the later and earlier traditions
but also how it may be illuminated and judged by them. The themes
thus announced—"Chalcedon judges the Bible," "Chalcedon judged
by the Bible," "Modernity judges Chalcedon," "Chalcedon judges
modernity"—make us feel the weight and the tensions of history.
Each of them opens up a complex ongoing play of judgment.

To put Chalcedon back in its historical context one would need
to grasp the history of Christology not as the slow assemblage of the
elements of the dogma but as a proliferation of possibilities often

occulted by the closure that the definitive dogma imposed. Origenian Christology, for example, does more justice than later Christology to a certain quasi-adoptionist dynamic in the New Testament. The terminology of "two natures" tends to objectify the humanity and divinity as two substances to be arranged in a satisfying ontological pattern, which impedes concrete perception of how the life, death, and resurrection of Christ connect with an opening up of humanity to the divine. The underlying objective basis constituted by the two natures overshadows the phenomenological reality of divine-human interplay in the Christ event. Likewise, the relation between these natures receives an objective foundation: the hypostasis. This clarification, which proceeds along the usual lines of metaphysical thought, in posing foundations, is less convincing today, for we mistrust any procedure that seeks to simplify complex phenomena by identifying their essence. Moreover, the phenomena of the humanity and divinity of Christ are more complex for us than for our fifth-century forebears, as also are the very notions of humanity and divinity in general.

Thus the apparent precision added by the word *nature* is again dissolved, and we see in it only the vague ostension of two "realities" to be contemplated and explored in a study of the sources. In this way the objectifying language of dogma is changed into a pragmatic language. We take the statement that the natures are united without confusion, alteration, division, or separation (*asunchutōs, atreptōs, adiairetōs, achōristōs*) as a practical injunction for a discipline of our ways of thinking and speaking. If for us the articulation of the relationship between the human and divine dimensions of the Christ event has become a task that the two-natures language only points to from afar, inadequately, we continue nonetheless to seek the equivalent of the Chalcedonian equilibrium.

The delicate balance of the *horos* of Chalceon was lost in subsequent quarrels where the formula became the point of departure for ulterior construction instead of being constantly referred back to the encounter with Christ in scripture and liturgy. A phobia toward natural language about the man Jesus undermined incarnational realism: "The condemnation of Nestorius was the most fateful event in the history of Christology, for it made simple and natural ideas impossible in Christology" (Seeberg, 303; see Harnack 1980, 2:374). In today's horizon the constraints imposed by Chalcedon have recovered some of their original subtlety and can be taken as challenges to the imagination of faith rather than as difficult protocols impeding spontaneous, unself-conscious talk of Jesus as a human being.

The more we question the apparent lucidity of the terms used in the dogma, both historically and in terms of contemporary reception, the more it turns out to be deceptive. Remarkably, Chalcedon itself comes halfway to meet our suspicions, exhibiting an unexpected modernity in its effort to avoid any unnecessary closure, any summary clarity, in its apophatic sense that dogma must be subordinate to the Christ of Gospel and church. Critics have underestimated the practical subtlety of the Council fathers who resisted imperial pressure by refusing to define the terms *nature, hypostasis,* and *person.* The conciliar "definition" is in reality a "border" or "horizon" (*horos*). It gives an abstract rule of speech to distinguish duality and unity in Christ, and it proposes an "enigma" in the four negations that indicate a greater reality, which eludes definition (see Coakley, 161; Halleux, 445–503). It has been argued that the beautiful style of the formula masks the heterogeneity of the elements making it up: "A formula thus fabricated from bits and pieces could not have any coherent theology behind it at the start. It would take as long as in the case of Nicea, or even longer, to compose for it such a background," in which, moreover, the Chalcedonian horizon is "brought back willy-nilly to Cyrilism" (G.-M. de Durand 2002a:25). "One might also ask how far the efforts of Maximus the Confessor to establish the physical existence of a human will of Christ really made up for the shelving of Theodore of Mopsuestia's suggestions on an authentic human psychology of that same Jesus Christ" (25). The positive terms of the formula—*natures, hypostasis, person*—are unusable, and one should retain rather "its negations, which delimit a field for our reflection" (25).

In resisting the desire for clear and well-defined foundations, the Council can be seen as overcoming metaphysics to witness to the living reality of faith. In general, the need to understand patristic debates in their historical thickness impedes speculative flights as much as does the thickness of the biblical text. One cannot extract the dogmatic formulas from that context to place them on an ahistorical pedestal and to make them the foundations of a system. A pragmatic reading of the dogma clarifies its meaning. Its strength is found in its use. The best approach to its historical significance and its contemporary relevance is to see it as presenting a set of rules of language, which steer Christological thought away from distortions that emerged in the early centuries and recur in various guises throughout Christian history. The dogma expresses a wisdom born of the experience of these dangers. It does not offer a synthetic theory, which at the limit could do without constant reference to the biblical sources.

The technical language of Chalcedon is a major advance of the scholastic spirit in theology. Though it was undoubtedly necessary, even salutary, its price was nonetheless high. The space held open by the *horos* is not that of a cold and neutral vision, in which hypostasis and natures are objectified, in abstraction from the context of a lived encounter. But an effort of reading is needed to see this and to overcome the long tradition of dogmatic formalization erected on this basis. "A conciliar formulation is *a datum open to actualization* in virtue of the plasticity of concepts" (Bourgine, 460). Thus one can ask if the churches are not "authorized, indeed urged, by patristic tradition itself to reformulate the Creed so as better to confront the present demands of their unity and their witness" (Halleux, 19).

(iii) The Critical Impact of a Christology from Below

If Chalcedon remains the gold standard within metaphysical Christology, it needs nonetheless to be referred back to the biblical realities it attests, at the same time as we register the limits of metaphysical Christology in general. This we can do by a step back to the Johannine Christ, the principal source for the Christology of the Councils. Then we repeat this process for John in turn, putting him in context by a step back to the historical Jesus. Jesus, in turn, can be understood only starting from his Jewish context. The dialectic we set up between different layers of the tradition is completed by the correlation of the Christ discerned in the depth of history with Christ as understood in contemporary paths of thought about liberation, including the reception of Buddhism, which permits a deeper appreciation of the kenotic character of Christ's humanity—its full participation in the dependently co-arisen texture of samsaric existence. Christ reveals God not because he combines divine and human substances but because in his self-emptying he reveals the true nature of humanity before God. Approached from below, on the paths of history and evolution, the figure of Jesus can emerge as a divine word spoken into the heart of history.

Having stepped back to the origins, can we then rethink Christology moving forward from them in a "theology from below"? This would entail putting the Jewish Jesus back in the center of the picture and keeping him there as long as possible before graduating to declarations on the eternal Word. Harnack diagnosed a wrong move in Christian theology when the Logos, at first a predicate of Jesus Christ, indicating the ultimate significance of his redemptive role and action, became instead the subject of redemption, with Jesus as its mere appearance (1927:82). Barth replied: "Strictly speaking, the Logos can never be predicate or object in a sentence in which the subject is other than God. . . . The Word became flesh, and only through this becoming of his, which is quite free and which is quite exclusively his becoming, did the flesh become Word" (*KD* 1/2:149). Liberal theology, in Barth's view, had dreamed up the historical Jesus in order to have "an access to Jesus Christ that bypasses his divinity" (150); it is the divine Word as subject that makes Jesus Christ who he is, so from the start our encounter with Christ has to be in this sense a "theology from above." Barth saw liberal Christology as having "made an unforgivable mistake, a mistake that rules out any understanding or even any discussion between it and a Christology which does not wish to make that mistake" (1/2:145). In liberal theology the irreducible mystery summarized in the slogan "True God and true man" was conveniently simplified, making the complex Christological debates of the past seem otiose, and preparing the way for an understanding of Jesus as at best a supremely gifted moral and spiritual teacher. Both sides in this quarrel tend to give themselves a bill of perfect theological health and to regard the other side as profoundly sick.

But if we broaden the base of a "theology from below" it need not entail the reduction of the status of Jesus to that of a merely human teacher. It must be conceded to Barth that an integral phenomenological approach to Jesus Christ cannot reconstruct or even postulate a human nature of Jesus anterior to or independent of his special relation to God. The air is bristling with the divine power and presence from the start. A phenomenology of Jesus must begin with a phenomenology of God, as known in Israel, and then go on to discern how the human figure of Jesus appears within that divine milieu. But this discernment may open up many avenues of contemplation, which need not all be peremptorily brought under the rubric of divine Word as subject. The pluralism of New Testament Christologies is overruled in Barth's drastic imposition of the full-fledged incarnational schema of the Councils. In the phenomenological approach, the divine Word appears as an ultimate horizon of the meaning of Jesus. Still later it comes into view as the subject acting in Jesus, in the Johannine prologue. But this needs to be interpreted. God is the ultimate subject acting in and through the human actions of Jesus. God may be seen as speaking his Word in and through these actions. A phenomenological approach that sees Jesus from the start in his special openness to and intimacy with God implicitly co-apprehends whatever will later be thematized as the Word made flesh. It grasps Jesus first as the event of the manifestation of God. Only as such is he Word made flesh. (Of course the notion of God as subject also needs to be recalled to its phenomenological base.)

This approach does not bypass Christ's divinity, but it does bypass the clumsy dogmatic constructions in which Barth is trapped. When Barth talks of the Word becoming Jesus, he reifies and anthropomorphizes the Word, projecting back onto it the personality of the human Jesus: "In appropriating this possibility [of fleshly existence] as its [or his] own and in actualizing it as such, in becoming Jesus, then, without ceasing to be what it was before, it became at the same time what it was not before, and now indeed was: a human being, this human being" (164). In personalizing the Word as the individual subject living and acting in Jesus Christ, this discourse renders the humanity of Jesus unreal. Christology "from above" leads straight into docetism. "God himself in person is the subject of a real human being and acting" (165). Instead, it would be enough to say that the true

God acts in and through Jesus Christ, and in so exceptional a fashion that we can speak of Jesus, in the full range of his activity and being, as the "eschatological event" (Bultmann), and as the Word of God expressed in the fleshly historicity of the human condition. That is a more cushioned and subtle way of addressing the question of Christ's identity. It is about as accessible and as credible to the modern mind as the preexistence myths of scripture or the metaphysical constructions of the Councils were in their time. Theological masochists who want faith to be a sheer *skandalon* are sacrificing their intellect not to what is revealed in scripture but to archaic frameworks of thought.

One of the effects of the prominence of dogma was to shift the center of Christian vision from the event of Christ's death and resurrection to his unique ontological status as the incarnate Word. The Platonic structuring of the Christian vision gave to Christology a two-tiered structure. In the foreground were earthly events such as the crucifixion, but these were merely shadows of the all-important hidden background event: the assumption of human nature by the Word. In the New Testament the meaning of Christ centers on his death and resurrection; it is here that the divine Word is spoken into history. The "incarnation" in the sense of his ontological constitution prior to or independently of this saving event is barely hinted at. Yet as Aloys Grillmeier's history of Christology shows, reflection on the death and resurrection of Jesus was overshadowed by disputes about the relation of his divine and human natures.

Lutheran dogmatics tried to adjust to the Gospels' picture of Jesus by stressing that the incarnate Word, in respect of its human nature, is the subject of self-emptying, in the historical event of Calvary, but that the self-emptying Word is not the subject of the Incarnation; to put the self-emptying and the Incarnation on the same level would make the Incarnation itself appear as something merely temporal (Kaftan, 415). However incarnational ontology and paschal event are mutually accommodated, the effect of the dogmatic viewpoint is that our understanding of the paschal mystery is always governed by awareness of the background conditions, which sometimes leap to the fore in speculative visions of the eternal divine Word itself emptying itself. If one must read the mythical language of the Philippians hymn as entailing such a vision, the Calvinist interpretation, that the Word's self-emptying consists only in its assuming a poor and humble human nature rather than one that would let its glory shine through, sensibly limits kenotic fantasy (416). But in all its forms the old dogmatic vision has lost its *immediate* relevance for Christian faith, as Schleiermacher saw. The question is no longer one of providing ontological foundations for the redemptive work of Christ. For Schleiermacher, "The understanding of the person and that of the office of the Redeemer are referred to one another, each limited and conditioned by the other" (Kaftan, 418). Rather than seeking to reconcile the historical Jesus and the Christ of dogma, let us seek to "make the evangelical life of Jesus comprehensible as the content of our faith in his divinity" (429), in the sense that he is "the complete revelation of God" (435, 440)—a phenomenological divinity, so to speak, the assurance that in Jesus we meet the true God.

Defenders of Chalcedon, if they admit that the personality of the man Jesus and that of the Word cannot be identical, for the Word is personal only in a sense infinitely different from the ordinary sense, will attempt to rethink the identity of Jesus and the Word in terms of event or process, as a coincidence of the human and historical career of Jesus with a divine revelational activity. The former is a linear story, like everything that happens in time; the latter is not so securely locatable in temporal terms: it is the general impact or upshot of the Jesus story, synchronic rather than diachronic. Even the Resurrection narratives could be regarded as synchronic comment on the story of Jesus rather than a new chapter in the story. Thinking the human story of Jesus as manifestation of the divine, Chalcedonians will avoid the word *nature*, which suggests an impossible synonymy, as if the nature of God and the nature of a man could be placed side by side on the same level. "Far worse than this wavering identification of the subject, and incapable of sustaining a more rigorous scientific examination, is the fact that the expression *nature* is used equivalently for the divine and the human. Any other expression used equivalently for both would already expose such a formula to the suspicion that it must give rise to many confusions. For how can divine and human be brought together under any concept, as if the two could be mutually coordinated precisions of one and the same general concept?" (Schleiermacher 2:51–52). "Once this formula imposed itself as the basis for all other determinations about the person of Christ, a complex and artificial procedure had to be introduced to handle these untenable expressions as faultlessly as possible" (2:55–56).

It is still rather schematic to focus the humanity of Jesus as illustrating or confirming the categories of the Council. A theology from below suspends those categories in order to expose itself to the basic data and to question the figure of Jesus as presenting a cluster of possibilities of placing oneself in contact with a liberating God. To parse his identity by parceling out the roles of his human aspect and his divine aspect is remote from the spirit of the New Testament and even more so from Jesus himself. The questions that dogma was called on to resolve are losing their necessity as the high titles bestowed on Christ are interpreted in terms of his saving impact rather than as topics for ontological discussion. To recover the New Testament milieu that suspends metaphysics, the best point of entry is Johannine thought, for it provided the chief foundation for dogma. We shall see that it in turn sends us back to earlier levels, to a Jewish Jesus for whom the precise explanations given in dogma are still more tangential.

(iv) Refocusing the Biblical Event

When we go to meet Christ we understand him from his human origin, in Israel, and from his divine origin, as the one "sent" by the Father— an expression not to be grasped straightaway in incarnational terms, as when Gordon Fee (63) and Emmanuel Durand (197) take the words "I have come" (Mk 2:17; Mt 11:19; Lk 12:49) to express the eternal Word's taking flesh. The ultimate horizon of the New Testament roots the mission of Jesus in the coming of the Word or Wisdom of God into the world from the beginning, and it takes one further step, inspired by the Wisdom books, to speak of the Word in its eternal relation to God (Jn 1:1–2; Heb 1:3). But we must beware of crudely telescoping these three levels of perception. We need to foreground the human Jesus as we encounter him, in his mission and preaching, and in his passion and ongoing glorified presence; only at a second level do we trace the ultimate significance of this, the numinous background, reaching back to the unimaginable depths of the divine. To treat the latter as a cut-and-dried donnée allowing us to measure and assess the former is an inversion of perspective that needs to be corrected today.

When Paul and John sought to articulate the intangible, enveloping, unmasterable reality of the risen Christ, they reached after words such as *light*, *Spirit*, and *Logos*, which offer little sustenance to literal or to speculative readings and function rather as metaphors, transporting us into a region of pneumatic event that cannot be objectified. All Christological propositions ultimately refer to the enveloping reality of Christ's pneumatic presence. In this encompassing "divine milieu" where God is encountered as "He who comes" in the Word and the Spirit, in judgment and grace, the terminology of Chalcedon has no privileged foothold. One can hold on to it as a sort of legal codicil, to be used if needed. Like law, dogma is less a matter of atemporal insights than a slow growth in function of particular cases. It serves as a fence around the burning bush of revelation; it would be idolatrous to venerate the fence more than the bush, or the bush more than what is revealed in it. As Christian thinkers, following the trail opened by Schleiermacher and Bultmann, reappropriate scriptural categories and find their contemporary "dynamic equivalents," dogma and the horizon of metaphysical explanation on which it depends come to appear ever less appropriate to what is to be thought. Christ is an event to be explored, not a substance to be defined. "Christ is everything that is asserted of him in so far as he is the Eschatological Event" (Bultmann, 286). The identity ("hypostatic union") of Jesus and the Word has to be rethought in terms of event and process, as a coincidence of the human historical career of Jesus with the revelational activity of God leading history to its goal.

Karlmann Beyschlag, denouncing the anemic concepts of Chalcedon, recalls that Christ is the eschatological advent of divine judgment and grace, their earthly personification, so that he is fully God precisely in the measure that he is fully man (133). Orthodoxy need not be shocked at this, for it continues to recognize an objective distinction between God, Word, and Spirit within the divine unity and continues to affirm that the ultimate meaning of Jesus is inseparable from the divine Word. But to measure this discourse by its capacity to satisfy dogmatic orthodoxy is again to introduce a distortion. Rather, once satisfied, the orthodox dogma must be shown its limited place as a historical guardian of the integrity of the revealed, a guardian who ideally should not be needed at all, as a lamp is not needed at midday.

Even if one roots the revelation of God in Jesus in the whole history of humanity, in a mutual openness of the divine mystery and the transcendence of the human mind, in the style of Rahner, the credibility of the Incarnation is still threatened if it is claimed that *"what has taken place has happened to God*, has occurred in God himself, and this can never be effaced or redone" (Moingt 2002:332). St. Thomas's view that the incarnation of the Word could happen several times encourages us to think that though in Christ humanity is opened to the divine in such wise that the divine is fully expressed in that humanity, any other hypothetical race could attain the same breakthrough to the divine or reception of the divine. God would love his Logos eternally in all these incarnations, but this would involve no change in the divine being.

But such argumentation misses the fact that the phenomenological horizon opened by Bultmann leaves behind as archaic the topography of the dogmatic world. Bultmann's horizon is itself inadequate, insofar as the categories of event and eschatology lose their anchorage in the real phenomenological data and become defensive apologetical constructions, based on a theological refashioning of the historical events, already perhaps under way in the great theologies of the New Testament itself. A useful tool of modern theological discourse, the notion of eschatological event imposes a false unity on a cluster of New Testament thoughts and experiences, masking their heterogeneity and the gaps between them and their basis in historical occurrence. It is as if one were to speak of a "revolutionary event" so as to impose a unity on all the incidents and discourses of the years of the French Revolution.

Brought back to its biblical basis, Chalcedon appears as a note to clarify the incarnational vision of John 1:14, a text inviting a subtler exegesis than what classical dogma worked with. "The Word was made flesh" can mean that the divinity manifested in the Wisdom with which the world was created and in the Torah which is the basis of the Covenant is now manifested in a fuller, fleshly presence in history, in and across the career of Jesus, not as an isolated individual but in the full reach of his relationships with the Jewish tradition and with the tradition inspired by him. God is made known in Israel, dwelling among them (the *shekinah*). This situation continues in the story of Jesus and its pneumatic extension in the community of the New Covenant; there is no stark break with the past, no leap to a totally new register, for the "grace and truth" brought by Christ translate the "*chesed wa emeth*, loving-kindness and faithfulness" that are the defining qualities of the God of Israel (Jn 1:17). The newness of the New Covenant concerns neither the presence of the Word, living and active from the beginning, nor "the revelation of the mystery of the Trinity," but the role of the flesh as what permits a more intimate conjunction of human and divine. If the prophets align the cause of God with that of the oppressed and with the struggle for justice, the kerygma of the cross seals that identification. The machinery of classical theologies of the Atonement obscures this first salvific aspect of the cross as confirmation of Israel's faith in the God who sustains the just. The fleshly history of Jesus gives new power to Old Testament presentations of God, God's Word, and God's Spirit. Thinking along these lines, we can do a lot to close the gap between the Jewish and Christian visions, while making the classical Christological doctrines more palatable. Theological judgment is oriented here by an ecumenical concern and by the discontent that the classical doctrines cause in many contemporary minds.

Taking "The Word was made flesh" as an utterance of the same order as "God is spirit" (Jn 4:24) or "God is light" (1 Jn 1:5), that is, as a summary of the entire Christian experience, communicating a contemplative vision to be appropriated by a continual opening of the mind, one can go beyond efforts to reduce the event to the ontological privileges of Jesus. Rather than a conjunction of two natures effected once for all at Jesus's conception, the Incarnation can be seen as the transformation of that particular human life into a locus of divine self-manifestation, as in the Eucharist the meal event is transformed into a communion in the paschal mystery, leaving no autonomous subsistence of its own "reality" or "substance." This more open interpretation of the Incarnation, which wants to hew close to the phenomena and to experience, reduces the gap between the New Testament revelation and other religious perspectives. The incarnation of God in Christ continues to unfold its meaning along the paths of fleshly and historical contingency as his Gospel and his paschal and pneumatic presence are received in different contexts.

The contemplative utterances of the Johannine community offer little support to a theologian seeking to define the ontological status of Christ. "The Logos was *theos*" (Jn 1:1)—not *ho theos*—is less an ontological definition than a pointer to the phenomenon of the Logos as the one who comes from the depth of God. "My Lord and my God—*ho theos mou*" (20:28) is less an assertion of equality with the Father than the last in a series of confessions of faith in the "Son of God," which 20:31, the original close of the Gospel, extends to all (see van Belle). The one who comes is also the one who returns, to the Father (the theme of Jn 13–20), but that departure is linked to an invisible coming of the Son (Jn 14:18, 28), an indwelling of the Father and the Son (14:23), and the gift of the Paraclete. Thus the meaning of the Gospel can be summed up as the coming of Christ into the world (3:13–16; 12:44–50) (see De Boer). The Johannine Christ appears only in the perspective of his coming into the world, as an event of illumination. He remains intimately subordinated to the God who sends him, even if this intimacy itself becomes a nonduality, making Father and Son one for believing contemplation. An echo of this double perspective, now translated into the terms of a metaphysical ontology, is found in Origen's contradictory views on the status of the Son. The post-Nicene strategy of attaching all subordinationist utterances to Christ's humanity (the *forma servi*) and to his divinity the declarations of preexistence or of unity with the Father is not satisfactory. It is insofar as he comes from God that the man Jesus is "one" with him (Jn 10:30), in a radical obedience that makes him God's agent and the vehicle of God's presence. Even when he refers to his preexistence (8:58; 17:5) he does not distinguish a specifically divine side of the totality of his person.

For Barth the human self-emptying of Jesus is only a reflection of a prior experience, that of the divine Word as it condescends to assume human form: "Thus the death on the cross is only the explication of the Incarnation" (Barth 1947:63). Phenomenologically, it might make more sense to say that the death on the cross *is* the Incarnation; it is here that Jesus is manifest as eschatological event and that his ultimate identity as "the power of God and the wisdom of God" (1 Cor 1:24) is realized. Between the adoptionist model and the "explication" model, we can perhaps draw on Buddhism for another approach based on the idea that Jesus lived and died in the key of emptiness (and that the Jewish tradition out of which Jesus came can be read as a tradition of emptiness). The Word is present in Jesus Christ as the ultimate horizon of emptiness to which all his words and actions point. He lives a human life and a human death in such a way that they constitute a cipher of that realm of emptiness. Thus the "word of the cross" (1 Cor 1:18) is not an explication of the Incarnation but is the Incarnation itself. In the cross a word is spoken from out the depths of the divine emptiness and it is spoken in the midst of human history. It is this, and not some story of miraculous birth, that is referred to in John 1:14, "The Word was made flesh." What lights up in the cross of Jesus is the ultimate interplay between human finitude and divine emptiness, a powerful expression of the "form of God" (Phil 2:6) or the Word of God in the forms of human, fleshly history.

This view is not adoptionist, for the whole being of Jesus is involved in this role of being the manifestation of the Word in human history; nor does it entail a merely accidental unity of the man Jesus and the divine Logos (Nestorianism), for the ultimate identity of Jesus is not expressible except in terms of his specific role. But neither does this view allow a docetist reduction of Jesus's life to the mere explication of a pregiven metaphysical arrangement. Jesus, acting from enlightened awareness, emptied out the Jewish tradition in such a way as to renew its power as a vehicle of ultimacy. The Word that had been present in that tradition (Jn 1:11–13; 8:58) now finds full expression (Jn 1:14, 16–17), pressing into the world in and across the deeds, teachings, and death of Jesus. The phenomenological perspective we adopt here is incommensurable with the metaphysical perspective of the Chalcedonian debates, but it can claim fidelity to Chalcedon if it succeeds in not clearly falling into either of the extremes denounced by Chalcedon.

The theses that the Word is the metaphysical subject (not the personal psychological one) of Jesus's actions and experiences, and that what is revealed in Jesus is somehow coterminous with the eternal light of the Word, cannot be allowed to override first perceptions of Jesus as a Jew of his time. The conjunction of Jesus and the Word is an event of meaning not reducible to its separate components, as in psilanthropism, adoptionism, and Nestorianism. In that sense Jesus is not known separately from the Word. The event of paschal communication confers retrospectively on the whole story of Jesus the meaning of an incarnation of the Word; the human subject and the divine subject of that story are inseparable; the divine subject constitutes the essential depth of the story, its ultimate horizon; the human subject does not become the incarnation of the Word at a given point in his linear history, for all that he is and has been has no other sense than that of a breakthrough of the Word into history. Thus God is shown in Jesus, as in the burning bush, without any prejudice to the natural texture of human history.

The Nicene clarification that the Son is *theos alethinos*, true God, leaves a space free for Christ to be truly man, not a preexistent mythical entity or a demigod, as he risked becoming in the previous subordinationist model. But when the story of salvation is told according to the schema "God became man" this possibility of leaving the humanity of Jesus free is lost again, in favor of the Word as direct agent of the acts of Jesus. It would have been better to hold together without mixing them the notion that God acts in Jesus Christ and that the man Jesus nonetheless acts as a human being to fulfill his Christic role. The doctrine of the Incarnation would then signify that God acts in a more particular manner in Jesus than in other humans, or that the action of God's coming into human history is focused in a unique way in Jesus. If the ultimate identity of this man is to be the Word of God in history, that identity is realized only in the manifestation of God across the whole of history.

Can the Incarnation be made contingent on the process of Jesus's becoming Christ? Is it in function of the manifestation of God in him that Jesus is seen as himself having a divine identity? Or is the divinity a superfluous redoubling of the messianity? "Jesus is the Messiah" and "Jesus is the Word incarnate" would then be rival and exclusive interpretations of the meaning of Jesus, the second defeating the first, so that the messianic status would figure only as an ornament of his humanity, while what is essential is his divine status. Is he Messiah because he is God or God because he is Messiah? A "theology from below" would say that it is because he became Christ that he is the prism through which we perceive God, the focusing of God in human history. What transpires across the human role as to the ultimate divine sense of Jesus is a limited concept, not to be taken as starting point, as in a "theology from above." The divinity of Christ is presented by Nicea and in Alexandrian theology as the first source of the entire Christian mystery, but today we might see it as a vanishing point, an ultimate horizon that eludes comprehension. So we seek a more concrete grasp of Jesus following the human and historical paths of his manifestation.

Jesus is inseparable from the Word, but can the Word be known separately from Jesus? Can the same fullness of revelation be found elsewhere? When the community adore Jesus, he transfers that adoration immediately to the Father, "greater" than he (Jn 14:28), and points as well to the Spirit (Jn 14:17, 26; 15:26; 16:7–14) who also surpasses him in a sense. To adore Jesus is to be caught up in the event that takes place in him, the divine movement that traverses him. This referentiality of Jesus is the antidote to a Christological concentration that freezes into Christomonism. But one does not adore an ordinary prophet or a man filled with the Spirit. The singular fullness of divine presence that is perceived in Jesus is such that it made the dogma of Chalcedon necessary in the ancient context of an objectifying metaphysics. In today's context it calls us to discern the ultimate identity of Jesus in the fact that he makes the divine presence historical and fleshly in a unique way.

Johannine and Chalcedonian Christology were in their day a resolution of chronic tensions, the emergence of a satisfying image of Christ. Today we need a similar moment of Christological resolution, overcoming the rigidity of uninterpreted dogma on the one hand, while on the other raising the low Christology diffused among liberal Christians to a firmer and richer apprehension of the mystery of Christ. The old linchpins of high Christology, such as the virgin birth and the empty tomb, have become too controverted to help here.

Rather, it must be from within the most evident phenomena of the life and death of Jesus—such as his commandment of love, his healing presence, his self-sacrificing death, his Kingdom preaching, and his paschal spiritual presence to the Christian community—that an interpretation of his being is attempted. A thoroughgoing theology from below, aiming to reduce the Christological tradition to a useful, clear, functional, pragmatic discourse, prescribes that everything said about Christ have a concrete significance for the human beings who seek to be enlightened and freed by him.

The variety of images of Jesus in the New Testament is surpassed by that of the literary, philosophical, and theological portraits of Christ over the centuries. Exposure to this pluralism clashes with the sentiment of having a direct knowledge of the Savior. In truth, if one could compare the variations of that sentiment one might exclaim with Blake, "The vision of Christ that thou dost see / Is my vision's greatest enemy." Yet despite this pluralism, the tradition preserves the unity of a reference to a precise name, individual, and history, and to the canonical texts. Caring for that unity but also obliged to be open to the pluralism, theological judgment seeks to give to each perspective its due weight, playing with them creatively and allowing their mutual deconstruction. Thus one may hope to liberate Christology from the dogmatic precipitation that has made it a painful and often sterile field of controversy.

(v) The Mobility of Historical Judgment

We may say that Chalcedon itself guides us to the encounter with the historical Jesus, even at the cost of overcoming its own metaphysical horizons. But there is no firm final point of arrival, and neither the step back from Chalcedon to Jesus nor the effort to move in the other direction in a theology from below can acquire the status of a smooth developmental process. Navigating back and forth, one must use judgment at every turn, not allowing the minute questions posed for historical judgment to enfeeble the larger theological questions presiding over the whole effort.

The perennial tension between the Christ of dogma and "the historical Jesus as he lives hidden in the Gospels" (Schweitzer, 47) has been exacerbated by clearer emergence of the historical Jesus, thanks to two centuries of scholarship. The "God incarnate" schema seems to impose an alien mythological framework on the prophet who announced the imminence of God's Kingdom and gave body to his message through exorcisms and healings, table fellowship with outcasts, and a fresh interpretation of Jewish law and wisdom. Jesus associated acceptance or rejection of his own message with the judgment to come and spoke in a way that gave rise to his identification as the Davidic Messiah and the coming Son of Man. Jesus's own messianological notions, or his rejection of them in favor of a more radically theocratic tradition, must be interpreted against the background of Jewish religion and culture (see Theissen, 223–25). The first interpretations of the significance of Jesus, by himself and his disciples, demand critical historical contextualization. The period was fertile in mythic schemas, and their application to Jesus was a human interpretative activity. The mythology surrounding Jesus is a product of the Jewish imagination of that time. The dogmatics based on it needs now to return to the phenomena, insofar as they can be extracted from the representations; but they cannot, so our interpretation of Jesus has to be constructed at our own expense.

The obsolescence of hellenistic myth does not entail any rejuvenation of Hebrew myth. The infant church left behind the repertory of thought forms of Jewish eschatology, replacing even the notion of Messiah with hellenized ideas of the preexistent Son or Logos. One can try to retrieve Jewish myth with the aid of Rosenzweig, Scholem, or Buber, and thus call on theology to leave its hellenistic rut, but these archaic representations can hardly form the basis of a new discourse of faith today. To enter into the reconstructed thought-world of Jesus does not provide a definitive sanctuary for our theological thought. Rather its foreignness sends us back to the task of rethinking the meaning of the Jesus tradition for today. The plurality of interpretations of Jesus within the New Testament further discourages any proclivity to take refuge in ancient categories. All of them rather point to the task of rearticulating in contemporary categories what the ancients envisaged in mythic terms.

Reference to the prepaschal historical reality of Jesus can be a source of resistance to the Christological tradition, preventing it from swelling into an empty idealism. The very difficulty of that reference weans us away from a positivism of hard facts as much as it does from naive trust in the theological portraits of Jesus. It thwarts inherited hellenistic habits of mind, but the imaginative Jewish categories it puts forward instead reveal a rich and satisfying vision for the people of the first century, not one we can appropriate immediately as our own. The challenge for theological imagination at all times is not to produce sharply defined doctrines but to generate a vision that can serve as skillful means for making Christ known in a given context. The conjectures of historical Jesus research prompt new ways of imagining Jesus, in a contrapuntal relationship to the visions of Christ fashioned in classical theology, and theological judgment, as it traverses this entire history, sounding its tensions and limits, is guided by the motivation of skillfully reimagining Christ for today.

Despite all the hermeneutical obstacles, the theological fascination with the question of the historical Jesus is far from sterile. Slowly, the phenomenological and interpretative structure of faith's encounter with the living God in and across the human figure of Jesus is yielding new possibilities for theological imagination. We begin to see that his historical Jewish, fleshly existence is the site of his revelatory and salvific status, and that this site is a bridge rather than an obstacle, at a time when our tradition is opening itself to other major sites of a revelatory breakthrough, from Judaism and Islam to Hinduism and Buddhism. The New Testament Christ has two faces, which are emerging with new clarity. While the strangeness of the historical context puts Jesus at a distance from us, some essential features, already reworked imaginatively within the New Testament—such as the Kingdom proclamation, the creation of an inclusive community, the forgiveness expressed in meals shared with sinners, the radical trust in God and the freedom that flows from this—can survive historical critique and provide a basis for thinking of the fleshly, Jewish Jesus as a compass and criterion of theological judgment today. On the other side, the paschal Christ is "reduced" to the pneumatic dimensions highlighted by Paul. The power of the Spirit is linked to the name and memory of Jesus. "Spirit-Christology" offers a frame for thinking these two aspects of Christ and connecting them.

The task of fundamental theology is not to construct a Christology but to explore the conditions under which doctrinal construction labors today. These may now appear as condemning us to a dizzyingly mobile critical play with models and conventions, remote indeed from a rocklike faith in the Savior. To allay this unease, let us engage in one more step back, again invoking the Buddhist economy of religious language as skillful means.

THE IMPACT OF EMPTINESS

The trajectories we have followed in studying the trinitarian and Christological dogmas set up a critical interaction between various levels of scriptural, dogmatic, and theological discourse, with a view to finding our bearings in a demystified reappropriation of these dogmas in their historical role as an attempt to attest biblical realities. Many other trajectories would be possible, and a struggle will go on between them as each tries to establish its distinctive illuminative force. Do these hermeneutical battles then subside into mere theological conversation, in which the merits and demerits of various approaches are desultorily reviewed? Each approach and its style of judgment should be systematically cultivated, to yield its fullest harvest of insight, so that in the confrontation of approaches a strong dialectic is set up. The process of theological judgment is an open-ended, ongoing one, an inescapable condition of the life of faith. The complexities of history and its ongoing theological assessment are dissolved neither by stepping back to origins nor by striving forward to eschatological goals, though both of these bring powerful instances of judgment to bear on study of the sources, ensuring that it never becomes mere history but rises to the status of historical theology. So all peremptory gestures that would put an end to the culture of theological judgment must be relinquished. But does this mean that the life of faith becomes a tissue of suppositions, theories, uncertainties, opportunistic adjustments, tentative revisions, in constant deferral of any closing in on the thing itself?

Let us consider how the entire fabric of theological tradition appears in a Buddhist perspective. The Buddhist critique of substantialism and fixed views might well compound our unease. Going beyond Harnack, it would unmask how the Christian tradition, even in its premetaphysical forms, invested massively in substance and identity. It was by strong affirmations of firm, substantial identity that Christianity made its way in the world. Dogma determined the identities of Father, Son, and Spirit as consubstantial hypostases of the one God, the identity of Jesus Christ as true God and true man united in one hypostasis, the real presence of Christ in the Eucharist, the unity, sufficiency, infallibility of the church and its scriptures, the continuity of the episcopal and papal ministries as transmitted from the apostles. The substantiality of what was proclaimed was matched by the total conviction of the faith that proclaimed it. Theologians might tinker with speculative elaborations, but the core of faith and dogma was untouchable, never subjected to doubt or questioning. It is a kind of metadogma that all this dogma was necessary. Substantialism (*astivāda*) slid into its opposite, nihilism (*nastivāda*), as the fight about the substance of the Savior reduced his being to a word, a shibboleth, an iota, on which everything was thought to hinge.

A Buddhist understanding of the nature and function of religion could be of key importance in bringing about a Christological thaw, putting an end to the old quarrels, in a very welcome "quiescence of fabrications." Then we could reread the tradition, discerning how it testified to the meaning of Christ and at the same time how its culture-bound substantialist representations thwarted its articulation of that meaning. The labor of dogma could be reinterpreted as the adroit cultivation of conventional truth, which is a skillful means at the service of ultimate truth. Dogma was taken as ultimate truth, pronounced in a determinative judgment, and shaping Christian thought as a well-defined system of ideas. Can we shift to seeing it as conventional truth, constantly sought and rethought in reflective judgment, and guiding Christian faith to an ever deeper appreciation of the theo-poetic language of scripture? Today the intellectual space or regime of truth within which dogmatic claims enjoyed an immovable security has become obsolete. What is left of dogma survives only on the strength of biblical support and within a space of Christian thinking quite foreign to that of the fathers, Councils, and scholastics. Little weight attaches to doctrinal claims unless they carry the mark of ultimacy—unless they could be candidates for a mystical level of contemplative apprehension. The Vedantic revelation "That art thou" (*tat tvam asi*) and the Mahāyāna paradox "*Saṃsāra* is *nirvāṇa*" are claims of that sort. "He was delivered for our sins and rose for our justification" (Rom 4:25) and "The Word became flesh" (Jn 1:14) are such claims too, if apprehended in their original contemplative context, without the intrusion of inappropriate ontology.

There are subtler forms of fixation or substantialism that attract Buddhists, at a deeper level than these dogmatic constructions. The three poisons of attachment, aversion, and delusion permeate religious thinking from childhood on, and to apply to them the therapy of emptiness is a lifelong task. The therapy of one's own unthinking habits reinforces the scrutiny of the mass of historical discourses and practices, where very often the same attachment, aversion, and delusion appear writ large, providing a vast collection of erring ontological investments, "views," to be analyzed and brought into healing perspective. That at every point we are dealing with conventional constructions, not the absolute truth absolutely expressed, invites an ironic undoing of all ill-considered affirmations and condemnations.

On another front, highly personalistic language about the Trinity fails to rejoin the majestic sense of the impersonality of ultimate reality that pervades philosophical Hinduism and Buddhism. Ultimate reality in these religions is a nirvanic being-consciousness-bliss free of all finite determinations. When we find ourselves thinking of numerical distinctions and sequences within ultimate reality, we cannot help feeling that there is something highly problematic about these conventions of thought. Eckhart placed the Godhead beyond these distinctions. We are obliged to speak conventionally of distinctions, as a negative method of warding off threats to the full reality of the encounter with God in God's Word and Spirit. That constraint corresponds to something in the divine reality. But how it corresponds, what exactly is its bearing on the abyssal simplicity of the divine, we cannot say.

At the same time as it uncovers fixations in Christian discourse, a Buddhist critique will also winkle out pockets of emptiness in the tradition, moments at which it becomes more critically aware of its fragile, broken status. Even Christian theology as shaped by Greek metaphysics is not irredeemably substantialist, totally the prey of naive reification and objectification. The definition of God as *ipsum esse subsistens* sufficiently eludes objectification to include the Plotinian sense of God as "beyond being." It can even be interpreted in the key of Buddhist emptiness. Again, the Christological debates of the early Christian centuries relied of necessity on substance-language, yet in placing that terminology at the service of a revealed mystery beyond the grasp of language or thought they introduced a ferment of paradox into the play of concepts and made of it a dance of traces, following the contours of a reality that cannot be brought under substantialist rubrics.

Buddhism radicalizes the "theology from below" by consigning all religious representations to the register of conventional truth, skillful means. But its sense of the nonduality between *saṃsāra* and *nirvāṇa*, conventional and ultimate, skillful means and wisdom, may allow it to do justice to the concerns of the "theology from above," above all the concern that in the broken body of the human Jesus the fullness of God's wisdom and power is manifest. Buddhist wisdom reveals the nonsubstantiality of historical and religious identities that have served as bulwarks of self-assertion. Candrakīrti observes that beings "have first generated self-infatuation through the thought 'I' and then attachment to objects through the thought 'This is mine,' so that like a paddlewheel they wander round and round devoid of self-determination" (Huntington, 149). The commentator Jay-tsun-pa adds: "The conception of true existence is an afflictive obstruction" (Newland 1984:82). Religions have become blindly flailing Leviathans because of their belief in their own intrinsic existence. They need to discover themselves as arising in dependence on a constantly changing array of contingent conditions and as having only a functional existence in their skillful response to these conditions.

Buddhism is happy to see itself thus, but can Christianity accept such a view of its own existence as merely functional? Christian faith is bound to historical claims about Israel, Jesus, and the church, claims that from the standpoint of Buddhist emptiness seem to be an absolutization of the conventional. We could attempt to reduce these claims to phenomenological terms as follows: Israel, Jesus, and the church are loci of ultimacy, that is, places we go back to again and again in the confidence that there we will be enabled to break through to ultimacy, places where the ultimate has emerged within history, forged for itself an effective historical vehicle, a tradition to be used as a skillful means by its adherents. Thus the historical fabric of Christian faith is subordinated to the spiritual realities at work in that history. An active and interventionist God is correlated with the breakthrough of ultimacy. Conversely, Buddhist emptiness acquires the associations of a powerful breakthrough, almost a theophany.

This way of talking might be seen as falsifying both Buddhism and the Bible by making emptiness an active power while reducing God to a mere impersonal ultimate. But what is afoot here can be seen as a quite legitimate mutual solicitation of the two traditions. As we work on our conceptions of God and empty them of delusive substantialism, there begins to emerge an image of God as Spirit, grace, freedom, rather than supreme being, substance, power. Emptiness arises in dependence on the conventional bases of which it is the emptiness. God as Spirit is also always discovered dialectically, as Spirit overcomes what is opposed to it (sin, the Law, flesh and blood, or the letter). Madhyamaka thought deabsolutizes emptiness by stressing the emptiness of emptiness itself. Perhaps we can analogously stress the spirituality of spirit itself, that is, that the divine freedom moves as it wills and cannot be frozen into an immutability that would be incompatible with freedom.

"With one voice all the Mahāyāna masters proclaim that analysis of objects, and not mere withdrawal of the mind from them, is the path to liberation" (Hopkins, 31). Similarly, religious bondage demands dissolutive analysis of the objects that cause it. Simply to "take leave" of God (Cupitt) is to be fixated in the counterposition, constantly fighting with the shadow of God or the shadowy "place of God." Rather, one must think through one's notions of God until they transform into traces of liberating emptiness or of the movement of the Spirit. Reification short-circuits the imaginative functioning of religious language and weighs it down with objects of clinging and defensiveness. When these are dissolved, religion becomes a style of discourse and practice that consistently heals, opens, frees the mind. Analytical reasoning in Madhyamaka, Tsong Khapa declares, is "only for the sake of sentient beings" attaining liberation (quoted in Hopkins, 32). So the deconstruction of "God" is quite meaningless if pursued as a purely disinterested philosophical exercise; rather, it must be a healing of painful and constricting conceptions accumulated in the course of a specific history of theistic imagining and thought. That nihilistic atheism is painful needs little demonstration, but in what manner is a reified theism painful? It is painful in that it is a projection of a basically deluded way of seeing things. The reification of God is on a continuum with the reification of self and of the data of experience. Conversely, if one acquired a fluid sense of self and a desubstantialized awareness of being, the residue of older substantializing habits of mind in one's received concept of God would be felt as painfully dissonant.

If God is conceived as massive substance, this gets in the way of understanding God as the enabling foundation for a lifestyle of emptying oneself through nondiscriminating embrace of the neighbor in an inclusive community. It is not to give glory to a supersubstantial God that one dissolves the false substantialisms of ego, but rather to tune in to the realm of Spirit and emptiness. The divine glory that is manifested in self-emptying love (as in the Torah the glory of God fills the sanctuary at the hour of sacrifice [Ex 40:34–35]) is to be conceived not as a substance but rather as in alignment with the ultimate thusness (*tathatā*) of things. For Buddhism, a world in which all phenomena are understood to be empty would be a paradise, *saṃsāra* itself would be *nirvāṇa*. That idea of nirvanic joy is close to the Christian idea of the divine glory blazing out in the renewed creation. Any language that presents God as an entity over against us who is intent on getting his rightful share of glory, or as fixed in place as the substance that founds the world, should be overcome in favor of a language evoking the Spirit that breaks through whenever the conventional fabric of the world is seen, by enlightened eyes, as an empty vehicle of ultimacy.

The patient analysis that corrects delusive reification is not a dry logic pursued for its own sake but an art of meditative judgment bent on freeing sentient beings from the shackles that cause suffering. Substantialist investments are not undercut by a deconstructive dialectic that functions automatically. One must first sound what is oppressive in the notions or dogmas in question and diagnose the condition of suffering of which they are symptoms; then one can adopt the aptest strategy for releasing the liberative potential these substantialist notions and habits may conceal. To overcome sclerotic thinking, something more than meditative analysis or the play of judgment is required. The theological imagination must be kindled by the grace of new encounters or challenges.

The reification of God is reflected in the processes of reification and fetishism that warp religious thinking at every level. The therapy of these replaces fixations with vital processes and communicative events. "Even a suspicion that emptiness—the lack of inherent existence—is the mode of being of phenomena disturbs the very causes that produce the rounds of powerless suffering" (Hopkins, 33). To season all religious cults and claims with the grain of salt of this suspicion encourages a reappropriation of the religious heritage as an arsenal of skillful means aiming at liberation. Religious representations are flowers of emptiness: their entire raison d'être, the air they breathe, is emptiness, liberation. The elaborate constructions of Christian theology, though heavily burdened with clumsy substantialism, are nonetheless pervaded by rumors of emptiness, of God as Spirit.

Church teaching, like Zen teaching, should aim to awaken people in the here and now, relying less on foundations provided by the past and promises of a future. Salvation history is a necessary background of the kerygma, but it is less substantial than is thought, as the changes in our conceptions of it over the centuries show. The meaning of the past and the discernment of future hope are always to be quarried anew from the horizons of present experience. Projecting our perspective on past and future starting from the lack of foundation and the emptiness of the present, no longer allowing the present to be overwhelmed and obscured by a domination of past and future, we refound past-oriented faith and future-oriented hope in the present movement of the Spirit, which has no stable foundation but is a breath, a wind.

If the texture of Christian truth is conceived in this way, then the function of dogma appears in a new light. Rather than defining substances, dogmas are guideposts to emptiness, valid conventions that keep us in touch with the empty ultimate. A dogmatics in this key would take up each topos of classical dogmatics—Christ, resurrection, eschatology, grace, Eucharist—and seek to bring out its meaning as a sign of the empty, pneumatic dimension. No longer anxious to shore up substance, but seeking instead to safeguard the freedom of emptiness, the labor of dogmatics would combine care for correct teaching with an equal care that the teaching fulfills its purpose of opening the minds of the faithful to the mystery it attests. The humbling of dogma through study of its historical roots thus spells a renewal for dogmatic theology, which can cultivate a flexible and functional language of faith. The constant exercise of theological judgment, as doctrinal utterance is assessed in relation to its audience and to the contemporary "signs of the times," will renounce the ambition to build an imposing system of theological truths and will cultivate instead an art of communication, in which the witness of the Creed is unfolded imaginatively in terms with full contemporary resonance. Lip service to conventions of the past, valid in their day but now an encumbrance, will yield to the embrace of new conventions, capable of focusing current spiritual insight, which will provide Christian doctrine with the elements for its current articulation.

References

Adorno, Theodor. 1966. *Kierkegaard: Konstruktion des Ästhetischen*. Frankfurt: Suhrkamp.

———. 1970. *Ästhetische Theorie*. Frankfurt: Suhrkamp.

Alexopoulos, Theodoros. 2007. "Gregor von Nyssa und Plotin zum Problem der Gottesprädikationen: Ein Vergleich." In Karfíková, Douglass, and Zachhuber, 411–22.

Alféri, Pierre. 1989. *Guillaume d'Ockham: Le singulier*. Paris: Éditions de Minuit.

Allemann, Beda. 1962. *Zeit und Figur beim späten Rilke*. Pfullingen: Neske.

Andia, Ysabel de. 1996. *Henosis: L'union à Dieu chez Denys l'Aréopagite*. Leiden: Brill.

———. 2001. "*Remotio-Negatio*: L'évolution du vocabulaire de saint Thomas touchant la voie négative." *Archives d'Histoire Doctrinale et Littéraire du Moyen Âge* 68:45–71.

Angot, Michel. 2012. *Le Yoga-sūtra de Patañjali: Le Yoga-bhāsya de Vyāsa. La parole sur le silence*. Paris: Les Belles Lettres.

Armstrong, A. H. 1992. "Plotinus and Christianity." In *Platonism in Late Antiquity*, ed. S. Gersh and C. Kannengiesser, 115–30. Notre Dame, IN: University of Notre Dame Press.

Arnold, Claus, and Giacomo Losito, eds. 2011. *"Lamentabili sane exitu" (1907): Les documents préparatoires du Saint-Office*. Rome: Libreria Editrice Vaticana.

Aubenque, Pierre. 1971. "Plotin et le dépassement de la métaphysique." In *Le Néoplatonisme*, 101–9. Paris: CNRS.

———. 1997. *Le problème de l'être chez Aristote*. Paris: Presses Universitaires de France.

Aubin, Paul. 1992. *Plotin et le christianisme*. Paris: Beauchesne.

Ayres, Lewis. 2004. *Nicaea and Its Legacy: An Approach to Fourth-Century Trinitarian Theology.* Oxford: Clarendon Press.

Barth, Karl. 1939–1970. *Die kirchliche Dogmatik.* Zollikon: Evangelischer Verlag.

———. 1947. *Erklärung des Philipperbriefs.* Zollikon: Evangelischer Verlag.

———. 1958. *Fides quaerens intellectum.* Zollikon: Evangelischer Verlag.

Barthes, Roland. 1986. "The Reality Effect." In *The Rustle of Language*, trans. Richard Howard, 141–48. Oxford: Blackwell.

Beckett, Samuel. 1980. *Company.* London: John Calder.

Beierwaltes, Werner. 1979. *Proklos: Grundzüge seiner Metaphysik.* Frankfurt: Klostermann.

———. 1994. "Unity and Trinity in Dionysius and Eriugena." *Hermathena* 157:1–20.

———. 2001a. *Platonismus im Christentum.* Frankfurt: Klostermann.

———. 2001b. *Das wahre Selbst: Studien zu Plotins Begriff des Geistes und des Einen.* Frankfurt: Klostermann.

———. 2002. "Le vrai soi." In *La connaissance de soi: Études sur le traité 49 de Plotin*, ed. Monique Dixsaut, 11–39. Paris: Vrin.

Beiser, Frederick C. 2002. *German Idealism: The Struggle against Subjectivism, 1781–1801.* Cambridge, MA: Harvard University Press.

Bergson, Henri. 2003. *Correspondances.* Paris: Presses Universitaires de France.

Bethune-Baker, J. F. 1908. *Nestorius and His Teaching.* Cambridge: Cambridge University Press.

Beyschlag, Karlmann. 1982. *Grundriss der Dogmengeschichte.* Vol. 1. Darmstadt: Wissenschaftliche Buchgesellschaft.

Biardeau, Madeleine. 1969. *La philosophie de Maṇḍana Miśra.* Paris: École française d'Extrême-Orient.

Blondel, Maurice. 1997. *Oeuvres complètes.* Vol. 2. Paris: Presses Universitaires de France.

Bouillard, Henri. 1957. *Karl Barth.* Paris: Aubier.

———. 1966. "Croire et comprendre." In Castelli, 285–301.

Boulnois, Olivier. 1999. *Être et représentation: Une généalogie de la métaphysique moderne à l'époque de Duns Scot.* Paris: Presses Universitaires de France.

———. 2008. "La philosophie analytique et la métaphysique selon Duns Scot." *Quaestio* 8:585–610.

Bourgeois, Bernard. 2012. "Hegel ou la métaphysique réformée." In Kervégan and Mabille, 25–36.

Bourgine, Benoît. 2005. "Que faire des premiers conciles?" *Revue Théologique de Louvain* 36:449–75.

Bradbury, Nicola. 1979. *Henry James: The Later Novels.* Oxford: Clarendon Press.

Bradley, Arthur. 2004. *Negative Theology and Modern French Philosophy.* London: Routledge.

Bréhier, Émile, trans. 1938. *Plotin: Les Ennéades.* Vol. 6. Paris: Les Belles Lettres.

Brons, Bernhard. 1976. *Gott und die Seienden: Untersuchungen zum Verhältnis von neuplatonischer Metaphysik und christlicher Tradition bei Dionysius Areopagita.* Göttingen: Vandenhoeck und Ruprecht.

Bultmann, Rudolf. 1955. *Essays Philosophical and Theological.* London: SPCK.

Cabezón, José. 1994. *Buddhism and Language.* Albany: State University of New York Press.

Caputo, John D. 1997. *The Prayers and Tears of Jacques Derrida.* Bloomington: Indiana University Press.

Carraud, Vincent. 2002. *Causa sive ratio: La raison de la cause de Suárez à Leibniz.* Paris: Presses Universitaires de France.

Casper, Bernhard. Forthcoming. "Die nicht-intentionale Intentionalität des Sich-ereignens des Verhältnisses zu dem Einzigen." *Archivio di Filosofia.*

Castelli, Enrico, ed. 1966. *Mito e fede.* Padua: CEDAM.

Chrétien, Jean-Louis. 2011. *Conscience et roman.* Vol. 2. *La conscience à mi-voix.* Paris: Éditions de Minuit.

Coakley, Sarah. 2002. "What Does Chalcedon Solve and What Does It Not? Some Reflections on the Status and Meaning of the Chalcedonian 'Definition.'" In Davis, Kendall, and O'Collins, 143–63.

Colish, Marcia L. 1994. *Peter Lombard.* Leiden: Brill.

———. 1996. "Christological Nihilianism in the Second Half of the Twelfth Century." *Recherches de Théologie Ancienne et Médiévale* 63:146–55.

Colson, F. H., and G. H. Whitaker, trans. 1929. *Philo.* Loeb Critical Library. Cambridge, MA: Harvard University Press.

Congregation for the Doctrine of the Faith. 2000. *Declaration "Dominus Iesus" on the Unicity and Salvific Universality of Jesus Christ and the Church.* www.vatican.va.

Corbin, Henry. 1972. *Le paradoxe du monothéisme.* Paris: Grasset.

Cornille, Catherine. Forthcoming. "Humility and Truth in Buddhist-Christian Comparative Theology." *Hōrin.*

Cornwell, Neil. 1992. *James Joyce and the Russians.* London: Macmillan.

Courcelle, Pierre. 1968. *Recherches sur les Confesions de saint Augustin.* Paris: De Boccard.

Courtine, Jean-François. 2003. *Les catégories de l'être: Études de philosophie ancienne et médiévale*. Paris: Presses Universitaires de France.

———. 2005. Inventio analogiae: *Métaphysique et ontothéologie*. Paris: Vrin.

Coward, Harold, and Toby Foshay, eds. 1992. *Derrida and Negative Theology*. Albany: State University of New York Press.

The Cowherds. 2010. *Moonshadows: Conventional Truth in Buddhist Philosophy*. New York: Oxford University Press.

Cross, Richard. 2005. "Duns Scotus and Suárez at the Origins of Modernity." In Hankey and Hedley, 65–80.

Cupitt, Don. 2001. *Taking Leave of God*. London: SCM.

Dalferth, Ingolf U. 2002. "Ganz Anders: Zur Hermeneutik Negativer Theologie." *Archivio di Filosofia* 70:117–45.

Daniélou, Jean. 1970. *Jean Chrysostome: Sur l'incompréhensibilité de Dieu*. Vol. 1. Sources chrétiennes 28bis. Paris: Éditions du Cerf.

Davis, Stephen T., Daniel Kendall, and Gerald O'Collins, eds. 2002. *The Incarnation: An Interdisciplinary Symposium on the Incarnation of the Son of God*. New York: Oxford University Press.

De Boer, Martinus C. 2005. "Jesus' Departure to the Father in John." In van Belle et al., 1–19.

De Botton, Alain. 2013. *Religion for Atheists: A Non-believer's Guide to the Uses of Religion*. New York: Vintage.

Denzinger, Heinrich. 1957. *Enchiridion Symbolorum*. Freiburg: Herder.

Derrida, Jacques. 1982. *Margins of Philosophy*. Chicago: University of Chicago Press.

———. 1992a. "How to Avoid Speaking: Denials." In Coward and Foshay, 73–142.

———. 1992b. "Post-Scriptum: Aporias, Way and Voices." In Coward and Foshay, 283–323.

Devynck, Jean-Christophe. 2000. *Logique du phénomène*. Paris: Diakom.

DiGiovanni, George. 1973. "Reflection and Contradiction: A Commentary on Some Passages of Hegel's *Science of Logic*." *Hegel-Studien* 8:131–61.

Dillon, John. 1996a. "Damascius on the Ineffable." *Archiv für die Geschichte der Philosophie* 78:120–9.

———. 1996b. *The Middle Platonists: 80 B.C. to A.D. 220*. London: Duckworth.

Dosse, François. 2002. *Michel de Certeau: Le marcheur blessé*. Paris: La Découverte.

Douglass, Scott. 2007. "Gregory of Nyssa and Theological Imagination." In Karfíková, Douglass, and Zachhuber, 461–71.

Downing, F. Gerald. 1964. *Has Christianity a Revelation?* London: SCM.

Drewermann, Eugen. 2000. *Hat der Glaube Hoffnung?* Düsseldorf: Patmos.

Duméry, Henry. 1963. *Raison et religion dans la philosophie de l'action.* Paris: Éditions du Seuil.

Dunne, John D. 2004. *Foundations of Dharmakīrti's Philosophy.* Boston: Wisdom.

Dupuy, Bernard. 1980. "Heidegger et le Dieu inconnu." In *Kearney and O'Leary*, 103–21.

Durand, Emmanuel. 2012. *L'offre universel du salut en Christ.* Paris: Éditions du Cerf.

Durand, Georges-Matthieu de. 2002a. "Réflexions sur les quatre premiers conciles oecuméniques." *Revue des Sciences Philosophiques et Théologiques* 86:3–26.

———. 2002b. "Sources et signification de Chalcédoine." *Revue des Sciences Philosophiques et Théologiques* 86:369–86.

Eckel, Malcolm D. 1987. *Jñānagarbha's Commentary on the Distinction between the Two Truths.* Albany: State University of New York Press.

Eckhart, Meister. 1936–2007. *Die lateinischen Werke.* Ed. E. Benz et al. Vols. 1–6 of *Meister Eckhart: Die deutschen und lateinischen Werke. Herausgegeben im Auftrage der Deutschen Forschungsgemeinschaft.* Stuttgart: W. Kohlhammer.

Ehrman, Bart. 2012. *Forgery and Counterforgery: The Use of Literary Deceit in Early Christian Polemics.* New York: Oxford University Press.

Eicher, Peter. 1977. *Offenbarung: Prinzip neuzeitlicher Theologie.* Munich: Kösel.

Eliot, T. S. 1957. *On Poetry and Poets.* London: Faber.

Evans, C. Stephen. 2002. "The Self-Emptying of Love: Some Thoughts on Kenotic Christology." In Davis, Kendall, and O'Collins, 246–72.

Falque, Emmanuel. 2013. *Passer le Rubicon. Philosophie et théologie: Essai sur les frontières.* Brussels: Lessius.

Fee, Gordon D. 2002. "St Paul and the Incarnation: A Reassessment of the Data." In Davis, Kendall, and O'Collins, 62–92.

Fenton, Paul B. 2002. "Le thème de la docte ignorance dans la pensée musulmane et juive médiévale." *Archivio di Filosofia* 70:555–73.

Feuerbach, Ludwig. 1994. *Das Wesen des Christentums.* Stuttgart: Reclam.

Fisher, Simon. 1988. *Revelatory Positivism: Barth's Earliest Theology and the Marburg School.* Oxford: Oxford University Press.

Flannery, Austin. 1984. *Vatican Council II: The Conciliar and Post Conciliar Documents.* Vol. 1. Collegeville, MN: Liturgical Press.

Frank, Manfred. 1997. *"Unendliche Annäherung": Die Anfänge der philosophischen Frühromantik.* Frankfurt: Suhrkamp.

———. 2007. *Auswege aus dem Deutschen Idealismus.* Frankfurt: Suhrkamp.

Freyer, Thomas. 2002. "Vergessener Monotheismus? Zur gegenwärtigen Trinitätslehre." *Jahrbuch Politische Theologie* 4:93–106.

Friedman, Michael. 1999. *Reconsidering Logical Positivism.* Cambridge: Cambridge University Press.

Gill, Joseph. 1961. *The Council of Florence.* Cambridge: Cambridge University Press.

Gonzalez, Francisco J. 2002. "Dialectic as 'Philosophical Embarrassment': Heidegger's Critique of Plato's Method." *Journal of the History of Philosophy* 40:361–89.

Greisch, Jean. 1985. *L'âge herméneutique de la raison.* Paris: Éditions du Cerf.

———, ed. 1999. *Philosophie, poésie, mystique.* Paris: Beauchesne.

———. 2002. *Le buisson ardent et les lumières de la raison.* Vol. 1. Paris: Éditions du Cerf.

Greshake, Gisbert. 1997. *Der dreieine Gott: Eine trinitarische Theologie.* Freiburg: Herder.

Griffiths, Paul J. 1994. *On Being Buddha.* Albany: State University of New York Press.

Guardini, Romano. 1953. *Rainer Maria Rilkes Deutung des Daseins: Eine Interpretation der Duineser Elegien.* Munich: Kösel.

———. 1955. *Hölderlin: Weltbild und Frömmigkeit.* Munich: Kösel.

Gunneweg, Antonius H. J. 1983. *Sola Scriptura.* Göttingen: Vandenhoeck und Ruprecht.

Gutwenger, Engelbert. 1959. *Bewusstsein und Wissen Christi.* Innsbruck: Rauch.

Guyer, Paul. 1990. "Hegel on Kant's Aesthetics: Necessity and Contingency in Beauty and Art." In *Hegel und die "Kritik der Urteilskraft,"* ed. Hans-Friedrich Fulda and Rolf-Peter Horstmann, 81–99. Stuttgart: Klett-Cotta.

Hadot, Pierre. 1968. *Porphyre et Victorinus.* Paris: Études Augustiniennes.

Halfwassen, Jens. 1999. *Hegel und der Spätantike Neuplatonismus: Untersuchungen zur Metaphysik des Einen und des Nous in Hegels spekulativer und geschichtlicher Deutung.* Bonn: Bouvier.

Hall, Stuart George, trans. 2007. "The Second Book against Eunomius," by Gregory of Nyssa. In Karfíková, Douglass, and Zachhuber, 59–204.

Halleux, André de. 1990. *Patrologie et œcuménisme.* Leuven: Peeters.

Hampson, Daphne. 2001. *Christian Contradictions: The Structures of Lutheran and Catholic Thought.* Cambridge: Cambridge University Press.

Hankey, Wayne J. 1999a. "French Neoplatonism in the 20th Century." *Animus* 4:135–67.

————. 1999b. "*Theoria versus Poesis:* Neoplatonism and Trinitarian Difference in Aquinas, John Milbank, Jean-Luc Marion and John Zizioulas." *Modern Theology* 15:387–415.

————. 2005. "Philosophical Religion and the Neoplatonic Turn to the Subject." In Hankey and Hedley, 17–30.

Hankey, Wayne J., and Douglas Hedley, eds. 2005. *Deconstructing Radical Orthodoxy.* Aldershot: Ashgate.

Harnack, Adolf. 1927. *Die Entstehung der christlichen Theologie und des kirchlichen Dogmas.* Gotha: Klotz.

————. 1980. *Lehrbuch der Dogmengeschichte.* Darmstadt: Wissenschaftliche Buchgesellschaft.

Harrison, Verna E. F. 1992. *Grace and Human Freedom According to St. Gregory of Nyssa.* Lewiston, NY: Edwin Mellen.

Hartkopf, Werner. 1986. *Studien zu Schellings Dialektik.* Meisenheim: Anton Hain.

Hayman, David. 1990. *The "Wake" in Transit.* Ithaca, NY: Cornell University Press.

Hegel, Georg Wilhelm Friedrich. 1934. *Wissenschaft der Logik.* Ed. Georg Lasson. Hamburg: Meiner.

————. 1988. *Phänomenologie des Geistes.* Ed. H.-F. Wessels and H. Clairmont. Hamburg: Meiner.

————. 2004. *Philosophie der Kunst: Vorlesung von 1826.* Ed. Annemarie Gethmann-Siefert et al. Frankfurt: Suhrkamp.

Heidegger, Martin. 1975–. *Gesamtausgabe.* Frankfurt: Klostermann.

Heisig, James W. 2013. *Nothingness and Desire: An East-West Philosophical Antiphony.* Honolulu: University of Hawai'i Press.

Holmes, Stephen R. 2009. "Three Versus One? Some Problems of Social Trinitarianism." *Journal of Reformed Theology* 3:77–89.

Honnefelder, Lotger. 1996. "Der zweite Anfang der Metaphysik." In *Philosophie im Mittelalter: Entwicklungslinien und Paradigmen*, ed. Jan P. Beckmann et al., 165–86. Hamburg: Meiner.

Hopkins, Jeffrey. 1996. *Meditation on Emptiness.* Boston: Wisdom.

Horn, Christoph. 2012. "Augustine's Theory of Mind and Self-Knowledge: Some Fundamental Problems." In *Le "De Trinitate" de saint Augustin: Exégèse, logique et noétique*, ed. Emmanuel Bermon and Gerard O'Daly, 205–19. Paris: Institut d'Études Augustiniennes.

Horstmann, Rolf-Peter. 1991. *Die Grenzen der Vernunft: Eine Untersuchung zu Zielen und Motiven des Deutschen Idealismus.* Frankfurt: Anton Hain.

Hulin, Michel. 1978. *Le principe de l'ego dans la pensée indienne classique.* Paris: Collège de France.

————. 2008. *La mystique sauvage.* Paris: Presses Universitaires de France.

Huntington, C. W. 1989. *The Emptiness of Emptiness.* Honolulu: University of Hawaii Press.

————. 2003. "Was Candrakīrti a Prāsaṅgika?" In *The Svātantrika-Prāsaṅgika Distinction: What Difference Does a Difference Make?*, ed. Georges B. J. Dreyfus and Sara L. McClintock. Boston: Wisdom.

Izutsu, Toshihiko. 1980. *Unicité de l'existence et création perpétuelle en mystique islamique.* Paris: Les Deux Océans.

Jaeschke, Walter. 2002. "Negative Theologie und philosophische Theologie." *Archivio di Filosofia* 70:303–14.

Joest, Wilfried. 1967. *Ontologie der Person bei Luther.* Göttingen: Vandenhoeck und Ruprecht.

Joyce, James. [1939] 1975. *Finnegans Wake.* London: Faber and Faber.

Jullien, François. 2008. *De l'universel: De l'uniforme, du commun et du dialogue entre les cultures.* Paris: Fayard.

Jüngel, Eberhard. 1992. *Gott als Geheimnis der Welt.* Tübingen: Mohr Siebeck.

Kaftan, Julius. 1908. *Dogmatik.* Tübingen: Mohr Siebeck.

Kant, Immanuel. 1986. *Kritik der Urteilskraft.* Stuttgart: Reclam.

Karfíková, Lenka, Scott Douglass, and Johannes Zachhuber, eds. 2007. *Gregory of Nyssa: Contra Eunomium II.* Leiden: Brill.

Kearney, Richard. 2004. *Debates in Continental Philosophy.* New York: Fordham University Press.

————. 2011. *Anatheism: Returning to God after God.* New York: Columbia University Press.

————. 2014. "Derrida and Messianic Atheism." In *The Trace of God: Derrida and Religion*, ed. Edward Baring and Peter Gordon, 199–212. New York: Fordham University Press.

Kearney, Richard, and J. S. O'Leary, eds. 1980. *Heidegger et la question de Dieu.* Paris: Grasset. 2nd ed. 2009. Paris: Presses Universitaires de France.

Keenan, John P. 1995. *The Gospel of Mark.* Maryknoll, NY: Orbis.

————. 2009. *Grounding Our Faith in a Pluralist World.* Eugene, OR: Wipf and Stock.

Kervégan, Jean-François, and Bernard Mabille, eds. 2012. *Hegel au présent: Une relève de la métaphysique?* Paris: CNRS.

Kierkegaard, Søren. 1968. *Attack upon "Christendom."* Trans. W. Lowrie. Princeton, NJ: Princeton University Press.

Kilby, Karen. 2012. *Balthasar: A (Very) Critical Introduction.* Grand Rapids, MI: Eerdmans.

Kimmerle, Heinz. 1970. *Das Problem der Abgeschlossenheit des Denkens: Hegels "System der Philosophie" in den Jahren 1800–1804.* Bonn: Bouvier.

Klein, Anne C. 1992. "Mental Concentration and the Unconditioned: A Buddhist Case for Unmediated Experience." In *Paths to Liberation*, ed. Robert E. Buswell and Robert M. Gimello, 269–308. Honolulu: University of Hawai'i Press.

Küng, Hans. 2008. *On Being a Christian*. New York: Continuum.

Künneth, Walter. 1963. *Glauben an Jesus? Die Begegnung der Christologie mit der modernen Existenz*. Hamburg: Wittig.

Lacan, Jacques. 2013. *Le séminaire, livre VI: Le désir et son interprétation*. Paris: Éditions de La Martinière.

Lacoste, Jean-Yves. 2009. Introduction to *Heidegger et la question de Dieu*, 2nd ed., ed. Richard Kearney and J. S. O'Leary. Paris: Presses Universitaires de France.

LaFleur, William R. 1994. *Liquid Life: Abortion and Buddhism in Japan*. Princeton, NJ: Princeton University Press.

Lamotte, Étienne. 1987. *L'enseignement de Vimalakīrti*. Louvain-la-neuve: Institut Orientaliste.

Lapide, Pinchas, and Jürgen Moltmann. 1979. *Jüdische Monotheismus—Christliche Trinitätslehre: Ein Gespräch*. Munich: Kaiser.

Laplanche, Jean. 2007. *Sexual: La sexualité élargie au sens freudien*. Paris: Presses Universitaires de France.

Larson, Gerald James, and Ram Shankar Bhattacharya. 1987. *Sāṃkhya: A Dualist Tradition in Indian Philosophy*. Encyclopedia of Indian Philosophies 4. Delhi: Motilal Banarsidass.

Leask, Ian, and Eoin Cassidy, eds. 2005. *Givenness and God: Questions of Jean-Luc Marion*. New York: Fordham University Press.

Lonergan, Bernard J. F. 1990. *Method in Theology*. Toronto: University of Toronto Press.

Lossky, Vladimir. 1998. *Théologie négative et connaissance de Dieu chez Maître Eckhart*. Paris: Vrin.

Luther, Martin. 1883–2009. *D. Martin Luthers Werke: Kritische Gesamtausgabe*. Weimar: Hermann Böhlau.

Mabille, Bernard. 2012. "Hegel, le dépassement de *quelle* métaphysique?" In Kervégan and Mabille, 311–31.

Mackey, James P. 1997. "The Preacher, the Theologian, and the Trinity." *Theology Today* 54:347–66.

Magliola, Robert. 1997. *On Deconstructing Life-Worlds*. Atlanta, GA: Scholars.

Mallarmé, Stéphane. 1945. *Oeuvres complètes*. Ed. Henri Mondor. Bibliothèque de la Pléiade. Paris: Gallimard.

———. 1995. *Correspondance: Lettres sur la poésie*. Ed. Bertrand Marchal. Folio. Paris: Gallimard.

Marenbon, John. 2005. "Aquinas, Radical Orthodoxy and the Importance of Truth." In Hankey and Hedley, 49–63.

Marion, Jean-Luc. 1991. *L'idole et la distance*. Paris: Grasset.

———. 1996. *Questions cartésiennes*. Vol. 2. Paris: Presses Universitaires de France.

———. 2001. *De surcroît: Études sur les phénomènes saturés*. Paris: Presses Universitaires de France.

———. 2008. *Au lieu de soi: L'approche de saint Augustin*. 2nd ed. Paris: Presses Universitaires de France.

———. 2010. *Figures de la phénoménologie*. Paris: Vrin.

———. 2012. "La question de l'Inconditionné." In *Dieu en tant que Dieu: La question philosophique*, ed. Philippe Capelle-Dumont, 239–61. Paris: Éditions du Cerf.

McBrien, Richard P. 2008. *The Church: The Evolution of Catholicism*. New York: HarperCollins.

Mehta, M. 1988. "The Advaitic Critique of 'Difference.'" In *Perspectives on Vedānta*, ed. S. S. Rama Rao Pappu, 78–91. Leiden: Brill.

Meijering, E. P. 1983. *Melanchthon and Patristic Thought*. Leiden: Brill.

Mélèze Modrzejewski, Joseph. 1995. *The Jews of Egypt*. Philadelphia: Jewish Publication Society.

Miernowski, Jan. 1998. *Le Dieu néant: Théologies négatives à l'aube des temps modernes*. Leiden: Brill.

Milbank, John. 1997. *The Word Made Strange*. Oxford: Blackwell.

Moingt, Joseph. 2002. *Dieu qui vient à l'homme*. Vol. 1. Paris: Éditions du Cerf.

———. 2004. "The Quest of Michel de Certeau." *Japan Mission Journal* 58:104–11.

Morrow, Glenn R., and John M. Dillon, trans. 1987. *Proclus' Commentary on Plato's "Parmenides."* Princeton, NJ: Princeton University Press.

Mortley, Raoul. 1986. *From Word to Silence*. Vol. 2. *The Way of Negation, Christian and Greek*. Bonn: Hanstein.

Muller, A. Charles. 2013. "Zen Views on Views (*dṛṣṭi*): Are We Ever Rid of Them?" *Japan Mission Journal* 67:28–33.

Munévar, Gonzalo. 2000. "A *Réhabilitation* of Paul Feyerabend." In *The Worst Enemy of Science? Essays in Memory of Paul Feyerabend*, ed. J. Preston, Gonzalo Munévar, and David Lamb, 58–79. New York: Oxford University Press.

Muralt, André de. 1993. *L'enjeu de la philosophie médiévale.* Leiden: Brill.

Murray, John Courtney. 1948. "The Root of Faith: The Doctrine of M. J. Scheeben." *Theological Studies* 9:20–46.

Murti, T. R. V. 1960. *The Central Philosophy of Buddhism.* London: Allen and Unwin.

Narbonne, Jean-Marc. 1993. *Plotin: Les deux matières.* Paris: Vrin.

———. 1999. "*Henōsis* et *Ereignis*: Remarques sur une interprétation heideg- gérienne de l'Un plotinien." *Études Philosophiques*, no. 1, 105–21.

Nef, Frédéric. 2004. *Qu'est-ce que la métaphysique?* Folio. Paris: Gallimard.

Newland, Guy. 1984. *Compassion: A Tibetan Analysis.* London: Wisdom.

———. 1992. *The Two Truths in the Mādhyamika Philosophy of the Ge-luk- ba Order of Tibetan Buddhism.* Ithaca, NY: Snow Lion.

Newman, John Henry. 1985. *An Essay in Aid of a Grammar of Assent.* Ed. Ian Ker. Oxford: Clarendon Press.

———. 1994. *Apologia pro Vita Sua.* Ed. Ian Ker. London: Penguin.

Nieden, Marcel. 1997. *Organum Deitatis: Die Christologie des Thomas de Vio Cajetan.* Leiden: Brill.

Nygren, Anders. 1953. *Agape and Eros.* London: SPCK.

O'Collins, Gerald. 2002. "The Incarnation: The Critical Issues." In Davis, Kendall, and O'Collins, 1–27.

O'Leary, Joseph Stephen. 1985. *Questioning Back: The Overcoming of Meta- physics in Christian Tradition.* Minneapolis: Winston-Seabury.

———. 1996. *Religious Pluralism and Christian Truth.* Edinburgh: Edinburgh University Press.

Otto, Rudolf. 1932. *Das Gefühl des Überweltlichen.* Munich: Beck.

Pabst, Adrian. 2002. "De la chrétienté à la modernité?" *Revue des Sciences Philosophiques et Théologiques* 86:561–99.

Pannenberg, Wolfhart. 1988. *Systematische Theologie.* Vol. 1. Göttingen: Vandenhoeck und Ruprecht.

Petzet, H.-W. 1977. *Bildnis des Dichters.* Frankfurt: Insel.

Philonenko, Alexis. 1980. *La liberté humaine dans la philosophie de Fichte.* Paris: Vrin.

Pinguet, Maurice. 1984. *La mort volontaire au Japon.* Paris: Gallimard.

Pleger, Wolfgang H. 1988. *Schleiermachers Philosophie.* Berlin: de Gruyter.

Poincaré, Henri. 1968. *La science et l'hypothèse.* Paris: Flammarion.

Potter, Karl. 1981. *Advaita Vedānta.* Encyclopedia of Indian Philosophies 3. Delhi: Motilal Banarsidass.

Pottier, Bernard. 1994. *Dieu et le Christ selon Grégoire de Nysse.* Namur: Culture et foi.

Prestige, G. L. 1981. *God in Patristic Thought.* London: SPCK.

Pusey, Edward B., trans. 1907. *The Confessions of Saint Augustine.* London: Dent.

Pye, Michael. 1978. *Skilful Means.* London: Duckworth.

Quantin, Jean-Louis. 1999. *Le catholicisme classique et les pères de l'Église: Un retour aux sources (1669–1713).* Paris: Institut d'Études Augustiniennes.

Quinn, John M. 1994. "Mysticism in the *Confessiones*: Four Passages Reconsidered." In *Augustine: Mystic and Mystagogue,* ed. Frederick Van Fleteren, Joseph C. Schnaubelt, and Joseph Reino, 251–86. New York: Peter Lang.

———. 2002. *A Companion to the "Confessions" of St. Augustine.* New York: Peter Lang.

Rachels, James. 1990. *Created from Animals: The Moral Implications of Darwinism.* Oxford: Oxford University Press.

Radde-Gallwitz, Andrew. 2009. *Basil of Caesarea, Gregory of Nyssa, and the Transformation of Divine Simplicity.* Oxford: Oxford University Press.

Rahner, Karl. 1967. *Schriften zur Theologie.* Vol. 4. Zurich: Benzinger.

———. 1975. *Schriften zur Theologie.* Vol. 12. Zurich: Benzinger.

———. 1976. *Grundkurs des Glaubens: Einführung in den Begriff des Christentums.* Freiburg: Herder.

Rahner, Karl, and Joseph Ratzinger. 1965. *Offenbarung und Überlieferung.* Freiburg: Herder.

Ratzinger, Joseph. 1966. *Das Problem der Dogmengeschichte in der Sicht der katholischen Theologie.* Cologne: Opladen.

Renaudet, Augustin. 2000. *Érasme et l'Italie.* Geneva: Droz.

Robinson, James M. 2005. *The Sayings Gospel Q: Collected Essays.* Leuven University Press.

Romano, Claude. 2010. *Au cœur de la raison, la phénoménologie.* Paris: Gallimard.

Röper, Anita. 1966. *The Anonymous Christian.* New York: Sheed and Ward.

Roques, René, ed. 1980. *Denys l'Aréopagite: La hiérarchie céleste.* Sources chrétiennes 58. Paris: Éditions du Cerf.

Rorem, P., and J. C. Lamoreaux. 1998. *John of Scythopolis and the Dionysian Corpus.* Oxford: Clarendon Press.

Santiago-Otero, Horacio. 1970. *El conocimiento de Cristo en cuanto hombre en la teologia de la primera mitad del siglo XII.* Pamplona: Universidad de Navarra.

Sartre, Jean-Paul. 1972. *La transcendance de l'ego.* Paris: Vrin.

Schillebeeckx, Edward. 1979. *Jesus: An Experiment in Christology.* New York: Crossroad.

Schleiermacher, Friedrich. 1999. *Die Christliche Glaube*. 2 vols. Berlin: de Gruyter.

Schmidt-Leukel, Perry. 1992. *"Den Löwen brüllen hören": Zur Hermeneutik eines christlichen Verständnisses der buddhistischen Botschaft*. Paderborn: Schöningh.

———. 2008. "On Claimed 'Orthodoxy,' Quibbling with Words, and Some Serious Implications: A Comment on the Tilley-D'Costa Debate about Religious Pluralism." *Modern Theology* 24:271–84.

Schürmann, Reiner. 1982. "L'hénologie comme dépassement de la métaphysique." *Études Philosophiques*, no. 3, 331–50.

Schweitzer, Albert. 1966. *Geschichte der Leben-Jesu-Forschung*. Munich: Silberstern.

Sèbe, Jean-Baptiste. 2012. *Le Christ, l'écrivain et le monde: Théologie et oeuvres littéraires chez Hans Urs von Balthasar*. Paris: Éditions du Cerf.

Seeberg, Reinhold. 1965. *Lehrbuch der Dogmengeschichte*. Vol. 2. Darmstadt: Wissenschaftliche Buchgesellschaft.

Semmelroth, Otto. 1949. "Erlösung und Erlöser im System des Ps.-Dionysius Areopagita." *Scholastik* 24:367–79.

———. 1950. "Gottes Überwesentliche Einheit: Zur Gotteslehre des Ps.-Dionysius Areopagita." *Scholastik* 28:209–34.

Sharma, Arvind. 1995. *The Philosophy of Religion and Advaita Vedānta*. University Park: Pennsylvania State University Press.

Sibony, Daniel. 1997. *Les trois monothéismes: Juifs, Chrétiens, Musulmans entre leurs sources et leurs destins*. Paris: Seuil.

Siderits, Mark, and Shōryū Katsura, trans. 2013. *Nāgārjuna's Middle Way: The Mūlamadhyamakakārikā*. Boston: Wisdom Publications.

Sloterdijk, Peter. 2013. *Mein Frankreich*. Berlin: Suhrkamp.

Smith, Jonathan Z. 1978. *Map Is Not Territory: Studies in the History of Religions*. Leiden: Brill.

Sorabji, Richard. 1983. *Time, Creation, and the Continuum*. Ithaca, NY: Cornell University Press.

Soskice, Janet M. 2002. "Philo and Negative Theology." *Archivio di Filosofia* 70:491–504.

Spurr, Barry. 2010. *"Anglo-Catholic in Religion": T. S. Eliot and Christianity*. Cambridge: Lutterworth Press.

Starobinski-Safran, Esther. 1978. "Exode 3, 14 dans l'oeuvre de Philon d'Alexandrie." In *Dieu et l'être*. Paris: Études Augustiniennes.

Stenlund, Sören. 1996. "Language and Metaphysics." *Theoria* 62:187–211.

Stolina, Ralf. 2000. *Niemand hat Gott je gesehen: Traktat über negative Theologie*. Berlin: de Gruyter.

———. 2008. "'Ökonomische' und 'immanente' Trinität? Zur Problematik einer trinitätstheologischen Denkfigur." *Zeitschrift für Theologie und Kirche* 105:170–216.

Tauscher, Helmut. 1995. *Die Lehre von den zwei Wirklichkeiten in Tson Kha Pas Madhyamaka-Werken.* Vienna: Arbeitskreis für tibetische und buddhistische Studien Universität Wien.

Taylor, Mark C. 2007. *After God.* Chicago: University of Chicago Press.

Ter Ern Loke, Andrew. 2009. "The Resurrection of the Son of God: A Reduction of the Naturalistic Hypotheses." *Journal of Theological Studies* 60:570–84.

Ternes, Bernd. 2008. *Karl Marx: Eine Einführung.* Konstanz: UVK.

Theissen, Gerd. 2003. *Jesus als historische Gestalt.* Göttingen: Vandenhoeck und Ruprecht.

Theobald, Christophe. 2007. *Le christianisme comme style: Une manière de faire de la théologie en postmodernité.* Paris: Éditions du Cerf.

Theunissen, Michael. 1980. *Sein und Schein: Die kritische Funktion der Hegelschen Logik.* Frankfurt: Suhrkamp.

Thibaut, George. [1896] 1962. *The Vedānta Sutras of Bādarāyana with the Commentary by Śaṅkara.* New York: Dover.

Todd, Warren Lee. 2013. *The Ethics of Śaṅkara and Śāntideva: A Selfless Response to an Illusory World.* Farnham, Surrey: Ashgate.

Tracy, David. 1987. "Christianity in the Wider Context: Demands and Transformations." *Religion and Intellectual Life* 4:7–20.

Trouillard, Jean. 1961. "Pluralité spirituelle et unité normative selon Blondel." *Archives de Philosophie* 24:21–28.

———. 1972. *L'Un et l'âme selon Proclos.* Paris: Les Belles Lettres.

———. 1982. *La mystagogie de Proclos.* Paris: Les Belles Lettres.

Vaihinger, Hans. 1927. *Die Philosophie des Als Ob.* Leipzig: Meiner.

van Belle, Gilbert. 2005. "Christology and Soteriology in the Fourth Gospel." In van Belle et al., 435–61.

van Belle, Gilbert, et al., eds. 2005. *Theology and Christology in the Fourth Gospel.* Leuven: Peeters.

Vaught, Carl G. 2004. *Encounters with God in Augustine's "Confessions," Books VII–IX.* Albany: State University of New York Press.

Vieillard-Baron, Jean-Louis. 2006. *Hegel: Système et structures théologiques.* Paris: Éditions du Cerf.

Viévard, Ludovic. 2002. *Vacuité (śūnyatā) et compassion (karuṇā) dans le bouddhisme madhyamaka.* Paris: Collège de France.

Virgoulay, René. 2002. *Philosophie et théologie chez Maurice Blondel.* Paris: Éditions du Cerf.

Voeltzel, René. 1956. *Vraie et fausse Église selon les théologiens protestants français du XVIIe siècle.* Paris: Presses Universitaires de France.

Völker, Walther. 1958. *Kontemplation und Ekstase bei Pseudo-Dionysius Areopagitica.* Wiesbaden: Franz Steiner.

Wear, Sarah Klitenic, and John Dillon. 2007. *Dionysius the Areopagite and the Neoplatonist Tradition: Despoiling the Hellenes.* Aldershot: Ashgate.

Weiss, Johannes. 1892. *Die Predigt Jesu vom Reiche Gottes.* Göttingen.

Welch, Claude. 1952. *In This Name: The Doctrine of the Trinity in Contemporary Theology.* New York: Scribner's.

Werckmeister, Jean. 2003. "Le droit de parler." In *Sujets à croire: Questions de théologie et de psychanalyse,* ed. René Heyer, 133–44. Strasbourg: Presses Universitaries de Strasbourg.

Westerink, L. G., ed., and Joseph Combès, trans. 1986. *Damascius: Traité des premiers principes.* Vol. 1. Paris: Les Belles Lettres.

Wiles, Maurice. 1989. "Eunomius: Hair-Splitting Dialectician or Defender of the Accessibility of Salvation?" In *The Making of Orthodoxy,* ed. Rowan Williams, 157–72. Cambridge: Cambridge University Press.

Williams, J. P. 2000. *Denying Divinity: Apophasis in the Patristic Christian and Soto Zen Buddhist Traditions.* Oxford: Oxford University Press.

Zachhuber, Johannes. 2013. "The Rhetoric of Evil and the Definition of Christian Identity." In *Rhetorik des Bösen/The Rhetoric of Evil,* ed. Paul Fiddes and Jochen Schmidt, 193–217. Würzburg: Eregon.

Žižek, Slavoj. 1997. *The Plague of Fantasies.* London: Verso.

———. 1999. *The Ticklish Subject: The Absent Centre of Political Ontology.* London: Verso.

Index

Joseph Stephen O'Leary

is The Roche Chair, Nanzan Institute for Religion and Culture, Nanzan University.